Smart Cards:
The Developer's Toolkit

Timothy M. Jurgensen
Scott B. Guthery

PH
PTR

Prentice Hall PTR, Upper Saddle River, NJ 07458
www.phptr.com

ISBN 0-13-093730-4

90000

9 790130 937307

Library of Congress Cataloging-in-Publication Data

Jurgensen, Timothy M.
   Smart cards : the developer's toolkit / Tim Jurgensen, Scott Guthery.
      p. cm.
   Includes index.
   ISBN 0-13-093730-4 (pbk.)
    1. Smart cards. I. Guthery, Scott B. II. Title.

TK7895.S62 J87 2002
004.5'6--dc21   2002070028

Editorial/Production Supervision: *Patti Guerrieri*
Acquisitions Editor: *Victoria Jones*
Editorial Assistant: *Michelle Vincenti*
Marketing Manager: *Debby VanDijk*
Buyer: *Maura Zaldivar*
Cover Design: *Nina Scuderi*
Cover Design Direction: *Jerry Votta*
Art Director: *Gail Cocker-Bogusz*
Interior Design: *Meg Van Arsdale*

Front cover photo: The original undersea photograph was provided by David Van Rooy (Ph.D., Rice University, 1971) currently a resident of the village of Ubud on the island of Bali. He can be contacted at *www.SeaBelow.com*.

© 2002 Pearson Education, Inc.
Publishing as Prentice Hall PTR
Upper Saddle River, NJ 07458

Prentice Hall books are widely used by corporations and government agencies for training, marketing, and resale. For information regarding corporate and government bulk discounts please contact:
Corporate and Government Sales (800) 382-3419 or corpsales@pearsontechgroup.com

All other products or services mentioned in this book are the trademarks or service marks of their respective companies or organizations. The 3GPP TS 31.102 Third Generation Mobile System Release 1999 v.3.2.0 is the property of ARIB, CWTS, ETSI, T1, TTA, and TTC who jointly own the copyright in it. It is subject to further modifications and is therefore provided to you "as is" for information purposes only. Further use is strictly prohibited.

Warning and Disclaimer: This book is designed to provide information about smart cards, including smart card systems, equipment, and standards. Considerable effort has been made to make this book as complete and as accurate as possible, but no warranty or fitness is implied. Information pertaining to various standards and specifications is approximate. Official versions of standards and specifications should be consulted for actual use reference. This information is provided on an as-is basis. The authors and Prentice Hall PTR shall have neither liability nor responsibility to any person or entity with respect to any loss or damage arising from the information contained in this book.

Printed in the United States of America

10 9 8 7 6 5 4 3 2 1

ISBN 0-13-093730-4

Pearson Education LTD.
Pearson Education Australia PTY, Limited
Pearson Education Singapore, Pte. Ltd.
Pearson Education North Asia Ltd.
Pearson Education Canada, Ltd.
Pearson Educación de Mexico, S.A. de C.V.
Pearson Education—Japan
Pearson Education Malaysia, Pte. Ltd.

Contents

3

Basic Standards for Smart Cards   55

4

Smart Card Applications   91

10

Smart Card System Management   317

11
Current Trends and Future Directions *355*

Glossary   *373*

Index   *397*

Foreword

Smart cards are now the most prevalent computer in the world. In particular, they are the central piece of the wireless revolution. The brain of 600 million mobile phones, they bring personal, secure computing to the world population in the most egalitarian spread of advanced technology.

Since the birth of the era of open smart card systems a little more than five years ago, the speed and memory of smart cards have multiplied ten-fold. The sophistication of both smart cards and their environment, their maturity in terms of concepts and applications, called for a book attempting to map the new technological landscape.

It is my pleasure to introduce a book written by two of the top experts in the world in smart card technology. Active in smart card standardization bodies, practitioners of smart card technology, actual participants in key projects, Scott and Tim have the perspective and knowledge needed to convey to a wide audience the fundamentals of smart card developments.

Smart cards are in the heart of our cell phone, in our wallet to secure your financial transaction, pinned on our clothes as a corporate badge, and we use them too as tickets for public transportation. Each time, they are our own, trusted, electronic representation, giving us keys to services that are fundamental for our interaction with the environment.

Scott and Tim have taken the challenge of explaining how this is all made possible. Each of us in the smart card business remembers our first months in the field, borne out of confusion, awe, and sometimes desperation; looking at the complexity of smart card systems. This book tries to peel each layer of complexity out of the smart card world.

The basic smart card concepts are grounded on interoperability, brought by an extremely rich web of standards covering everything from physical appearance to arcane details of software interactions. The book not only presents established practices, it also tries to convey in a very effective way today's hot debates and their implication for the future of the technology.

Once the basics are mastered, the challenge is to assemble the knowledge acquired, into systems assembling the chain of trust needed to securely build smart card systems. By going in detail into the description of card infrastructure software, the authors help the reader understand how smart cards are the cornerstone of computer security.

The tools can then be played out for building applications in the critical domains of smart card deployment: mobile telephony, financial exchanges, information technology, digital rights, and transport. Thanks to very specific examples, readers should be able to translate the book's illustrations into applications related to their own business and specialty.

Finally, no technical panorama would be complete without an attempt to look beyond the horizon. I appreciate that Scott and Tim wandered into the unknown and, if they may not show us the future, they show us very candidly how experts in the field think about the future.

I now let you enjoy the book. Once you've passed the maelstrom of new concepts and techniques, I hope that you will participate in the smart card adventure where these ubiquitous, secure, and cheap computers are core components of the information infrastructure at the beginning of the 21st century.

Bertrand du Castel
Schlumberger Fellow, Head of Smart Card Research

Preface

The technical groundwork has been laid for wide-spectrum exploitation of smart card technology in both commercial and enterprise venues. Our goal in this book is to provide IT managers, system architects, system analysts, and application developers with the basic information about smart card technology that they need to open the tap on the incredible value stored in this technology.

Information about smart cards and the technical detail needed to harness the technology has historically been very hard to come by. This, more than any other factor, has been the barrier to the use of smart cards. Whereas they once had a unique value offer, smart cards now have many technical substitutes. Belatedly, the smart card industry has realized that either applications carry cards into the mainstream of everyday use or they will join eight-track tapes, monorail trains, cold fusion, magnetic bubbles, and Betamax video in the dustbin of technical curiosities.

A smart card is just a computer. We know how that story plays out. We've seen it in mainframes, mini-computers, desktop computers, and laptops. You have apps and you connect or you die. The smart card will follow the same path.

Some computing device will capture the next and, yet again, more personal level of computing. It will be our avatar on the Internet. It will be our digital wallet. It will be the keeper of our digital persona. The smart card is in the race. It's cheap. It's portable. It's about as secure as you can make a computer that fits in your pocket. And if you're willing to spend the time, it can deliver a surprising amount of performance. Take it out for a spin. See what you think.

ACKNOWLEDGMENTS

The authors would like to express thanks to Schlumberger and to Mobile-Mind respectively for their support in the development of this book. Schlumberger was most gracious in allowing us to discuss and present technical details about their Cryptoflex and Cyberflex Access smart cards and to allow us to use selected graphical material from various Schlumberger sources.

We would especially like to recognize David Corcoran of M.U.S.C.L.E. for his contribution of material to the book and his review of other material in the book. Much of the discussion of Unix, Mac OS, and Linux implementations of smart card stacks in Chapter 7 came from Dave.

We would like to thank Nigel Barnes, Dan Butnaru, Bertrand du Castel, Paul Curtis, Ed Dolph, Susanna Eskola, Olivier Franchi, Gillian Harris, Michael Johnson, Roger Kehr, Ksheerabdhi Krishna, Rune Lindholm, Scott Marks, Gregory Maulion, James McLaughlin, Mike Montgomery, Michael Meyer, Maria Nekam, Neville Pattinson, Jean-Claude Perrin, Joachim Posegga, Renaud Presty, Jean-Francois Rubon, Wim Ton, Jean-Paul Truong, Harald Vogt, and Marc Valderrama for various conversations that contributed to the book and for various reviews of material in the book.

Remaining errors are the sole responsibility of the authors. They would greatly appreciate hearing about them. Opinions expressed are those of one or both of the authors and do not necessarily reflect those of the publisher, Schlumberger, or Mobile-Mind.

Tim Jurgensen
tmjurgensen@jump.net
Scott Guthery
sguthery@mobile-mind.com

1

Overview of Smart Cards and Their Programming

A smart card is a computer. It doesn't include the keyboard and display screen that stare at us from our desktop personal computers, but it has all the elements of a general-purpose computing platform nonetheless. From a distance, it looks like a credit card with a small metal plate on its face. That plate is the electrical interface for a very small and very highly integrated computer buried in the plastic beneath it. This computer includes a processor and several types of memory; sometimes it even includes an auxiliary processor that helps it in particularly intense computations. So, while it's something less than the PC on your desk, it is also something more: it's a reasonably secure computing platform.

Slightly more formally, we can say that a smart card is a portable, tamper-resistant computer with a programmable data store. It is the exact shape and size of a credit card, can hold 32 KB or more of sensitive information, and can do a modest amount of data processing as well. The central processing unit (CPU) in a smart card is typically an 8-bit microcontroller that has the computing power of the original IBM PC; however, 32-bit processors are beginning to make inroads in smart cards. To make a computer and a smart card communicate, you place the card in or near (in the case of what are called *contactless* smart cards) a smart card reader, which is connected to the computer.

Smart cards cost between $1 and $20, depending primarily on the size of the memory in the card and the software functionality included. Smart card software, depending on the specific card, can range from a rudimentary on-board operating system with file system, communication, authorization, encryption, and access control primitives to a more sophisticated on-board operating system supporting the use of advanced languages and/or interpreted languages (such as C, Java, or Basic) to add new applications onto the cards even after they're in the hands of the cardholder. Smart cards are particularly useful components of computer systems that need to address data security, personal privacy, and user mobility requirements.

Smart card programming is characterized by a constant and consuming concern for two system requirements: data security and data integrity. Data security means that a data value or a computational capability contained on the card can be accessed by those entities that are authorized to access it, and not accessed by those not authorized. Data integrity means that at all times the value of information stored on a card is well known; the value is not corrupted, even if power to the smart card is cut during a computation involving some piece of information stored on the card.

Unlike many software applications commercial programmers deal with daily, smart card applications are typically public systems. This means first that smart cards are used in settings and situations in which using a computer is not the first thing on the user's mind. Furthermore, the smart card computer must fit seamlessly and, to the greatest extent possible, unnoticed into existing behaviors and relationships. Paying for a newspaper with electronic money on a smart card should, for example, be very much like paying for the newspaper with cash. Furthermore, unlike applications that are run on corporate computers in physically guarded environments and on private networks, smart card computers are "on the street" and subject to attack by a range of interests and agendas that are not fully known—let alone understood—by the smart card programmer and system designer.

The amount of data processed by a smart card program is usually quite small and the computations performed are typically quite modest. Subtracting 50 cents from a smart card's electronic purse, for example, entails neither many numbers nor much arithmetic. However, making sure that the expectations of all the parties to this transaction (i.e., the cardholder, the card issuer, and the merchant) are met during and after the transaction places an unfamiliar and relatively unique set of demands on software system designers and computer programmers. The merchant expects to be exactly 50 cents richer, the cardholder expects to be exactly 50 cents poorer, and the card issuer expects that the smart card will be left in a consistent state and not have leaked information about its inner workings.

HISTORY OF SMART CARDS

The smart card—a term coined by French publicist Roy Bright in 1980—was invented in 1967 and 1968 by two German engineers, Jürgen Dethloff and Helmut Gröttrupp. Dethloff and Gröttrupp filed for a German patent on their invention in February 1969 and were finally granted patent DE 19 45 777 C3, titled "Identifikanden/Identifikationsschalter," in 1982. Independently, Kunitaka Arimura of the Arimura Technology Institute in Japan filed for a smart card patent in Japan in March 1970. The next year, in May 1971, Paul Castrucci of IBM filed an American patent titled simply "Information Card" and on November 7, 1972, was issued U.S. Patent 3,702,464. Between 1974 and 1979 Roland Moréno, a French journalist, filed 47 smart card–related patent applications in 11 countries and founded the French company Innovatron to license this legal tour de force.

THE GENERIC SMART CARD APPLICATION

In the course of this book, our goal is to present the essential information you'll need to evaluate the use of smart cards in your computer environment or for your specific task. As a preface to that, it is useful to examine just what purposes a smart card can serve in some mainstream computer and other application areas. To that end, let's examine the use of smart cards in four areas that are of increasing significance in the general Information Technology (IT) environment. Each of these uses is aimed at an existing problem; each of these problems may well be solved in some fashion without a smart card today. Our aim is to illustrate how the use of a single smart card in attacking all of these problems offers a superior solution when compared to other approaches. In this cursory review, we'll confine ourselves to examining the general capabilities offered by the smart card and how its use appears to cardholders and system administrators of the environments in question. In the remainder of this book, we'll then examine in more detail specifically what smart cards are "doing" in applications such as those described in the next section.

A smart card is used in an application as a portable token, which can be carried on the person of an individual who can use it (the smart card) in the context of an application system. The smart card will typically carry sensitive information that the cardholder, and the system, want to keep private from others. In addition to carrying sensitive information, the smart card also can provide services to the cardholder or application system in the form of secure, and therefore trusted, computations. The sensitive information mentioned might include account information, either for financial accounts or for computer or network accounts, to be used by or on behalf of the cardholder. Trusted services to be provided might include establishing the identity of the cardholder to the application system.

Through discussions with many IT managers in various large and small business and government entities, the following applications are among the most often suggested as needing new, convenient solutions—solutions for which smart cards seem uniquely suited.

MAJOR IT APPLICATIONS—THE BIG FOUR

Smart cards have been used throughout the world in a variety of applications. Their use to convey user subscription and identification information for **Groupe Spécial Mobile** (GSM cellular) telephones is widespread, as is their use to convey account information for credit, debit, and cash financial services. The use of smart cards in the IT environment, although growing, is still a relatively small market segment. In examining the potential IT use of smart cards, four applications (or application areas) arise as being particularly suited to exploiting the characteristics of smart cards:

- ID badge
- Token for building and office door access
- Token for computer and network access
- Token for small (cash) financial transactions

These distinct uses are valuable individually; however, if they are supported by a single token, the value increases significantly. If they are provided by a token that can subsequently support as yet undefined applications, then the solution becomes even more attractive.

Let's take a close look at the specific characteristics of these applications to which smart cards are such an attractive solution.

Physical ID Token

The need for a reliable, trusted ID badge is widespread. Such a badge is needed to offer a trusted means for authenticating the true identity of a person in a variety of situations. In some of these situations, a connection to a wide area communications network may be available; in other situations, perhaps not. The end result is that the badge needs to convey identity authentication in a trusted fashion, even in isolated (off-line) environments.

The ID badge can offer a variety of ways for the identity of the bearer to be authenticated; some involve simple visual comparison while others involve electronic checks.

Picture ID

The smart card identity token should include a picture of the valid cardholder on its surface. Like a driver license or passport, the picture enables someone to visually compare the appearance of the valid holder of the smart card (i.e., the person whose identity the smart card will authenticate) with the appearance of the person presenting the smart card. As we'll see in later chapters, personalizing a smart card with a picture of the cardholder presents some security and logistic problems in the large-scale deployment of the cards, but there are techniques available in card management systems that satisfactorily solve these problems. Figure 1.1 illustrates the general appearance of such an ID token.

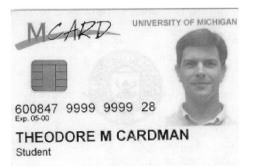

A smart card provides a significant enhancement over other ID badge mechanisms through the capabilities of the embedded computer. Specifically, the picture of the cardholder can be reduced through pattern recognition and facial feature parameterization to a digital template of the picture, which can be stored in the on-card integrated circuit chip (ICC). Automatic image capture devices and pattern recognition software can then be used to view the face of the cardholder and match an analysis of that face to the template stored on the smart card. The face becomes like a fingerprint in determining that the cardholder is really the individual that the smart card is supposed to "represent."

Printed Personal Information

The name and address of the cardholder can be printed on the surface of the card, along with other personal information that might be of value in establishing the identity of the cardholder. Conveying such information in a printed form on the card is something of a two-edged sword. While the information might be of value in authenticating the identity of the cardholder, having it so easily accessible to the casual viewer of the ID badge makes it a threat to the privacy of the cardholder. As we will see later, it is quite feasible to keep the printed information on the card to a minimum and to store further information electronically within the ICC embedded within the card. Information stored within the ICC can be protected in a variety of ways that we'll be discussing throughout the course of this book. At this point, suffice it to say that the access to such information can be significantly inhibited to other than "trusted" applications.

Embossing

Along with a name on the face of the ID badge, it will usually be acceptable to include some type of identifying number: a personal ID number or an account number. Such numbers are obviously useful in overcoming redundancy in ordinary names.

In many instances, it is useful to imprint such an ID number in raised or embossed print. Embossing allows the card to be used to easily render a copy of the number on paper through the use of a small printing machine. This technique is still used as a backup technique for creating a receipt, which includes an account number for an ID (perhaps a credit) card. As we will see in the later chapters, a large body of standards has been created to govern, among other things, the size and positioning of embossed printing such that equipment can be made available to process such cards in a uniform manner.

Magnetic Stripe

A smart card ID token also can include information encoded on a magnetic stripe. This allows all of the information printed on the face of the card, and perhaps even additional information, to be extracted from the card by equipment that can read the magnetic stripe. Again, the positioning and the electrical encoding formats for magnetic stripes are governed by a variety of standards.

It should be noted that information encoded on a magnetic stripe is not necessarily secure. Information stored here is typically not encrypted and because the encoding is done according to international standards, there is a lot of equipment available to read and process magnetic stripe information.

While information encoded on magnetic stripes is not necessarily secure, one can generally count on it to be accurate. Checksums of the information encoded also can be included on the magnetic stripe. This makes it possible to confirm the checksum as information is read from the magnetic stripe. Thus, information can be conveyed accurately via magnetic stripe, albeit not always securely.

Bar Code

A bar code also can be printed on the face of the smart card ID badge. This allows information from the card to be extracted via bar code readers such as those found at the checkout counters of most grocery stores. Bar codes are a particularly efficient way to encode indexing numbers on the card in order to tie the card to database entries, which can then be easily accessed, given the index number obtained from the bar code.

Anti-counterfeiting

Finally, a variety of anti-counterfeiting mechanisms can be included on the face of the smart card ID badge. Probably the most prevalent such mechanism is a white light hologram. Such holograms are typically not easily duplicated and they serve the function of a "signet ring" in marking the ID badge as having come from a specific, well-identified source.

In some instances, special printing characteristics, which make it difficult to reproduce the printing on the card through normal copying mechanisms, can be used. If those who look to such an ID badge to authenticate the identity of the cardholder are trained in what to look for (in the way of anti-counterfeiting mechanisms), then the smart card ID badge can form a moderately secure identity authentication mechanism, and cannot be easily counterfeited just by a hacker with a color printer.

Other anti-counterfeiting mechanisms also can be built into the ICC, but these require computer access to and processing of the information stored within the ICC. These mechanisms will come into play when we discuss the use of this smart card to gain physical access to buildings and offices in the next section.

The Application in Practice

The ID token that we've described is actually an identity card created according to a number of international standards (which we'll examine in some detail in a subsequent chapter) that actually pre-date the creation of smart cards. In order to take advantage of the physical infrastructure that was put in place to handle such ID cards, smart cards were defined as an extension to these standards. So, provision of such an ID badge is not really a "new" application. Rather, it simply illustrates the characteristics of a good ID badge.

What significantly enhances the use of this new badge is the power to build additional capabilities into the smart card ICC, as we'll see later. This means that the same card can be used in a variety of circumstances. The support and operating infrastructure can be shared among all of the applications.

Physical Access

An ID badge based on a smart card provides a good vehicle to establish the identity of a person in a large work environment where one doesn't necessarily know everyone else with whom he or she comes in contact. The ID badge even goes beyond merely a picture and name of the bearer; it also allows for a cursory electronic examination of the badge, allowing identification information and authenticating information to be extracted. Let's now look at extending that ID badge so that it can be used systematically in an electronic fashion to establish the identity of the bearer and to establish the rights or permissions that person has to enter various buildings or offices.

Chip Card

The addition of an ICC to the ID badge makes it a true smart card. By way of the contact pad on the face of the card, a telecommunication protocol can be established between the ICC (computer) and an off-card computer, which, for example, controls the access to a doorway to a building or office. Once the communication pathway is established, the ICC can convey to the control computer some set of information that identifies the card bearer and establishes the right of that card bearer to pass through the doorway in question.

The communication protocol established between the two computers in question allows for the exchange of relatively complex identity information. In fact, the protocol can support a very high security exchange through which both computers authenticate themselves to each other. Once this mutual authentication is achieved, the two computers are relatively free to actually believe the information that they received from the other machine. Thus, the control computer can ask the ICC for a code identifying the card bearer. On receiving this code, the control computer can check it against an entry list to determine whether the card bearer can pass through the door. As we'll see later, a number of additional operations can be added to this relatively simple, yet reasonably secure procedure in order to make it extremely secure.

Contactless and Combi Cards

Using the contact pad on the face of the smart card to enable a communication pathway between the smart card's ICC and the control computer requires the card to be inserted into a reader. This can be a somewhat time-consuming step in gaining access to a doorway. For moderate security portals, use of a card that operates in mere proximity to a reader, rather than being inserted completely into a reader, increases the efficiency of the operation considerably. For this application, a variant of the smart card, called a contactless card, has been developed. This card actually communicates by way of electromagnetic radiation, essentially working at Radio Frequency (RF) frequencies. Power to make the ICC on the card work is transmitted via this RF pathway. Information can then be transferred between the on-card and the off-card computers.

Contactless cards that operate at a variety of distances between the card and the reader are available. Typically, distances from a few millimeters to a few centimeters can be supported. If the amount of information exchanged is held to a minimum, then access to a doorway can be achieved within a second or so, considerably faster than the time required to insert the card into an electrical reader. Bear in mind, of course, that operation in this mode really just requires the card. That is, there is no opportunity for the card to authenticate the card bearer; simple possession of the card is deemed sufficient to allow the bearer through the door. In order to authenticate the card bearer, it is necessary to be able to extract information from the card bearer and allow that information to be checked by the card—typically either a Personal Identification Number (PIN) or biometric information, such as a fingerprint. This type of interaction is generally more convenient when done via an electrical interface.

So, for handling both moderate- as well as high-security environments, sometimes a combination card is used—that is, a smart card that contains an ICC accessible through the contact pad on the face of the card and another ICC that is accessible through an RF antenna embedded in the plastic of the card.

Permission Conveyance

The four application areas we're considering each represent four distinct administrative domains of control for the solution system. That is, each area has its own standards for authenticating identities and each has its own policies for governing authorizations based on those authenticated identities. In the case of the ID badge, some "flag" printed on the face of the card might be used to differentiate areas (of a facility) into which the badge bearer is allowed. In the case of a physical access system, information contained within the ICC might be used to determine to which buildings or offices the card bearer should have access. Similar authorization controls will be considered in the remaining applications. If a single smart card is to be used for all of these environments, then a significant problem presents itself in the form of just how the administrative systems of the various environments are to be coordinated.

One approach would be to revise each system to run off of the same administrative system. To a certain extent, this will be the case in that a common card management system, one that encompasses all of the individual environments, must be used to issue the smart cards that then operate in the various environments. Smart cards provide an interesting extension to this, however, in that they actually can be used to convey authorization information from system to system. For example, the authorization for the card bearer to enter a particular set of rooms could be encoded into a digitally signed document stored in the smart card. By presenting this document (certificate) to the physical access system, an authorization to enter a particular room could be conveyed from the certificate (on the card) to the control system computer. The smart card acts as the conveyance mechanism for this authorization.

Electronic ID Token

In a previous section, we examined the characteristics of an ID badge based on a smart card platform. That badge contained a variety of information that could either be directly read by another person or could easily be accessed by a variety of relatively simple scanning devices. Such an ID token serves to authenticate the identity of the cardholder and to make a variety of auxiliary services available to the cardholder in a person-to-person environment. Now, let's look at extending such authentication services to the distributed, electronic (computer and network) environment. For this, we will make use of the capabilities of the computer chip embedded in the smart card ID token. The goal is to establish trust on the part of each of the entities so that they actually know the identities of the other entities involved in the environment. If fact, they should have enough trust to know that these various entities can engage in a transaction and can, in fact, exchange goods and services with each other, perhaps in exchange for money or for other goods and services.

For this application, let's consider the environment illustrated in Figure 1.2. In this environment, we have a personal computer (PC) with an attached smart card reader. The PC also includes a display screen and a keyboard in which the cardholder (also known as the PC user) can communicate with PC applications, including the application that can access the smart card chip embedded in the ID badge.

The object of this application is to authenticate the bearer of the smart card ID badge to the PC system. Moreover, if the PC is connected to a wide area net-

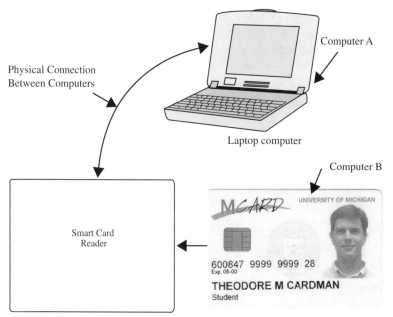

▶ **Figure 1.2**   Computer user's identity authentication. (Reprinted by permission of Schlumberger. All rights reserved.)

work (e.g., the Internet), then we'd like for the badge to authenticate the cardholder's identity to other entities (e.g., servers) located throughout the network. You might recognize this situation as one that exists today and typically is solved by having account and password access defined for the PC and for various servers throughout the network that want to authenticate the identity of the users accessing each server. If this situation is familiar, the maze of accounts and passwords that a user has to manage to navigate through the various servers in the network might be familiar as well. Our goal with a smart card–based solution to this problem is to minimize the amount of information a cardholder (user) needs to know in order to access services throughout the network.

The general approach to solving this problem is to require the smart card token and the PC system (that is, the authenticating authority) to share a secret. If the token and the PC can prove to each other that they each possess the secret, then they have authenticated their identities to each other. Of course, the trick to approaches such as these is how well the various entities involved can protect that secret and keep other parties from learning it. As we'll consider later in the book, there are several approaches, each involving various forms of cryptography, which can be used in this situation.

Cardholder Authentication

Consider the environment illustrated in Figure 1.2. You'll notice that there are actually three entities involved in the act of authenticating identities:

- the cardholder
- the smart card token
- the PC system

To authenticate the identities involved requires three separate actions. First, the cardholder must authenticate himself to the smart card token. This step guards against the loss of a token resulting in some unknown person being able to impersonate the real cardholder. Once the card is convinced that it is being asked to perform operations on behalf of the real cardholder, the remaining authentication steps can occur. That is, the smart card token can now authenticate its identity, or more appropriately, the identity of its cardholder to the PC system. Likewise, the PC system can authenticate itself to the smart card token. When each of these pair-wise authentications is completed, the transaction can proceed with each party confident that it is dealing with a known entity at the other end of the communication channel. So, what mechanisms are used to authenticate identity? Generally, it is the proof of knowledge of a shared secret between each side.

To authenticate the cardholder to the card, the cardholder is usually asked to enter a PIN. This is typically a four- to eight-digit number that can be entered through a ten-digit (numeric) PIN pad or a PC keyboard. The PIN is passed over to the card, which verifies that it matches a stored PIN value on the card. It should be noted that the cardholder must explicitly trust the host computer when entering the PIN; that is, if the PC is not trustworthy, then the PIN could be compromised. In that case, an imposter could use the PIN to authenticate to the card and have the card act on behalf of someone other than the true cardholder.

Authenticated Identity

To authenticate the PC and the card to each other generally involves the use of communication protocols through which each side can prove knowledge of a shared secret without passing that secret directly across the communications line linking the two computers. Such a protocol usually involves one side encrypting a random number provided by the other side and then passing the encrypted information back to the source side. If this is done with the card first creating a random challenge value and passing it to the PC to be encrypted and passed back, and then the PC creating a random challenge to be encrypted by the card, then both sides can be mutually authenticated. When this is accomplished, each entity in the (subsequent) transaction can know precisely which identity it is dealing with.

It should be noted that this process of mutual authentication of identities makes use of a couple of very useful characteristics of smart cards. First, all of the shared secrets are stored on the smart card in a secure fashion. That is, an imposter, on gaining control of a card, cannot easily extract the secret information from the card. In fact, it will likely take the destruction of the card by some extremely expensive equipment to (perhaps) be able to extract information from the card. In such a case, the card can no longer function as an "electronic identity token." Next, the exchange of secret information between the card and the PC, without passing that secret information across the communication pathway between the two computers, requires an ability to perform complex cryptographic algorithms. The smart card processor provides this capability; it functions as a secure computing platform.

Digital Signature

The smart card can perform another useful service associated with authenticating the identity of the cardholder. It can digitally sign electronically stored information in a fashion that will allow the signature to be validated by someone who receives a copy of the signed information. This is done through a mechanism called a *digital signature*. While we'll go through the details of this operation in Chapter 4, the general mechanism is relatively straightforward.

The electronically stored copy of the information in question, perhaps a file stored on a computer disk, is processed through a variant of a checksum algorithm, which produces a relatively short string of bits that is associated with the exact (but very much longer) string of bits that makes up the stored information. Such an algorithm is called a *hash function*. The resulting checksum, called a *hash code*, can now be encrypted by an encryption key stored on the smart card; either all or part of the application of the hash function is done on the card as well. The resulting encrypted form of the hash code is called a *digital signature*. If we have available a cryptographic process called *public key encryption*, we have a situation where two complementary keys can be created to represent the identity of a cardholder. One of the keys is kept secret on the smart card, and can be used to form a digital signature. The other key is presented to the external (to the smart card) world as open information; it can be used to decrypt the digital signature to retrieve the hash code. By recalculating the hash code from the electronically stored copy and comparing it to the decrypted value, it can be determined that the smart card's cardholder was the source of the information and that the information has not been modified since being provided by the cardholder.

There are a lot of additional wrinkles that can be exercised from this process and we'll look at them in some detail later on.

Personal Information Storage

In addition to the secret keys that are stored on the smart card and used to authenticate identities, other information about the cardholder can be securely stored on the smart card as well. Then, this information can be provided to a host PC application to which the cardholder wishes to entrust the information. If the host PC application is not able to perform a satisfactory mutual identity authentication with the smart card, then the card does not give up the personal information stored there.

The Application in Practice

This electronic identity badge provides a number of extremely useful services for computer systems, wide area networks interconnecting a large number of such computer systems, and the exchange of information among these various computer systems across this network. First, by inserting the smart card into a reader attached to a computer system, the cardholder can initiate an action requesting secure access to the computer. By performing a mutual authentication between the computer and the smart card, it can be determined that (a) this is a computer system the cardholder can feel secure in using, (b) this user is allowed to use this computer system, and (c) this strong identification of the cardholder by the computer can be passed across the network to other computers this computer trusts.

If the smart card is removed from the reader, it can provide a signal that the cardholder wants to terminate this "secure session" with the computer in question. The authenticated identity state is destroyed and no other person can use the computer to impersonate the cardholder.

By also being able to use the smart card to digitally sign information (e.g., electronic mail messages), it is possible for the cardholder to communicate with others on the network (at a distance) and for that person to trust that the message(s) actually came from the cardholder. Further, by using other mechanisms available in the general field of public key cryptography, other people can send private (encrypted) messages that can be deciphered only by the cardholder.

So, the electronic identity badge allows the cardholder and other people to carry on trusted exchanges of information across wide area computer networks which are inherently untrusted.

Financial Services

The first major application area for smart cards was one of financial services. These services generally fall into one of three distinct areas: credit, debit, and cash. For credit and debit applications, the smart card provides identity authentication of the cardholder and connects that identity with an account at a bank. The real (unique) value of a smart card for financial transactions is in enabling a "cash purse" on the smart card and allowing any amount of money to be immediately debited (spent) from that purse.

Cash Payment

A major use of smart cards is to support an on-card purse. The purse is a data area that contains a balance of currency "resident on" the card. When presented to a proper point-of-sale terminal, and with the cardholder properly authenticated, a transaction can proceed in which an amount is debited from the smart card contained purse and immediately credited to the point-of-sale terminal. Periodically (at the end of the day perhaps), the point-of-sale balance can be deposited (via telephone line) into a normal bank account.

To support purse operations, the smart card supports a number of commands especially designed to provide purse transactions in a secure fashion and also as an "atomic operation." This means that if the goal is to identify the cardholder and then to debit the purse variable by some amount of money (while crediting an external account with this same amount of money), all of the operations can be performed as a single procedure. This operation either completely succeeds, or it completely fails. The transaction neither creates nor destroys value (i.e., currency stored on the smart card) the amount debited from the card is credited to an account elsewhere in the financial network.

Credit/Debit Payment

A debit or credit transaction facilitated by a smart card can either cause the account to be immediately debited by the amount of the transaction or can issue a credit charge against the account. Of course, these operations can be supported by a simple credit card (i.e., a card with a magnetic stripe rather than an embedded ICC). However, if a simple magnetic stripe card is used, the transaction typically will require approval from a centralized clearinghouse that is contacted in real-time by telephone. If a telephone line is not immediately available, the transaction may be allowed, within defined financial limits, but with a recognized increased risk for fraud. This increased risk can be addressed by a true smart card.

The use of a smart card for these transactions simply enhances the security framework. The identity of the cardholder can be better determined than with a simple magnetic stripe card. This improves the security of performing these transactions in an off-line mode; that is, where the point-of-sale terminal being used for the transaction cannot make immediate contact (via telephone line) with a central clearinghouse. With a smart card–enabled transaction, the risk of fraud is greatly diminished in the situation where the transaction is completed off-line.

The Applications in Action

If the four applications we've considered are addressed with four separate smart cards, then we really haven't improved the situation much beyond the ways such problems are addressed today. However, if we can solve all four with a single smart card, then we've made some significant progress in efficiency and convenience and, if the truth be known, we've probably significantly enhanced the overall security environment as well.

Consider the corporate environment. We now have a single ID badge that will first of all get an employee in the front door of the corporate workplace. This same badge can be worn on the person of the cardholder, thus offering assurance that this person properly belongs in the office area. The badge can be used to open a private office door through an action that requires authentication of the cardholder via a PIN or perhaps biometric information. At this point, more than simple possession of the ID badge is required.

Once in the office, the ID badge can be used to log in to the desktop computer system and to authenticate the identity of the cardholder (user) across a world-wide computer network. The badge can be used to digitally sign information, thus attesting to its authenticity and integrity.

If the cardholder leaves the office, the ID badge will need to go along. Thus, the desktop computer is no longer working in the name of the cardholder. It becomes impossible to impersonate the cardholder and it does not leave a sensitive, desktop machine accessible or connected to a network. This enforces good security policy.

Finally, when the cardholder goes to lunch in the company cafeteria, lunch can be paid for from a cash purse carried on the card. This greatly enhances book-keeping in the cafeteria and removes a need to deal with large amounts of cash.

SMART CARD PROGRAMMING

So, assuming that the four applications discussed previously present an interesting scenario for the use of smart cards in a corporate or personal work environment, let's look at a preliminary overview of the elements that went to make up those applications. We'll be looking at all these areas in some detail throughout the course of this book, but a brief survey will give us some context as we delve into the more detailed discussions.

Host Software

Most smart card software is host software; it is written for personal computers and workstation servers and it accesses existing smart cards and incorporates these cards into larger systems. Host software (aka off-card software, PC software, or terminal software) will typically include end-user application software, system-level software that supports the attachment of smart card readers to the host platform, and system-level software that supports the use of the specific smart card needed to support the end-user application. In addition, host software includes application and utility software necessary to support the administration of the smart card infrastructure.

Host software usually is written in one of the high-level programming languages found on PCs and workstations (e.g., C, C++, Java, BASIC, COBOL, Pascal, or Fortran), and linked with commercially available libraries and device drivers to access smart card readers and smart cards inserted into them. Card software is usually written in a "safe" computing language such as Java, a precursor "safe" machine-level language such as Forth, or assembly language.

Card Software

Card software (aka on-card software) includes software that runs on the smart card itself. It usually is classified as operating system, utility, or application software, much as is the case with host software. For many applications, rather generic smart cards with their general on-card software will suffice; special software for the card is not required. Where application-specific software is required, it typically is written either in assembly language for the chip architecture of the microprocessor found embedded in the smart card or it is written in a higher level language that can either be interpreted directly on the card, or compiled into card assembly language and loaded onto the card.

It is useful to occasionally further categorize smart card software into application software or system software. Application software uses the computational and data storage capabilities of a smart card as if they were those of any other computer and is relatively unaware of the data integrity and data security properties of the smart card. These are of more concern to the person using the card than to the application software accessing it. System software, on the other hand, explicitly uses and may contribute to and enhance the data integrity and data security properties of the smart card.

Host application software substitutes the smart card for an alternative implementation of the same functionality (e.g., when an encryption key or a medical record is kept on a smart card rather than in a hard disk file on the local computer or in a central database on a server somewhere). Host system software harnesses the unique and intrinsic computing and data storage capabilities of the smart card by sending data and commands to it and by retrieving data and results from it.

Card application software typically is used to customize an existing off-the-shelf smart card for a particular application and amounts to moving some functionality from host application software onto the card itself. This can be done in the interest of efficiency, in order to speed up the interaction between the host and the card—or security, in order to protect a proprietary part of the system. Card system software is written in a low-level machine language for a particular smart card chip and is used to extend or replace basic functions on the smart card. Table 1.1 lists some simple relationships among host or card platforms and the type of software they might contain.

Table 1.1 Types of Smart Card Software with Sample Applications

Software Type	Application	System
Host	Digital signal	Electronic purse
Card	Lottery game	Encryption algorithm

Host and Card Software Integration

Both kinds of smart card software—host software outside the card looking in, and card software inside the card looking out—are treated in this book, but they are fundamentally different in their orientation and outlook. Card software focuses on the contents of a particular card, provides computational services for applications in accessing these contents, and protects these contents from many applications that might try incorrectly to access these contents. Host software, on the other hand, might make use of many different cards, and typically is aware of many cardholders (and possibly many card issuers) as well as many different kinds of cards.

Card software implements the data and process security properties and policies of a particular smart card. For example, a program running on the card might not provide an account number stored on the card unless presented with a correct PIN. Or, a program running on the card might compute a digital signature using a private key stored on the smart card, but it would under no condition release the private key itself. Software running in a smart card provides secure, authorized access to the data stored on the smart card. It is only aware of the contents of a particular smart card and entities "out there" (e.g., people, computers, terminals, game consoles, set-top boxes, etc.) trying to get at these contents.

Host software connects the smart cards and the users carrying them to larger systems. For example, software running in an automatic teller machine (ATM) uses the smart cards inserted by the bank's customers to identify the customers and to, in turn, connect the customers to their bank accounts. Or, software running in a soda machine verifies that the card inserted into the card reader is a valid cash card and decrements the amount of cash on the card before triggering the release of a can of soda. Host software is aware of many smart cards and tailors its response based on the particular smart card presented.

Unlike most computer software, which relies on supporting services from its surrounding context, smart card software begins with the assumption that the context in which it finds itself is hostile and is not to be trusted. Until presented with convincing evidence to the contrary, smart cards don't trust the hosts they are inserted into and smart card hosts don't trust cards that are inserted into them. A smart card program only trusts itself. Everything outside the program has to prove itself trustworthy before the program will interact with it.

Host Programs

By far, most smart card software will be host software and written against existing smart cards, either commodity off-the-shelf smart cards available from smart card manufacturers or smart cards created by major smart card issuers such as bank associations, telecommunication companies, retailers, or national governments. The operating system on these widely distributed smart cards implements a characteristic set of commands (usually 20 or 30) to which the smart card responds. Host software sends commands to the card operating system that executes them on the smart card processor and returns the results. Some examples of commands are "Decrement the amount of money in purse 1 by $1.50," "Authenticate user with PIN 1234," and "Read and return the second record from file 5."

There are more functions you might like a smart card to perform than can fit in the resources of today's smart cards; at this time, there is no one all-purpose smart card operating system or one all-purpose, off-the-shelf smart card. For example, some standard cards are particularly good for payment and loyalty applications, some standard smart cards are particularly good for network and cryptological applications, and some smart cards are particularly good for mobile telephone applications. Also, some off-the-shelf cards offer collections of general-purpose (if low-level) functions. One of the first tasks of a host software programmer is to choose the smart card that will be included in the system.

A host smart card program must accomplish two tasks before it begins to conduct business with a smart card. First, it must ensure that the smart card it is dealing with is authentic. Second, it must convince the card that it is authentic. No business can be conducted before this mutual trust has been established. Actually filling the role the smart card was intended to perform—provide some digital cash or produce a digital signature—typically is only a very small part of the total interaction between a command language host program and the smart card operating system.

High-Level Language Card Programs

Late in 1996, the smart card manufacturer Schlumberger introduced the first off-the-shelf smart card that could accept and run programs written in a high-level programming language, namely Java. Until the advent of the Java card, the only way to get software onto a smart card was to have it written and loaded into a smart card by a smart card manufacturer. This was a long, tedious, and surprisingly error-prone process. It also was a very expensive process and precluded all but the largest organizations from creating purpose-built smart cards. Some smart card manufacturers used high-level languages such as Forth and C to create card software, but the capability of using these tools to program the card itself was not passed on to the owner of the card and certainly not to the cardholder.

One use of a Java program running on a smart card is to implement a specialized set of commands for use by a host program. The Java program receives commands from the host program, executes them on the card, and returns results just like the operating system in an off-the-shelf smart card. Using this technique, a Java card can either emulate an existing non-Java card, it can extend an existing card with new commands, or it can become a wholly new card for use by host software.

Theoretically, a Java smart card program could implement any command set whatsoever. However, due to both memory constraints for containing the program on the card and time constraints for running the program, the functionality of the Java program is constrained by the functionality of the underlying operating system services on which it can call. For example, you likely would not want to perform encryption using very secure keys purely in Java on the card (because of the computational loading on the card), but rather would call on cryptographic functionality in the native card operating system and perhaps in a crypto coprocessor in the microcomputer itself. In Chapter 6, we'll look at two smart cards that provide cryptographic services: one of them specifically designed for such services and the other, a Java card, allowing for the development of cryptographic services in applets on the card.

Java programs that are both stored and executed on the card also have opened up the possibility of breaking out of the master/slave relationship between host software and card software and thus have enabled new classes of smart card applications. Although the underlying communication channel is still a half-duplex channel (i.e., a channel over which either end can send information to the other end, but in only one direction at a time), a smart card programmer can now arrange for the card to control and send commands to the host rather than the other way around. In Chapter 8, we'll look at the use of smart cards in the GSM telephone system, an area where the smart card often acts as the commanding agent of applications.

Assembly Language Card Programs

Although they're the least likely and most demanding of the smart card programming scenarios, there are situations in which a system designer will want to consider extending an existing smart card operating system or creating a wholly new and unique smart card. For example, you might wish to add a new encryption algorithm or mode of communication to a smart card. The Mondex™ and Visa® Cash electronic cash cards are good examples of such cards.

To build a custom smart card, an application system designer would typically work with a smart card manufacturer such as Schlumberger or Gemplus and possibly a smart card chip manufacturer such as Infineon or STMicroelectronics. It might be possible to modify and extend existing operating systems and libraries owned by these manufacturers to incorporate custom features as opposed to creating a completely new operating system for the smart card. Both

Schlumberger and Gemplus produce off-the-shelf cards that can be extended after manufacture. Some functions on smart cards, such as communications and card file services, are common to almost all smart cards; the creator of a custom card would not want to reproduce these.

Creating a custom-built smart card is expensive both in time and in money; Table 1.2 lists some hypothetical cases; you should probably budget at least two years and at least $1 million. Furthermore, it is unlikely that the resultant card will interoperate with any existing host software or systems, so there might be additional time and money expenses on the host side of the system. For all but the largest organizations and applications, assembly language programming of smart cards should be considered only for closed, mission-critical systems where compatibility is not a consideration.

Each smart card chip manufacturer has its own procedures for building a smart card chip containing a custom assembly language program and operating system. These procedures are discussed in detail in Chapter 3, "Some Basic Standards for Smart Cards," as are procedures for getting these chips made into cards.

Table 1.2 Comparison of Smart Card Programming Projects

Software Type	Application Development Time	Typical Program Size	Card Type Used	Difficulty	Expense
Host	6 months	10 KLOC	Off-the-shelf	Medium	Low
Application	1 year	1 KLOC	Java card	Medium	Medium
System Card	2 years	4 KLOC	Custom	High	High

ELEMENTS OF SMART CARDS

Smart cards or smart card application systems have many recurring themes and elements. During the course of this book, we will talk about many of these in some detail. In the following section, let's introduce some of them as a means of creating a context for further discussions.

Smart Card Software Security

Smart card software security is, not surprisingly, based on cryptography. Keys are stored in files on the card and algorithms and protocols are implemented in software on the card. Cryptography is used primarily to authenticate system entities such as users, cards, and terminals and to encrypt communications between the smart card and the outside world. The cryptographic functions built into a smart card for its own security requirements also can be used to implement security functionality in other systems. The protections provided by the former obviously enhance the security of the latter.

Before a smart card can provide access to its resources, it must determine with whom it is dealing. Similarly, before it is accepted by other entities, it must be able to prove who it is. Therefore, one of the first tasks a smart card performs when it is activated is to authenticate entities outside itself, primarily the person who inserted it into the terminal and the terminal into which it has been inserted, and to authenticate itself to some or all of these entities.

An authentication procedure might be as simple as demonstrating the possession of a shared secret such as a four-digit PIN, or it might be as complicated as demonstrating the ability to encode an offered message, called a *challenge*, with a particular key and algorithm or continuously following a defined transaction protocol. If at any point in an authentication process an entity reveals that it is not who it claims to be, all further communication with the entity is blocked. A record of these failed attempts may be kept on the smart card and, after a certain number of failures with no intervening success having been reached, the card may block all further access or destroy itself and its contents completely.

Encryption can be applied to all message traffic to and from the smart card or only to particular messages. If a smart card is communicating with two applications simultaneously, it might be using a different encryption key or technique with each.

Smart card programmers typically do not have to design new authentication or encryption algorithms. Rather, they use the facilities that are built into the smart card. These facilities have been field tested and come with a certain level of assurance of correctness. Designing new algorithms is not easy, and validating the correctness of a new algorithm is probably not a subtask that a smart card application developer wants to assume. Table 1.3 lists a number of cryptographic algorithms that find use in various smart cards.

Table 1.3 Examples of Smart Card Encryption Algorithms

Algorithm	Sample Uses
DES and TDES	Communication channels
A3 and A8	GSM mobile telephone
Elliptic curve	Digital signature
TSA7	Health records
RSA	Digital signature

Smart Card Operating Systems

Smart card operating systems, at least those that pre-date post-issuance programmable smart cards, are not operating systems in the sense that today's mainstream programmers and software developers think of them. Smart card operating systems certainly don't have the functionality of Windows or UNIX or even DOS. Rather, they are more like pre-DOS collections of on-card commands to which the smart card responds. New variants of smart cards are evolving toward classical operating system functionality.

The basic relationship between a smart card terminal (such as a PC) into which a smart card is inserted and the smart card itself is one of master and slave. The terminal sends a command to the smart card, the smart card executes the command, returns the result if any to the terminal, and waits for another command.

In addition to describing the physical characteristics of a smart card and the detailed formats and syntaxes of these commands and the results they return, smart card standards such as ISO 7816 and CEN 726 also describe a wide range of commands that conforming smart cards can implement. Most smart card manufacturers offer off-the-shelf smart cards with operating systems that implement some or all of these standard commands, together with manufacturer-specific extensions and additions; Table 1.4 lists a few examples.

Table 1.4 Examples of Operating Systems for Off-the-Shelf Smart Cards

Card Type	Manufacturer	Maximum Memory Size	Extensible
Cryptoflex™	Schlumberger	32 KB	Yes
MPCOS-EMV 128k™	Gemplus	16 KB	Yes
Cyberflex Access™	Schlumberger	32 KB	Yes
GemXpresso211/V2	Gemplus	32 KB	Yes
SIMphonIC™	Oberthur	32 KB	Yes
SIMtelligence 32/J Java™	Orga	32 KB	Yes

Smart Card File Systems

Many smart card operating systems support a modest file system based on the ISO 7816 smart card standard. Because a smart card has no peripherals, a smart card file is really just a contiguous block of smart card memory. A smart card file system is a singly rooted, directory-based, hierarchical file system in which files can have long alphanumeric names, short numeric names, and relative names.

You usually can't extend or expand an already allocated file, so you have to create files at the maximum size they are expected to need to be. Furthermore, there is no notion of garbage collection or compacting in a smart card file system. So, for example, if file A and file B are created in this order in the same file system directory and then file A is deleted, the space occupied by A is lost until file B also is deleted. If file B is deleted because it was the last file created, the space occupied by file B is reclaimed and can be reused by file C, for example.

Smart card operating systems support the usual set of file operations such as create, delete, read, write, and update on all files. In addition, operations are supported on particular kinds of files. Linear files, for example, consist of a series of fixed-size records that can be accessed by record number or read sequentially using read-next and read-previous operations. Furthermore, some smart card operating systems support a limited form of seek on linear files. *Cyclic files* are linear files that cycle back to the first record when the next record after the last record is read or written. Purse files are an example of an application-specific file type supported by some smart card operating systems. *Purse files* are cyclic files, each of whose records contains the log of an electronic purse transaction. Finally, *transparent files* are single, undifferentiated blocks of smart card memory that the application program can structure any way it pleases.

Associated with each file on a smart card is an access control list. This list records what operations, if any, each card identity is authorized to perform on the file. For example, identity A might be able to read a particular file but not update it, whereas identity B might be able to read, write, and even alter the access control list on the file.

One of the key design tasks of a smart card programmer in building a new smart card application is defining and laying out the files that the application will expect to find on the smart card; see, for example, Table 1.5. Size and usage of smart card real estate is a key concern, but the names of the files, their hierarchical relationship to one another, and their access authorizations must also be thought through.

Table 1.5 Examples of Smart Card File Types

Type	Special Operations	Sample Uses
Linear	Seek	Credit card account table
Cyclic	Read next, read previous	Transaction log
Purse	Debit with certificate	Loyalty points, e-cash
Transparent	Read and write binary	Picture
SIM file	Encrypt, decrypt	Cellular telephone

Smart Card Communications

The typical single-chip computer on a smart card is able to transmit and receive data at speeds up to 115,200 bits per second (bps), but most smart card terminals drive smart cards at 9,600 bps for contact smart cards and 7,800 bps for contactless smart cards. Because only a small amount of data is being transmitted and because the channel can be quite noisy, reliable communication is more important than high-speed communication. As we'll discuss later in the book, movement toward other I/O mechanisms is one of the major directions for the evolution of smart card technology. Two of the cards that we'll examine in some detail make use of the Universal Serial Bus (USB) as a communication channel, allowing for much higher speed I/O.

The communications pathway to and from a smart card is *half-duplex*, that is, data is either flowing from the terminal to the smart card or from the smart card to the terminal, but not both at the same time. The result is that the smart card and the terminal have to be synchronized and always agree on whose turn it is to talk and whose turn it is to listen. If both the terminal and the card transmit at the same time, data will be lost. If they both believe it is their turn to listen, the system enters a deadlock situation and nothing further happens. Half-duplex communication matches the processing paradigm in most smart card systems today; that is, single-threaded, single-tasking operations. Another evolutionary path for smart cards that we'll examine later in the book is a move toward multithreaded operations.

Data received by and transmitted from a smart card is stored in a buffer in the smart card's very limited random access memory (RAM). Therefore, only relatively small packets (10's to 100's of bytes) of information are moved in each message. Although the ISO and CEN standards describe in detail the format and coding of these messages, nothing prevents the smart card programmer from designing messages specifically tuned to his or her application. You must ensure that other surrounding systems don't make assumptions about the messages based on the ISO or CEN standards (which you'll learn more about in Chapters 3 and 4).

Smart Card Hardware

The computer on a smart card is a single ICC that includes the CPU, the memory system, and the input/output lines of a general-purpose computer. A single chip is used in order to make tapping into information flows inside the computer more difficult. If more than one chip were used to implement the smart card computer, the connections between the chips would be obvious points of attack.

The Smart Card Memory System

Smart cards have a memory architecture that will be unfamiliar—if not downright bizarre—to most mainstream programmers. Programmers typically think in terms of having available large amounts of homogeneous RAM that is freely available for reading and writing. This is definitely not the case on a smart card. There are, in fact, three kinds of memory on a smart card: read-only memory (ROM), nonvolatile memory (NVM), and a relatively tiny amount of RAM.

ROM is where the smart card operating system is stored and is of interest only to assembly language programmers. General-purpose smart cards have between 8 KB and 96 KB of ROM. Here, one finds various utility routines such as those for doing communication and for maintaining an on-card file system along with encryption routines and special-purpose arithmetic routines. Code and data are placed in ROM when the card is manufactured and cannot be changed; this information is hardwired into the card.

NVM is where the card's variable data—such as account numbers, number of loyalty points, or amount of e-cash—is stored. NVM can be read and written by application programs, but it doesn't act like and cannot be used like RAM. NVM gets its name from the fact that it happily retains its contents when power is removed from the card; data written to NVM, if not overwritten, will last ten years. NVM presents two problems:

- *Slowness*. It generally takes 3 to 10 milliseconds to write data into NVM.
- *Data loss*. NVM wears out after it has been written to a number of times (around 100,000 times).

The typical programmer is not familiar with either of these two problems, but must take them into account when writing smart card software.

There is some familiar RAM on a smart card, but not very much—usually only 2,000 bytes or less. This is unquestionably the most precious resource on the smart card from the card software developer's point of view. Even when using a high-level language on the smart card, the programmer is acutely aware of the need to economize on the use of temporary variables. Furthermore, the RAM is not only used by the programmer's application, but also by all the utility routines, so a programmer has to be aware not only of how much RAM he or she is using, but also how much is needed by the routines he or she calls.

The Smart Card CPU

The CPU in a smart card chip is most typically an 8-bit microcontroller using the Motorola 6805 or Intel 8051 instruction set. Hitachi's H8 smart card chip is a notable exception. These instruction sets have the usual complement of memory and register manipulations, addressing modes, and input/output operations. Some chip manufacturers have extended these basic instruction sets with additional instructions that are of particular use on smart cards. Smart card CPUs execute machine instructions at the rate of about 400,000 instructions per second (400KIP) although speeds of up to 1 million instructions per second (1MIP) are becoming available on the latest chips.

The demand for stronger encryption in smart cards has outstripped the ability of software for these modest computers to generate results in a reasonable amount of time. Typically, 1 to 3 seconds is all that a transaction involving a smart card should take; however, a 1,024-bit key RSA encryption can take 10 or more seconds on a typical smart card processor. As a result, some smart card chips include coprocessors to accelerate specifically the computations done in strong encryption.

A smart card CPU will not necessarily execute code from all parts of the smart card memory system. Most smart card chips, for example, will not execute code stored in RAM. Furthermore, some chips make it possible to reconfigure sections of NVM so that a program loaded into NVM cannot be overwritten (essentially turning the NVM into ROM) or so that the CPU won't take instructions and therefore execute code from this part of memory.

Smart Card Input/Output

The input/output channel on a smart card is a unidirectional serial channel. This means that it passes data 1 bit and, hence, 1 byte at a time and that data can flow in only one direction at a time. The smart card hardware can handle data at up to 115,200 bps, but smart card readers typically communicate with the card at speeds far below this.

New cards are now becoming available, which use hybrid forms of communication channels between the card and the host computer. Later in this book, we'll discuss a card that can be plugged directly into a USB port of a computer.

The communication protocol between the host and the smart card is based on a master (host) and slave (smart card) relationship. The host sends commands to the card and listens for a reply. The smart card never sends data to the host except in response to a command from the host. Some new card variants are starting to experiment with the use of TCP/IP-like protocols to allow peer-to-peer communication between the card and the host computer.

Smart card operating systems support either character or block transfers, but usually this level of detail is hidden from the smart card programmer.

Smart Card System Design

Most smart card programming consists of writing programs on a host computer that sends commands to and receives results from predefined or application-specific smart cards. These applications read data from and write data to the smart card and perhaps make use of the modest computing powers of the processor on the smart card. Smart cards in these applications typically are secure stores for data pertaining to the individual bringing the card to the system, such as personal identification data.

In situations where no off-the-shelf card contains all the functionality needed by the application, the programmer may be able to extend the capabilities of an off-the-shelf card by writing software that runs on the card itself. This software may implement special-purpose or higher level function on the card that is a combination of existing operating system functions, or it may provide additional protections for the data stored on the card.

Finally, there may be situations where the operating system capabilities of an existing smart card need to be extended or where a wholly new and unique smart card needs to be manufactured. Examples of such situations include a closed system application where cost or a particularly high level of security is a critical factor or where a particular encryption algorithm is needed to connect the smart card to an existing host system. In these situations, smart card programmers write new operating system software for smart cards partially or completely in the assembly language of the processor on the smart card.

Regardless of the type of software being written, the smart card programmer must be constantly aware of the two central concerns of smart card software: data security and data integrity.

Data Security

Data security means simply providing data only to those who are authorized to receive it. It requires that neither data values nor even information about these data values are revealed to unauthorized parties or systems. Wherever data is stored and whenever data is moved, the smart card programmer must ensure that this requirement is satisfied.

Although there are many methods for obscuring data, data security doesn't make use of data encryption as much as it does the notion of an authorized entity. One of the most obvious attacks on a smart card is for an unauthorized entity to become authenticated as an authorized entity and then use the provided facilities of the card to access data. Because keys, passwords, and PINs stored on the card are all used to authenticate entities, particular care must be exercised in protecting this kind of data.

One way to ensure the data security of a smart card is to control physical access to the card. This technique is often used early in the life cycle of the card. For example, cards are manufactured under tight physical security procedures and shipped to the card customer under equally tight procedures. The keys used to protect the card during transit from manufacturer to customer are called *transport keys* and they are given only to the customer. Using the transport keys, a smart card customer can access all files on the smart card and set up a particular file system and access an authorization scheme. Transport keys are like a superuser password for the card and they typically are deleted from the card by the customer after they have been used to configure the card for the customer's application.

Data Integrity

Data integrity requires that all parties to a smart card transaction agree on the state of the data in the transaction. If vending machine software intends to charge a smart card electronic purse $1 for a can of soda, then at the end of the transaction, there should be $1 less on the smart card, $1 more in the vending machine, and a soda in the hands of the cardholder. Any variation—$1 added but $1 not subtracted; $1 transferred, but no soda vended; and so on—is a violation of data integrity.

The primary source of breakdowns in data integrity is system failure in the middle of processing a transaction. Such failure can be accidental—for example, when a communication line from an ATM goes down—or deliberate, for example, when the cardholder prematurely removes the smart card from the reader. Programming to ensure data integrity means both guarding against its loss and detecting and repairing its loss when it occurs.

Smart Card System Architectures

Because it carries neither power nor clock, there is no such thing as a standalone smart card. All smart cards are integrated into larger systems that themselves typically contain additional computers and data stores. For example, an ATM system will include a computer in each ATM machine, transaction servers to concentrate requests coming from many ATMs, and database machines that contain identity and account information. In fact, it is in large, distributed, multiparty systems where smart cards play one of their unique roles as a secure identity token.

There have been a number of efforts to specify and de facto standardize smart card systems in addition to just smart cards themselves. Three bank card associations, Europay, MasterCard, and Visa, teamed up in early 1996 to produce EMV'96, which specifies an overall system architecture for debit and credit card applications of smart cards. Late in 1996, a work group headed by Microsoft and including Schlumberger, Bull CP8 Transac, Hewlett-Packard, and Siemens Nixdorf Information Systems produced a specification called PC/SC (personal computer/smart card) for connecting smart cards to personal computers and for surfacing application program interfaces to smart cards on personal computers. Next, in early 1997, IBM published a specification called the Open Smart Card Architecture, and the Open Group published an architecture for Personal Security Modules. Finally, version 2.0 of the Secure Electronic Transactions (SET) specification published by MasterCard and Visa in the summer of 1997 contained yet another smart card system architecture specification based on the EMV specification and is specifically tailored for credit and debit applications of smart cards.

One of the design challenges for a smart card programmer is distributing system functionality among the multiple computers that deal with a smart card and with which a smart card must deal. Deciding what functions go on the smart card itself, what functions go on the machine into which the smart card is inserted, and what functions go on the various machines upstream from the terminal machine comprises the heart of the application design process. Not surprisingly, these are not solely technical decisions; they directly affect both the business interests and security concerns of owners of all these various computers.

ORGANIZATION OF THE BOOK

Our goal in this book is to provide you with a view of the essential information you'll need to consider the use of smart cards in your application. Our approach to this will be to first look at the basics of smart cards. Over the course of three chapters, we'll look at the physical structure and construction of smart cards. This will give us a general appreciation for the intrinsic security (tamper resistance and tamper evident) characteristics plus the ability of smart cards to live and operate in a relatively hostile environment.

Next, we'll look at the grounding of smart card technology in a variety of standards. A comprehensive set of international standards form the common heart of smart cards. Over the years, these have been augmented by specifications developed by various industry consortia, which stabilize the operation and use of smart cards in a number of areas. Finally, we'll look at a few instances of proprietary intellectual property adopted in some highly useful areas.

Extending the standards basis for smart cards, we'll examine in some detail the specifications for an interindustry command set that has shaped the evolution of smart cards for the last two decades. Presented as international standards, this command set describes a complete telecommunication protocol for smart cards, from physical connectivity to application-level support. This command set can be found in various levels of completeness on a number of smart cards from various vendors. Such cards are usually aimed at supporting one, or at most a very few, distinct application(s).

Then, we'll look at the evolution of smart cards from fixed command sets to extensible or "post-issuance programmable" smart cards. These cards form the cutting edge of smart card deployment today. We'll look at the basic architecture of these cards and provide some general comparisons of their utility for a variety of application areas. To close out this look at the basics of smart cards, we'll discuss in detail the command sets provided by two "high-performance" smart cards on the market today: one, a fixed command set card and the other, a multi-application card.

With a good foundation in smart card basics, we'll move on to look at the software found on host computer systems, which allows the use of smart cards. Here, we'll concentrate on the smart card stacks found on most PC or workstation operating systems. We'll look at the architecture of these software components and illustrate how large-scale applications make use of the software to access the services of various smart cards.

GSM telephones offer a look at a high-volume use of smart cards as well as a look at an extremely demanding host system environment. We'll spend one full chapter delving into the details of the GSM system.

Following this, we'll then close out our technical review by looking at an application using one of the cards that we examined in some detail. We'll also look at the elements of card infrastructures and card management systems, which are required to actually deploy and support large numbers of smart cards.

Finally, we'll take a bit of a crystal ball look at where we see smart card systems evolving. This final (chapter) gaze is largely the personal perceptions of the authors; others may see the pathway into the future along a very different route.

That said, let's now delve into some of the gory details of smart cards and their applications.

2

Physical Characteristics of Smart Cards

Smart cards present a variety of faces depending primarily on the type of integrated circuit chip (ICC) embedded in the plastic card and the physical form of the connection mechanism between the card and the reader. They can be very inexpensive tokens for financial transactions such as credit cards, telephone calling tokens, or loyalty tokens from a variety of businesses. They can be access tokens for getting through locked doors, for riding on a train, or driving an automobile on a toll road. They can function as identity tokens for logging in to a computer system or accessing a World Wide Web server with an authenticated identity. Of particular interest are several such variants, including cards with

- surface contacts leading to a memory-only ICC
- an electromagnetic connection to a microprocessor ICC
- surface contacts leading to a microprocessor ICC
- high-level physical network connections (e.g., Universal Serial Bus, or USB)

The very earliest smart cards were *memory cards* containing an ICC comprising only nonvolatile memory (NVM) and the necessary circuitry to read and write that memory. Today, such cards still constitute the largest number of smart cards in use. These cards are relatively inexpensive and provide modest security for a variety of applications, ranging from transportation fee tokens to telecommunications fee tokens (such as phone cards).

A *memory card* is used for storing information in a permanent or semipermanent fashion. The circuitry of the smart card exposes, through a standard electrical connector, the control lines for addressing selected memory locations as well as for reading and writing those memory locations through the electrical connectors on the face of the card. There is no on-board processor to support a high-level communications protocol between the reader and the card. Rather, memory cards use a synchronous communication mechanism between the reader and the card. Essentially, the communication channel is always under the direct control of the reader side and the card circuitry responds in a very direct (synchronous) way to the very low-level commands issued by the reader for addressing memory locations and for reading from or writing to the selected locations. In some recent memory cards, security enhancements have been incorporated through the provision of memory addressing circuitry within the chip that requires a shared secret between the terminal (which is writing to the card chip) and the chip itself.

A *contactless card* has an ICC embedded within the card; however, it makes use of an electromagnetic signal to facilitate communication between the card and the reader. With these cards, the power necessary to run the chip on the card is transmitted at microwave frequencies from the reader into the card. The separation allowed between the reader and the card is quite small—on the order of a few millimeters. However, these cards offer a greater ease of use than cards that must be inserted into a reader. This ease of use can be mitigated by other factors.

With the current state of the technology, the data transfer rate between the reader and the contactless card may be restricted by the power levels that can be achieved in the card; that is, for such cards without an internal power source (e.g., a battery) the power to run the on-card processor must be derived from a signal transmitted to the card from the reader. The power levels achieved typically allow only very small separation (a few millimeters) between the card and the reader. Further, a feedback mechanism from the reader to the card through which cardholder verification is done is a bit more awkward with the contactless card. Consequently, these cards are most popular for uses where the possession of the card is deemed to be adequate authorization for card use.

A *smart card*, that is, the card that is most commonly viewed as a "smart card," is one that makes use of an electrical connection between the on-card ICC and the off-card computer. The physical connection is made through a contact plate on the face of the card; the contact plate providing eight distinct electrical connections to the embedded ICC as illustrated in Figure 2.1. The most common such physical connection makes use of two connectors on the face plate to effect a half-duplex input/output (I/O) channel to and from the card.

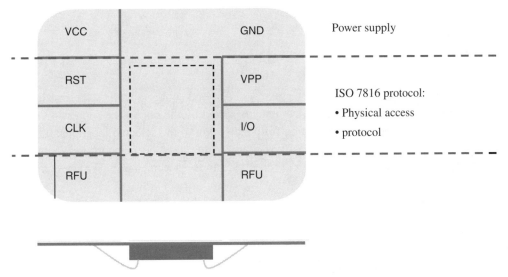

▶ **Figure 2.1**   A standard smart card contact face plate.

A second variant of such cards, which is just starting to come into being, makes use of two additional connectors on the face plate to effect a full-duplex channel through a USB connection. This is illustrated in Figure 2.2. This variant greatly simplifies the host computer connectivity in that a special smart card reader is no longer required; connectivity is achieved through the USB port to the host.

Except for the physical mechanism used to transfer information between the reader and the card, contactless and contact-based cards are very similar in overall architecture. This book focuses mainly on smart cards that make use of electrical connections between the cards and the readers. The two cards that we will review in some detail can actually be interfaced through a smart card reader or through a USB port, but this impacts only the physical interconnection. This type of microprocessor-based smart card combines all the necessary ingredients for an enhanced-security computing platform. It integrates both memory and a central processing unit (CPU) into a single ICC. This minimizes the opportunity to intercept well-defined electrical signal patterns moving between processor and memory elements. Keep in mind that the security resulting from this integrated packaging is not infallible. The smart card is tamper resistant, not tamper proof.

The impetus for creating smart cards was the need for secure tokens that could contain information and that could provide a secure platform for certain processing activities. These capabilities were greatly facilitated with an innovative packaging approach for the principal elements of a computer system, as illustrated in Figure 2.3. Specifically, all the basic components of a computer

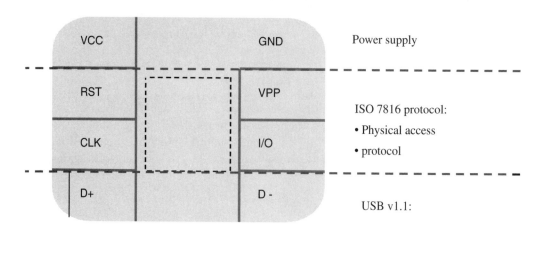

▶ **Figure 2.2**   Smart card face plate with USB connections.

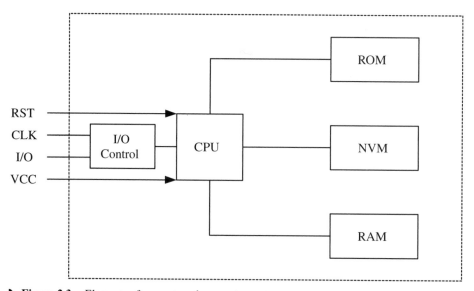

▶ **Figure 2.3**   Elements of a smart card computer system.

system are incorporated into a single ICC. This means that the physical connections between these components are embedded within a monolithic (silicon) structure. This, in turn, means that it is difficult for an observer to intercept signals passing between these components (within the chip). The net result is a more secure computer system than is normally achieved with macroscopic physical connections between components.

PHYSICAL SECURITY

Central to the overall security architecture is the concept of physical security. The smart card figures very prominently in this. From the cardholder's standpoint, being able to have the smart card computer platform in physical possession is a large step toward overall security. In this case, attacks against the security of the overall system have to be made against the system components while in operation or through examination of information gained while the system was in operation. This means, for example, that attacking encryption algorithms used by the smart card must typically proceed from captured cyphertext, not from active examination of the card while in use.

Conversely, the overall security architecture of the smart card-enabled system must be such that if a card is no longer in the cardholder's possession, the damage to the system through a security attack can be limited through the knowledge that the card is no longer in the cardholder's possession. Further, the vulnerability to the entire system must be minimized if the information related to a single cardholder is compromised.

Complementing the concept of physical security is the concept of tamper resistance and tamper evidence on the part of smart cards and their constituent parts. Central to this concept is the packaging of the ICC and its connections into a module that is encased in an epoxy resin as illustrated in Figure 2.4. This packaging provides for both tamper resistance and tamper evidence. The epoxy is nontrivial to penetrate in a nondestructive fashion and to do so requires possession of the card. If the module packaging is penetrated, it requires destruction of the packaging, thus providing evidence of the tampering.

Processor and Memory Architecture

An adjunct to physical security, at least in the case of the smart card, is the enhanced security architecture of the microprocessor-based computer installed in the card and the tamper-resistant packaging of the card itself. This chapter examines the architecture of the smart card's computer. Packaging the processor, memory, and I/O support in a single ICC enhances the security of the entire configuration. It is difficult, though certainly not impossible, to connect electrical probes to lines internal to an ICC. The equipment to insert such probes is reasonably expensive. Consequently, for an attacker to extract information directly from a chip requires physical possession of the card, costly equipment,

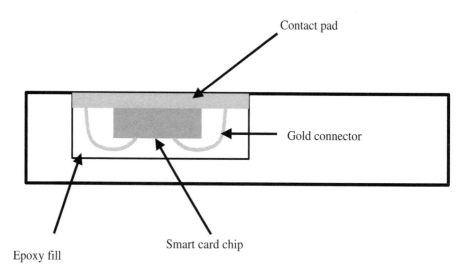

▶ **Figure 2.4**   An ICC module.

and detailed knowledge of both the hardware architecture of the chip and the software loaded onto the chip.

Tamper-Resistant Packaging

As we noted earlier, the ICC is packaged into a "module" which is then inserted into the card body. The module itself is a tamper-resistant and tamper-evident package. When the module is, in turn, embedded into the card body, it actually forms a second layer of tamper resistance and tamper evidence. Tamper resistant refers to the characteristic that, given physical possession of a smart card, it's a nontrivial task to get to the chip and even more nontrivial to extract information from the chip. Further, tamper apparent or tamper evident refers to the characteristic that, to do so, will typically leave an obvious trail that the card has been tampered with. Thus, it is difficult to learn the secrets contained within a smart card without the cardholder knowing that the card has been compromised.

CARD CONSTRUCTION

The construction of a smart card is a nontrivial manufacturing problem, particularly given the volume of cards produced, the environmental conditions under which cards must operate, and the length of time they're expected to provide undiminished service. The details of card construction typically are a closely held secret of each manufacturing company. The general features of the process are, however, relatively standard.

The construction process proceeds from the beginning in two threads:

- the manufacture and printing of the card body
- the preparation of the ICC module and its insertion into the card body

The last stage in the preparation of the card itself is typically the final printing of information on the face and back of the card. This is the point in the process where the card is tied to a unique cardholder, and it generally entails both the printing operation and storing a set of information into the ICC of the card— information that uniquely identifies the cardholder.

The card construction operation, including its personalization for each individual cardholder, is done under the auspices of a "card management system" which controls and tracks the manufacturing and deployment operations on a population of cards. In Chapter 10, we will examine the characteristics of card management systems and smart card application infrastructures in a bit more detail.

Card Body

Smart card bodies, according to international standards, must be composed of polyvinyl chloride (PVC) or an "equivalent material." The physical requirements placed on the card body by its operating environment are quite rigorous. The smart card is generally carried on the person of the cardholder, either in a purse or perhaps in a pocket wallet. Consequently, the card is subjected to a large amount of bending and flexing. The material from which it is constructed must be sufficiently resilient to return to an essentially flat shape after it is flexed. This flat shape is required in order for the electrical contacts to be stable when the card is inserted into a reader or when it is swiped through a magnetic stripe reader.

The card body material must also be resistant to the effect of infrared or ultraviolet radiation, which is sometimes used as a fixing process in the printing operation. A recurring problem is an induced brittleness from the printing process, which makes cards crack during normal operations. Sometimes, this cracking can be so severe as to cause embedded ICC modules to be ejected from the card.

The most modern card construction sometimes makes use of the layering of dissimilar materials. The layering itself enhances the mechanical properties of the card against failure during flexing and bending. In addition, the layering diminishes the depth (into the card) of any failure induced by the printing operation. Finally, the layering process allows specially printed components (e.g., white light holograms) to be affixed to the card during the construction process. This greatly increases the difficulty of counterfeiting a card.

ICC

The computer on a smart card is a single ICC that includes the CPU, the memory system, and the I/O lines. A single chip is used in order to make tapping into information flows inside the computer more difficult. If more than one chip were used to implement the smart card computer, the connections between the chips would be obvious points of attack. Signals passing across these connections would typically not be protected (e.g., by encrypting information) from eavesdropping. Hence, extracting information from the card would likely be greatly enhanced.

Most smart card programming consists of writing programs on a host computer that sends commands to and receives results from predefined or application-specific smart cards. These applications read data from and write data to the smart card and perhaps make use of the modest computing powers of the processor on the smart card. Smart cards, in these applications, typically are secure stores for data pertaining to the individual bringing the card to the system, such as personal identification data.

In situations where no off-the-shelf card contains all the functionality needed by the application, the programmer may be able to extend the capabilities of an off-the-shelf card by writing software that runs on the card itself. This software may implement special-purpose or higher level function on the card that is a combination of existing operating system functions, or it may provide additional protections for the data stored on the card.

Finally, there may be situations where the operating system capabilities of an existing smart card need to be extended or where a wholly new and unique smart card needs to be manufactured. Examples of such situations include a closed system application where cost or a particularly high level of security is a critical factor or where a particular encryption algorithm is needed to connect the smart card to an existing host system. In these situations, smart card programmers write new operating system software for smart cards partially or completely in the assembly language of the processor on the smart card.

Regardless of the type of software being written, the smart card programmer must be constantly aware of the two central concerns of smart card software: data security and data integrity. The invocation of operations on the smart card must be allowed only by entities whose identities can be authenticated by the smart card. Conversely, the smart card's identity must be authenticated by the off-card (host computer) application. In some instances, the privacy of information flowing to and from the card must be guaranteed by encrypting the information.

An interesting problem that must be handled with the computer in a smart card is the integrity of information in the ICC in the midst of transaction computations. Power to the ICC is provided through the reader connections to a smart card. Because the smart card typically can be removed at any time, it is not unusual for the card to be removed in the midst of a computation (transaction). This particular error condition is actually given a name: *tearing*. When this happens, it is important that information not be left in an ambiguous state within the ICC. In particular, when some form of value is stored on the smart card, for example, in a cash purse, it is important that value not be "created" on the card during the conduct of a transaction operation. That is, no intermediate state of the purse should ever be greater than the final intended value of the purse at the completion of operations.

A number of antitearing mechanisms are used in smart cards. The most common is a mechanism similar to the transaction mechanisms of database systems. A "transaction flag" is set when the operation is started, and this flag is the last thing to be cleared at the completion of the operation. If, at the start of an operation, the transaction flag is noted to be set, it is an indication that a previous transaction was interrupted and not completed. When this state is identified, the transaction can be "rolled back" to the state at the beginning of the previous transaction. In later sections, we'll look at smart card transaction operations in much greater detail.

Magnetic Stripe

Most smart cards belong to a family of standardized cards referred to as Class I ID cards. We'll look at the specifications for these cards in a bit more detail in Chapter 3. Such cards have a well-defined size, including length, width, and thickness. These cards also have fixed positions for all the printing and information storage mechanisms typically used on cards. One such mechanism, which is quite prevalent on smart cards, is a magnetic stripe. This is a narrow strip of material affixed to the "back" of the smart card. The back of the card is the face of the card opposite the contact face plate.

The magnetic stripe material is typically a ferrous alloy, which will retain a magnetic field imprinted on it by an electromagnetic write head such as is used in a tape recorder. Characters can be imprinted on this magnetic stripe according an ISO/IEC specification. The information is redundantly recorded in two or three tracks defined within the stripe. By swiping the card past a read head, the information recorded on the stripe can be extracted for use on an attached computer system.

Information is typically stored on a magnetic stripe in a redundant fashion; that is, information is stored more than once at various positions within the magnetic stripe. When the information is read off of a magnetic stripe, the redundant components can be checked for integrity (e.g., a checksum) and for consistency. This allows the retrieval of information even if the magnetic stripe is worn or damaged.

Embossing

Embossing is a technique for printing characters on the surface of a card such that the characters are raised above the general level of the face of the card. By inserting such a card into a printing press-like mechanism, it is easy to print a copy of the characters found on the card onto a paper receipt. The characters printed on the card are usually an account number, which provides an unambiguous connection back to an account of the cardholder.

Other scanning techniques that can be used on other elements of the card (bar codes, magnetic stripe) are more reliable and provide better integration of the card information into host systems than does embossing. Consequently, embossing is perhaps not as important or used as routinely as in years past. Embossing is, however, perhaps the most straightforward and externally visible technique for monitoring information on the card. Thus, it is perhaps the preferred "method of last resort."

Printing

The face (and back) of a card also can be printed in a "normal," multicolor printed format. This printing may include uniquely identifying material related to the cardholder, for example, a picture of the cardholder. This provides a mechanism for connecting the cardholder to the card. Anyone presented with such a card can easily compare the picture to the actual person presenting the card.

Printing on the face and back of the card also can be used to identify other entities associated with the card. For example, the name of a bank that issued the card might be included, or the name and logo of a bank association responsible for the standards associated with the card.

Security

The smart card is largely about security. In the construction of the card, security comes in several guises, in the

- structure of the ICC and its modular packaging
- embedding of the ICC module in the card body
- techniques used to communicate with the card
- techniques used to manipulate information within the ICC in the card

Much of the way that the smart card is constructed, programmed, and used is replete with measures designed to enhance the security of the system. We'll examine both directly and indirectly many of the attacks used to try to compromise the smart card. It should be noted that security measures for smart card systems are in a constant state of evolution in response to the constant evolution of attack mechanisms.

Historically, there are a variety of attacks against smart cards, which are facilitated by the external provision of power and programming (clock) control to the card. One such class of attack is termed "power analysis." This approach makes use of knowing sequences of commands that are to be executed by the smart card processor and, by monitoring in very fine-grained steps the power consumed by the smart card processor, determining which commands are being executed; including determining the values of parameters used to trigger switching among processing pathways in the command sequences. This approach is particularly adept at isolating cryptographic operations involving the use of keys; that is, encryption and decryption operations. In some instances, the breaking of cryptographic keys can be greatly enhanced (speeded up) by power analysis.

The counter to this type of attack is to be cognizant of the attack mechanism while creating the on-card code which will effect the cryptographic operations. The cryptographic algorithms can be coded so that power analysis is greatly diminished as a viable attack. Of course, it should be remembered that to make use of such an attack means that the card must be in the hands of the attacker. This means that the cardholder should be able to detect the loss of the card and report it, allowing the information (e.g., keys) contained on the card to be invalidated.

Another attack, which is somewhat similar, is termed "differential fault analysis." In this form of attack, a particular (usually cryptographic) operation is initiated and then an error is induced into the card operation causing an error response from the algorithm. If the error can be induced repeatedly, it is possible to glean information from the error responses that is useful in breaking the on-card keys. As we'll discover when we look at a couple of specific (commercial) smart cards in Chapter 6, this type of attack can be diminished by reducing the information returned by an error condition within the computation.

Attacks such as these are damaging to a system at large in the case where information from a single card can somehow be used to compromise a larger segment of the system in which it works. If the information gleaned from a single card can only impact that single cardholder, then the integrity of the overall system can generally be maintained. Specifically, if the attacker must have physical possession of the card in order to pursue a particular attack mechanism, then the cardholder has an opportunity to notice the missing card and report it to the system's administrators. In this case, strictly personal information, such as a (cryptographic) key used to establish the identity of the cardholder, can be invalidated and reissued.

Probably the greater risk to the individual cardholder are attacks aimed at intercepting information as it flows between the card and the terminal configuration. If an attacker can access this information stream and extract useful information without the knowledge of the cardholder, then damage might well be done to the cardholder. We will look at a number of such attack mechanisms and the defenses against them throughout the remainder of this book.

Again, the bottom line is that new attacks are being discovered or refined all the time. Then, defenses of those attacks are developed and made part of the smart card methodology. Continuing vigilance of attacks and defenses is necessary on the part of those who develop and deploy smart card-based systems.

Anti-counterfeiting

Printing or other preparation of a smart card can contain a variety of elements that guard against the card being counterfeited. One such mechanism is a white light hologram affixed to the face of a card. Such holograms cannot be directly copied with normal electrostatic copying machines. Further, it is typically quite expensive to create a copy hologram. Consequently, it is difficult, if not impossible for a counterfeiter to correctly reproduce the physical appearance of a specific smart card.

Just as with currency, certain printing elements may be included on the face of a card that are difficult or impossible to copy with normal copying machines. One such mechanism is extremely fine-line artwork. If line widths much finer than the resolution of copying machines are used, then running a copy of the card will result in fuzzy areas on the face of the card.

Perhaps the best anti-counterfeiting mechanism provided by a smart card is the ability of the ICC on the card to support complex identification protocols. Such protocols, generally based on the sharing of secret information between the on-card and off-card computers, are very difficult (and expensive) to crack. This means that it can be virtually impossible for an attacker to get a card to communicate (with an attacking system) long enough to extract any useful information from the card.

Contactless Cards

Contactless smart cards are a variant which makes use of a wireless communication mechanism between the card and the card reader. A contactless card contains an embedded ICC but does not require a contact face plate on the front of the card. Rather, an antenna is embedded within the plastic body of the card. This antenna is connected to the ICC. The card, or more correctly the card antenna, must be brought into physical proximity to a card reader, which also includes an antenna. Power, in the form of electromagnetic radiation, is transmitted from the reader antenna and is received by the card's antenna. The power received is quite small, but it is sufficient to power the on-card ICC.

Once power is received by the card and applied to the on-card ICC, a communication protocol is initiated between the card and the host computer. Most contactless cards make use of two distinct frequencies for this communication channel, which allows a full duplex channel to be created. Data is transferred between the card and the host at approximately 100 Kbps.

Contactless cards are most useful for transactions where it is reasonable to assume that possession of the card is adequate authorization for participation in the transaction(s) that the card supports. Paying a toll at a tollbooth, or opening a door that many people use are good examples of such transactions. In such systems, the cardholder is not authenticated to the card as a prelude to the transaction.

During the course of this book, we will, from time to time, discuss the ramifications of using contactless smart cards. However, our main thrust will always be contact-based cards.

Combination Cards

Another variant of the smart card features a card with both a contactless ICC and a contact-based ICC. These two processors may be interconnected on the card or they may operate autonomously. This type of card is of particular use for supporting operations that require specific cardholder authentication and other operations that only require possession of the card. The latter is typical of transportation systems, while the former is typical of credit or debit card operations.

While combi-cards have some very useful applications, it should be remembered that having two processors on the card, particularly if they are interconnected, goes against one of the main tenets of smart cards; that is, the monolithic processor and memory combination of the smart card ICC makes it harder to effect a physical attack against the card.

ICC ARCHITECTURE

The generally recognized (most secure) smart card packaging approach consists of putting the CPU, all the memory, and the I/O electronics into the same ICC, rather than presenting them in the form of various chips, which are then tied together through electrical connections of some type. Why is this simple packaging approach so profound? Because it provides all the necessary capabilities in a very small physical package and it conceals the interconnections between the various computer elements inside the chip itself, thereby enhancing the security of what's going on (or what's stored) in the computer.

Once the elements of the computer are integrated into a single chip, it becomes very difficult for an outside observer to intercept signals flowing among the various elements and to subsequently discern the information content of those signals. The connection to the outside world through which information flows is a simple I/O port that can be guarded to a large extent by the processor included within the chip. This is done through the use of high-level telecommunications protocols through which the chip's processor element filters all information passed to or from the other components of the chip. Through these protocols, it is possible to require authentication of the identity of the reader-side program that is communicating with the computer on the smart card. In this manner, the smart card can protect itself by communicating only with entities that can prove who they are and that the smart card's computer trusts.

In addition to enhancing the security of the smart card, the ICC packaging also provides a small unit that is amenable to being embedded in a credit card-sized card, which can be carried on the person of the card bearer. When embedded in the plastic card and carried, for example, in a person's wallet, the chip is subject to a variety of physical forces. The card is bent and flexed and might be subjected to sudden shocks. In typical electronic equipment, in which components are tied together through macroscopic electrical wiring or even conducting lines on a printed circuit board, this physical environment is an excellent recipe for many failures. When all the elements are packaged in a single chip, however, the stresses tend to be applied to all the elements equally. So, if the chip itself can hold together, then the components will tend to operate successfully. Empirical evidence indicates that when chips are reduced to a size of approximately 25 square millimeters (in roughly a square configuration) they are able to withstand the day-to-day stresses encountered through normal credit card-type uses.

Achieving these small sizes for the chip to be embedded in a smart card is dependent on several criteria:

- the resolution of the technology used for the chip, which is often characterized by "feature size" (e.g., the size of a single transistor element within the chip) in microns
- the width of the internal bus of the processor (i.e., is it 8 bits, 16 bits, 32 bits, or 64 bits?)
- the type of memory utilized
- auxiliary elements (such as power line frequency, voltage filters, and memory-mapping registers) included in the chip for security or functionality reasons

The small size needed for chip features requires leading-edge technology. However, in order for chips to be inexpensive and reliable, we often need to turn to older, more mature technologies. The makeup of memory, that is the amount of ROM, EEPROM, and RAM is a design decision based on the amounts of each memory necessary to address particular problem areas. To meet the constraints of the physical environment, ICCs generally do not exceed 25 mm2. At the same time, the amount of chip area required to implement the various types of memory varies significantly, as shown in Figure 2.5.

The width of the internal bus structure indicates the number of memory address lines running between components within a chip; that is, width is generally indicative of the number of bits in individually addressable sections of memory. Minimizing chip size generally tends to call for selection of fewer address lines; therefore, most smart card chips are currently based on 8-bit microprocessors. These microprocessors also tend to be the older and more mature technologies.

With higher resolution manufacturing techniques becoming more mature, we can expect to see significantly larger memory sizes in coming years; sizes in the 500-kB to 1-MB range are predicted in some quarters. If this evolution does occur, then the smart card will surely become more of a general-purpose computing element in future systems.

Processor

The CPU in a smart card chip is typically an 8-bit microcontroller typically using the Motorola 6805 or Intel 8051 instruction set. Hitachi's H8 smart card chip is a notable exception. These instruction sets have the usual complement of

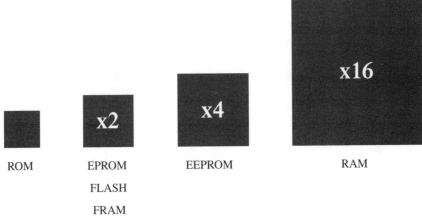

▶ **Figure 2.5**   Relative size of 1 bit of various memory types.

memory and register manipulations, addressing modes, and I/O operations. Some chip manufacturers have extended these basic instruction sets with additional instructions that are of particular use on smart cards. Smart card CPUs execute machine instructions at the rate of about 400,000 instructions per second (400KIP) although speeds of up to 1 million instructions per second (1MIP) are becoming available on the latest chips.

In the next few years, 32-bit processors will likely become the norm. This enhancement, coupled with much larger memory sizes, will open up whole new classes of problems that can be addressed by the smart card as a secure and truly personal computing system.

Physical Interface

The I/O channel on a smart card is a unidirectional serial channel. This means that it passes data 1 bit and subsequently 1 byte at a time and that data can flow in only one direction at a time. The smart card hardware can handle data at up to 115,200 bps, but smart card readers typically communicate with the card at speeds far below this.

The communication protocol between the host and the smart card is based on a master (host) and slave (smart card) relationship. The host sends commands to the card and listens for a reply. The smart card never sends data to the host except in response to a command from the host.

Smart card operating systems support either character or block transfers, but usually this level of detail is hidden from the smart card programmer.

As was indicated earlier, two smart cards to be discussed in some detail later in this book will allow the direct use of a USB channel. This channel offers both full-duplex operation and higher speed operation. Higher speeds can be exploited with existing smart card O/S architectures. However, some architectural changes will be required to take advantage of full-duplex and essentially peer-to-peer communication protocols. Word is proceeding in this direction, but it will likely be a few years before it makes its way to commercial viability.

Power. Power is supplied from the reader to the card. Virtually all smart cards in use today operate at 5 volts. Some ICCs are able to operate at a lower voltage, nominally 3 volts. In this case, the reader will typically power the card to 5 volts and then the ICC and the reader negotiate a lower voltage as part of the protocol negotiation sequence.

I/O. Two interface lines are used to carry I/O traffic between the reader and the card. One line, the I/O line, carries the data bits. This line is found in one of two states, which nominally represent a "0" in one position and a "1" in the other position. The second line, the clock, indicates when the I/O line is to be sampled in order to determine a data bit.

For the USB interface that we've mentioned, two additional lines are used to carry a second I/O channel. Thus a full-duplex connection can be achieved.

Synchronization. The typical link-level protocols that are used between the reader and the card are half-duplex protocols. That is, data is either written to the I/O line by the reader and read by the card or data is written by the card and read by the reader. Thus, each end of the communication line keeps track of whether it is in a talking state or a listening state. The protocols are not terribly sophisticated, so it is possible to get into a sequence of error conditions that may leave one or both of the ends of the channel in an ambiguous state. When this happens, it is the responsibility of the reader to reset the entire protocol sequence, which it can do with the reset line.

Security Features

Physical security of information stored in a smart card starts with the combination of computer memory and processor in the same small package. It is difficult, though not impossible, to physically examine the contents of memory cells within the chip. It is also difficult, though not impossible, to intercept the electrical signals passing between the processor and memory or between processor elements during selected computations. To examine or intercept such information requires the use of fairly expensive equipment and unfettered access to the smart card itself, usually without the smart card's owner being aware of it.

Security features are sometimes enhanced by randomizing the sequence of memory cells to be accessed by the processor. That is, the address lines for various memory cells don't proceed in a linear sequence, but rather are varied from one cell to the next through some complex algorithm. The net result is that an external observer is less likely to be able to discern any information about where data is stored or how it is being used by simply watching the sequencing of access to individual memory cells.

As the use of smart cards has grown, the number of attempts to thwart the security features of smart cards has grown. Several techniques to coax information out of a card have been identified. Some of these involve manipulation of the power supplied to a card. Defenses against these techniques have been developed as well. Some chips have additional sensors that monitor characteristics of the power supplied to the chip. This information can be used by programs within the chip and allow it to lock down the card when it detects that it is under attack. In extreme circumstances, the card can destroy sensitive information in such cases in order to prevent it from being extracted by the attacker.

Memory

Smart cards have a memory architecture that will be unfamiliar—if not down-right bizarre—to most mainstream programmers. Programmers typically think in terms of having available large amounts of homogeneous random access memory (RAM) that is freely available for reading and writing. This is definitely not the case on a smart card. There are, in fact, three kinds of memory on a smart card: read-only memory (ROM), nonvolatile memory (NVM), and a relatively tiny amount of RAM.

ROM is where the smart card operating system is stored and is of interest only to assembly language programmers. General-purpose smart cards have between 8 KB and 96 KB of ROM. Here one finds various utility routines such as those for doing communication and for maintaining an on-card file system along with encryption routines and special-purpose arithmetic routines. Code and data are placed in read-only memory when the card is manufactured and cannot be changed; this information is hard-wired into the card.

NVM is where the card's variable data—such as account numbers, number of loyalty points, or amount of e-cash—is stored. NVM can be read and written by application programs, but it doesn't act like and cannot be used like RAM. NVM gets its name from the fact that it happily retains its contents when power is removed from the card; data written to NVM, if not overwritten, will last 10 years. NVM presents two problems:

- *Slowness*. It generally takes 3 to 10 milliseconds to write data into NVM.
- *Data loss*. NVM wears out after it has been written to a number of times (around 100,000 times).

The typical programmer is not familiar with either of these two problems, but must take them into account when writing smart card software.

There is some familiar RAM on a smart card, but not very much—usually only 2,000 bytes or less. This is unquestionably the most precious resource on the smart card from the card software developer's point of view. Even when using a high-level language on the smart card, the programmer is acutely aware of the need to economize on the use of temporary variables. Furthermore, the RAM is not only used by the programmer's application, but also by all the utility routines, so a programmer has to be aware not only of how much RAM he or she is using, but also how much is needed by the routines he or she calls.

A smart card CPU will not necessarily execute code from all parts of the smart card memory system. Most smart card chips, for example, will not execute code stored in RAM. Furthermore, some chips make it possible to reconfigure sections of NVM so that a program loaded into NVM cannot be overwritten (essentially turning the NVM into ROM) or so that the CPU won't take instructions and therefore execute code from this part of memory.

These various types of memory used in smart card chips bring in a very interesting wrinkle with respect to the chip design for smart card ICCs. The implementation technologies used for chip memories vary greatly in the size of individual memory cells as we saw illustrated in Figure 2.5. The smallest memory element is read-only memory. This type of memory, as the name implies, can be read by typical computer elements, but it requires very special equipment in order to write information into the memory. In fact, the writing of ROM can be incorporated very early into the chip fabrication process itself; this technique tends to enhance the security of the chip because it is difficult to examine the contents of the ROM without destroying the chip, even with very expensive probing equipment. So this type of memory is very useful for permanently encoding stored programs for the smart card, but it is useless for storage of dynamic information that needs to be changed during the normal use of the card.

Significantly larger is the electrically erasable and programmable read-only memory (EEPROM). The contents of this type of memory in a smart card chip can actually be modified during normal use of the card. Hence, programs or data can be stored in EEPROM during normal operation of the card and then read back by applications that are using the card. The electrical characteristics of EEPROM memory are such that it can only be erased and then reprogrammed a finite (but reasonably large) number of times, generally around 100,000 times. While somewhat limited, techniques have evolved which make this type of memory quite useful for typical smart card uses. EEPROM memory cells tend to be about a factor of four larger than ROM memory cells. EEPROM, like ROM, does have the nice characteristic of being nonvolatile memory; that is, the information content of the memory is unchanged when the power to the memory is turned off. So information content is preserved across power-up and power-down cycles on the smart card chip.

Larger still is a memory type known as RAM. This is the type of memory used in typical computer systems such as a desktop PC. Information can be written and erased in this type of memory a very large number of times. In the smart card chip, however, a RAM memory cell is approximately four times larger than an EEPROM memory cell. RAM is also volatile memory; that is, the contents of the memory are lost when power is removed from the memory cell. So information in RAM is not preserved across a power-down and power-up cycle on a smart card. RAM is, nevertheless, essential for certain operations in smart card applications; in particular, it requires much less time for RAM locations to be read or written by the chip's processor unit. This can be extremely important when the smart card is interacting with a PC application in which the timing of responses from the card to the PC are important; this is often the case in the mobile telecommunications area (i.e., smart card-based cellular telephones).

The net result is that smart card chips tend to make use of varying amounts of each memory type depending on the specific application for which the smart card is intended to be used. The most powerful chips used in smart cards today have RAM sizes in the 1-kB to 2-kB range, ROM sizes in the 16-kB to 96-kB range, and EEPROM sizes in the 8-kB to 64-kB range.

Cryptographic Assist

The demand for stronger encryption in smart cards has outstripped the ability of software for these modest computers to generate results in a reasonable amount of time. Typically, 1 to 3 seconds is all that a transaction involving a smart card should take; however, a 1024-bit key RSA encryption can take 10 or more seconds on a typical smart card processor. As a result, some smart card chips include coprocessors to accelerate specifically the computations done in strong encryption.

A typical smart card processor is an 8-bit microprocessor. Such a processor is capable of manipulating only 1 byte of information at a time. This manifests itself in the support of 8-bit integer arithmetic as the primary computational facility of the computer. Handling larger integer arithmetic or floating-point arithmetic operations requires significant additional programming beyond the basic instruction set of the processor. This presents something of a problem when you need to support public key cryptography on a smart card chip.

Public key cryptography is predicated on the use of integer arithmetic on a scale that severely taxes the capabilities of a typical smart card processor. Performing encryption or decryption operations can be extremely time-consuming, taking several seconds or even minutes. Because these delays are not acceptable given the time it should take to conduct a typical transaction, enhancements to smart card processors are needed. This enhancement has been accomplished by adding to the chip a second processor that is capable of enhanced performance for selected integer arithmetic operations, such as fast integer multiply operations. This greatly speeds up the public key cryptography operations; however, it affects the overall size of the chip (slightly) and the cost of the chip (more significantly).

Security Hardening

One of the security threats to smart cards is the ability of an attacker to probe the ICC with high-powered magnification devices such as scanning electron microscopes (SEM). This form of attack is essentially destructive of the smart card. That is, one must disassemble the card in order to extract the ICC from it. One must then chemically (and perhaps physically) remove layers of the chip and then examine the constituent layers with an SEM. Through this technique, however, one can extract much about the software and information stored on the card if one is willing to invest the time, energy, and money. Given the knowledge that can be gained when it is combined with other forms of attack (e.g., power analysis), it is conceivable that multipronged attacks could be devised which would threaten an individual cardholder's personal card.

One approach to mitigating such a physical attack is to harden the ICC itself. That is, as part of the manufacturing process, a hardened shell is deposited over the top surface of the chip. This shell is difficult for a probe to penetrate and is very brittle. This means that if some physical means is used to remove the shell, there is a high probability that the ICC will fracture. This will greatly increase the difficulty in this type of attack.

SUMMARY

Smart cards have a very uniform physical footprint. Standardization has been accomplished through a number of international standards. This approach was taken in order to standardize the worldwide infrastructure needed to support the use of smart cards, and allows equipment vendors in all parts of the world to create cards and equipment to use cards that are interchangeable throughout the world.

The construction of smart cards and their internal structure are also highly standardized, which allows them to be used in large-scale systems without having to resort to single source providers. This much standardization, of course, offers the prospect of uniform methods of attacking smart cards and their constituent systems in an attempt to extract the value they represent.

Our review in this chapter of the physical characteristics of smart cards gives us a good grounding from which to begin to examine the software systems contained within smart cards. We'll delve into these aspects in the coming chapters.

3

Basic Standards for Smart Cards

Smart cards, perhaps more than most other technologies, have been subject to tremendous pressures across their lifetime to conform to *standard* implementation and deployment strategies. The form factor, electrical characteristics, and model of computation are firmly established by internationally recognized standards. This has the attractive benefit of guaranteeing that no one approach can attain a monopoly or near-monopoly stranglehold on the technology (e.g., PC operating systems). However, it does encumber the use of smart cards with a tremendous load of baggage. The chances for true, revolutionary advances are greatly minimized, if not eliminated, by the need to conform to established equipment and operations trails that stretch for decades into the past.

At least three distinct approaches to standardization are present in today's smart card world:

- international standards
- de facto standards from consortia
- patent and copyright protection for Intellectual Property (IP)

The precursors to today's smart cards were the plastic credit cards used as identity tokens in the retail financial marketplace. These tokens, when introduced, represented a significant improvement in the ability of merchants to accept payment in an abstract form (essentially "on credit") from customers whose identity they could not personally vouch for. The credit card represented (and actually still does) a certification of identity and financial situation from an issuer functioning as a trust broker.

In the trust infrastructure provided by the credit card (although a merchant might not be personally inclined to extend credit to an unknown customer to make a purchase), it was reasonable for the merchant to trust the issuer of a credit card, in no small part because of the known financial strength of the issuer and because of financial agreements entered into when the merchant became "certified" to accept the (credit card) tokens of the card issuer.

As the convenience of credit cards became established and their use spread, it became highly desirable to achieve an unprecedented level of interoperability among cards from different issuers and transaction equipment from a variety of vendors in merchants' stores around the world.

The start of the journey toward worldwide interoperability lay in the establishment of international standards regarding first the cards themselves, and then the equipment that would work with them and with the environments in which they would be used. The venue of choice for establishing such standards was the International Standards Organization (ISO). In some fields of technical activity, the International Electrotechnical Commission (IEC) collaborates with the ISO in the development of standards. Similarly, in the United States, the American National Standards Institute (ANSI) functions as a primary standards-setting body. Consequently, in the following discussion, some standards are ISO standards and others are joint ISO/IEC/ANSI standards accepted by all three bodies.

ID Card Standards

ISO/IEC (and in some instances, ANSI) standards have been established to fully describe plastic identification cards. The various standards have evolved over time and are found in a variety of ISO/IEC/ANSI classifications, the more pertinent of which are listed in Table 3.1.

Table 3.1 ISO Standards Pertaining to Smart Cards

ISO/IEC Standard	Title
ISO/IEC 7810 – 1995-08-15	Identification Cards – Physical Characteristics
ANSI/ISO/IEC 7811-1 – 1995: Part 1	Identification Cards – Recording Technique Embossing
ANSI/ISO/IEC 7811-2 – 1995: Part 2	Identification Cards – Recording Technique Magnetic Stripe
ANSI/ISO/IEC 7811-3 – 1995: Part 3	Identification Cards – Recording Technique Location of Embossed Characters on ID-1 Cards
ANSI/ISO/IEC 7811-4 – 1995: Part 4	Identification Cards – Recording Technique Location of Read-Only Magnetic Tracks – Tracks 1 and 2

Table 3.1 ISO Standards Pertaining to Smart Cards (Continued)

ISO/IEC Standard	Title
ANSI/ISO/IEC 7811-5 – 1995: Part 5	Identification Cards – Recording Technique Location of Read/Write Magnetic Tracks – Track 3
ANSI/ISO/IEC 7812-1–1993	Identification Cards – Identification of Issuers Part 1: Numbering System
ANSI/ISO/IEC 7813 – 1995	Identification Cards – Financial Transaction Cards
ISO 7816-1	Identification Cards – Integrated Circuit(s) Cards with Contacts – Physical Characteristics
ISO 7816-2	Identification Cards – Integrated Circuit(s) Cards with Contacts – Dimensions and Location of the Contacts
ISO 7816-3	Identification Cards – Integrated Circuit(s) Cards with Contacts – Electronic Signals and Transmission Protocols
ISO 7816-3 Amendment 1	Protocol Type T=1, Asynchronous Half-Duplex Block Transmission Protocol
ISO 7816-3 Amendment 2	Revision of Protocol Type Selection
ISO 7816-4	Identification Cards – Integrated Circuit(s) Cards with Contacts – Inter-Industry Commands for Interchange
ISO 7816-5	Identification Cards – Integrated Circuit(s) Cards with Contacts – Number System and Registration Procedure for Application Identifiers
ISO 7816-6	Identification Cards – Integrated Circuit(s) Cards with Contacts – Inter-Industry Data Elements
ISO 1177 - 1985	Information Processing – Character Structure for Start/Stop and Synchronous Character-Oriented Transmission

PHYSICAL CHARACTERISTICS OF IDENTIFICATION CARDS

A seminal specification that ultimately leads to smart cards is ISO/IEC 7810: Identification Cards—Physical Characteristics. This standard defines nominal physical characteristics for three types of identification cards, labeled ID-1, ID-2, and ID-3. Card type ID-1 deals with the generally accepted size and shape of a *credit card* or *smart card* and is the primary focus of this discussion. The ID-2 and ID-3 card types are simply larger sizes, but with all the other physical characteristics the same as ID-1 card types.

The basic function of an ID-1 identification card is to contain information in a visual, tactile, and electronic form that identifies its bearer and that may support transactions the card is to enable. Visual information may be presented through artwork, personal pictures, anti-counterfeiting mechanisms such as holograms, or machine-readable mechanisms such as bar codes. Embossing is used to convey information in a tactile form suitable for creating impressions of characters on other media, a capability often used in transactions based on such identification cards. Information may be conveyed in electronic form through two mechanisms: magnetic stripes, which are prevalent on credit cards, and an embedded integrated circuit chip (ICC), which is the defining characteristic of smart cards.

The elements of an ID-1 identification card include:

- the card backing (the plastic)
- optional embossing areas on which alphanumeric information may be stamped
- an optional area to which a magnetic stripe may be attached

Information then can be magnetically encoded on the magnetic stripe. As illustrated in Figure 3.1, an ID-1 identification card is a rectangle 85.6 mm wide, 53.98 mm tall, and 0.76 mm thick. ISO/IEC 7810 places stringent restrictions on the distortions allowed in the card backing, particularly near the area that might contain a magnetic stripe. The intent of these exacting specifications is to ensure that reader or imprinting devices that ID-1 cards are inserted into can be expected to reliably read the information off a magnetic stripe and imprint the embossed numerals reliably without causing any damage or significant deterioration of the card.

The material characteristics of ID-1 identification cards are also established by ISO/IEC 7810; specifically, the card must be composed of polyvinyl chloride (PVC), PVC acetate, or "materials having equal or better performance." There are correspondingly stringent deformation characteristics for the card. In general, the specifications require that after one end of a card is flexed by up to 35 mm (which corresponds to about half the width of a card), it should return to its original flat state to within 1.5 mm. Further, it is specified that it be possible to bring the card to within an acceptable flat state through the uniform application of a moderately light pressure across the face of the card. Interestingly, the actual durability of a card is not established by the ISO/IEC specifications, but rather is left to a "mutual agreement between the card issuer and the manufacturer."

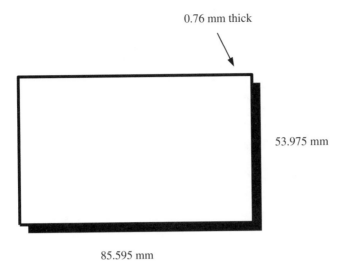

0.76 mm thick

53.975 mm

85.595 mm

▶ **Figure 3.1**   ID-1 identification card form factor.

ENCODING OF INFORMATION FOR IDENTIFICATION CARDS

Building on the base formed by ISO/IEC 7810, the ANSI/ISO/IEC 7811 specification establishes standards for the encoding of information on an identification card through embossing or magnetic stripe techniques. This specification is divided into five parts:

- embossing (recording technique)
- magnetic stripe (recording technique)
- location of embossed characters on ID-1 cards
- location of read-only magnetic tracks (tracks 1 and 2)
- location of read-write magnetic track (track 3)

Embossing means causing the shape of characters to rise above the backing plane of the card. The embossed characters essentially form a typeface that can be used to print these characters onto some other material through the use of a rudimentary "printing press": before online printing of transaction receipts became prevalent, merchants used these credit card imprinting devices to prepare credit card invoices and receipts. ANSI/ISO/IEC 7811-1 establishes the allowed characteristics of embossing itself, including the relief height of the embossed characters (0.46 mm to 0.48 mm), the spacing between embossed characters (2.54 mm to 3.63 mm), and the size of the characters (4.32 mm). Auxiliary ISO specifications identify the characters and font sizes that render embossed characters suitable for optical recognition devices, along with the test procedures to be used to determine that a specific identification card meets all of these specifications; these include:

- ISO 1073-1, Alphanumeric character sets for optical recognition–Part 1: Character set OCR-A–Shapes and dimensions of the printed image.
- ISO 1073-2, Alphanumeric character sets for optical recognition–Part 2: Character set OCR-B–Shapes and dimensions of the printed image.
- ISO 1831, Printing specifications for optical character recognition.
- ISO/IEC 10373, Identification cards–Test methods.

ANSI/ISO/IEC 7811-2 specifies the recording techniques to be used to encode characters into a magnetic stripe affixed to an ID-1 card. Provisions are made for three different types of information recording, referenced as Track 1, Track 2, and Track 3. Track 1 can contain up to 79 alphanumeric characters encoded at a write density of 8.27 bits per mm (210 bits per inch); this track can contain both alphabetic and numeric information. Track 2 can contain up to 40 characters of numeric information encoded at a write density of 2.95 bits per mm (75 bits per inch). Both Track 1 and Track 2 are intended to be write-once/read-many channels; essentially, once the card is issued, these are read-only channels. Track 3 is both a write-many and a read-many facility (that is, a read/write track). It can contain up to 107 characters encoded at 8.27 bits per mm (210 bits per inch). The encoding for each of the data tracks includes a "longitudinal redundancy check" character that can be used by the card reader to detect any errors in the information read versus what was originally written onto the card.

ANSI/ISO/IEC 7811-3 specifies in detail the location of embossed characters on an ID-1 card, and Part 4 specifies the location of magnetic stripes. As illustrated in Figure 3.2, two areas for embossing are specified. The first, whose center line is 21.42 mm above the bottom edge of the card, or just below the center line of the card, allows for up to 19 card identification number numerals to be embossed. Just below this is an additional area of approximately 14.53 mm × 66.04 mm in which 4 rows of 27 characters each can be used to form a name and address field, which is offset at least 2.41 mm from the bottom of the card and 7.65 mm from the left edge. The embossed characters are raised toward the front side of the card. If a magnetic stripe is included on the card, it is found near the top, on the back side of the card. The specifications state that the magnetic stripe and the embossing may not overlap.

Two variants of magnetic stripes can be found on ID-1 identification cards; the form and location of these are defined in ANSI/ISO/IEC 7811-4 (for read-only tracks) and Part 5 (for read/write tracks). One of these is 6.35 mm tall × 79.76 mm wide, positioned no more than 5.54 mm from the top edge of the card

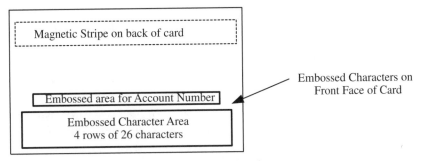

Magnetic Stripe on back of card

Embossed Characters on
Front Face of Card

Embossed area for Account Number

Embossed Character Area
4 rows of 26 characters

▶ **Figure 3.2**   Embossing and magnetic stripe locations.

and on the back face of the card. This magnetic stripe supports two recording tracks, each of which is intended to be a read-only track.

THE BUSINESS MODEL FOR IDENTIFICATION CARDS

By following the ISO standards through several interconnected specifications for identification cards, it is possible to go beyond just the description of physical and electronic characteristics of the card, arriving at a business model from which inferences can be made regarding how cards will be manufactured, what groups will actually distribute the cards to end-users, and some of the operations to be performed by the end-users of the identification cards. For example, the ANSI/ISO/IEC 7811-1 specification defines two terms reflecting the *distribution state* of a card:

- *Unused card.* A card that has been embossed with all the characters required for its intended purpose but has not been issued.

- *Return card.* An embossed card after it has been issued to the cardholder and returned for the purpose of testing.

ANSI/ISO/IEC 7811-2 further defines similar states for magnetic stripe cards:

- *Unused unencoded card.* A card possessing all components required for its intended purpose that has not been subjected to any personalization or testing operation. The card has been stored in a clean environment without more than 48-hour exposure to daylight at temperatures between 5 degrees C and 30 degrees C and humidity between 10% and 90%, without experiencing thermal shock.

- *Unused encoded card*. An unused, unencoded card that has only been encoded with all the data required for its intended purpose (for example, magnetic encoding, embossing, electronic encoding).
- *Returned card*. An embossed and/or encoded card after it has been issued to the cardholder and returned for the purpose of testing.

ANSI/ISO/IEC 7812: "Identification of Issuers—Part 1: Numbering System" further develops the business model by establishing a standard for the card identification number, which is displayed in embossed characters on the front face of an ID-1 card. The card identification number, which may be up to 19 characters long, is subdivided into three components:

- Issuer identification number. A six-digit component that includes the following:
  - Major industry identifier. A one-digit indicator of the industry designation of the card issuer; it is one of the following:
    - 0 - Tag reserved to indicate new industry assignments
    - 1 - Airlines
    - 2 - Airlines and other future industry assignments
    - 3 - Travel and entertainment
    - 4 - Banking/financial
    - 5 - Banking/financial
    - 6 - Merchandizing and banking
    - 7 - Petroleum
    - 8 - Telecommunications and other future industry assignments
    - 9 - For assignment by national standards bodies
  - Issuer identifier - A five-digit number associated with the specific issuing organization
- Individual account identification number. A variable-length component up to 12 digits maximum.
- Check digit. A cross-check number that is calculated from all the previous digits in the identification number according to an algorithm called the Luhn formula that is defined in an appendix of ANSI/ISO/IEC 7812.

The path toward standards-based specification of a general business mode (for financial transactions) becomes very explicit with ISO/IEC 7813: Identification Cards—Financial Transaction Cards. This specification does not consider any new technical areas, but makes a strict enumeration of the standards that must be adhered to in order to call a card a *financial transaction card*.

ISO/IEC 7813 specifies the content of the two read-only tracks of a magnetic stripe included on the card; this augments the content definition for ISO 4909 for the read/write track. The end result is a complete description of both the technical characteristics and the information content of cards suitable to support financial transactions, all rooted in international standards and acceptable for worldwide deployment.

SMART CARD STANDARDS

ISO 7816: Identification Cards —Integrated Circuit(s) Cards with Contacts provides the basis to transition the relatively simple identification card from a token that can be compromised through forgery, theft, or loss into a tamper-resistant and "intelligent" *integrated circuit chip* (ICC) card, more popularly known as a *smart card*. It is a multiple-part standard through which the smart card is specified in sufficient detail to achieve the same level of interoperability that has been achieved with the simpler cards discussed in the section "ISO Standards for Cards." Although ISO 7816 includes many approved parts and has several additional parts under review, the discussion here is aimed primarily at Parts 1 through 5. Consideration of other parts of ISO 7816 will occur in various later chapters.

- Part 1 - Physical characteristics
- Part 2 - Dimensions and location of the contacts
- Part 3 - Electronic signals and transmission protocols
- Part 3, Amendment 2 - Revision of protocol type selection
- Part 4 - Inter-industry commands for interchange
- Part 5 - Numbering system and registration procedure for application identifiers

Note

In the ISO standards related to ICCs, the device into which the ICC is inserted is referred to as an interface device (IFD). In the course of this book, the terms ICC, card, and smart card tend to be used interchangeably. Similarly, the terms IFD, reader, and terminal are used to mean the same thing.

ISO 7816-1 extends the physical characteristics definition of simpler ID-1 identification cards from the realm of plastic cards with perhaps an associated magnetic stripe to the more complex environment supporting an ICC within the card. This includes accommodation of exposure limits for a number of electromagnetic phenomena such as x-rays, ultraviolet light, electromagnetic fields, static electrical fields, and ambient temperature of the card (with embedded chip), as indicated in Table 3.2.

Table 3.2 Exposure Limits for Physical Phenomena

Phenomenon	Limit
Ultraviolet light	Ambient (depends on card vendor)
X-rays	Two times acceptable annual human dosage
EMI (electromagnetic interference)	No interference with magnetic stripe
Electromagnetic fields	Less than 1,000 Oe
Static electricity	1,500-volt (v) discharge through 1.5-K ohm resistor from 100-pF capacitor
Heat dissipation	Less than 2.5 watt; card temperature less than 50° C

The specification is also concerned with defining the characteristics of the card when it is bent or flexed. The concern, of course, is that an environment amenable to operation of the chip in the card—with its microelectronic connections between surface connectors and chip I/O pins, as well as its integrated circuitry—be maintained. Two tests of flexibility for the card are specified: Figure 3.3 illustrates the bending requirements of the card and Figure 3.4 illustrates the torsion requirements of the card.

In the cases of both bending tests and torsion tests, the concern is that through the normal wear and tear on a card (e.g., keeping the card in one's wallet), either

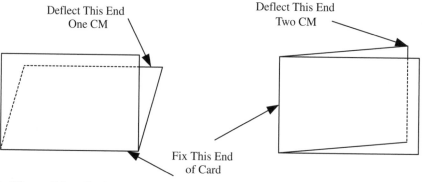

Deflect This End
One CM

Deflect This End
Two CM

Fix This End
of Card

▶ **Figure 3.3**   Card-bending testing.

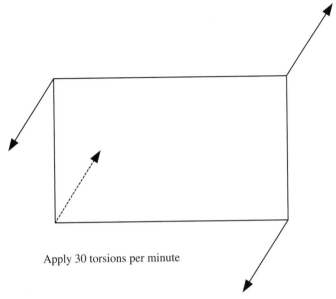

Apply 30 torsions per minute

▶ **Figure 3.4**   Torsion testing of a smart card.

the chip itself or the microconnection wires from the chip to the surface contacts will be damaged or broken. Practical experience with these tests has shown that a chip size on the order of 25 mm^2 is the largest that can routinely meet these flexibility constraints.

CHARACTERISTICS OF SMART CARDS

The mechanical tolerances required of smart cards are relatively stringent in order to ensure that cards can be properly aligned such that a reader's contact points can make a good electrical connection with the correct card contacts. In general, the card's contacts cannot vary from the surface of the card by more than 0.1 mm. The card must be sufficiently strong to resist permanent deformation when bent; it must be possible to return the card to a flat position with a very modest pressure over the face of the card. Finally, the electrical resistance of the card's contacts must fall within the acceptable limits established by ISO 7816-1.

ISO 7816-2 specifies an ICC with eight electrical contacts present in a standardized position on the front face of the card; these are referred to as C1 through C8. Some of these contacts are electrically connected to the microprocessor chip embedded within the card; some are not, having been defined to allow for enhancements but unused at the present time. The specific definitions for the contacts are shown inTable 3.3.

Table 3.3 Contact Definitions for Smart Cards

Contact	Designation	Use
C1	Vcc	Power connection through which operating power is supplied to the microprocessor chip in the card.
C2	RST	Reset line through which the IFD can signal to the smart card's microprocessor chip to initiate its reset sequence of instructions.
C3	CLK	Clock signal line through which a clock signal can be provided to the smart card's microprocessor chip to control the speed at which it operates and to provide a common framework for data communication between the reader and the smart card.
C4	RFU	Reserved for future use.
C5	GND	Ground line providing a common electrical ground between the reader and the smart card.
C6	Vpp	Programming power connection providing a separate source of electrical power (from the operating power) that can be used to program the NVM on the microprocessor chip.
C7	I/O	Input/output line that provides a half-duplex communication channel between the reader and the smart card.
C8	RFU	Reserved for future use.

The location of the contacts is illustrated in Figure 3.5. The contacts are almost always found on the front face of the card (which is the side of the card with the primary graphic and opposite the side with any magnetic stripe). However, the ISO 7816-2 standard does not mandate that the contacts appear on the front; the contacts can appear on the back of the card as long as care is taken to make sure the contacts do not intersect the magnetic stripe area.

Many of the earliest smart cards adhered to a different standard for contact locations that positioned the contacts toward the upper-left portion of the front face of the card. The standard on which this positioning was based became obsolete in 1990. Cards designed according to this standard were deployed primarily in Europe to support credit and debit applications.

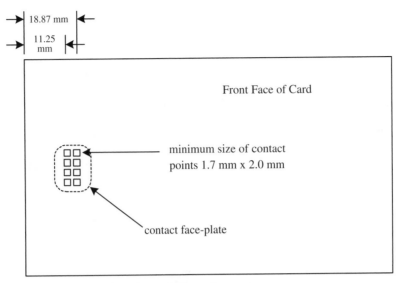

▶ **Figure 3.5**   Location, size, and shape of contacts.

ISO 7816-3 begins to delve into the specification of the "intelligent" aspects of the smart card. This standard describes the relationship between the smart card and the reader as one of "slave" (the smart card) and "master" (the reader). Communications are established by the reader signaling to the smart card through the contacts noted previously and are continued by the smart card responding accordingly. Communication between the card and reader proceed according to various state transitions illustrated in Figure 3.6. The communication channel is single-threaded; once the reader sends a command to the smart card, it blocks until a response is received.

When a card is inserted into a reader, no power is applied to any of the contacts. The chip on the card could be seriously damaged by applying power to the wrong contacts, and this situation could easily occur if a card were inserted across powered contact points. The contacts remain unpowered until an edge detector determines that the card is properly aligned with the contact points to within some acceptable (for the reader) mechanical tolerance.

Note -

Security mechanisms on many chips could be triggered if the cards were inserted across powered contact points, resulting in the possible disabling of the chip.

Reader State Diagram

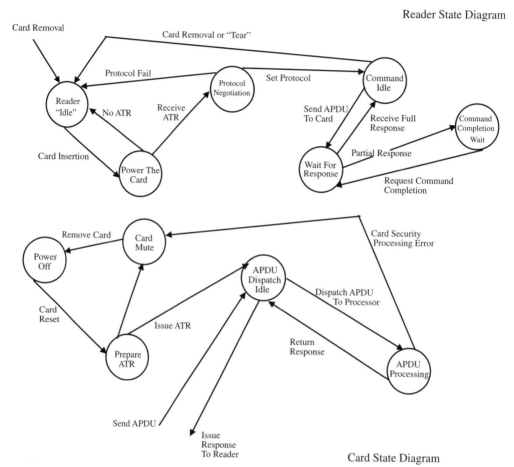

▶ **Figure 3.6**   Reader and smart card general state diagrams.

When the reader detects that the card is properly inserted, power is applied to the card. First, the contacts are brought to a coherent idle state, as shown in Table 3.4; then, a reset signal is sent to the card via the RST contact line. The idle state is characterized as being when the power (VCC) contact is brought up to a normal, stable operating voltage of 5 v; an initial power setting of 5 v is always applied first, even though some microprocessor chips being introduced operate at 3 v when in an I/O state. The I/O contact is set to a reception mode on the reader side and a stable clock (CLK) is applied. The reset line is in a low state. It must remain in a low state for at least 40,000 CLK cycles before a valid reset sequence can be started by the reader raising the reset line to a high state.

As illustrated in Figure 3.7, powering up a smart card occurs according to a well-defined sequence. Once power has been satisfactorily applied to the card,

Table 3.4 Contact States Prior to Card Reset

Contact	State
VCC	Powered and stable
VPP	Stable at idle state
RST	State – low
CLK	Suitable and stable clock signal applied
I/O	Reception mode in interface device

the RST line is raised to a high state that signals to the card to begin its initialization sequence. The specific initialization operations can vary from card to card, but the sequence should result in the sending of an answer to reset (ATR) from the card back to the reader. In general, the first byte of the ATR must be received by the reader within 40,000 clock cycles. Following that, each successive byte of the ATR must be received by the reader at a rate of at least 1 byte per second.

Data transfer between the reader and the card occurs through the concerted action of two of the contact lines: CLK and I/O. The I/O line conveys a single bit of information per unit of time as defined by the CLK depending on its voltage

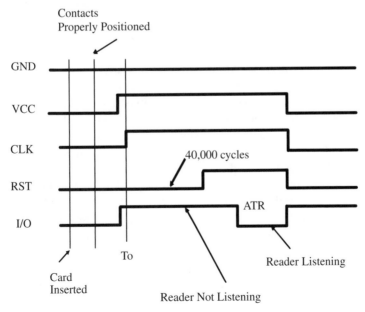

▶ **Figure 3.7**   The reader reset sequence.

relative to GND. One bit can be conveyed either through a +5 v value or through a 0 v value. The actual convention used is determined by the card and is conveyed to the reader's *initial character* of the ATR, which is referenced as *TS*. To transfer 1 byte of information, 10 bits are actually moved across the I/O line; the first is always a *start bit* and the last is always a parity bit used to convey even parity. Considering that the I/O line can be (in one bit period) either in a high (H) state or a low (L) state, the TS character being of the form HLHHLLLLLH signals that the card wants to use the *inverse convention*, meaning that H corresponds to a 0 and L corresponds to a 1. A TS character of the form HLHHLH-HHLLH signals that the card wants to use the *direct convention*, meaning that H corresponds to a 1 and <u>L</u> corresponds to a 0.

The direct convention and the inverse convention also control the bit ordering with each byte transferred between the card and the reader. In the direct convention, the first bit following the start bit is the low-order bit of the byte. Successively higher order bits follow in sequence. In the inverse convention, the first bit following the start bit is the high-order bit of the byte. Successively lower order bits follow in sequence. Parity for each byte transferred should be even; this means that the total number of 1 bits in the byte, including the parity bit, must be an even number.

The I/O line comprises a half-duplex channel; that is, either the card or the reader can transmit data over the same channel, but they both cannot be transmitting at the same time. So as part of the power-up sequence, both the reader and the card enter a receive state in which they're listening to the I/O line. With the commencement of the reset operation, the reader remains in the receive state while the card must enter a send state in order to send the ATR back to the reader. From this point on, the two ends of the channel alternate between send states and receive states. With a half-duplex channel, there is no reliable way for either end to asynchronously change a state from send to receive or from receive to send. Rather, if this is desired, that end must go into a receive state and allow a timeout of the operation in progress; then a reader end will always try to re-establish a known sequence by re-entering a send state.

The CLK and I/O lines can support a rather wide variety of data transmission speeds. The specific speed is defined by the card and is conveyed back to the reader through an optional character in the ATR. The transmission speed is set through the establishment of *one bit time* on the I/O line, which means that an interval is established at which the I/O line may be sampled in order to read a bit and then each successive bit. This time is defined as an *elementary time unit* (etu) and is established through a linear relationship between several factors. Note that the TS character was returned before any definition of the etu could be made; this is possible because the etu during the ATR sequence is always specified to be

$$etu_0 = 372/(CLK \text{ frequency})$$

where the CLK frequency is always between 1 MHz and 5 MHz; in fact, the frequency is almost always selected such that the initial data transfer rate is 9,600 bps.

Once an RST signal is sent from the reader to the card, the card must respond with the first character of the ATR within 40,000 CLK cycles. The card might not respond with an ATR for a number of reasons, the most prevalent being that the card is inserted incorrectly into the reader (probably upside down). In some instances, the card might not be functioning because it has been damaged or broken. Whatever the case, if the ATR is not returned within the prescribed time, the reader should begin a sequence to power down the card. During this sequence, the reader sets the RST, CLK, and I/O lines low and drops voltage on the VCC line to nominal 0 (that is, less than 0.4 v).

The ATR is a string of characters returned from the card to the reader following the successful completion of the power-up sequence. As defined in ISO/IEC 7816-3, the ATR consists of 33 or fewer characters comprising the following elements:

- *TS*. A mandatory initial character.
- *T0*. A mandatory format character.
- *TA_i TB_i TC_i TD_I.* Optional interface characters.
- *T1, T2, ~TK*. Optional historical characters.
- *TCK*. A conditional check character.

The historical characters can be defined at the discretion of the card manufacturer of the card issuer. These characters are typically used to convey some type of designation of the type, model, and use of this specific card. When used in this way, the historical characters provide a modest mechanism through which systems can automatically detect the use to be made of an inserted card (within that system) and can initiate other actions (or software) accordingly. The check character provides a mechanism through which the integrity of the ATR can be measured, that is, whether a transmission error has occurred in sending the characters from the card to the reader.

The structure of the ATR is illustrated in Table 3.5. As discussed previously, the initial TS character is used to establish the bit-signaling and bit-ordering conventions to be used between the reader and the card. The T0 character is used to signal the presence or absence of subsequent interface characters or historical characters. The interface characters are used to tailor the characteristics of the I/O channel, including the specific protocol to be used by the card and reader during subsequent exchange of commands (from the reader to the card) and responses (from the card to the reader). The historical characters, if present, are used to convey card manufacturer–specific information from the card to the reader, and hence to the application system being served by the reader. There is really no established standard for the information presented in the historical bits.

Table 3.5 The Answer to Reset Structure

Character ID	Definition
	Initial Character Section
TS	Mandatory initial character
	Format Character Section
T0	Indicator for presence of interface characters
	Interface Characters Section
TA_1	Global, codes F1 and D1
TB_1	Global, codes 11 and P11
TC_1	Global, code N
TD_1	Codes Y2 and T
TA_2	Specific
TB_2	Global, code P12
TC_2	Specific
TD_2	Codes Y3 and T
TA_3	Tai, Tbi, and Tci are specific
TD_i	Codes Yi+1 and T
	Historical Character Section
T1	(Maximum of 15 characters)
…TK	Card-specific information
	Check Character Section
TCK	Optional check character

The interface characters are used as a selection method for the protocol to be used for subsequent higher level communication between the reader and the card. Two such protocols are defined by ISO 7816-3: the T=0 protocol and the T=1 protocol. T=0 is an asynchronous protocol, meaning that there is no strict timing connection between one command sent from the reader to the card and the next command sent from the reader to the card. When the card receives a command from the reader, it performs the requested operations and sends back to the reader a response relative to that command. The reader is then free to send the next command to the card whenever it needs to. The T=1 protocol is an asynchronous block transmission protocol. This means that in one transmission packet (from the reader to the card), from one to several commands are sent. The card responds to this (these) command(s), at which point the reader can send another command or block of commands. Designations for additional protocols are defined as indicated in Table 3.6.

Table 3.6 Protocol Designations

Designation	Definition
T=0	Asynchronous (single) command/response protocol
T=1	Asynchronous (multiple) command/response protocol
T=2	Reserved for future full-duplex protocol
T=3	Reserved for future full-duplex protocol
T=4	Reserved for enhanced asynchronous protocol
T=5	Reserved for future use
T=6	Reserved for future use
T=7	Reserved for future use
T=8	Reserved for future use
T=9	Reserved for future use
T=10	Reserved for future use
T=11	Reserved for future use
T=12	Reserved for future use
T=13	Reserved for future use
T=14	Reserved for vendor-defined protocol
T=15	Reserved for future extension

The ATR sequence that initializes the physical communication channel between the reader and the card allows a number of characteristics of the channel to be defined or manipulated. The ISO/IEC 7816-3 standard defines a more elaborate adjunct to the ATR sequence called the *Protocol Type Selection* (PTS) facility. Actually, the PTS can be thought of as an extension of the ATR. Through the PTS, the reader-side of the channel and the card-side of the channel can negotiate to an optimum set of characteristics for the channel. For most current smart card systems, there is a strong correlation between the reader-side development and the card development. Consequently, the optimum communication characteristics are almost always derived through the ATR sequence without performing a PTS sequence. Therefore, we will not delve into the details of the PTS. However, in the future, with an expanding marketplace for smart cards encouraging more disconnected development of readers, terminals, and cards, the need to go through a PTS sequence on card initialization may significantly increase.

OTHER SMART CARD STANDARDS AND SPECIFICATIONS

ISO 7816 is unquestionably the most widely known and followed general-purpose smart card standard, but it is by no means the only one. There are standards for the use of smart cards in specific applications such as health, transportation, banking, electronic commerce, and identity. And there are standards for new kinds of smart cards, such as proximity and contactless smart cards. Because a smart card is always part of a larger information technology, it is subject to a wide range of information-processing standards such as character sets, country encodings, monetary representations, and cryptography. Finally, since many smart card applications intersect a number of governmental concerns such as monetary systems, national identity, and benefit eligibility, there are national and regional smart card standards in addition to international standards.

Due to the deliberate pace of international standards efforts, there also is a growing number of smart card specifications issued by organizations such as governmental laboratories, professional societies, trade associations, academic institutions, and private firms not associated with standards bodies. These specifications have no force other than the force of the marketplace of products and ideas, but they do serve the useful role of stimulating discussion and discovering consensus, which can be fed into official standards efforts. As smart cards become embraced within other technologies such as cellular telephones, watches, automobiles, and Internet browsers, we can expect that these technologies and their application domains will make rules and regulations about the nature of the smart card component. For the near term, as smart card usage explodes, it probably will be as much the marketplace as it is the international standards process that will say how smart cards are supposed to be.

As by no means an exhaustive list but rather to simply give you some starting points for further search, Tables 3.7 and 3.8 list some further standards and specifications that are influencing the deployment and evolution of smart cards.

Table 3.7 Examples of Smart Card Standards

Standard	Subject Area
International Standards Organization	
ISO 639	Languages, countries, and authorities
ISO 646	7-bit coded character set
ISO 3166	Names of countries
ISO 4217	Currencies and funds
ISO/IEC 7501	Travel documents
ISO/IEC 7810, 7811, 7812	Magnetic stripe cards
ISO/IEC 7813	Financial transactions
ISO 8601	Dates and times
ISO 8859	8-bit coded character set
ISO 9564	Personal identification number (PIN) management
ISO 9797	Data cryptographic techniques
ISO 9992	Messages between card and terminal
ISO 10202	Financial transaction cards
ISO 10536	Contactless ICCs
ISO 11568	Cryptographic key management
ISO 11694	Optical memory cards
European Telecommunications Standards Institute (ETSI)	
ETSI TE9	Card terminals
ETSI TS 102.221	UICC-Terminal Interface; Physical and Logical Characteristics

Table 3.7 Examples of Smart Card Standards (Continued)

Standard	Subject Area
ETSI TS 102.222	Administrative Commands for Telecommunications Applications
ETSI TS 102.223	Card Application Toolkit
ETSI TS 102.240	UICC Application Programming Interface
Third Generation Partnership Project (3GPP)	
3GPP TS 31.113	USAT Interpreter Byte Codes
3GPP TS 31.131 C	Language Binding to the (U)SIM API
3GPP TS 43.019	SIM API for Java Card
3GPP TS 51.011	Specification of the Subscriber Identity Module – Mobile Equipment (SIM-ME) Interface
European Committee for Standardization (CEN)	
TC 224	Machine-readable cards
EN 726	Requirements for ICCs and terminals for telecommunications use
Commission of the European Union (CEU)	
ITSEC	Information technology (IT) security evaluation criteria
European Computer Manufacturers Association (ECMA)	
ECMA-219	Key distribution
International Telecommunication Union (ITU)	
X.400	Secure email
X.509	Authentication framework
American National Standards Institute (ANSI)	
ANSI X9.15-1990 (R1996)	Specification for financial message exchange between card acceptor and acquirer

Table 3.7 Examples of Smart Card Standards (Continued)

Standard	Subject Area
ANSI X9.8-1995	Banking—PIN management and security, Part 1: PIN protection principles and techniques; and Part 2: approved algorithms for PIN encipherment
ANSI X3.15-1975 (R1996)	Bit sequencing of the American National Standard Code for Information Interchange in serial-by-bit data transmission
ANSI X3.118 (1984)	PIN pad specification
U.S. National Institute for Standards and Testing (NIST)	
FIPS 140-1	Cryptographic tokens

Table 3.8 Examples of Smart Card Specifications

Specification	Sponsor(s)	URL
Integration of Smart Cards into the Pluggable Authentication Module (PAM)	Open Group	*www.opengroup.org*
RFC 86.0 - Unified Login with PAM	Open Group	*www.opengroup.org*
RFC 57.0 - Smart Card Introduction	Open Group	*www.opengroup.org*
ISI-3 - (IBM Smartcard Identification)	IBM and the University of Twente	*www.iscit.surfnet.nl*
International Chip Electronic Commercial Standard	Visa	*www.visa.com*
Integrated Circuit Card (ICC) Specification	Visa	*www.visa.com*
Java Card	Java Card Forum	*www.javacardforum.org*
Java Card 2.1.3	Sun Microsystems	*www.javasoft.com*
IATA 791 - Airline Ticketing	International Airline Travel Association	*www.iata.org*

Table 3.8 Examples of Smart Card Specifications (Continued)

Specification	Sponsor(s)	URL
PKCS #11 Cryptographic Token Interface Standard	RSADSI	*www.rsa.com*
Electronic ID Application	Secured Electronic Information in Society (SEIS)	*www.seis.se*
ICC Specification for Payment Systems (EMV'96)	Europay, MasterCard, Visa	*www.mastercard.com*
Standards 30 and 40 - Card Terminals	Association for Payment Clearing Services (APACS)	
OpenCard Framework	Open Card Consortium	*www.opencard.com*
PC/SC	PC/SC Workgroup	*www.smartsys.com*

LINK-LEVEL PROTOCOLS TO SMART CARDS

When talking about communications protocols, you can generally analyze the situation in terms of the Open Systems Interconnection (OSI) Reference Model, which is shown in Figure 3.8. The OSI Reference Model describes the general communication problem between two entities in terms of seven distinct protocols that layer on top of each other (hence the term *seven-layer model*) and provides a complete mechanism through which two applications on disparate platforms can effectively exchange information with each other. A central theme of the OSI Reference Model is the strict separation of layers. That is, a layer communicates only with the layer immediately above or below it through a well-defined interface, and each layer provides a specific set of services to the entire protocol stack. In the case of the T=0 and T=1 smart card protocols, the T=1 protocol fits the OSI Reference Model fairly well as a *data link* (or link-level) protocol layer, but the T=0 protocol tends to mix elements from several different protocol layers (as defined by the OSI Reference Model).

At this point, it should be reiterated that the host and the card communicate through a very strict command-and-response protocol. That is, the reader side of the link sends a command to the card, possibly including data to be used on the card in the execution of the command, and the card then executes that command and sends a response back to the reader. This response may include data result-

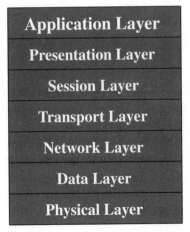

▶ **Figure 3.8** The OSI Reference Model.

ing from the execution of the command on the card as well as a status response regarding the execution of the command. The data structures exchanged by the reader and the card in this command-and-response protocol are referred to as *transmission protocol data units* (TPDUs). The TPDU structures used in the T=0 protocol are quite different from those used in the T=1 protocol.

Once the T=0 or T=1 protocol is established between the reader and the card, it is used to support application-level protocols between application software on the card and application software on the reader side of the link. These application protocols exchange information through data structures referred to as *application protocol data units* (APDUs). The details of the various TPDU and APDU structures are reviewed in the following sections. One conclusion that can be drawn from this discussion is the fact that the T=0 protocol provides very poor layer separation between the link-level protocol and the application-level protocol. Consequently, it is found that mechanisms that would normally be based on intervening protocol layers (between the application layer and the data link layer) can be extremely awkward to implement on top of the T=0 protocol. Principal among these is *secure messaging* between application software on the card with application software on the reader side of the link. Secure messaging refers to the use of cryptographic techniques to limit access to information conveyed between application components on the reader side and application elements on the card side of the channel. Specifically, only the application components on each end of the channel should be able to understand the information transferred between them; the intervening layers should simply see the information flowing as unintelligible collections of bytes. In Chapter 6, when we discuss the Cyberflex Access card, we will see a form of secure messaging defined through the Open Platform (OP) specifications to which the card conforms.

The poor protocol layering of the T=0 protocol is not the product of design. Rather, it is the result of an attempt to make the protocol as responsive as possible in order for communication between the reader and the card to be as efficient as possible. The data transmission speed across the reader-to-card interface is relatively slow (nominally 9,600 bps) and this channel is in the critical path of all transactions that involve the card. To maximize consumer satisfaction, it is desirable that such transactions proceed as quickly as possible—instantaneously would be very nice. Consequently, in the T=0 protocol, the error handling and the application protocol support are optimized so as to minimize the amount of information that flows across the reader-to-card interface and thereby to minimize the transaction time.

The T=0 Protocol

The T=0 protocol is a byte-oriented protocol. Like all other ISO-compliant smart card protocols, it functions in a command-response mode in which the reader side of the connection issues a command to the card, which then performs the commanded operation and sends back a response.

Note

- -

Byte-oriented means that a byte is the minimum unit of information transferred across a channel and that error handling is handled one byte at a time as well.

In the T=0 protocol, error detection is done by looking at the (even) parity bit on each byte transferred across the reader-to-card interface. The transfer of each byte of information requires the use of 11 bits, as illustrated in Figure 3.9. The parity bit is cleared or set to make the total number of bits set (per character transferred) be an even number. The receiver side of the channel can look at the bit values transferred prior to the parity bit and determine whether the parity bit should be set. If the actual parity bit transferred does not match what was expected, then it can be assumed that an error exists in the byte of data just transferred and some recovery procedure must be undertaken. The recovery procedure used with the T=0 protocol is triggered by the receiving side, which, on detecting a parity error, signals that it expects the transmitting side to retransmit the byte (that was received in error). It provides the signal to the transmitting side by holding the I/O line in a low state. Normally, the I/O line is in a high state immediately preceding the transfer of a byte, so a low state acts as an error feedback signal to the transmitter. On detecting this, the transmitting side of the channel waits for at least two character times and then again sends the byte that was previously received in error.

Those well versed in communication protocols might see this error detection and recovery mechanism as being somewhat prone to less-than-perfect behavior.

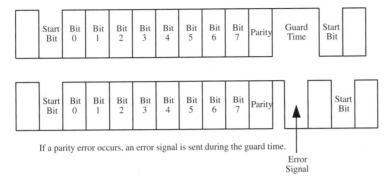

If a parity error occurs, an error signal is sent during the guard time.

Error
Signal

▶ **Figure 3.9** Reader-to-card byte transfer and error feedback loop.

This indeed tends to be the case in actual practice. For most readers, however, the channel tends to be very good or very bad. If it's very good, then this error detection and recovery mechanism is seldom used; if it's very bad, then the error detection and recovery mechanism is likely to fail at some point. This leads to the transmitting and receiving sides of the channel getting out of synchronization. If this situation is detected by the card, it usually will be programmed to go mute and quit responding to commands from the reader. At this point, or if the reader detects the ambiguous state first, the reader will issue a reset signal to the card that forces the communication protocol to be brought up from scratch.

The TPDU for the T=0 protocol comprises two distinct data structures: one that is sent from the reader to the card (as a command) and one that is sent from the card to the reader (as a response). The command header (sent from the reader to the card) includes five fields:

- *CLA*. A 1-byte field that establishes a collection of instructions; this is sometimes referred to as the class designation of the command set.

- *INS*. A 1-byte field that specifies a specific instruction (to the card) from within the set of instructions defined within the CLA designation; this is sometimes referred to as the *instruction designation* within the class of commands.

- *P1*. A 1-byte field used to specify the addressing used by the [CLA, INS] instruction.

- *P2*. A 1-byte field also used to specify the addressing used by the [CLA, INS] instruction.

- *P3*. A 1-byte field used to specify the number of data bytes transferred either to the card or from the card as part of the [CLA, INS] instruction execution.

The *procedure bytes,* which are sent from the card to the reader, used to respond to the reader's command, include three or four fields:

- *ACK.* A 1-byte field that indicates reception (by the card) of the [CLA, INS] command.
- *NULL.* A 1-byte field used by the card to essentially do flow control on the I/O channel; it sends the message from the card to the reader that the card is still working on the command and signals the reader not to send another command just yet.
- *SW1.* A 1-byte field used by the card to send a status response back to the reader regarding the current command.
- *SW2.* A 1-byte field that may be included in the procedure bytes, depending on the specific command being executed. If included, it also conveys a status response back to the reader.

As indicated previously, the T=0 protocol tends to mix elements of application-level protocols with elements of link-level protocols. The definition of the CLA byte is one such case in point. Each value of CLA defines an application-specific set of instructions; the individual instructions have a unique INS value. The first set of application-oriented commands is found in ISO/IEC 7816-4; the specific command sets are aimed at manipulation of a file system on a card and at accessing "security" commands on a card. Other standards documents define additional sets of commands (that is, additional values of the CLA byte). Some of these are listed in Table 3.9. The specific instructions found in these classes will be reviewed a little later in this chapter.

Table 3.9 CLA Instruction Set Definitions

CLA Byte	Instruction set
0X	ISO/IEC 7816-4 instructions (files and security)
10 to 7F	Reserved for future use
8X or 9X	ISO/IEC 7816-4 instructions
AX	Application- and/or vendor-specific instructions
B0 to CF	ISO/IEC 7816-4 instructions
D0 to FE	Application- and/or vendor-specific instructions
FF	Reserved for protocol type selection

Within a given CLA value (that is, within a class of instructions identified by a common value of CLA), the INS byte is used to identify a specific instruction. As indicated in Table 3.9, several different standards identify collections of instructions. The ISO/IEC 7816-4 standard identifies a number of instructions used to access an on-card file system and security functions that serve to limit access to the file system and to the card in general. This instruction set is listed in Table 3.10.

Table 3.10 ISO/IEC 7816-4 INS Codes

INS Value	Command Name
0E	Erase Binary
20	Verify
70	Manage Channel
82	External Authenticate
84	Get Challenge
88	Internal Authenticate
A4	Select File
B0	Read Binary
B2	Read Record(s)
C0	Get Response
C2	Envelope
CA	Get Data
D0	Write Binary
D2	Write Record
D6	Update Binary
DA	Put Data
DC	Update Record
E2	Append Record

Note

At this point, a portion of the discussion related to how EEPROM memory is programmed should be reiterated. In early microprocessor chips that included EEPROM memory, a separate power source (VPP) was needed to program (i.e., erase and write) EEPROM memory. ICCs used in current smart cards are able to derive "programming power" for NVM from the VCC power, so any significant discussion regarding VPP has been omitted. When the ISO/IEC 7816 Standard was adopted, however, the proper manipulation of the VPP power was necessary and was subsequently embedded rather deeply into the T=0 protocol. Specifically, the manner in which the INS byte is defined and in which the ACK procedure byte is returned are, in effect, the control mechanisms for VPP. Suffice it to say that all INS values must be even because the low-order bit allows control over VPP to be exercised. Further, in the absence of any manipulation of VPP, the ACK procedure byte is always returned as an exact copy of the INS byte in the command TPDU to which the procedure bytes form a response.

There are additional constraints on the values the INS byte can take; specifically, the high-order half-byte cannot have the value of either 6 or 9. In both cases, the restricted values are related to control mechanisms used to manipulate the VPP power source. The reader is referred to the ISO/IEC 7816-4 standard if further discussion is desired.

Note

ISO/IEC standards are available from:
ISO/IEC Copyright Office
Case Postale 56
CH-1211 Geneve 20
Switzerland

Copies of international standards, catalogs, and handbooks (ISO and IEC), as well as all foreign standards from ISO member body countries (DIN, JISC, BSI, AFNOR, and so on), are available in the United States from:
ANSI
11 West 42nd Street
New York, NY 10036
212-642-4900 (voice)
212-302-1286 (fax)

The command header parameters P1 and P2, although defined at what should be the link-protocol level, are actually dependent (for their specific definition) on the actual instruction specified; that is, their definition is actually dependent on application protocol information. P1 and P2 provide control or addressing parameters for the various application-specific instructions. For example, one application instruction, which is examined later, involves the selection of a specific file within the card's file system; selecting a file then allows subsequent operations such as reading or writing to be performed on the selected file. For this specific instruction, the parameter P1 is used to control how the file will be referred to in the select operation (i.e., Will it be referred to by an identifier, by name, or by path?). When the Select File instruction is reviewed, the strict definitions of those terms will be considered; however, for the reader familiar with general file systems on various computer systems, the meanings can be readily inferred. For the Select File instruction, the parameter P2 offers further refinement of just which file is to be selected.

The command header parameter P3 also is an application-level parameter. For many instructions, the P3 parameter can take on rather complex connotations (e.g., multiple parameters are defined within it). When the TPDU structure is examined, it is found that P3 generally defines the number $\underline{n}$ of data bytes that are to be transmitted during the execution of the INS-specified instruction. The direction of movement of these bytes is dependent on the instruction. The convention of movement of data is card-centric; that is, *outgoing* means data moving from the card to the reader, while *incoming* means data moving from the reader to the card. A value of P3=0 for an instruction specifying an outgoing data transfer means that 256 bytes of data will be transferred from the card to the reader.

Each time a command TPDU is sent from the reader to the card, a response TPDU is returned from the card to the reader. This response TPDU is made up of a number of procedure bytes. The first byte of this TPDU is an ACK byte. This byte is simply a repeat of the INS byte from the command TPDU to which this response is made. The second byte is the NULL byte. This byte is simply a way for the card to mark time while it processes the indicated command. While it is processing, the reader side of the channel is waiting for the response TPDU. If the response does not arrive within a specified timeout period, the reader may start an RST sequence to reinitialize the protocol between the reader and the card. This is prevented if at least a NULL response is received by the reader from the card.

SW1 is a status byte from the card to tell the reader the result of the requested instruction. The allowed values for SW1 are actually defined as part of the application protocol. For certain instructions, the card may have data bytes to be returned to the reader. In this case, a second status byte labeled SW2 is returned to the reader. This acts as a trigger for the reader to now execute another command called a GetResponse command, which will actually return the data bytes generated by execution of the previous command.

As you can see, the T=0 protocol is a relatively optimized protocol for moving commands and responses between the card and reader. It tends to blur the distinctions between the application-layer protocol and the link-layer protocol, with many of its constituent elements actually being defined within the application-layer protocol.

The T=1 Protocol

The T=1 protocol is a block-oriented protocol. This means that a well-defined collection of information (i.e., a *block*) is moved as a single unit between the reader and the card. Embedded within this block structure may be an APDU defined for a specific application. This facility is a good illustration that the T=1 protocol provides excellent layering between the link protocol layer and the application protocol layer. Moving information in a block, however, requires that the block be transferred (between the reader and the card) error free, or else the protocol can rather easily get lost. The error detection and correction, then, is a significantly more complex operation than was the case with the T=0 protocol.

Error detection in the T=1 protocol is done by using either a *longitudinal redundancy character (LRC)*, which is essentially a slightly more complex form of parity checking than was done in the T=0 protocol, or by using a *cyclic redundancy check (CRC)* character, which (unlike any parity check) is guaranteed to detect any single-bit errors in a transmitted block. The specific CRC algorithm used is defined in detail in the ISO 3309 Standard. When an error is detected within a block by the received end of the channel, it signals the transmitting end to repeat sending the block received in error.

The T=1 protocol makes use of three different types of blocks, as illustrated in Figure 3.10. Each has the same structure, but serves a different purpose:

- *Information block.* This block is used to convey information between application software in the card and application software on the reader side of the channel.
- *Receive ready block.* This block is used to convey either positive or negative acknowledgments from one end of the channel to the other. A positive acknowledgment indicates that a block was correctly received while a negative acknowledgment indicates that an error was detected (via checking the LRC or CRC) in the received block.
- *Supervisory block.* This block is used to convey control information between the card and the reader.

Prologue Field			Information Field	Epilogue Field
Node Address	Protocol Control Byte	Length	APDU	Error Detection
NAD	PCB	LEN	Data Length	LRC/CRC
1 byte	1 byte	1 byte	0 to 254 bytes	1 or 2 bytes

▶ **Figure 3.10** T=1 protocol components.

Each T=1 block comprises three fields:

- *Prologue field*. A mandatory field in the block that is 3 bytes in length. It includes the following three elements:
  - *NAD. Node address.*
  - *PCB. Protocol control byte.*
  - *LEN. Length.*
- *Information field*. An optional field in the block, which may be up to 254 bytes in length.
- *Epilogue field*. A mandatory field in the block, which is either 1 or 2 bytes in length.

The NAD element is used to identify the addresses of the source of the block and the intended destination for the block. This addressing facility is of greatest use when the T=1 protocol is being used to support multiple logical connections between the card and multiple application connection points on the reader side of the channel. When used, the NAD contains two subfields:

- *SAD*. Source address is indicated by the low-order three bits of the NAD byte.
- *DAD*. Destination address is indicated by bits five through seven of the NAD byte.

In situations where multiple logical channels are not being used, the NAD byte is set to all zeros. The two other bits of the NAD byte, those not used for the SAD or the DAD, are used to convey information related to controlling the VPP (EEPROM programming power).

The PCB element is used to indicate the type of block (i.e., either an information, a receive ready, or a supervisory block). The two high-order (most significant) bits of the PCB byte are used to denote the various types:

- A high-order bit set to 0 indicates an information block.
- The two high-order bits set to 1 indicate a supervisory block.
- The high-order bit set to 1 and the next bit set to 0 indicate a receive ready block.

T=1 is a relatively complex protocol. As a block-oriented protocol, error detection and retransmission occur at a block level. Much of the complexity comes from establishing the correct ordering of message blocks as errors occur and are corrected for. For purposes of this discussion, the protocol is viewed as was the T=0 protocol (i.e., as a reliable channel for moving APDUs between application software elements on the card and on the reader side of the communication channel). The other protocols that can be defined through the ATR and/or PTS sequence (i.e., T=2, ..., T=14, T=15) serve this same purpose.

APPLICATION-LEVEL PROTOCOLS

The ISO/IEC 7816-4 standard moves from the realm of defining base system functionality for smart cards into the realm of functionality directly useful to application software found on the smart card. Two areas of functionality are addressed:

- First, a file system is defined with a completely specified hierarchical structure. A set of functions are defined; these functions comprise an API through which application software on the reader side of the channel can access the files and information in those files within this file system.
- Second, a series of security functions are defined, which can be used to limit access to application software on the card or to files and information in those files within the card's file system.

This application software makes use of a protocol to exchange control and information between the reader and the card. This protocol is based on a block structure called an APDU. These APDUs are exchanged by making use of the T=0 and T=1 link-layer protocols. A software component on the card interprets these APDUs and performs the specified operation; this architecture is illustrated in Figure 3.11.

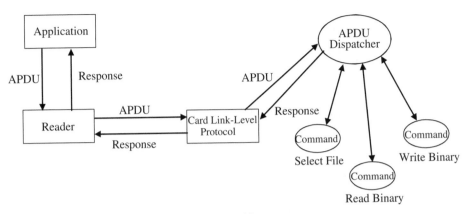

▶ **Figure 3.11**   Application communications architecture.

The APDU structure defined in ISO 7816-4 is very similar to the TPDU structure defined in ISO 7816-3 for the T=0 protocol. When the APDU structure is transported by the T=0 protocol, the elements of the APDU directly overlay the elements of the TPDU; hence, the comments earlier about the lack of effective protocol layering with the T=0 protocol.

An ISO 7816-4 APDU is

- Link-level protocol independent
- Defined at the application level

An instruction APDU is a message structure that carries a command or instruction (and perhaps data) from the reader to the card. A response APDU is a message structure that carries a response (and perhaps data) from the card back to the reader. We'll examine the ISO 7816-4 command set in some detail in Chapter 4.

Summary

Throughout their history, smart cards have been subjected to a stringent requirement that their development and deployment be controlled through standards; standards which come from a variety of sources. Standards defined through international standards bodies establish much of the framework for classical smart card infrastructures. The physical and electrical characteristics of the card and its embedded ICC along with the operational paradigm and essential security characteristics are so defined.

In addition, many specifications for card operational characteristics are defined through consortia. In some instances, such specifications have evolved into international standards. Finally, many characteristics of the latest generation cards are subject to definition and protection as intellectual property. All of these mechanisms, taken together, establish a very well-defined framework into which smart cards must fit. While this certainly establishes a well-regulated marketplace for vendors and customers alike, it does make for a tough environment for rapid or revolutionary developments to occur.

The initial startup sequence for smart cards is defined through well-established standards. In this chapter, we have reviewed this procedure and had a brief overview of the base-level communication protocols used between cards and terminals. In the following chapter, we will move "up" the protocol stack to look at the application-level mechanisms used to communicate between cards and terminals.

4

Smart Card Applications

Smart cards provide a personal component of applications, whatever the complete purpose of the application might be. The smart card is carried by an individual and is periodically utilized in various equipment configurations to achieve the results or obtain the services provided by those configurations. The most common feature of smart cards in an application is to establish or authenticate the identity of the cardholder and the cardholder's right (permission) to access and use the application in question. In other cases, besides authenticating identity, the smart card may carry additional information needed by the application. For example, in financial debit and credit applications, the smart card may carry an account number (or numbers), which are to be accessed in backend servers involved in the application.

A common aspect to virtually all smart card–enabled applications is that they involve establishing a communication channel between the smart card and some other computer processor acting as the general controller for the application. This translates into a situation of two application-level programs running on peer-level computers needing to communicate with each other. This is exactly the scenario of the International Standards Organization (ISO) Reference Model for communication protocols illustrated in Figure 4.1.

Essentially, all of the layers described in the ISO Reference Model are found in the communication channel between an off-card application and the corresponding application on the smart card. We'll look at a more detailed comparison in Chapter 7 where we'll recognize that the layering in the smart card environment is not quite what was envisioned in the ISO Reference Model, but the sum total of the layers is pretty well there.

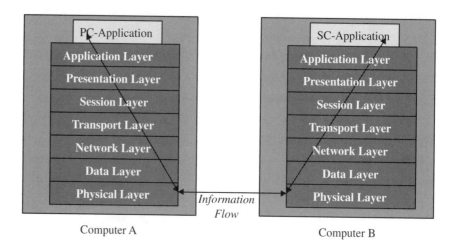

Computer A   Computer B

▶ **Figure 4.1**   ISO 7-Layer Reference Model.

The smart card protocols do present some rather eccentric characteristics relative to a true peer-to-peer communication protocol. Most noteworthy, perhaps, is the fact that the host and the smart card actually operate in a master-slave mode. The host requests an operation of the card and the card performs the operation and tells the host the results.

GENERAL ARCHITECTURE OF APPLICATIONS

The earliest smart cards were designed from scratch with the larger application in mind and the function of the smart card well established from the beginning. A command set was implemented on the card to provide the necessary functionality for the application. This approach, of course, tended to argue against having multiple smart card (and other equipment) vendors provide components for the application. In an effort to provide some commonality among applications, an interindustry command set was ratified by the ISO organization and published as the ISO/IEC 7816-4 standard.

The ISO 7816 standard makes an assumption for the basic paradigm of smart card–aware applications; that is, the smart card provides information storage in the form of an abbreviated file system, accessed through a command set comparable to that used on a general-purpose computer system. It is further assumed that the smart card provides a relatively secure platform on which to store information. Consequently, a general protocol for authenticating identities and then authorizing operations based on those identities was defined. Finally, because true general transaction operations were extremely difficult to provide, a reduced form of transaction operation was defined that would allow simple operations to be performed on smart card files in a highly secure and reliable fashion.

INFRASTRUCTURE

Deploying a smart card–aware application on a typical PC or workstation system generally requires provision of the complete smart card infrastructure to support the application. That is, the base operating system of the host computer must be upgraded to include a smart card protocol stack, which allows the transfer of information between the host application and the smart card application. In addition, the host computer (hardware) configuration must be enhanced to include a smart card reader, which provides the physical connectivity between the smart card's integrated circuit chip (ICC) and the host computer. We'll look in some detail at this smart card stack in Chapter 7.

Few, if any, computer systems have smart card readers as an integral input/output (I/O) channel of the systems. Rather, a variety of smart card readers have been developed that attach to computer systems through existent I/O ports. The most common such reader attaches through a serial port. Readers that interface in this fashion range from extremely simple devices, which simply serialize the byte streams that convey commands and responses between the PC application and the smart card, to very complex devices, which incorporate personal identification number (PIN) pads, display screens, and hardcopy printers to support the smart card application.

Some variants of smart card readers have been built directly into the standard keyboard of a computer. Some such configurations have further modifications that allow the keyboard to interrupt the transfer of characters to the CPU in the case where the input characters constitute a PIN destined to be sent to the smart card.

Another smart card reader takes the form of a floppy disk plug-in, which conveys the smart card I/O traffic through the floppy disk port. This particular device requires a floppy disk–like module that the card plugs into, and which contains an independent power source for the smart card.

The simple fact that most general computer systems do not, today, contain a smart card reader means that deploying a smart card–aware application immediately runs up against the "infrastructure problem." That is, a piece of equipment (a smart card reader) must be added to a configuration, but which contributes no other benefit than to allow a smart card to be used. This makes the economics of adding a smart card to an application bend out of shape a bit. For every card that we want to issue, we also must issue a smart card reader. Use of a smart card starts to look like a $50 to $100 option (depending on the cost of the reader) rather than a $2 to $15 option (which looks like the price of just a smart card).

That said, by standardizing smart card components such that they are usable across a wide range of smart card–aware applications, the economics of adding smart cards can be greatly mitigated.

SECURITY

One of the primary reasons smart cards exist is security. The card itself provides a computing platform on which information can be stored securely and computations can be performed securely. The smart card also is highly portable and convenient to carry around on one's person. Consequently, the smart card is ideally suited to function as a token through which the security of other systems can be enhanced.

In financial systems, sensitive information such as bank account numbers can be stored on a smart card. In electronic purse applications (cash cards and the like), the balance of some negotiable currency can be stored on a card and this currency can be credited or debited by external terminals (systems) in a local transaction.

In physical access systems (e.g., opening the door to your office), a smart card can hold the key through which an electronic system can be enticed to unlock the door and allow entry. In network systems or even local computer systems, the smart card can hold the password through which a user is identified to the network or local system and through which privileges are granted by those systems to access information or processing capabilities.

When viewed in the abstract, all these seemingly disjointed systems have very similar needs and operational characteristics, particularly with regard to the security of those systems. On that basis, let's examine some of the general characteristics of systems that collectively are referred to as *security*.

The term *security* is often used in a rather loose fashion to refer to a variety of characteristics related to the performance of transactions between two or more parties in such a manner that everyone involved in the transaction trusts the integrity and, perhaps, the privacy of the transaction. With the advent of computer networks and of highly distributed financial transactions, it is often the case that all the necessary parties to a transaction cannot be physically at the same place, or even at the same time, in order to participate in the transaction.

Consider the purchase of an item with a credit card at an airport gift shop while on a trip. This transaction includes a number of distinct steps:

- presentation of the consumer's credit card to the vendor
- validation by the vendor that the cardholder is really the owner of the card

- validation by the vendor that the credit card account represented by the card is valid
- validation by the vendor that the account maintains a sufficient credit balance to cover the cost of the item being purchased
- debiting the credit account represented by the card by the amount of the item purchased
- crediting the account of the vendor with the amount of the item purchased (less any fees due to the bank, etc. related to the credit card transaction)

In the performance of this transaction, the cardholder would also like some assurances that much, if not all, of the information related to the transaction is held private. The credit card name, account number, and validation code should not be obtained by some unscrupulous character bent on making fraudulent purchases with the purloined information.

In the performance of a credit card transaction, there are actually many more components than previously mentioned. However, in just the steps noted, you can see that physical separation of the various parties to the transaction makes it difficult to guarantee that all these parties are satisfied about the integrity and privacy of the transaction.

This section discusses the characteristics of security involved in supporting such a transaction. To facilitate this discussion, the objectives of a security environment are first presented in somewhat abstract terms. After, some of the elements (we'll call them *players*) of a widely distributed transaction system are examined. Then, some of the mechanisms currently in wide use to provide the desired characteristics through the identified players are examined. Finally, some of the attacks used to thwart these security mechanisms are reviewed.

Objectives and Characteristics of Security Systems

Security within physical or electronic systems can be viewed as the provision of one or more general characteristics:

- authentication
- authorization
- privacy
- integrity
- nonrepudiation

When part or all of these characteristics are provided to the extent required to satisfy all the participants of the transaction, the transaction can be said to be secure.

Authentication

Authentication means establishing an identity within a transaction. Consider a very simple (nonelectronic) transaction such as a student providing homework to a teacher. In general, the teacher wants to confirm that a specific set of homework comes from a specific student. What's involved in establishing identities in such a transaction? Well, when the homework is turned in to the teacher, the teacher will likely just visually recognize the student and accept the homework. In order to identify the homework of a specific student, the teacher may inspect the homework when it is turned in to confirm that the student's name is on it. Then, at some later time after the teacher has reviewed the homework and graded the paper, the grade can be recorded next to the name. In such a transaction, an environment of trust must be established; the teacher can associate (visually) a student, the student's homework, and the student's name on the homework, and the teacher believes this association to be true. Establishing this trust environment for a classroom setting is typically a subtle—and not usually rigorous—procedure.

In general, the rigor applied to establishing trust is commensurate with the value of the transaction. If the transaction does not involve simply homework, but something much more valuable (to one or both parties), such as a final examination or an SAT examination, then establishing the trust environment can be much more involved. Verification of identity may be required at the door of the testing facility; the form of this verification might be a student ID card or a state drivers license. Such forms of authenticated identity suffice to introduce the concept of a trust broker or a trusted third party that both of the parties to the transaction can look to for establishment of a trust environment if they don't know each other. The test monitor might not be able to visually recognize a student, but does know what a valid student ID looks like. So if the student presents such an ID with a picture on it that matches the bearer of the card and a name on it that matches a name on the test list, then the monitor can believe that the bearer of the ID card is really the person authorized to take the examination and hence received the grade derived from taking the examination.

If the transaction in question involves something of even greater value (to one or both parties), then establishing the trust environment can be even more involved. For example, purchasing a house with a mortgage loan may require that a wide variety of information be collected and the validity of that information be attested to in legally binding ways.

The object then of a security system is to provide authentication mechanisms through which a trust environment can be established among all the participants in a transaction even though the participants might not know each other, might not be physically together during the transaction, and might even be participating in the transaction at widely different times (i.e., the transaction requires a significant elapsed time to complete).

Authorization

Authorization is the establishment of privileges within a transaction. That is, after the identity of a participant in a transaction has been authenticated, what that participant is allowed to do as part of the transaction must be established. In a financial transaction, this authorization might consist of simply confirming that the authenticated individual has enough money to make the desired purchase or enough money to provide the desired loan. In the earlier exam example, authorization might consist of finding a student's name on the class roster; that is, if the student can authenticate that her identity is Jane Doe and the name of Jane Doe is found by the monitor on the class roster, then that student will be allowed to take the final examination.

Just as in establishing identity (authentication), the length to which various parties in the transaction will go to establish authorization is generally related to value ascribed to the transaction by one or more parties. To gain entry to a room containing particularly sensitive information in a high-security facility, your name might have to be on an access list that can be checked by a guard of that room. To enter that room, you must meet at least two criteria. First, you must present the correct identification information to the guard to establish (authenticate) your identity. Then the guard must find your identity on the list of individuals allowed access to the room.

In some situations, the concepts of authentication and authorization might be merged together. In many office buildings, each office has a physical key. The key patterns might be such that a master key can open any office door. In this case, authentication is established by physical possession of the key. From the standpoint of the lock on the door (which is one of the participants in the transaction of unlocking and opening the door), both the authenticated identity of the individual and that individual's authorization to enter the room guarded by the door is satisfied by that individual physically presenting the key.

Privacy

Privacy is the concept of allowing only the participants in a transaction to know the details of the transaction, and it might even mean that only the participants know that a transaction is occurring.

When a credit card purchase is made, the protocol of presenting the card to the vendor, performing the financial transaction, and returning a receipt of the transaction to the cardholder is set up to minimize the conveyance of sensitive information such as the account name, number, or validation number to those who might be casually observing the transaction. Similarly, when using a telephone calling card at a public telephone, conventional wisdom mandates that one be very cautious to hide the entry of the card number, lest it be seen by someone who will make note of it and use it to make cardholder telephone calls that the cardholder has not authorized.

Integrity

Integrity is the concept that none of the information involved in a transaction is modified in any manner not known or approved by all the participants in the transaction, either while the transaction is in progress or after the fact. In the previous homework example, when the student turns in the homework, the total transaction may not actually be concluded until the teacher reviews the homework and records a grade. In this simple example, the integrity of the information is maintained by the teacher keeping the homework in controlled possession until it is graded and the grade recorded. The student's integrity facility in this case is to get the homework back from the teacher and to be able to review it to make sure that it's in the same state as when it was submitted.

For the homework example, the integrity of the transaction system is typically not of paramount importance to the student because teachers don't often maliciously modify homework in their possession. The teacher might be more concerned with the integrity of the information: first, in the sense of knowing that the homework hasn't been modified since it was turned in (usually not too likely) and second, in knowing that the homework was actually done by the student.

This latter aspect is often not guaranteed by any stringent mechanism in the case of homework. In the case of examinations, which might be viewed as more valuable, more proactive mechanisms are sometimes used. For example, some universities make use of an "honor code" under which a student might be required to attest to the fact that an examination was completed by the student and that the student neither gave nor received any assistance during the examination proper. Providing mechanisms to facilitate this concept in the highly dispersed environment of electronic transactions across a wide area computer network is a bit more challenging.

Nonrepudiation

Nonrepudiation is establishing the fact of participation in a particular transaction by all the parties to the transaction such that none of the parties can claim after the fact that they did not actually take part in the transaction. Mechanisms to facilitate this concept are typically closely related to the mechanisms used to authenticate identity. In many discussions, the two concepts are viewed as essentially equivalent.

Of these five characteristics of security, it is the concept of privacy that precipitates the greatest concerns on the part of governmental entities. As you will see, encrypting information through mechanisms that allow only the intended participants of a transaction to be able to understand it is often a highly regulated capability. The same encryption mechanisms used to establish privacy can often also be used to authenticate identity. When used for authentication, encryption is viewed much more benignly by governmental entities than when used for privacy.

SECURITY MECHANISMS

The previous sections define some of the abstract concepts of security as well as the major components of the systems for which a secure environment is desired. In this section, some of the mechanisms that the various players can use to facilitate the various security concepts are examined.

Authentication

The field of cryptography is dedicated to the development of mechanisms through which information can be shared in a secure fashion. A variety of mechanisms have thus been developed through which the security concepts discussed earlier can actually be realized. Several different mechanisms have been developed to support the authentication of identity among widely diverse participants in a transaction. A few of the more prevalent of these mechanisms are described in the following sections.

Symmetric Key Authentication

Most, if not all, authentication mechanisms involve the sharing of a secret among all the participants in a transaction. Two such mechanisms involve distinct forms for encryption and decryption of information; the first makes use of a symmetric key encryption algorithm and, the second, a public key encryption algorithm. Both of these mechanisms involve a shared secret; however, the manner in which the secret is shared in each case makes the two mechanisms preferable in different situations. Specifically, symmetric key algorithms are most useful in providing bulk encryption of information because they are less processor intensive than public key algorithms.

Symmetric encryption algorithms make use of a single key for both the encryption and the decryption of information. This is illustrated in Figure 4.2.

In a symmetric key approach, the same key is fed into the encryption algorithm to both encrypt information and decrypt information. Plain text information is passed into the encryption process, where it is modified through the application of the key value. The resulting ciphertext contains all the information present in the original plain text; however, due to the manipulation of the encryption algorithm, the information is in a form not understandable by a reader that does not possess the key. When the ciphertext is passed back through the encryption algorithm with the same key applied (as was used for the encryption process) then the plain text is recovered.

It is apparent that this approach can be used to keep secret the plain text information from anyone who does not have the required key. The approach also can be used, however, to allow each side of a pair-wise transaction to confirm that the other side holds the same key and thereby authenticate a known identity.

This symmetric key identity authentication for a smart card environment is illustrated in Figure 4.3.

In the case shown in Figure 4.3, the application spans both the off-card environment and the on-card environment. In most common instances today, the application is created by the card issuer, who installs the shared secret (the key) in both environments. It should also be pointed out that the case shown in Figure 4.3 could be extended to make use of two distinct authentication operations, each using a different key. This approach would be quite useful if, for many different

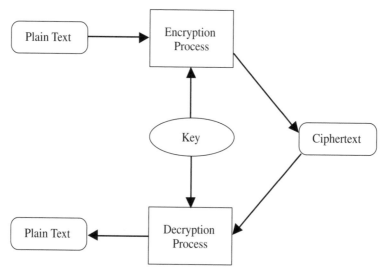

▶ **Figure 4.2**   Symmetric key encryption.

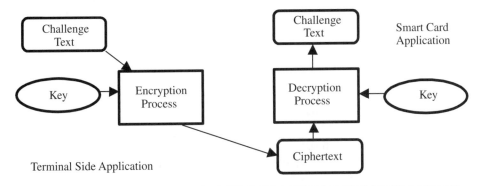

If "challenge text" matches, then the card and the terminal know they share the same "secret" (i.e., they both have the same "key," so they've established a mutually authenticated identity).

▶ **Figure 4.3**   Authentication via shared secret.

cards (with different cardholders), all of the cards simply need to authenticate a single identity for the off-card application while the off-card application needs to authenticate the unique identity of each individual card.

With this approach, each card would need to know two keys: one to be used to authenticate the off-card application and one to use in authenticating itself to the off-card application. The off-card application, however, would need to know a large number of keys; the one it uses to authenticate itself to all the various cards and one for each card it uses when each card authenticates itself to the off-card application. From the standpoint of the cardholder, this is a less than optimal situation in that the secret key used to authenticate the identity of the card is known outside the card. Similarly, the secret key used to authenticate the identity of the off-card application is known to every card that can access this application. If this key can be retrieved from the card, then perhaps an attacker could use it to gain access to the application.

A shared secret approach typically is used by a smart card to authenticate the cardholder to the card. This is done through a cardholder verification (CHV) command set, listed among the interindustry commands defined in the ISO/IEC 7816-4 specification that we'll consider a bit later in this chapter. This verification process often is referred to as PIN entry or PIN checking. In this process, a file is written within the file structure of a smart card. A PIN value is then written in this file. When a cardholder inserts a card into a terminal, the off-card application requests the bearer to enter a PIN through a terminal keypad. The number sequence then entered is passed through an application protocol data unit (APDU) command to the card, which then compares the value supplied by the terminal (which was entered by the cardholder) to the value in the CHV file.

If they match, the cardholder is then identified (so far as the card is concerned) as the person for whom the card will act.

This CHV process can be significantly more complex than depicted here; multiple PINs can be required or supported by a single card. In addition, multiple steps can be required for the cardholder to finally be authenticated to the card.

Asymmetric Key Authentication

A second approach that is widely used for identity authentication makes use of an encryption process called asymmetric key encryption; this technique is commonly called *public key cryptography.* As the name implies, the technique makes use of different keys for the encryption operation and the decryption operation. This is illustrated in Figure 4.4.

With this technique, one key is used to encrypt information and the other is used to decrypt the ciphertext to get back the original plain text. There is actually a shared secret between the encryption and decryption keys; that is, the keys are generated as different components of a common algorithm. What's so interesting about this approach, as opposed to the symmetric key approach, is that the proliferation of keys alluded to in the symmetric key discussion can be greatly reduced.

Of the two keys used in the asymmetric key mechanism, one of the keys can be held as a closely guarded secret (and indeed should be) by the entity that will subsequently use this key for identity authentication; this key is termed the *pri-*

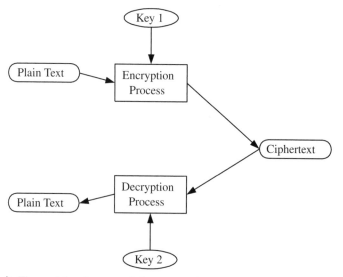

▶ **Figure 4.4**   Asymmetric key encryption.

vate key. The other key can now be distributed to anyone; hence, it's referred to as the *public key.* The public/private key pair can be used to establish authenticated identity, as illustrated in Figure 4.5.

What's shown in Figure 4.5 is actually just authentication in one direction; that is, the off-card application can authenticate its identity to the smart card–side application. To do this, the off-card application keeps secret the private key, which essentially represents its identity. The public key corresponding to this private key can be freely distributed; hence, it can be stored on every smart card that might want to access the off-card application. So, the card can use this public key to encrypt some type of challenge text string; that is, some arbitrary string that the card knows and wants to see if the terminal can find out. It then sends the ciphertext generated from this challenge text to the off-card application. If the off-card application really possesses the identity (private key) corresponding to the public key possessed by the card, then it can decrypt the challenge and return the plain text to the card for validation.

Obviously, the inverse of this procedure can be used to allow the card to authenticate its identity to the off-card application. In this case, the off-card application needs to know only the public key component related to each card's identity. So if it is to be able to authenticate a large number of cards, it needs to keep a list of, or at least be able to obtain, the public keys of the cards it wants to authenticate. This is considerably better from a security standpoint than the symmetric key situation described in the previous section.

Of course, there's never a free lunch. Computationally, a public key encryption and/or decryption algorithm is much more intensive than a symmetric key algorithm. Therefore, it is unrealistic to think about encrypting or decrypting large amounts of information on a smart card processor in a short time. However, the challenge text noted previously does not have to be too voluminous. So

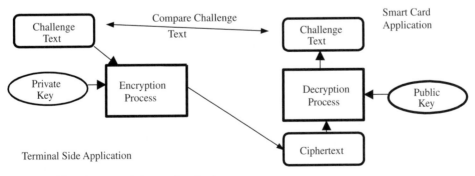

▶ **Figure 4.5** Asymmetric key authentication.

for establishing authenticated identity, public key mechanisms can be used effectively even given the limited processor capacity of a smart card.

Integrity

The mechanisms described previously are useful for authenticating identities among a variety of parties to a transaction. Although it may not always be thought of as a transaction, the same mechanisms are useful for establishing identities related to documents or procedures—that is, performing the function of allowing an identity to sign a document or a process. Thus, this identity authentication procedure can form part of what can be referred to as a *digital signature*. The other aspect of a digital signature is the confirmation that the information that has been digitally signed has not been modified from the time that it is signed until it is read (and the signature's identity is authenticated). This, then, is a means of addressing another of the concepts of security: integrity.

One-Way Hash Codes

In the case illustrated by Figure 4.5, when the smart card encrypts the challenge text with a public key, the smart card authenticates the identity of the off-card application when it demonstrates possession of the private key, which can decrypt the challenge text. The smart card application knows that only the possessor of the private key can decrypt that message. So if the process is reversed and the off-card application generates some piece of text and encrypts it with its private key, the smart card application knows that the text, when decrypted with the public key (of the off-card application's identity) must have come from the off-card application. Thus, the off-card application has digitally signed the text in question; that is, it has essentially affixed an identifying symbol that conveys the same information that the signature at the bottom of a contract does.

As mentioned previously, public key encryption and decryption can be very processor intensive. Further, the public key encryption and decryption operations being discussed are (for purposes of the current discussion) intended to authenticate identity, not assure privacy. This being the case, it is not actually necessary to encrypt all the information in question in order to digitally sign it and to validate that it hasn't changed (i.e., that the integrity of the information has been preserved). Rather, all that is necessary is to calculate some type of unique checksum over the information in question and then encrypt that checksum. A *checksum* is the result from a computational algorithm acting on the information in question such that if a single bit of that information changes, the resulting checksum will change.

Generation of such checksums is possible with a family of computational algorithms known as *one-way hash functions*. Through these functions, you can process a large collection of information and derive a much smaller set of information, referred to as a *hash code*. You might think of a hash function as a logical, nondestructive meat grinder. When you grind a piece of meat with it, you don't destroy the meat, but you get out a pile of ground round that is unique for every piece of meat you put into it. So, if I put the same piece of meat through the grinder twice, I get two identical batches of ground round.

Some very desirable traits of useful one-way hash functions are the creation of a unique hash code for a unique collection of bits comprising the source document and the inability (or at least great computational difficulty) to predict what hash code will be generated (without passing the information in question through the one-way hash code algorithm) from a given collection of bits. Probably, the most popular one-way hash code in use in the smart card world is the SHA-1 algorithm.

A variant of one-way hash functions has been developed that also requires a key, in addition to the information in question, before a one-way hash code can be computed. These functions are referred to as *message authentication codes*, or MACs. They are useful for confirming integrity of information as well as authenticating identities associated with the information, but without guaranteeing the privacy of the information. A variant on this theme involves the use of public key cryptography in conjunction with one-way hash functions; this is the mechanism that is most generally called a *digital signature* as opposed to the definition suggested earlier.

Digital Signatures

If a one-way hash function is computed on a collection of information and that hash code is not encrypted with the private key of a public/private key pair, the encrypted information that results provides both authentication of the identity of the entity which encrypted the hash code (essentially signed the original information) and the integrity of the original information. This mechanism is illustrated in Figure 4.6.

From Figure 4.6, you can see that if the original document along with the digital signature of that document (i.e., the private key–encrypted hash code calculated from the document) is now passed to a another entity, that entity can validate the digital signature, authenticate the identity of the entity that digitally signed the original document, and confirm the integrity of the original document (i.e., confirm that the same one-way hash code is calculated from the document on receipt as was calculated from the document at signing time).

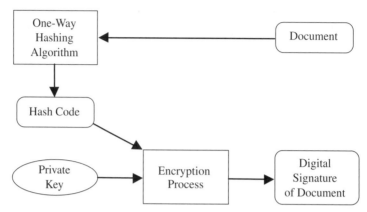

▶ **Figure 4.6**   A digital signature using a one-way hash code.

Authorization

After the identity of an entity is established through some authentication procedure, what that entity is allowed to do in the context of a given system is the subject of another security concept termed *authorization*. It is useful to think of
authorization in the context of a server that is being accessed by a client—the
server provides information or some other abstract service to the client based on
what privileges the client has with respect to that server; the model is illustrated
in Figure 4.7.

   This model indicates that if a client wants to gain some type of access to an
object of interest, it must first authenticate its identity to the server. The server
can then consult a list of privileges, which that client (identity) has with respect to
that object of interest. Figure 4.7 denotes this list of privileges as an access control list (ACL); most such mechanisms can be abstracted back to something that
looks like an ACL. This mechanism is widely used within smart cards for access
to information (in files or objects) and/or processing capabilities (functions).

ACLs

   ACLs are authorization or privileges lists that link identities, and what those
identities are allowed to do, to specific objects of interest. The ACL is typically
viewed from the perspective of the object of interest and the server that makes
that object of interest accessible to clients. It is the server that interprets the ACL
and decides, based on the authorizations it finds there, what access to allow to
the object of interest by the client. For a particular object of interest, a well-

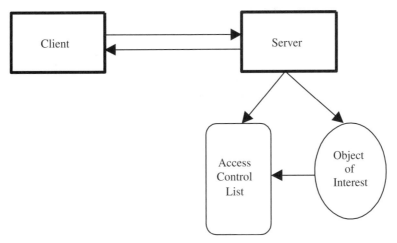

❱ **Figure 4.7**   The authorization model.

defined set of authorizations typically can be defined. For a file, for instance, the following privileges typically are defined:

- create
- delete
- read
- write
- modify
- execute

An ACL for such a file might then look as shown in Table 4.1.

Table 4.1 The ACL for the File abc.txt

Identity	Create	Delete	Read	Write	Execute	Control
Jane Doe	X	X	X	X	X	X
Good Person			X	X	X	
Iffy Person			X			

This ACL says that the identity Jane Doe can really do anything at all to the file. The identity Good Person can read, write, and execute any code found in the file, while the identity Iffy Person can only read the contents of the file.

Capabilities List

A relatively orthogonal way of looking at this same authorization model (i.e., one represented by an ACL) is called a capabilities list. In most instances, the way this variant of the model is implemented, the capabilities list is passed along to the server essentially merged with the identity authentication. That is, there is assumed to be an administration function that decides, external to the actual server, what capabilities (privileges) a specific identity is to have with respect to the object of interest.

In both variants, the security procedures followed are essentially the same. First, authenticate the identity, and then go to an authorization list to determine what privileges that identity has with respect to the object of interest. The most straightforward mechanism for doing this is to include the capabilities list in the digital certificate through which identity is tied to a key that can be used to authenticate that identity.

Privacy

The final concept of security to be dealt with is privacy, which is keeping the details of a transaction secret from everyone not involved in the transaction. The cryptographic mechanisms previously discussed are adequate to provide transaction privacy. In general, the major design factor (i.e., deciding which mechanism to actually use) is one of performance in the actual operational environment.

As mentioned previously, public key cryptography is significantly more processor intensive than is symmetric key cryptography. Consequently, most systems make use of symmetric key algorithms to actually encrypt the information flow between two disparate points involved in the same transaction. In point of fact, however, public key mechanisms are still quite useful in even this case. Specifically, public key mechanisms are useful in order to exchange the symmetric key needed by both ends of the communication channel. Such shared secrets are well-recognized risk areas in security systems; the longer and more often that the same symmetric key is used, the better the chance for an attacker to figure out what it is and use that knowledge to compromise the privacy of the transaction channel.

If public keys are well known throughout the specific security system, then the mechanisms discussed earlier can be used in which one end of the transaction channel can generate a random symmetric key and send it, under cloak of encryption by the other end's public key knowing that only the other end possesses the private key necessary to decrypt the message containing the secret symmetric key.

If public keys are not well known throughout the system, or actually even if they are, another mechanism exists that is useful specifically for distributing secret symmetric "session" keys (so named because a new key can be generated for each "session" in which a transaction of some type is to occur) among disparate participants in the transaction. The mechanism is known as the Diffie-Helman protocol. It has the very nice feature that, by agreeing in advance to make use of a common algorithm, each end of the channel can calculate a secret key based on information that it can exchange in the clear. The mechanism cannot be used to actually encrypt information, but rather just to exchange a secret symmetric key, which can then be used to encrypt the actual transaction information.

Bulk Encryption

The encryption of transaction information often is referred to as *bulk encryption*. In general, smart cards are not involved in bulk encryption processes. The data transfer rate across the I/O port from a smart card reader to the card is very low (on the order of 10 Kbps) relative to typical transmission speeds across local area or even wide area networks. Consequently, most cryptographic operations that are actually performed on a smart card are related to establishment of identity.

The dominant algorithms used for bulk data encryption include the DES algorithm, the Triple-DES algorithm, the RC4 algorithm, and the AES algorithm.

ACCESS CONDITIONS

The ISO/IEC 7816-4 specification provides a paradigm for identity authentication that is found consistently across most smart card applications. Moreover, it defines an authorization mechanism that builds upon this authentication facility so as to allow the definition of security policies that limit access to information stored in the file systems found on smart cards or to standard computations performed on information found in the file system of a smart card.

In the course of a typical smart card application, there are three distinct actors whose identities need to be authenticated:

- host (off-card computer) application
- smart card (on-card computer) application
- cardholder

The host and the smart card computers need to authenticate themselves to each other. After they do this, they can communicate information and services because each knows that the other belongs to the same security domain. It is possible for these two entities to establish a private (encrypted) channel and thus preclude any eavesdropper from listening in on the proceedings of the transaction. These two computer systems can then participate in the application on behalf of the cardholder, assuming that the cardholder is truly the owner (holder) of the smart card. So, an additional authentication mechanism is needed to authenticate the identity of the cardholder to the smart card. After this is done, the card can participate in the application on behalf of the cardholder.

The method used for authenticating the two computer systems to each other (i.e., the smart card ICC to the host computer) consists of each computer proving to the other that it knows a secret shared between the two machines. To enhance the long-term security of the two systems, it is desirable that this mechanism not involve actually moving the secret between the two systems. So, in the approach used, the shared secret is a key that can be used by a cryptographic algorithm to encrypt information. The approach can use either symmetric key cryptography or asymmetric key cryptography. In the authentication process, a key is used by one side of the operation (either the card or the host computer) to encrypt a random piece of information that has been specified by the other side of the operation. If both sides are using (know) the same key, then the "other" side will be able to decrypt and recover the random piece of information.

When the card has authenticated the off-card computer's identity, the card is then said to be in an AUTH state relative to the key used in the authentication process. Various commands can be tagged such that the on-card system must be in an AUTH state before the command can be executed. Since the off-card computer sends commands to the on-card computer, this mechanism means that the off-card system has to be authenticated to the on-card system in order execute these commands. Since the various commands provide access to information or computational services on the card, this defines an authorization mechanism which limits access to that information of those services.

There can be multiple key files stored on a card and there can be multiple keys in each of those files. This means that, in theory, a very large number of identities can be authenticated by the card and given access to various pieces of information or services.

Another authentication mechanism uses a PIN stored in a file. If an off-card computer can provide a command containing the correct PIN, it can cause the on-card system to enter a state called CHV (cardholder verified). Commands can be predicated upon being in the CHV state just as for the AUTH state. So, by proper design of the information structures on the card, various information and various capabilities (in essence, various applications) can be made available to different off-card identities. In this case, the off-card identities are the "owners" of the application systems in which the on-card components work.

In the following sections, we'll examine the details of the specific commands used to authenticate identities. Plus, we'll see a standard information storage system and the commands that, under authorization control such as we've just discussed, are able to operate on this storage system.

INTERINDUSTRY SMART CARD COMMANDS (ISO 7816-4)

As was mentioned previously, in an effort to provide some standardization among smart cards, an interindustry command set was defined in the ISO/IEC 7816-4 specification. This command set included commands in two distinct areas, as well as several general-purpose, administrative commands. The two specific areas are:

- security features
- on-card file systems

The commands aimed at security provide mechanisms that allow the authentication of identity among the participants in smart card–based transactions. That is, computers can authenticate to computers and a person (a cardholder) can authenticate to a computer (the smart card). These mechanisms are based in well-established cryptographic operations.

APDUs

The messages used to support the ISO 7816-4–defined application protocol(s) comprise two structures: one used by the reader side of the channel to send commands to the card and the other used by the card to send responses back to the reader. The former is referred to as the *command APDU* and the latter as the *response APDU*.

As illustrated in Figure 4.8, the command APDU comprises a *header* and a *body*, each of which is further subdivided into several fields. The header includes CLA, INS, P1, and P2 fields. CLA and INS define an application class and instruction group as described, for example, in ISO 7816-4. The P1 and P2 fields are used to qualify specific instructions and are therefore given specific definitions by each [CLA,INS] instruction. The body of the APDU is a variable size (and form) component that is used to convey information to the card's APDU processor as part of a command or to convey information from the card back to the reader as part of a response to a command. The Lc field specifies the number of bytes to be transferred to the card as part of an instruction; it contains the length of the data field. The data field comprises data that must be conveyed to the card in order to allow its APDU processor to execute the command specified in the APDU. The Le field specifies the number of bytes that will be

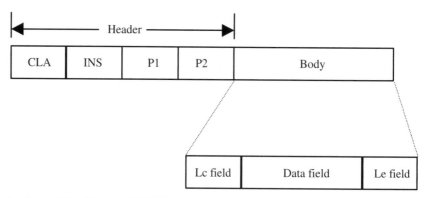

▶ **Figure 4.8**   Command APDU structure.

returned to the reader by the card's APDU processor in the response APDU for this particular command. The body of the APDU can have four different forms:

- No data is transferred to or from the card, so the APDU includes only the header component.
- No data is transferred to the card but data is returned from the card, so the body of the APDU includes only a non-null Le field.
- Data is transferred to the card but no data is returned from the card as a result of the command, so the body of the APDU includes the Lc field and the data field.
- Data is transferred to the card and data is returned from the card as a result of the command, so the body of the APDU includes the Lc field, the data field, and the Le field.

Figure 4.9 illustrates the much simpler structure of the response APDU structure. It includes a body and a trailer. The body is either null or includes a data field, depending on the specific command that it is a response to and depending on whether that command was successfully executed by the card's APDU processor. If the response APDU does include a data field, its length is determined by the Le field of the command to which the response corresponds.

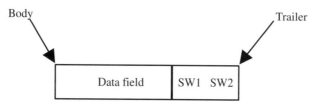

▶ **Figure 4.9**   Response APDU structure.

Error Responses

The response APDU also includes a trailer field, which can comprise two fields of status information that are referenced as SW1 and SW2. These fields return (from the card's APDU processor) to the reader-side application a status code that, according to ISO 7816-4, has a numbering scheme in which one byte is used to convey an error category and the other byte is used to convey a command-specific status or error indication. This numbering scheme is illustrated in Figure 4.10.

The CLA code that is included in each command APDU has two additional components to be noted:

- The two low-order bits of the CLA byte can be used to designate a logical communication channel between the reader-side application and the card's APDU processor.

- The next two higher order bits of the CLA byte can be used to indicate that secure messaging is to be used between the reader-side application and the card's APDU processor.

After the link-level protocol is established between the reader-side application and the card's APDU processor, a base-level (command) logical channel is created. This is indicated (in the CLA byte) by both of the low-order bits being 0. Additional logical channels can be created by using the `Manage Channel` command, which is defined by ISO 7816-4.

ISO 7816-4 also defines a modest secure messaging protocol, which can be used to ensure privacy and integrity of APDUs transferred between the reader-side application and the card's APDU processor.

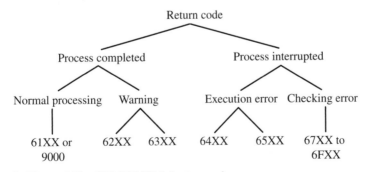

▶ **Figure 4.10**   ISO/IEC 7816-4 return codes.

Security Commands

Associated with each component of the file system is a list of access properties. Through these access properties, a state can be defined such that the smart card system must be put into that state, through the successful execution of a series of commands by the reader, before that component of the file system can be accessed. At the most basic level, the operations to be performed on the file system are to select a specific file and then write information to that file or read information from that file. As shown in the following sections, the access properties may be as simple as requiring the reader to provide a predefined PIN or as complex as the reader proving that it possesses some shared secret (e.g., a key) with the card. These mechanisms will be reviewed in more detail in the following sections.

The *Verify* Command

CLA	INS	P1	P2	Lc	Data
$C0_{16}$	20_{16}	00_{16}	00_{16}	03_{16}	$53_{16}\ 61_{16}\ 53_{16}$

The Verify command is a command sent by a reader-side application to the security system on the card to allow it to check for a match to password type information stored on the card. This command is used to allow the reader-side application to convince the card that it (the reader-side application) knows a password maintained by the card to restrict access to information on the card.

The password type information may be attached to a specific file on the card or to part or all of the file hierarchy on the card. Successful execution of this command indicates that the reader-side application did know the correct password and it puts the card into a state such that a subsequent access to a file guarded by this password information will succeed.

If the Verify command fails (i.e., the password required by the card is not correctly provided by the reader-side application), then an error status indicator is returned by the card to the reader-side application.

The *Internal Authenticate* Command

CLA	INS	P1	P2	Lc	Data
$C0_{16}$	88_{16}	00_{16}	00_{16}	03_{16}	$02_{16}\ 01_{16}\ 03_{16}$

The Internal Authenticate command is a command sent by a reader-side application to the security system on the card to allow the card to prove that it possesses a secret key that is shared with the reader-side application. To prepare this command, the reader-side application creates a set of challenge data (i.e., essentially, the reader-side application generates a random number). This number is then encrypted with some agreed-on algorithm (with the card); this constitutes a challenge to the card.

When given the command, the card then decrypts the challenge with a secret key stored in a file on the card. The information derived from the decryption is then passed back to the reader-side application as a response to the command. If the card really does have the correct secret key, then the information passed back will be the random number generated by the reader-side application prior to issuing the Internal Authenticate command.

This command is used by the reader-side application to authenticate the card's identity. That is, when successfully completed, the reader-side application knows the identity of the card and can give to the card access to information or services within the reader-side application.

The *External Authenticate* Command

CLA	INS	P1	P2	Lc	Data
$C0_{16}$	82_{16}	00_{16}	00_{16}	03_{16}	$03_{16}\,02_{16}\,01_{16}\,03_{16}$

The External Authenticate command is used by a reader-side application, in conjunction with the Get Challenge command (described in the next section) to allow the reader-side application to authenticate its identity to the card.

Through the Get Challenge command, the reader-side application receives a set of challenge data from the card (i.e., a random number generated by the card). The reader-side application then encrypts this information with a secret key. This then forms a challenge, which is sent to the card via the External Authenticate command. If the reader-side application knows the same secret key that is stored on the card, then when the card decrypts the challenge, it will find the same random number generated by the last Get Challenge command. Therefore, the card now knows the identity of the reader-side application and can give it (the reader-side application) to data on the card.

The attractive characteristic of this method (from a security standpoint) is that the secret key used to authenticate identity between the reader-side application and the card was never transferred between the reader-side application and the card.

The *Get Challenge* Command

CLA	INS	P1	P2	Lc	Data
$C0_{16}$	84_{16}	00_{16}	00_{16}	06_{16}	empty

The `Get Challenge` command is used by the reader-side application to extract information that can be used to formulate a challenge to the card that can be validated through an `External Authenticate` command. The result of this command is the generation of a random number by the card, which is then passed back to the reader-side application.

File System

A central application for smart cards defined by the ISO/IEC 7816-4 standard is a file system. The file system is actually applied to the nonvolatile memory on the smart card, generally electrically erasable and programmable read-only memory (EEPROM). The file system defined is a relatively straightforward hierarchical structure comprising three basic elements:

- a master file (MF) component
- a directory file (DF) component
- an elementary file (EF) component

The MF component is the root of the file hierarchy; there is only one MF on a smart card. An MF may contain as elements a DF, or even many DFs, and it may contain none to many EFs. The DF component is essentially a container for EF components; a DF may contain none to many EFs. An EF component may contain only records. This simple hierarchical structure is illustrated in Figure 4.11.

Several characteristics of the smart card file system are significantly different from typical (e.g., disk-based) file systems. These differences are almost exclusively due to the physical characteristics of the EEPROM memory system—specifically, the facts that EEPROM memory can only be subjected to a modest number of erase and write cycles and that it is significantly faster to write to EEPROM memory in a cumulative fashion than in a pure erase and then write fashion. The first of these characteristics resulted in the definition of a rather unique file structure called a *cyclic* file. The second characteristic resulted in rather unique definitions of the various file write commands.

The cyclic file is actually a ring buffer of physical files that are addressed and accessed as a single file. On successive write operations, the next physical file (in the ring of physical files) is accessed. The net result is that erase and write operations can be spread across a wider selection of EEPROM memory loca-

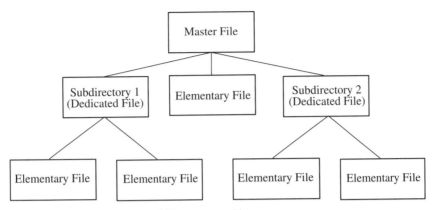

▶ Figure 4.11   The smart card file system architecture.

tions. This mitigates somewhat the limit (generally on the order of 100,000 cycles) on the number of times that a specific EEPROM memory location can be erased and rewritten.

EEPROM memory has the additional interesting characteristic that it is significantly faster to set additional bits in a memory location than it is to erase all the currently set bits and then rewrite them. This fact becomes doubly useful in certain operations (e.g., manipulating a purse value on a smart card) where it is required that operations on a file be performed in such a fashion that the values stored in the file are well understood at any point in time, even if power is removed from the smart card in the middle of a file operation. To facilitate the exploitation of these characteristics, the write operations to a smart card file are typically bit-set operations while the update operations are actually erase and rewrite operations, which we generally associate with file-writing operations. These characteristics will be examined in a bit more detail in the following sections.

MF Characteristics

Each smart card file system has exactly one MF. The MF serves as the root of the hierarchical file structure. In the parlance of general file systems, the MF is a container or a directory; it may contain other dedicated (or directory) files (DFs) or it may contain EFs.

Any file can be identified by a 2-byte file identifier. The file identifier 3F00 is reserved for the MF; that is, there is only one file with a file identifier of 3F00, and the file with that identifier is the MF.

DF Characteristics

The DF also is a container or a directory file in the same vein as the MF. The DF forms a subdirectory within the file hierarchy rooted in the MF. A DF also can be identified by a file identifier. A DF must be given a unique file identifier within the DF (or MF) that contains it. This allows for the creation of a unique path designation for a file (i.e., a path is simply the concatenation of the file identifiers of the file in question, and of all the DFs between the file in question and its containing DF or MF).

A DF also can be referenced by a name that may be from 1 to 16 byes long. The naming conventions for the DF name are found in the ISO/IEC 7816-5 specification.

EF Characteristics

The EF is the leaf node of the file hierarchy. It is the file that actually contains data. There are two variants of EFs: an internal EF, which is to be used by applications on the card, and a working EF, which is used as a storage mechanism for information used by an off-card application.

Within a specific DF, an EF may be identified by a short (5-bit) identifier. There are four variants of EFs as illustrated in Figure 4.12:

- a transparent file
- a linear, fixed-length record file
- a linear, variable-length record file
- a cyclic, fixed-length record file

A transparent file can be viewed as a string of bytes. When a command is used to read or write information from a transparent file, it is necessary to provide a byte offset (from the start of the file) to the specific byte (within the transparent file) where reading or writing should begin. A command to read or write information from/to a transparent file will also contain a counter or length of the byte string to be read or written to the file.

Fixed- or variable-length record files are, as the name suggests, files that comprise subdivisions called *records*. Records (within a file) are identified by a sequence number. In a fixed-length record file, all the records contain the same number of bytes. In a variable-length record file, each record in the file can contain a different number of bytes. As might be suspected, a variable-length record file generally has a significantly higher overhead in read/write access time and in the amount of administrative (data storage) overhead required by the file system.

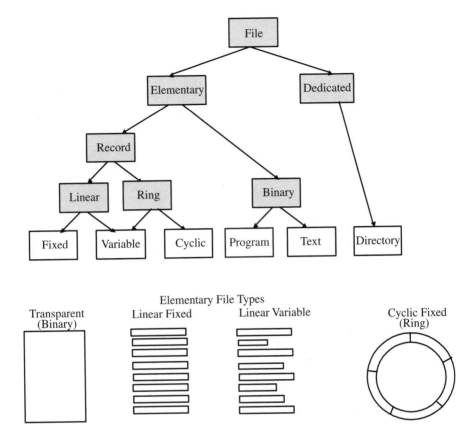

▶ **Figure 4.12**   Smart card file system file types.

A cyclic file is a rather unique (to smart card file systems) structure. It allows applications to access a file in a consistent, transparent fashion and yet have the file system itself map this access into a variety of different physical files. This allows the limits of erase and rewrite cycles on EEPROM memory to be somewhat mitigated.

A cyclic file is best thought of as a ring of records. Each successive write to the file performs the operation on the next physical record in the ring. Read operations are performed on the last physical record that was actually written to.

File Access Commands

To manipulate the smart card file system, an application-level protocol is defined in the form of a collection of functions for selecting, reading, and writing files. These functions are discussed qualitatively in the following sections.

The *Select File* Command

CLA	INS	P1	P2	Lc	Data
$C0_{16}$	$A4_{16}$	00_{16}	00_{16}	02_{16}	$3F_{16}\ 00_{16}$

The Select File command is used to establish what may be thought of as a logical pointer to a specific file in the smart card's file system. After a file is selected by this command, any subsequent commands, such as those to read or write information, will operate on the file pointed to by this logical pointer. Access to the smart card's file system is not multithreaded (from the card's viewpoint), but it is possible to have multiple such logical pointers in play at any point in time. This is done by using the Manage Channel command to establish multiple logical channels between the reader-side application and the card. Commands to access different files can then be multiplexed (by the reader-side application) allowing different files on the card to be in various states of access by the reader-side application at the same time.

The primary piece of information the command must convey (from the reader-side application to the smart card's APDU processor) is the identification of the file to which this logical pointer must point. This identification can be provided in three ways (with the specific addressing mechanism being indicated in the data field of the Select File command APDU):

- by file identifier (2-byte value)
- by DF name (string of bytes identifying the DF)
- by path (concatenation of file identifiers)

The *Read Binary* Command

CLA	INS	P1	P2	Lc	Data
$C0_{16}$	$B0_{16}$	00_{16}	00_{16}	10_{16}	empty

The Read Binary command is used by a reader-side application to retrieve some segment of an EF on the card. The EF being accessed must be a transparent file; that is, it cannot be a record-oriented file. If a Read Binary command is attempted on a record-oriented EF, the command will abort with an error indicator being returned by the card to the reader-side application.

Two parameters are passed from the reader-side application to the card for this command: an offset pointer from the start of the file to initial byte to be read, and the number of bytes to be read and returned to the reader-side application.

The *Write Binary* Command

CLA	INS	P1	P2	Lc	Data
$C0_{16}$	$D0_{16}$	01_{16}	01_{16}	01_{16}	FF_{16}

The `Write Binary` command is used by a reader-side application to put information into a segment of an EF on the card. The file being accessed must be a transparent file; that is, it cannot be a record-oriented file. If a `Write Binary` command is attempted on a record-oriented EF, the command will abort with an error indicator being returned by the card to the reader-side application.

Depending on the attributes passed from the reader-side application to the card in the `Write Binary` command, the command can be used to set a series of bytes in the EF (i.e., set selected bits within the designated bytes to a value of 1), clear a series of bytes in the EF (i.e., set selected bits within the designated bytes to a value of 0), or do a one-time write of a series of bytes in the EF.

The *Update Binary* Command

CLA	INS	P1	P2	Lc	Data
$C0_{16}$	$D6_{16}$	01_{16}	01_{16}	01_{16}	FF_{16}

The `Update Binary` command is used by a reader-side application to directly erase and store a set of information (bytes) into a segment of an EF on the card. The file being accessed must be a transparent file; that is, it cannot be a record-oriented file. If an `Update Binary` command is attempted on a record-oriented EF, the command will abort with an error indicator being returned by the card to the reader-side application.

The `Update Binary` command provides the functions that would normally be associated with a file write command. That is, a string of bits provided in the command are actually written into the EF on the card, with those byte positions in the file on the card being erased first. The net result is that the string of bytes found in the designated position within the EF on the card is exactly the string sent by the reader-side application in the `Update Binary` command.

Input parameters for the command include an offset pointer from the start of the file and a byte count of the total number of bytes to be written.

The *Erase Binary* Command

CLA	INS	P1	P2	Lc	Data
$C0_{16}$	$0E_{16}$	01_{16}	01_{16}	01_{16}	06_{16}

The `Erase Binary` command is used by a reader-side application to erase (set the value to $\underline{0}$) a string of bits within an EF on a card. The file being accessed must be a transparent file; that is, it cannot be a record-oriented file. If an `Erase Binary` command is attempted on a record-oriented EF, the command will abort with an error indicator being returned by the card to the reader-side application.

Two parameters are specified as part of the command: an offset from the start of the EF to the segment of bytes within the file to be erased and the number of bytes within that segment.

The *Read Record* Command

CLA	INS	P1	P2	Lc	Data
$C0_{16}$	$B2_{16}$	06_{16}	04_{16}	14_{16}	empty

The `Read Record` command is a command sent by a reader-side application to read and return the contents of one or more records in an EF on a card. This command must be executed against a record-oriented EF. If it is applied to a transparent EF, the command will abort and an error indicator will be sent from the card back to the reader-side application.

Depending on the parameters passed through the command, the one designated record is read and returned, or all the records from the beginning of the file to the designated record are read and returned, or all the records from the designated record to the end of the file are read and returned.

The *Write Record* Command

CLA	INS	P1	P2	Lc	Data
$C0_{16}$	$D2_{16}$	06_{16}	04_{16}	14_{16}	$53_{16}\,61_{16}\,6C_{16}\,6C_{16}\,79_{16}\,20_{16}\,47_{16}$ $72_{16}\,65_{16}\,65_{16}\,6E_{16}\,00_{16}\,00_{16}\,00_{16}$ $00_{16}\,00_{16}\,00_{16}\,00_{16}\,00_{16}\,00_{16}$

The `Write Record` command is a command sent by a reader-side application to write a record into an EF on the card. This command must be executed against a record-oriented EF. If it is applied to a transparent EF, the command will abort and an error indicator will be sent from the card back to the reader-side application. In the sample command sequence noted previously, 14 (hexadecimal) characters will be written into the currently selected record beginning at the sixth character position in that record. The characters to be written are contained in the Data field (i.e., the hexadecimal representation for "Sally Green").

As with the Write Binary command, this command can actually be used to achieve one of three results: a one-time write of a record into the EF, setting of specific bits within a specific record in the EF, or clearing of specific bits within a specific record in the EF.

Several addressing shortcuts may be used in this command to specify the record to be written to, including the first record in the EF, the last record in the EF, the next record in the EF, the previous record in the EF, or a specific record (identified by number) within the EF.

The *Append Record* Command

CLA	INS	P1	P2	Lc	Data
$C0_{16}$	$E2_{16}$	00_{16}	00_{16}	14_{16}	$53_{16}\,61_{16}\,6C_{16}\,6C_{16}\,79_{16}\,20_{16}\,47_{16}$ $72_{16}\,65_{16}\,65_{16}\,6E_{16}\,00_{16}\,00_{16}\,00_{16}$ $00_{16}\,00_{16}\,00_{16}\,00_{16}\,00_{16}\,00_{16}$

The Append Record command is a command sent by a reader-side application to either add an additional record at the end of a linear, record-oriented EF on a card or to write the first record in a cyclic, record-oriented EF on a card. If it is applied to a transparent EF, the command will abort and an error indicator will be sent from the card back to the reader-side application.

In the preceding example, P1 is an unused parameter and is always 00_{16}. P2 is the short identifier of the file to which the record append will apply. Lc specifies the number of characters in the record to be appended and the Data field contains the characters to be appended—in this case, the hexadecimal representation of "Sally Green." That is, for whatever end, this command appends the words "Sally Green" in a record onto the end of the selected file.

The *Update Record* Command

CLA	INS	P1	P2	Lc	Data
$C0_{16}$	DC_{16}	06_{16}	04_{16}	14_{16}	$53_{16}\,61_{16}1\,6C_{16}\,6C_{16}\,79_{16}\,2_{16}0\,47_{16}$ $72_{16}\,65_{16}\,65_{16}\,6E_{16}\,00_{16}\,00_{16}\,00_{16}$ $00_{16}\,00_{16}\,00_{16}\,00_{16}\,00_{16}\,00_{16}$

The Update Record command is a command sent by a reader-side application to write a record into an EF on the card. This command must be executed against a record-oriented EF. If it is applied to a transparent EF, the command will abort and an error indicator will be sent from the card back to the reader-side application.

As with the `Update Binary` command, this command is used to write a specific record into an EF. The net result of the operation is that the specific record in the EF is erased and the new record specified in the command is written into the EF.

Administrative Commands

The master-slave command protocol specified by ISO/IEC 7816-4 is quite restrictive in its ability to accommodate the wide variety of commands that you might want to access on a smart card. In an attempt to compensate for some of the syntactic shortcomings, ISO/IEC 7816-4 also defines a number of administrative commands that allow a wider latitude of command structures and responses.

The *Get Response* Command

CLA	INS	P1	P2	Lc	Data
$C0_{16}$	$C0_{16}$	00_{16}	00_{16}	14_{16}	empty

The `Get Response` command is another command that allows the use of the T=0 link-level protocol for conveying the full range of APDUs. Specifically, the Case 4 type of APDU body cannot be supported with the T=0 protocol. That is, you can't send a body of data to the card and then receive a body of data back as a direct response to that command. For this type of command, using the T=0 protocol, the initial command results in a response that indicates more data is waiting (in the card). The `Get Response` command is then used to retrieve that waiting data.

It should be noted that no other command can be interleaved between the original command and the `Get Response` command.

The *Manage Channel* Command

CLA	INS	P1	P2	Lc	Data
$C0_{16}$	70_{16}	00_{16}	01_{16}	00_{16}	empty

The `Manage Channel` command is used by the reader-side application to open and close logical communication channels between it and the card. When the card initially establishes an application-level protocol with the reader-side application (i.e., following the ATR sequence) a basic communication channel is opened. This channel is then used to open and/or close additional logical channels via the `Manage Channel` command.

The *Envelope* Command

CLA	INS	P1	P2	Lc	Data
$C0_{16}$	$C2_{16}$	00_{16}	00_{16}	07_{16}	$C0_{16}\ A4_{16}\ 00_{16}\ 00_{16}\ 02_{16}\ 3F_{16}\ 00_{16}$

The `Envelope` command is a command that supports the use of secure messaging via the T=0 link-level protocol. In secure messaging, the full command APDU should be encrypted. However, because the CLA and INS bytes from the APDU overlay elements of the transmission protocol data units (TPDU), these bytes (in the TPDU) cannot be encrypted if the link-level protocol is still to work correctly. So the `Envelope` command allows a full APDU to be encrypted and then included in the `Envelope` command's data section (of its APDU). The card's APDU processor can then extract the "real" command and cause it to be executed.

The *Get Data* Command

CLA	INS	P1	P2	Lc	Data
$C0_{16}$	CA_{16}	02_{16}	01_{16}	14_{16}	empty

The `Get Data` command is a command sent by a reader-side application to read and return the contents of a data object stored within the file system on the card. This command is essentially the complement of the `Put Data` command (defined in the next section). This command tends to be very card specific in its internal implementation. However, the semantics of the command are well defined. That is, the definition of just what constitutes a data object varies widely from card to card, but what the command does should be consistent from card to card. Thus, for retrieving a small amount of information, this command might well be preferable to retrieving information from a specific file.

The *Put Data* Command

CLA	INS	P1	P2	Lc	Data
$C0_{16}$	DA_{16}	02_{16}	01_{16}	01_{16}	FF_{16}

The `Put Data` command is a command sent by a reader-side application to put information into a data object stored within the file system on the card. This command tends to be very card specific in its implementation; however, it is relatively general in its specification. So, the fact that the definition of just what constitutes a data object varies widely from card to card does not necessarily mean that the semantics of the command varies from card to card. In fact, the attractive feature of this command is the fact that you do not need to know the identity of a specific file into which the "data" is to be stored. This tends to make the command similar across a variety of different smart cards. An application, should it need to store only a modest bit of information, can do so with this command and be moderately assured that the command will work on a variety of different smart cards.

SUMMARY

This chapter has hopefully provided you with a fairly extensive introduction into the structure of the smart card–side of a smart card–aware application. The most interesting facets of this environment are the security mechanisms that are defined through a set of international standards and which find themselves present on most smart cards in use today. Further, these same international standards establish a paradigm for smart card applications in the form of an on-card file system replete with an authentication and authorization mechanism that is firmly rooted in the use of cryptographic services to achieve the desired characteristics of security. A series of commands for manipulating this on-card file system forms the backbone of many smart card applications in use today.

5

Multiapplication Smart Cards

Since the early to mid-90s, much of the evolution of smart card technology has been in the direction of defining and adding on-card code later and later in the development and deployment phases of smart card applications. This "late binding" of application definition to smart card infrastructure has culminated in a variety of systems which allow application software to be loaded onto a card even after it is in the hands of a cardholder. In this chapter, we'll examine several of these multiapplication card systems. Each has a variety of advantages and detractions, and for the most part all are still being pushed in the marketplace of ideas.

In terms of deployment of cards in real-world systems, the Java Card technology would appear to be in a leading role. This is due in no small part to its acceptance as a Subscriber Identity Module (SIM) used in GSM cellular telephone systems. Overall, the number of multiapplication cards in use, relative to single-application smart cards, is still in the minority; however, the numbers are increasing at a rapid pace. Let's examine, then, some of the aspects of multiapplication smart cards.

WHY MULTIAPPLICATION SMART CARDS

There are a number of reasons to want to add commands and applications to cards after they have been issued. For example:

- *Faster Transaction Times*: In reaching for general utility, the commands on off-the-shelf cards are necessarily low level and least common denominator. This means you can accomplish almost anything you like with them but it also means that, like grains of sand, you might need many of them to build your application. If transaction time is of the essence, which it usually is in building smart card applications—and recalling that communication between the terminal and the card is the most time-consuming—the application designer is led to building application-specific application protocol data units (APDUs) that accomplish in one go the combined effect of multiple general-purpose commands.

- *Application-Specific Processing*: Due to the domain in which they function, applications might have unique cryptographic algorithms or regional requirements for data privacy. By allowing for the construction of special-purpose APDUs and on-card applications, these programmable cards can be used in situations where their fixed-command, off-the-shelf brethren cannot.

- *Rapid Application Deployment*: Increasingly, smart cards have to compete with other trust-bearing application platforms such as PDAs, pagers, set-top boxes, cell phones, and personal multimedia players, not to mention the various programmable identity tokens that are in the R&D pipeline. Regardless of the level of security offered by the smart card, if the turnaround time to roll out a new application is years rather than days or weeks as it is with these competitors, the smart card will lose.

- *Chip Independence*: Technologies that permit post-issuance loading of applications onto large card populations will have to solve the problem of running the application on different chip hardware. A side benefit of this will be that card issuers and their applications become independent of the underlying chip and, more importantly, its supplier.

In a sense, programmable smart cards are a return to the early days of smart cards when the entire card was application specific. The difference is that now, the application runs out of electrically erasable and programmable read-only memory (EEPROM), and the application can be deleted and replaced with another application anytime the card is used. The strategy of building an application's needs into the smart card's ROM-based operating system worked well when the number of cards needed for a particular application was large, when the application didn't do much, and was very stable over time—Carte Bancaire's Carte Blue, for example. As cards started to be used for smaller and more quickly evolving applications, however, the economic advantage of building the application's needs into ROM diminished. The turnaround time for a new version of the card was too long, the cost of development was too high, and the lifetime of the card was too short.

Another development that energized the quest for programmable cards was the empirically and painfully derived realization that smart card programs—whose business models had to stand on their own two feet and not be propped up by governmental mandates—had to offer more than one function. Because it was clearly impossible for all practicable functions to be ground into the card and activated on an as-needed basis, and because it was clear that the suite of functions of interest to one cardholder would differ from that of another, the notion of a multiapplication card—where applications could be loaded, used, and then deleted at the whim of the cardholder, the issuer, the application provider or, in all likelihood, all three—was quickly reached.

Finally, of course, application programmers and system architects, both those inside the established development organizations and those espousing new ideas and methods, needed smart cards for experimentation, testing and debugging, pilot projects, and special event business opportunities. Neither the skills demands, nor the tools requirements, nor the security protocols, nor the development cycle of assembly-language, ROM-based, single-application smart cards could begin to meet the new, emerging demands of the smart card marketplace. The stage was set for a new approach to on-card programming.

A BRIEF HISTORY OF ON-CARD INTERPRETERS AND VIRTUAL MACHINES

Adding executable code to cards after their manufacture was in and of itself not new. Card manufacturers used it from the day the first bug in ROM code was discovered to patch bugs or meet late-breaking customer requirements. The technique, familiar to all programmers as illustrated in Figure 5.1, was to plant some jump table–driven hooks at strategic places in the ROM code and to transfer out as needed to executable code in EEPROM to fix up a broken computation or to put an extra wrinkle on a stock ROM-based command. In fact, each of the card manufacturers semicommercialized this feature of their cards and would offer it to large, trusted customers as a way to differentiate their cards from their competitors.

While very useful in special situations, linking executable native code into the operating system clearly wouldn't work as a general on-card programming paradigm. It didn't solve the skill set problem—you still had to program in 8051 assembler—and because code linked in like this could theoretically read ROM and write EEPROM freely and undetected by the access protections of the operating system, there were a number of less than totally compelling security implications of this technique. What was needed was a way of running a program on the card in way that guaranteed that it didn't misbehave.

The use of source code interpreters as a way to execute programs on constrained computing resources achieved widespread popularity with the version of Beginner's All-purpose Symbolic Instruction Code (BASIC) created by Bill Gates and Paul Allen for the MITS Altair in 1975. The use of interpreters to

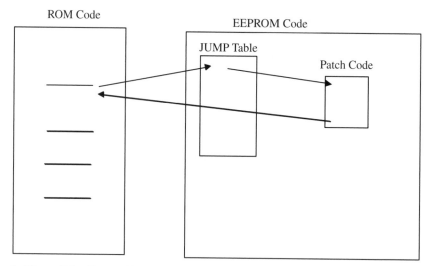

▶ **Figure 5.1**   Jump tables used to patch ROM code.

ensure safe and controlled execution of programs can be traced to IBM's Series/1 data communications computer introduced in 1977. The issues addressed by the Series/1, whose entire operating system was interpreted, was making sure that one malfunctioning application program couldn't bring down an ultra-reliable computing platform used for 24×7 online transaction processing.

Thus, when the need to run application programs on a smart card under tight control began to arise, one approach, at least, had some historical standing. The available resources were, however, yet another order of magnitude more meager than those enjoyed by Messrs. Gates and Allen.

As often happens when an idea is in the air, work on smart card interpreters sprang up independently in more than one location. In 1990, at the RD2P (Research & Development on Portable Files) research laboratory in France (run jointly by Gemplus, Lille University, Pierre Paradinas, and others), the Card Virtual Machine (CAVIMA) was developed, which focused on the use of an on-card interpreter for data retrieval as part of a medical smart card application. This work led to Gemplus's CQL card and, subsequently, the ISO 7816-7 standard. Concurrently, Jelte van der Hoek and Jurjen Bos working at DigiCash in the Netherlands built the J-Code engine for use on the electronic purse smart card that was part of a toll-road project. The J-Code engine went on to become part of the famous DigiCash "Blue" mask, which can still be licensed today from DigiCash's phoenix, eCash Technologies.

The (apparently) first patent for an interpreter on a smart card was French patent FR 2 667 171 B1 issued to Edouard Gordons, Georges Grimonprez, and

Pierre Paradinas on March 27, 1992. The title of the patent is "Support Portable A Microcircuit Facilement Programmable et Procede de Programmation de ce Microcircuit."

The mid-1990s saw the creation of a number of smart card interpreters and on-card virtual machines. The SCIL interpreter by Eduard de Jong went on to become Integrity Art's Clasp interpreter for the TOSCA language. Tony Guilfoyle, one of the programmers of the GeldKarte, created ZeitControl's Basic interpreter. Keycorp introduced the OSSCA operating system that sported a Forth interpreter and Europay also flirted with a Forth card called the Open Card Architecture (OCA) built by Forth, Inc. Oberthur announced the HOST smart card operating system that included an on-card interpreter.

Portability of applications among cards with different chips was the primary driving force during this era. Ease of programming, including the use of standard high-level languages, was less of an issue. It was generally thought that there would be few applications, that they would be small, that they would have to be carefully written, and that as the cost of creating the application was such a small part of creating a new smart card, that efficiencies provided by software tools such as the use of high-level languages simply weren't worth the effort.

The Nat West (National Westminster) Development Team led by David Peacham and David Everett created the first e-purse, Mondex. In May 1995, NWDT set out to design a multiapplication smart card that was to contain a virtual machine with exactly these criteria in mind. Strict separation of applications and ITSEC Level 6 certification were the two design goals. NWDT started with the public domain Pascal virtual machine and byte codes in the book *Programming Language Processors* by David A. Watt. These byte codes were modified primarily by making them variable length to achieve higher density code at a slight expense of runtime efficiency. This card, completed in the summer of 1996, met both of its design desiderata and is now the Multos card.

Still in the mid-1990s, none of these interpreters or multiapplication cards garnered much more than tire-kicking attention from heavyweight issuers and scheme sponsors that were looking for a multiapplication, programmable smart card platform. It may have been the language, the organization behind the product, the experimental patina of the offerings, or simply that the time was not quite right.

This situation changed abruptly in late 1996 when Schlumberger announced the creation of the first Java Card smart card. Supporting a subset of the Java language subsequently labeled as Java Card and a subset of the Java byte codes executed by a 4-Kb on-card virtual machine built at Schlumberger's Austin product development center, Schlumberger's Java Card smart card was quickly embraced by the other major smart card manufacturers, Visa International and, eventually, the GSM mobile telephone community. While probably Java buzz, as much as technical prowess, fueled the success of Java Card, it did have the effect of changing the perception of programmable cards with on-card virtual machines from technical curiosity to commercial opportunity.

Java Card smart cards can, practically speaking, only be programmed in Java. In 1998, Microsoft introduced a smart card with a virtual machine called the Runtime Environment (RTE) that was programming language–independent. It was a Harvard architecture virtual machine that (for those with long memories) could easily have been mistaken for software Intel 8048. Microsoft initially provided a compiler for a subset of the Visual Basic (VB) language for the RTE.

In early 2000, Rowley and Associates broke—for once and for all—the connection between the on-card virtual machine and the source language used to create on-card applications by introducing a suite of software tools that enabled programs written in C, Java, Basic, or Modula-2 to be compiled for and run on both the Multos and Microsoft virtual machines. These tools have since been acquired by Aspects Software.

As is often the case with travels to unknown places, you don't know what's wrong with them until you get there. There are moats around the El Dorado that on-card interpreters sought: Actually installing and deleting lots of programs on the smart card generated large administration requirements and the running programs were pigs. As it usually the case, bridges can be built over moats; both of these shortcomings of installed interpreted applications are being addressed.

In 1998, engineers in a Swedish company, then called Across Wireless, came up with an elegant solution to the administrative costs problem: Don't install the programs on the card. Download the byte-coded program when you need to run it, run the program, and then throw the byte codes away. Because this is just exactly what your World Wide Web browser does when it downloads a page from the Internet, the interpreter that ran these Just-In-Time (JIT) byte codes came to be known as a "mini-browser." However, you aren't in fact browsing in the Web sense at all. Not only is the cost of managing fire-and-forget byte codes much less than managing byte codes that are installed on the card, but issuers can also offer a much broader universe of on-card applications because they don't have to just go with the most generic—and thus least personal—applications. Of course, just as with real Web browsers, the security infrastructure involved in identifying loadable code that is "safe" is highly problematic.

Interpreted programs on an 8-bit smart card run at about 2 Dhrystones per second. The 8-bit processor itself runs at about 80 Dhrystones per second. Now the integer Dhrystone benchmark is arguably not representative of the compute profile of a typical interpreted program, but there can be no question that a stiff performance penalty is being paid every time an interpreted program is run. Originally, this was the price of the runtime checks that ensured the program didn't misbehave. As performance became an issue, however, these checks were moved from runtime to preloading program verification so that very few runtime checks were left in the on-card interpreter. All that's left (if this is done) is pure interpretation overhead. Because it is (to the first order of approximation) as easy to verify microprocessor assembly language as it is to verify arbitrary byte codes, more and more attention is being paid to downloading native code applications. Of course, as we pointed out above, this still doesn't address the "skill set" problem; curiouser and curiouser.

But today, the on-card interpreter—whether for functional languages like Basic, Java, or JIT languages like XML—is the mainstream for building on-card applications. This chapter is about building applications for these multiapplication cards.

APPLICATION SELECTION AND AIDS

On-card application programming for a specific application is essentially nothing more than a matter of defining custom APDUs and implementing them on the card. The off-card application is aware of these custom APDUs and uses them to access the on-card functionality of the application. The off-card application sends an APDU (Table 5.1) to the on-card application:

Table 5.1 APDU Command Structure

CLA	INS	P1	P2	Data Field

and the on-card application returns a response (Table 5.2) to the off-card application:

Table 5.2 APDU Command Response Structure

Response Data	SW1	SW2

just like all the other APDUs we've discussed in previous chapters.

The on-card and off-card application programs can imbue the custom APDUs with whatever semantics they wish, but the basic APDU message format of ISO 7816-4 and master-slave between the host and the card must be maintained because these characteristics of the communication channel are ground into the physical and data-link layers of the T=0 and T=1 smart card protocol stacks.

The problem presented to off-card smart card programs by on-card programming is determining if the card that it has just shocked to life with a reset signal contains an application it can talk to and, if so, how it is to be activated so that the preceding APDU conversation can begin. This is called the application selection problem and it has been around for a surprisingly long time in smart cards.

There are some primitive but effective application selection methods built into ISO 7816-4 that go back to 1994 that we discuss later in this chapter. A patent for application selection was issued to Georges Grimonprez and Pierre Paradinas of Gemplus on October 11, 1995. The title of the patent is "Secured Method for Loading a Plurality of Applications into Microprocessor Memory Card."

In early 1997, the United States made a proposal to the International Standards Organization (ISO) to expand the methods in ISO 7816-4. The proposal was titled "Card Structure and Enhanced Functions for Multi-application Use." It would have become ISO 7816-11 had it been pursued, but it wasn't. The proposal (in a slightly modified form) did go on to become U.S. patent 5802519 issued on September 1, 1998, to Eduard De Jong and titled "Coherent Data Structure with Multiple Interaction Contexts for a Smart Card."

With the commercial acceptance of multiapplication smart cards in the late 1990s and the perception that money (perhaps the "real money") was to be made in managing the applications on card populations and not just in writing and licensing them, a number of start-ups and old-line transaction processing companies proposed proprietary application management schemes, and a number of patents for application management were applied for and issued. Principal among the latter was U.S. patent 6005942 titled "System and Method for a Multi-application Smart Card Which Can Facilitate a Post-Issuance Download of an Application onto the Smart Card" issued on December 21, 1999, to Alfred Chan, Marc Kekicheff, Joel Weise, and David Wentker, and assigned to Visa International Service Association.

The smart card application selection problem has three subproblems: naming card applications (knowing what you are looking for), finding applications on the card (knowing where to look), and activating on-card applications (knowing what to do when you find it).

Note in passing that the "microbrowser" approach to applications finesses all of these problems, if one assumes that there is to be no inter-leaving of applications on the card (a good assumption with current systems, but not necessarily for the future). The terminal doesn't have to wonder if the card can perform its application because it gives the card the application it wants performed at the time it needs it to be performed.

APPLICATION IDENTIFIERS

The application naming subproblem has a widely agreed upon solution. ISO 7816-5 establishes a standard—a universal name space for smart card applications creatively called Application Identifiers (AIDs). An AID has two parts. The first is a Registered Application Provider Identifier (RID) of 5 bytes that is unique to the application provider. Acme Smart Card Software, for example, might have an AID of 0xA0 0x00 0x00 0x00 0x88.

The second part of an AID is a variable-length field of up to 11 bytes called the Proprietary Application Identifier Extension (PIX) that an application developer uses to identify specific applications. It is up to the individual application developer to manage the PIX name space and, thus, to make sure that the RID plus the PIX uniquely identifies one and only one application. Acme could decide to use a 3-byte PIX where the first byte was the product identifier, the second byte was the major version, and the third byte was the minor version number. 0xA0 0x00 0x00 0x00 0x88 0x05 0x01 0x02 would be Version 1.2 of Acme's application number 5.

Every smart card application developer should get an RID to identify his or her applications. RIDs are assigned by the Copenhagen Telephone Company, KTAS, which is also the ISO 7816-5 Registration Authority. KTAS's address is Teglholmsgade 1, DK-1790, Copenhagen, V, Denmark, but the application has to be approved by your national ISO body. RIDs cost about 500 Euros. For those in the U.S., the American National Standards Institute, or ANSI (*www.ansi.org/*), will handle requests for both national and international numbers. Forms for applying for an RID can be found in ISO 7816-5 and at *www.scdk.com*. If you want to issue a single-application smart card, then you need an Issuer Identification Number (IIN) that is specified in ISO 7812. For U.S. residents, forms for an IIN are also available through ANSI. The cost of an IIN is $600.

ISO-7816 APPLICATION SELECTION

ISO 7816-4 and -5 define three methods of application identification and selection-based AIDs called implicit, direct, and DIR file.

Implicit application means that the card runs an application automatically when it is reset and includes the AID of the application in the historical bytes of the ATR or in the ATR file, 0x2F01. Initially, this was used for single-application cards where the AID in the ATR identified the application hard-wired to the card. More recently, on multiapplication cards, implicit application selection is used to launch an on-card shell program that can, in turn, run other applications. The Multos card discussed later in this chapter includes such a shell program capability.

Direct application selection uses the SELECT FILE command wherein the data field contains an AID rather than a dedicated file name. Application selection in this case is not so much a matter of launching an application program on the card as it is setting the current directory using an AID rather than a path name. After direct application selection, normal 7816-like APDU commands would be used to perform application operations on the files in the selected directory and its subdirectories. Direct application selection is typical for applications on multiapplication cards that store data but not executable code on the card.

The most elaborate application selection mechanism defined by ISO-7816 is selection by means of the DIR file. The *DIR file* is the file with identifier 0x2F00 in the root directory. Each constructed TLV object in the DIR file describes one application on the card. The application description must include the AID of the application and, optionally, may include the path to the directory containing the files relevant to the application and a sequence of commands that are to be executed to initiate the application. This is essentially a general-purpose shell file or BAT file capability for smart cards but the authors have never seen it used as such.

OTHER APPLICATION SELECTION SCHEMES

In addition to the three alternatives offered by ISO-7816, a number of smart card consortia and major issuers have come up with their own methods for doing application selection. EMV2000, for example, defines a very elaborate scheme. Visa Open Platform, the Open Card Framework, the European Telecommunications Standards Institute and the Java Card Forum, Europay and the Small Terminal Interoperability Platform consortium among others have also weighed in with their own homegrown approaches. There are also patents held by Fujitsu, Microsoft, Gemplus, Visa, Citibank, and American Express covering application selection on a smart card. Finally, each of the multiapplication cards comes with its own application selection and activation method that we will cover when we discuss the cards themselves. Most of these application selection methods are based on AIDs and all are—in the finest tradition of the smart card industry—wholly incompatible with each other.

Application selection is intimately connected on one hand to the way applications are loaded, unloaded, and generally managed on card populations and, on the other hand, to the way applications on a particular card share data and activate one another. Indeed, some of the application selection methods referred to previously are created in the midst of proposing solutions to one or the other or both of these allied problems. As a result, application selection will probably not stabilize on its own but will have to wait for consensus resolution of these other problems.

THE SCADA CARD

In this section, we will describe the on-card components of a hypothetical smart card application. After describing the application in generic terms, we will implement the application on each of four programmable, multiapplication smart cards. By considering the same application across all cards, the reader will more easily be able to compare the cards and decide which one is best for his or her own application.

There are two on-card application programs in our example: One is used when the card is in action and the other is used for card administration. The application itself is not one of the long-in-the-tooth smart card applications such as electronic cash, loyalty, stored value, or workstation logon. Rather, it is the application of a smart card to industrial control, also known by the acronym SCADA (System Control And Data Acquisition).

Imagine a smart card that is inserted into an electromechanical system of some sort. The system could, for example, be an automobile, a food processing plant, or a utility meter. While the card is inserted, it gathers performance data from the system and provides control commands back to the system. From time to time, the card is collected and brought back to an administration station where the data it has collected is retrieved and the algorithms it uses to provide control commands to the system are updated.

Imagine also that the control algorithms are like secret formulae. This is why we want to store them and the data we are gathering in a tamper-resistant capsule when they are out on the factory floor or in the field doing their work. For the automobile manufacturer, they control fuel consumption and emissions; for the food manufacturer, they control the taste and consistency of the product; and for the utility meter, they balance power consumption among the devices governed by the meter. For all three, the control algorithms are part of the card issuer's competitive edge. The process control card is a good example of a smart card that is a candidate for on-card programming.

Our hypothetical process control smart card has two applications: the online application and the administrative application. The *online application* is what is running while the card is inserted into the electromechanical system. The *administrative application* is what is used back at the office to collect the data and to update the algorithms.

SCADA Card APDUs

Each on-card application handles two APDUs. The online application has one APDU to accept performance data from the system and one APDU to provide control commands back to the system. The administrative application has one

APDU to retrieve the performance data from the card and one APDU to update the control algorithms. Table 5.3 gives the particulars of each of these APDUs.

Table 5.3 APDUs of the Applications on the SCADA Card

APDU	CLA	INS	P1	P2	Data Field	Response
Online Application						
Store Data	C0	10	Point	Flags	Point reading	
Command	C0	20	Point	Flags	Point reading	Control command
Admin Application						
Get Card ID	C0	10				Card identification
Get Data	C0	20	Point	Rec #		Stored data
Update Algorithm	C0	30	Point	Flags	Algorithm parameters	

The details of how the performance data are accumulated and how the control algorithms are represented inside the card can be expected to vary widely from system to system.

For the sake of being explicit for our discussion on the various programmable cards, we will assume that the card keeps a running total of the data and the data squared for each control point and that each control algorithm is simply a table of control value intervals with each interval being associated with an output control command. Thus, associated with each control point, k, are two files. The file with file identifier 1000+k holds the accumulating data for control point k and the file with file identifier 2000+k holds the control table for control point k.

The data accumulation file begins with one byte that counts the number of records in the file. This count is followed by a series of 10-byte records, each having the following structure:

```
struct {
    WORD  n;  /* number of readings accumulated */
    DWORD v;  /* sum of all accumulated readings */
    DWORD v2; /* sum of squares of all accumulated readings */
} record;
```

Each record accumulates a batch of readings and the card can hold a number of batch accumulations.

The control table file similarly begins with 1 byte that counts the number of rows in the table. This count is followed by a series of 12-byte records, each having the following structure:

```
struct {
    WORD lb;    /* lower bound of reading */
    WORD ub;    /* upper bound of reading */
    BYTE c[8]; /* control command for readings in interval */
} row;
```

The interpretation of a row is that if the reading provided by the system in its request for a control command for a control point is greater than the lower bound and less than or equal to the upper bound, then the associated command is returned to the system. The meaning of the command is, of course, purely dependent on the system.

The SCADA Card Online Application

Here is a C sketch of the generic version of the online application:

Code for the Online Application

```
main()
{
    BYTE recs, rows;
    BYTE record[10], row[12];
    short d, n, lb, ub;
    int i, v, v2;

    if(CLA != 0xC0)
            return CLA_ERROR;

    d = MAKEWORD(APDUdata[0], APDUdata[1]);

    switch(INS) {

    /* Accumulate Data */
    case 0x10:
            SelectFile((WORD)(1000 + P1));
            ReadBinary(0, &recs, 0, 1);
            if((recs == 0) || (P2 && NEW_RECORD)) {
                    recs++;
                    WriteBinary(0, &recs, 0, 1);
            }
            recs--;
            ReadBinary((BYTE)(recs*8+1), record, 0, 10);
            n  = MAKEWORD(record[0], record[1]);
            v  = MAKEDWORD(MAKEWORD(record[2], record[3]),
                MAKEWORD(record[4], record[5]));
            v2 = MAKEDWORD(MAKEWORD(record[6], record[7]),
```

```
                 MAKEWORD(record[8], record[9]));
         n++;
         v += d;
         v2 += d*d;
         memset(record, 0, sizeof(record));
         memcpy(&record[0], &n, 2);
         memcpy(&record[2], &v, 4);
         memcpy(&record[6], &v2, 4);
         WriteBinary((BYTE)(recs*8+1), record, 0, (BYTE)10);
         break;

/* Provide Control Command */
case 0x20:
         SelectFile((WORD)(2000 + P1));
         ReadBinary(0, &rows, 0, 1);
         for(i = 0; i < rows; i++) {
                 ReadBinary((BYTE)(i*12+1), row, 0, 12);
                 lb = MAKEWORD(row[0], row[1]);
            ub = MAKEWORD(row[2], row[3]);
            if(d> lb && d <= ub) {
                    SetResponse(row, 4, 8);
                    return SUCCESS;
            }
         }
         return TAB_ERROR;

default:
         return INS_ERROR;
    }

    return SUCCESS;
}
```

The SCADA Card Administration Application

The administration application is simpler than the online application. We will
assume that if the control table is to be updated during an administrative session,
then it will be completely rewritten.

Here is a C sketch of the generic version of the administrative application:

Code for the Administrative Application

```
main()
{
    BYTE recs, rows;
    BYTE record[10];

    if(CLA != 0xC0)
            return CLA_ERROR;

    switch(INS) {

    /* Return Card Identifier */
    case 0x10:
            SelectFile((WORD)0x0002);
            ReadBinary(0, record, 0, 10);
            SetResponse(record, 0, 10);
```

```
            break;

     /* Return Stored Data Record */
     case 0x20:
            SelectFile((WORD)(1000 + P1));
            ReadBinary(0, &recs, 0, 1);
            if(recs < P2)
                    return REC_ERROR;
            ReadBinary((BYTE)((P2-1)*8+1), record, 0, 10);
            SetResponse(record, 0, 10);
            break;

     /* Update Control Table */
     case 0x30:
            SelectFile((WORD)(2000 + P1));
            ReadBinary(0, &rows, 0, 1);
            if(P2 && TAB_RESET) {
                    rows = 0;
                    WriteBinary(0, &rows, 0, 1);
            }
            WriteBinary((BYTE)(rows*12+1), APDUdata, 0, 12);
            rows++;
            WriteBinary(0, &rows, 0, 2);
            break;

     default:
            return INS_ERROR;
     }

     return SUCCESS;
}
```

Some of the API functions we used to access the card from the off-card application, such as `SelectFile`, `ReadBinary`, and `WriteBinary`, also show up in the on-card application. This makes sense because all we have really done is move functionality from the off-card application to the on-card application and, in effect, eliminated the communication overhead. The basic services provided by the card operating system are the same whether you are accessing them locally or remotely.

THE MULTOS CARD

The Multos card is the most mature and arguably the most secure, programmable multiapplication card on the market today. Multos card applications were originally conceived of as being written in byte code assembly language. This language, called the Multos Executable Language (MEL), is based on Pascal P-codes and the virtual machine described in David A. Watt's book _Programming Language Processors_. These byte codes underwent some modification to increase their density and the result was the MEL assembly language. While it was not a design constraint at the time, these modifications did not destroy the possibility of compiling high-level languages to the byte codes and today, MEL byte code compilers exist for both C and Java.

The Multos Virtual Machine

The core Multos virtual machine consists of the 31-byte code instructions given in Table 5.4.

Table 5.4 Byte Codes of the Multos Virtual Machine

Mnemonic	Description
ADDB	Add literal to byte
ADDN	Add n-byte blocks
ADDW	Add literal to word
ANDN	Bitwise AND of n-byte blocks
BRANCH	Branch to relative address
CALL	Call a function
CLEARN	Zeroize n-byte block
CMPB	Compare literal to byte
CMPN	Compare n-byte blocks
CMPW	Compare literal to word
DECN	Decrement n-byte block
INCN	Increment n-byte block
INDEX	Index an array
JUMP	Jump to code address
LOAD	Load data to stack
LOADA	Load address
LOADI	Load indirect
NOTN	Bitwise NOT of n-byte blocks
ORN	Bitwise OR of n-byte blocks
PRIMRET	Call primitive or return
SETB	Set byte to literal
SETW	Set word to literal

Table 5.4 Byte Codes of the Multos Virtual Machine (Continued)

Mnemonic	Description
STACK	Push or pop the stack
STORE	Store data from the stack
SOTREI	Store indirect
SUBB	Subtract literal from byte
SUBN	Subtract n-byte blocks
SUBW	Subtract literal from word
SYSTEM	Various system functions
TESTN	Test n-byte block against 0
XORN	Bitwise XOR of n-byte blocks

Every implementation of the Multos card must support these byte codes and a mandatory set of operating system services that include bit manipulation, division, multiplication, and low-level memory operations. The mandatory set of operating services can be extended with services that support advanced services such as cryptographic algorithms and modular arithmetic. Implementers of the Multos card are not free to add their own extensions, so if an optional service is present on a Multos card, it is the same as that service on all other Multos cards regardless of card manufacturer.

Besides the byte codes in Table 5.4, every Multos card supports 24 operating system service calls called *primitives*. These include various byte array copy and compare operations, bit manipulation operations, integer multiply and divide, and card-oriented operations such as set ATR that ask the host for more time.

An advantage of a modest byte code and primitive operation set with a simple execution context is that it is feasible to write assembly language subroutines that can be called by high-level language applications and even to write inline byte codes in high-level language programs. This is a unique feature of the Multos card. We will see some examples of this later in this chapter.

There are a number of assemblers available for MEL. For small, time-critical, relatively stable applications, one of these may be the appropriate software development tool to use. For the purpose of comparing programming of a Multos card to programming of other cards, we will confine our attention to Multos's standard high-level programming language, C. There are also compilers of Java, Basic, and Modula-2 for the Multos virtual machine. Compilers for all these languages on the Multos card are provided by Rowley Associates Limited and Aspects Software in the U.K.

The Multos Programming Model

Multos does not support a file system for an application's nonvolatile data but rather simply provides a static block of EEPROM memory to the application that the application can structure how it pleases. This static data segment is protected against access by all other applications. An application in execution can also access two volatile data segments. The dynamic data segment is private to the application and contains the stack and other session data. The public data segment contains the communication buffers that handle traffic to and from the terminal and a common global area used to pass data between applications.

Virtually no structure is imposed on an application by the Multos programming model. In the spirit of Unix, an application consists of a main function that can define and call other functions as well as functions provided by the operating system.

Once a Multos application has been activated, each arriving APDU causes the main function to be called. The four header fields of the APDU (CLA, INS, P1, and P2) are preloaded into global variables by the Multos operating system. Subsequent calling of the CheckCase system service within the application causes the APDU's data field to be loaded into the application's public data segment and the Lc and Le global variables to be set. The argument to CheckCase is the ISO 7816-4 case of the APDU that the application expects, and CheckCase returns a Boolean flag indicating whether or not the APDU received from the host matches the application's expectations. For Case 2 and 4 APDUs for which the card returns data in addition to the status word to the host, the application places the data to be returned in the public data segment before exiting with a status code.

The C library for Multos applications includes many of the standard library functions known and loved by C programmers everywhere, including the ctype functions, the heap management functions, the string functions, setjmp/longjmp, and even good old printf. There is also a good collection of both high- and low-level cryptographic functions.

A unique feature of the Multos programming model is the ability to include inline byte codes and to write byte-coded subroutines. The ability to mix assembly code in with high-level language statements is standard fare in the world of microcontroller programming and is entirely missing in the other programmable cards. Notice that there is no downside security implication of this feature because execution is still controlled by the Multos virtual machine.

Some of the library functions are implemented using inline code. For example, the library function COPYN, which copies *n* bytes from a source pointer to a destination pointer is defined by:

```
#define COPYN(N, DEST, SRC)
do {
    __push(__typechk(unsigned char *, DEST)); \
    __push(__typechk(unsigned char *, SRC)); \
```

```
      __code(PRIM, 0x0e, N);
} while(0);
```

where `0x0e` is the opcode of the Multos operating system primitive to copy *n* bytes from one location to another.

The SCADA Application on Multos

Here is the online SCADA application rendered for the Multos card using the Rowley C compiler.

Code for SCADA Application on Multos Card

```c
#include <string.h>
#include <multoscomms.h>

#define BYTE unsigned char

#define CONTROL_POINTS 10
#define DATA_RECORDS 10

#define SUCCESS 0x9000
#define CLA_ERROR 0x6999
#define CSE_ERROR 0x6999
#define TAB_ERROR 0x6999
#define INS_ERROR 0x6999

#define NEW_RECORD 0x01

#define CONTROL_INTERVALS 10

#pragma melpublic

union
{
  BYTE as_bytes[8];
  int as_int[4];
} apdu_data;

#pragma melstatic

typedef struct
{
  short m_n;
  long m_v;
  long m_v2;
} record_t;

typedef struct
{
  short m_lb;
  short m_ub;
  BYTE m_data[8];
} row_t;

static BYTE records[CONTROL_POINTS];
static record_t record[CONTROL_POINTS][DATA_RECORDS];
```

```
static BYTE rows[CONTROL_POINTS];
static row_t row[CONTROL_POINTS][CONTROL_INTERVALS];

void main(int argc, char *argv[], char *envp[])
{
 BYTE r, i;
 short d;
 row_t *rowp;
 record_t *recp;

 if(CLA != 0xC0)
  ExitSW(CSE_ERROR);

 switch(INS) {

 /* Accumulate Data */
 case 0x10:

  if(!CheckCase(2))
   ExitSW(CLA_ERROR);

  d = apdu_data.as_int[0];
  r = records[P1];
  if ((r == 0) || (P2 && NEW_RECORD))
    records[P1] = ++r;
  r--;

  recp = record[P1] + r;
  recp->m_n++;
  recp->m_v += d;
  recp->m_v2 += d*d;
  break;

 /* Provide Control Command */
 case 0x20:
  r = rows[P1];
  for (rowp = row[P1]; rowp < row[P1]+r; ++rowp)
    if (d > rowp->m_lb && d <= rowp->m_ub) {
       memcpy(apdu_data.as_bytes, rowp->m_data, 8);
       ExitLa(8);
   }
  ExitSW(TAB_ERROR);

 default:
  ExitSW(INS_ERROR);
 }

 ExitSW(SUCCESS);
}
```

The Multos C version of the SCADA online application compiles to 459 MEL byte codes using Version 1.0 of the Rowley C compiler.

The three Multos data segments are identified in the C code through the use of the pragma statements, #pragma melstatic, #pragma melpublic, and #pragma melsession. In the preceding program, the array apdu_data is the incoming and outgoing communication buffer and is placed at the beginning of the public data segment. The data accumulation records and the control tables are non-volatile data and, therefore, like the code itself, are placed in the static data segment.

Pointers and bit shifting operations are very handy to have when building resource-constrained applications such as those for a smart card. The fact that the Multos card has received the E6 High ITSEC security certification—the highest certification possible—which included the separation of applications, says that there is no connection between the use of a programming language with pointers and card security.

The Multos Application Development Cycle

Any text editor or program development environment can be used to create the Multos C source code. The code is compiled to a MEL byte code file by the Rowley DOS command-line compiler. This file can be loaded into a byte code simulator for single-step debugging or downloaded to the application directory on the card. Once on the card, the application can be selected using its AID or its name (as determined by the name of the first file in the C compilation). After the selection APDU, all subsequent APDUs are routed to the main entry point of the application for processing.

Multos has perhaps the most elaborate security scheme of all the programmable cards for loading and deleting applications. This is because the Multos scheme serves security and business purposes, with the business purposes keeping track of each load and unload operation in a nonreputable way. Fortunately, all of this machinery can be turned off during application development so that very quick edit/test/debug cycles are possible.

THE JAVA CARD

The first Java Card virtual machine was created in the spring of 1996 at Schlumberger's Austin product development center. The Schlumberger Java Card team worked top down, first prioritizing Java features versus their utility in the current smart card arena, and then discarding less useful features of Java until the Java Card virtual machine fit in 4 Kb of 6805 code.

The first implementation of the Java Card virtual machine implemented 74 Java byte codes (*www.slb.com/et/*). It ran on the SC49 chip, which has 11.2 Kb of ROM, 4 Kb of EEPROM, and 512 bytes of RAM (*www.mot.com*). The interpreter and its runtime support took all of the ROM and 1 Kb of the EEPROM, leaving 3 Kb for user programs and data. The runtime library for the card supported on-card file system operations, identity and security features such as PIN handling and file access control, and T=0 host communication functions.

This work received a U.S. patent, "US6308317: Using a High Level Programming Language with a Microcontroller" on October 23, 2001.

Following its initial development, Schlumberger transferred the specification of Java Card 1.0 to Sun Microsystems and, in the same time frame, established with Gemplus and other members of the "smart card community" the Java Card

Forum. The Java Card Forum offers a venue for Java Card licensees to review, discuss, and offer suggestions to Sun Microsystems for the evolution of the Java Card specifications. As of this writing, the latest released version is Java Card 2.2 with Java Card 3.0 requirements assessment well underway.

Almost all of the Java Card smart cards on the market consist of an interpreter for the Java Card subset of Java byte codes running on top of a single-application smart card operating system. Some of the cards hide this fact and present a pure Java programming model exactly as described in the Java Card specification. Other cards, principally the Schlumberger Cyberflex Access™ series of cards, let the capabilities of the underlying operating system come through to the programming interface presented to the application.

Because the unadulterated Java Card API provides only a modest set of services outside cryptography, this latter approach holds some benefits for the application developer who is concerned with getting the application built. There is an ongoing tension between programming (application) efficiency and maintaining the integrity (purity) of the Java language, although this is not too unlike similar tensions that we've always seen between language and operating system implementations.

The Java Card Virtual Machine

As of Java Card Version 2.1.2 of May 2001, the 108 Java card byte codes were as shown in Table 5.5.

Table 5.5 Java Card 2.1.2 Byte Codes

Mnemonic	Description
aaload	Load from array reference
aastore	Store to array reference
aconst_null	Push a null
aload	Load a local variable
aload_<n>	Load reference from local variable
anewarray	Create a new array
areturn	Return from a method
arraylength	Get length of array
astore	Store into local variable

Table 5.5 Java Card 2.1.2 Byte Codes (Continued)

Mnemonic	Description
astore_<n>	Store to local variable
athrow	Throw an exception
baload	Load byte or Boolean from array
bastore	Store into byte or Boolean array
bipush	Push a byte
bspush	Push a short
checkcast	Check type of an object
dup	Duplicate top of stack
dup_x	Duplicate top of stack and insert below
dup_2	Duplicate top two operands on stack
getfield_<t>	Fetch field from object
getfield_<t>_this	Fetch field from current object
getfield_<t>_w	Fetch field from object using wide index
getstatic_<t>	Get static field from class
goto	Branch always
goto_w	Branch always with wide index
i2b	Convert integer to byte
i2s	Convert integer to short
iadd	Add integer
iaload	Load integer from array
iand	Boolean AND integer
iastore	Store into integer array
icmp	Compare integers

Table 5.5 Java Card 2.1.2 Byte Codes (Continued)

Mnemonic	Description
iconst_<i>	Push constant integer onto stack
idiv	Divide integers
if_acmp<cond>	Branch if comparison succeeds
if_acmp<cond>_w	Branch if comparison succeeds (wide index)
if_scmp<cond>	Branch if short comparison succeeds
if_scmp<cond>_w	Branch if short comparison succeeds (wide index)
if<cond>	Branch if short comparison with zero succeeds
if<cond>_w	Branch if short comparison with zero succeeds (wide index)
ifnonnull	Branch if reference is not null
ifnonnull_W	Branch if reference is not null (wide index)
ifnull	Branch if reference is null
ifnull_w	Branch if reference is null (wide index)
iinc	Increment local integer variable by a constant
iinc_w	Increment local integer variable by a constant (wide index)
iipush	Push integer
iload	Load integer from local variable
iload_<n>	Load integer from local variable
ilookupswitch	Access jump table by key match and jump
imul	Multiply integers
ineg	Negate an integer
instanceof	Determine if object is of a given type
invokeinterface	Invoke interface method

Table 5.5 Java Card 2.1.2 Byte Codes (Continued)

Mnemonic	Description
invokespecial	Invoke instance method with special handling
invokestatic	Invoke a class method
invokevirtual	Invoke instance method based on class
ior	Boolean OR of integers
irem	Remainder of integer division
ireturn	Return integer from a method
ishl	Shift integer left
ishr	Shift integer right
istore	Store integer into local variable
istore_<n>	Store integer into local variable
isub	Subtract integers
itableswitch	Access table by integer index and jump
iushr	Logical shift right of an integer
ixor	Boolean XOR of integers
jsr	Jump to a subroutine
new	Create a new object
newarray	Create a new array
nop	Do nothing
pop	Pop top operand on stack
pop2	Pop top two operands on stack
putfield_<t>	Set value of field in an object
putfield_<t>_this	Set value of field in current object

Table 5.5 Java Card 2.1.2 Byte Codes (Continued)

Mnemonic	Description
putfield_<t>_w	Set value of field in object (wide index)
putstatic_<t>	Set value of field in static class
ret	Return from subroutine
return	Return void from method
s2b	Convert short to byte
s2i	Convert short to integer
sadd	Add shorts
saload	Load short from array
sand	Boolean AND of shorts
sastore	Store short into an array
sconst_<s>	Push short constant
sdiv	Divide shorts
sinc	Increment short by constant
sinc_w	Increment short by constant (wide index)
sipush	Push short
sload	Load short from local variable
sload_<n>	Load short from local variable
slookupswitch	Access jump table by short key match and jump
smul	Multiply shorts
sneg	Negate short
sor	Boolean OR of shorts
srem	Remainder of short division

Table 5.5 Java Card 2.1.2 Byte Codes (Continued)

Mnemonic	Description
sreturn	Return short from method
sshl	Shift left of short
sshr	Shift right of short
sspush	Push a short
sstore	Store short into local variable
sstore_<n>	Store short into local variable
ssub	Subtract shorts
stableswitch	Access jump table by short index and jump
sushr	Local shift right of short
swap_x	Swap top two operand stack words
sxor	Boolean XOR of shorts

Due to the complex state of the Java Card virtual machine, it is virtually impossible to write assembly language subroutines using Java Card byte codes, let alone inline Java Card byte codes in Java Card application programs. It is also forbidden by the Java Card specification.

The Java Card Programming Model

The Java Card smart card has the most complex application programming model of the commercially available programmable smart cards. This is because Java Card removes the notion of an underlying operating system and uses the Java Card programming language to serve the dual—and, at times, contradictory—roles of computational process description and runtime context administration. The result is that a Java Card program is a mixture of application logic and job control logic.

A Java Card application provides four routines that allow it and its data to be controlled by the Java Card framework. Three of these routines—*install*, *select*, and *deselect*—concern only job control logic, including memory management and data sharing. The fourth—*process*—is called each time an APDU arrives for the application and is analogous to the main entry point of a Multos card application.

A Java Card application's *install* entry point is called once by the Java Card framework when the application is loaded onto the card. The *install* routine allocates all the nonvolatile data space that the application might ever need. Data space can be allocated as needed by the process routine, but this approach is not recommended by the Java Card specification because if the space should turn out to be unavailable, the application aborts. The *install* routine must also call the framework's register routine to make the framework aware of the application's AID. Even though it is only used once, the *install* routine code stays on the card and the space it occupies is lost.

Because Java Card's language features are used to provide what would normally be operating system services, a Java Card application's data and code are closely bound together. On the one hand, this makes it difficult to update the application's code to a new version without disturbing the data associated with the application. Conversely, it minimizes discrepancies between data definitions and data processing code, which can occur when the two are allowed to evolve independently. On specialized Java Cards that support file operations, files can be used to hold the data associated with an application, thus providing a more "classic" smart card software architecture. On more orthodox Java Cards, you can create a data repository application that just holds the application's data and shares read and write methods with the application itself. Essentially, each application has to provide its own file system code. There has been some successful prototyping of a relational database data store on a Java Card smart card that allows various applications to access information in a common data store. As the memory available on smart card chips increases, this approach may see increasing merit.

The Java Card 2.1.2 API consists of 119 entry points that include APDU reception and transmission services, volatile memory management, array manipulation services, transaction services, a large number of cryptographic services, and runtime exceptions. Like the Multos card, the Java card specification does not support a file system of any sort. However, rather than simply making a block of memory available that can be used in a manner that is natural for the application, Java card binds nonvolatile memory management, including the data security constructs to the Java programming language. Thus, nonvolatile data objects are created within the language and controlled by the Java card runtime environment. Once created, they cannot be freed nor, because of the strict typing of the Java language, can the EEPROM space they occupy be used for other purposes by the application. Upcoming releases of the Java card specification will support the reclamation of unused data space (garbage collection) but it will be a while before these cards are in the field.

The SCADA Application on a Java Card

Code for Online SCADA Application for Java Card

```java
/*
** online.java - On-Line Application for the SCADA Card
*/
import java.lang.reflect.Array;
import javacard.framework.*;
import javacardx.framework.*;
import javacardx.crypto.*;

public class online extends javacard.framework.Applet {

    /* SCADA card on-Line application parameters and sizing val-
ues */
    final static byte SCADA_CLA = (byte)0xC0;

    final static byte DATA_ACQUISITION_INS = (byte)0x10;
    final static byte SYSTEM_CONTROL_INS   = (byte)0x20;

    final static byte NEW_RECORD = (byte)0x01;

    final static byte POINTS  = 4;
    final static byte RECORDS = 8;
    final static byte ROWS    = 8;

    /* The input/output buffer */
    byte apdu_data[];

    /* The data acquisition records and system control tables */
    static byte records[];
    static byte record[];
    static byte rows[];
    static byte row[];

    private online() {

            records = new byte[POINTS];
            record  = new byte[POINTS*RECORDS*10];
            rows    = new byte[POINTS];
            row     = new byte[POINTS*ROWS*12];

            register();
    }

    /* Called when the applet is instantiated. */
    public static void install(APDU apdu) {
            new online();
    }

    /* Called when the applet is selected. */
    public boolean select() {
            return true;
    }

    /* Called when an APDU is received. */
    public void process(APDU apdu) throws ISOException {
```

```
        short d;
        byte p;

        apdu.setIncomingAndReceive();

        apdu_data = apdu.getBuffer();

        if ((apdu_data[ISO.OFFSET_CLA] == ISO.CLA_ISO) &&
                (apdu_data[ISO.OFFSET_INS] == ISO.INS_SELECT)){
                ISOException.throwIt(ISO.SW_NO_ERROR);
        }

        if (apdu_data[ISO.OFFSET_CLA] != SCADA_CLA)
                        ISOException.throwIt(ISO.SW_CLA_NOT_
SUPPORTED);

        p = apdu_data[ISO.OFFSET_P1];

        d = Array.getShort(apdu_data, 0);

        switch (apdu_data[ISO.OFFSET_INS]) {

        case DATA_ACQUISITION_INS:
                AccumulateData(p, d, apdu_data[ISO.OFFSET_P2]);
                break;
        case SYSTEM_CONTROL_INS:
                ProvideControl(p, d);
                apdu.setOutgoingAndSend((short)0, (short)8);
                break;
        default:
                ISOException.throwIt(ISO.SW_INS_NOT_SUPPORTED);
        }

        ISOException.throwIt(ISO.SW_NO_ERROR);
}

/*
** Accumulate a Data Value from a Control Point
*/
private void AccumulateData(byte p, short d, byte flags) {
        short r, n, v, v2;

        r = records[p];

        if((r == 0) || ((flags & NEW_RECORD) != 0)) {
                r++;
                records[p] = (byte)r;
        }
        r--;

        n  = Array.getShort(record, p*r*10+0);
        v  = Array.getShort(record, p*r*10+2);
        v2 = Array.getShort(record, p*r*10+6);

        n  += 1;
        v  += d;
        v2 += d*d;

        Array.setShort(record, p*r*10+0, n);
        Array.setShort(record, p*r*10+2, v);
```

```
                Array.setShort(record, p*r*10+6, v2);
        }

        /*
        ** Provide a Control Command to a Control Point
        */
        private void ProvideControl(byte p, short d) {
                short r, i, lb, ub;

                r = rows[p];

                for(i = 0; i < r; i++) {

                        lb = Array.getShort(row, p*r*12+0);
                        ub = Array.getShort(row, p*r*12+2);

                        if(d > lb && d <= ub) {
                                Util.arrayCopy(row, (short)(p*r*12+4),
                                                apdu_data, (short)0,
(short)8);
                                return;
                        }
                }
                ISOException.throwIt(ISO.SW_RECORD_NOT_FOUND);
        }
}
```

The Java card version of the SCADA online application compiles to 680 Java byte codes using Schlumberger's mksolo32 byte code converter.

The need to preallocate the data acquisition and command tables to their maximum possible size means that a lot of EEPROM space is wasted. Files could be used to store this data, but files are not part of the Java Card specification; those Java cards that extend the specification by including file objects require preallocation if the file is to maximum size.

The lack of multidimensional arrays in Java Card Java is only a slight irritation as is having to constantly cast everything to a short. You should, however, abandon the "write once, run everywhere" notion when it comes to Java Card versus "pure" Java. Java Card is a special-purpose offshoot of Java that, because of the smart card architectural and processing environment, has abandoned some elements of consistency with its parent. This is particularly true in the area of data access control and data sharing, which we discuss later.

The Java Card Application Development Cycle

The process of creating an executable Java card application consists of the following steps:

1. Edit and compile the application's Java card source code.
2. Convert the resulting class files to a Java card byte code file (CAP file).

3. Verify the CAP file (optional).
4. Translate the CAP file to a vendor-specific application image file.
5. Download the application image file to the vendor's Java card.
6. Install the application into the Java card framework.

At this point, the application can be selected and run. The translate step and the download step are combined in some Java Card implementations.

While this process is straightforward, the eight Java card software development kits currently on the market differ markedly in how they present this process to the application developer. Work is underway to standardize this process among a particular subset of the eight cards.

Each Java card SDK takes as its starting point the collection of application class files created by any one of the commercially available Java compilers from the application's Java source code. Because none of these full Java compilers recognize the Java Card subset or extensions, it falls to the task of the converter, the verifier, and the translator to check for compliance with the Java Card specification. Unfortunately, because the source code has been left behind, it can be a challenging task to tie the error messages generated by these programs back to the Java source code line that is causing the problem. Furthermore, because Java Cards differ in their loading mechanisms from one vendor to another, an application that successfully passes through the convert/verify/translate process from one vendor might fail the same process of another vendor.

Many of the Java card SDKs leave in place the security machinery that is used in production to ensure that only authorized applets get onto the card. While this is helpful if you are doing end-to-end testing, it can get in the way if you are at the initial stages of developing, testing, and debugging a Java card application. One of the kits, the one from Giesecke & Devrient, includes a very nice Java card simulator that can be very useful in initial debugging of a Java card application.

The Java Card specification mandates the step of installing an application into the on-card framework. Because Java Card implements classic operating system features such as data security, access control, and interapplication communication using programming language constructs, there must be a "first among equals" application that knows and manages all the other applications. This overseer application is essentially the Java card framework, and installing a new application into the framework connects the language features and name space of the new application with the language features and name space of the framework. The result is that a Java card is essentially one giant application—the framework—that contains all the applications loaded onto the card.

The "firewall" between Java card applications is provided by the rules of variable name visibility defined for the Java Card language. All applications are part of the framework's name space and all execute in the same sandbox—the framework's. As we will see later, the unified name space provided by the Java card framework is the language feature also used to implement data sharing between applications.

Java cards have perhaps the most involved application development cycle of all the cards discussed in this chapter. This is due both to the innate complexity of the process and the lack of integration of the steps. The inability of standard compilers to handle the distinct specifications of Java Card Java means that simple programming errors are caught farther downstream than is desirable. The use of language features to perform operating system services begets the installation step.

THE WINDOWS-POWERED SMART CARD

Microsoft's Windows for Smart Cards (WfSC) operating system was developed in the summer of 1998 and made its debut at Cartes'98 in November of that year. Rather than designing *de novo* for the smart card, the Microsoft development team, like Multos's Nat West Development Team before it, started with battle-hardened designs from "big iron" and adapted them to the resources available on the smart card. The philosophy was to embed smart card computing in the skill sets and programming models of existing application programmers rather than require that these application programmers learn new skills and programming models in order to use smart cards. Of course, handling the limited resources environment of the smart card will probably always constitute a re-learning process for typical PC-level application programmers.

The file system design of the Windows card is the tried and true File Access Table (FAT) file system of DOS and Windows. Because smart cards are used internationally, file names are represented in Unicode rather than ASCII. To support the fine-grain, multipersonality requirements for access control and data security, the team adopted the access control list (ACL) design created by Bob Daley and Peter Neumann in 1964 for the Multics operating system and found in many Multics descendants such as George, Unix, VMS, and Windows NT. The virtual machine is a compact version of the Intel 8048 and the on-card application programming interface is a greatly scaled-down version of the Windows API.

The Windows Card Virtual Machine

The Microsoft Windows Card virtual machine (or as the documentation refers to it, the Windows Card Runtime Environment, or simply RTE) is arguably the most well-designed and most parsimonious of all the smart card virtual machines.

Like the Multos virtual machine, the Microsoft virtual machine has a Harvard architecture with a single 8-bit accumulator and an optional stack. Also, like the Multos virtual machine, it is defined in terms of a small core byte code set to which application-specific extensions can be added. The 27 core byte codes are shown in Table 5.6.

Table 5.6 Byte Codes for Windows Card Virtual Machine

Mnemonic	Description
ADD	Add literal to the ACC
SUB	Subtract literal from the ACC
AND	AND literal with the ACC
OR	OR literal with the ACC
XOR	XOR literal with the ACC
LDA#	Load ACC with a literal
LDA	Load ACC from an address
LDAI	Load ACC from address and increment address
STAI	Store ACC to address and increment address
LDAD	Decrement address and load address to ACC
STAD	Decrement address and store ACC to address
LDAC	Load the ACC with contents of PC+A+offset+2
JMP	Jump to a location
JZ	Jump if Z flag is set
JNZ	Jump if Z flag is not set
JC	Jump if C flag is set
JNC	Jump if C flag is not set
CALL	Call subroutine
RET	Return from a subroutine

Table 5.6 Byte Codes for Windows Card Virtual Machine

Mnemonic	Description
CLR	Clear an address to zero
DEC	Decrement contents of an address
INC	Increment contents of an address
NOP	Do nothing
END	Terminate execution
STOP	Break-point in debug mode
ESC	Transfer control to extension
SYS	Call an operating system service

The Windows Card Programming Model

The Windows card programming model is very much like the Multos programming model. There is no over-arching framework as there is on the Java card. After being selected, the application has complete control of the card and calls upon the WfSC operating system for services such as communication, file access, and cryptography—classic platform computing.

Selection of an application is accomplished by associating a unique APDU with the application and then sending that APDU to the card. In other words, it is not by way of AIDs. In this regard, WfSC is like the Basic card (see later in this chapter) except that an APDU is associated with an entire application, not entry points in the application. Once activated, the application receives all APDUs transmitted to the card until it terminates. Associating an APDU with an application can be a\ bit awkward because it requires editing and overwriting the APDU dispatch table on the card. The dispatch table itself is a very powerful construct and, as its full utility gets integrated into the development environment, the process of associating an APDU with an application should become painless.

A compiled WfSC program consists of two files: a byte code file (.RTE) and a data space file (.DAT). This separation of code and data, at one time a basic tenet of good programming practice, together with the existence of a full-featured file system, means that code that implements a WfSC application on a card can be updated without destroying the data that has become associated with the application. It is, in fact, possible for two code files to share the same data space file but this is not typically done. Rather, the file system is used to share data between applications.

The SCADA Program on a Windows-Powered Smart Card

Code for SCADA Program on a Windows Smart Card

```
Const CLA = &HC0
Const INS = &H20
Const P1 = &H0
Const P2 = &H0

Const NEW_RECORD = &H1

Const SUCCESS = &H9000
Const CLA_ERROR = &H6D00
Const INS_ERROR = &H6E00
Const TAB_ERROR = &H6F00

Const SHIFT8 As Integer = &H100
Const SHIFT16 As Long = &H10000
Const SHIFT24 As Long = &H1000000

Function MAKEWORD(ByVal a As Byte, ByVal b As Byte) As Long
    MAKEWORD = a * SHIFT8 + b
End Function

Function MAKEDWORD(ByVal a As Long, ByVal b As Long) As Long
    MAKEDWORD = a * SHIFT16 + b
End Function

Sub Main(ByVal CLA As Byte, _
         ByVal INS As Byte, _
         ByVal P1 As Byte, _
         ByVal P2 As Byte, _
         ByVal lc As Byte)

    Dim APDUdata(0 To 10)
    Dim recs, rows As Byte
    Dim record(0 To 9) As Byte, row(0 To 11) As Byte
    Dim d, n, lb, ub As Integer
    Dim v, v2 As Long
    Dim hFile As Byte
    Dim i, Status, ActualBytes As Byte
    Dim fileName(0 To 3) As Byte

    If (CLA <> &HC0) Then
        ScwSendCommInteger CLA_ERROR
        Exit Sub
    End If

    d = MAKEWORD(APDUdata(0), APDUdata(1))

    Select Case INS

    ' Accumulate Data
    Case &H10:
        fileName(0) = &H10
        fileName(1) = P1
```

```
        fileName(2) = 0
        fileName(3) = 0
        Status = ScwCreateFile(fileName, "", hFile)
        Status = ScwReadFile(hFile, recs, 1, ActualBytes)
        If recs = 0 Or P2 = NEW_RECORD Then
            recs = recs + 1
            Status = ScwSetFilePointer(hFile, 0, FILE_BEGIN)
            Status = ScwWriteFile(hFile, recs, 1, ActualBytes)
        End If
        recs = recs - 1
        Status = ScwSetFilePointer(hFile, recs * 8 + 1,
FILE_BEGIN)
        Status = ScwReadFile(hFile, record, 10, ActualBytes)
        n = MAKEWORD(record(0), record(1))
        v = MAKEDWORD(MAKEWORD(record(2), record(3)), MAKE-
WORD(record(4), record(5)))
        v2 = MAKEDWORD(MAKEWORD(record(6), record(7)), MAKE-
WORD(record(8), record(9)))

        n = n + 1
        v = v + d
        v2 = v2 + d * d

        record(0) = n \ SHIFT8
        record(1) = n - record(0) * SHIFT8

        record(2) = v \ SHIFT24
        record(3) = v \ SHIFT16 - record(2) * SHIFT8
        record(4) = v \ SHIFT8 - (record(2) * SHIFT16 + record(3)
* SHIFT8)
        record(5) = v - (record(2) * SHIFT24 + record(3) *
SHIFT16 + record(4) * SHIFT8)

        record(6) = v2 \ SHIFT24
        record(7) = v2 \ SHIFT16 - record(6) * SHIFT8
        record(8) = v2 \ SHIFT8 - (record(6) * SHIFT16 +
record(7) * SHIFT8)
        record(9) = v2 - (record(6) * SHIFT24 + record(7) *
SHIFT16 + record(8) * SHIFT8)

        Status = ScwSetFilePointer(hFile, recs * 10 + 1,
FILE_BEGIN)
        Status = ScwWriteFile(hFile, record, 10, ActualBytes)

    ' Provide Control Command
    Case &H20:
        fileName(0) = &H20
        fileName(1) = P1
        fileName(2) = 0
        fileName(3) = 0
        Status = ScwCreateFile(fileName, "", hFile)
        Status = ScwReadFile(hFile, rows, 1, ActualBytes)
        For i = 0 To rows
            Status = ScwSetFilePointer(hFile, i * 12 + 1,
FILE_BEGIN)
            Status = ScwReadFile(hFile, row, 12, ActualBytes)
            lb = MAKEWORD(row(0), row(1))
            ub = MAKEWORD(row(2), row(3))
            If d > lb And d <= ub Then
                ScwSendCommBytes row, 4, 8
```

```
            ScwSendCommInteger SUCCESS
            Exit Sub
        End If
    Next
    ScwSendCommInteger SUCCESS
    Exit Sub
  End Select

End Sub
```

The SCADA application compiles to 1753 bytes of executable byte codes for the Version 1.0 Microsoft Runtime Environment (RTE).

The fact that FAT files can grow and shrink as needed means that there is no wasted space on the Microsoft card for storing either the acquired data or the process control rules. The lack of bit operations in Visual Basic does, however, mean that unnatural computation acts to efficiently store multibyte values in the files have to be performed.

The Windows Card Application Development Cycle

Microsoft has integrated application development for Windows for Smart Cards completely into Visual Studio and its popular and widely used Visual Basic IDE. In fact, Windows for Smart Cards is just another type of Visual Basic project. When you compile a Windows for Smart Cards Visual Basic application, all of the constraints on Visual Basic to enable it to be compiled for the WfSC virtual machine are taken into account and violations of those constraints are flagged at the source code level and immediately available for editing and fixing. At the time of this writing, Microsoft has discontinued their support for Windows for Smart Cards. The product may well be supported by others; however, its continued support in Visual Studio and other Microsoft toolkits may become an issue.

The Visual Basic IDE also includes a Windows for Smart Cards simulator into which a successfully compiled application can be loaded. The simulated card can be connected to an off-card VB application and the two run in tandem, but the off-card application is running in a separate VB IDE. You can single-step from off-card to on-card and back to off-card code, but it is much more awkward than the "double debugger" environment offered by the ZeitControl Basic card (see later in this chapter).

After the on-card application has been run in the simulator, it can be downloaded to the card from within the VB IDE. Like some of the other programmable cards, the security mechanisms surrounding code downloading in the field can be turned off to speed debug turnaround time. After the code has been downloaded, the off-card application can be pointed at the card rather than the simulator and debugging with the card itself commenced.

Besides writing and downloading VB applications, the free-for-the-download Microsoft SmartCard Toolkit provides a number of additional capabilities that enable the smart card architect to design a complete smart card including the file system, access control policies, and cryptography. This multifaceted smart card design capability tends to lead to a complex development context within which it is easy to lose your simple VB application. Nevertheless, the integration of Source Safe and continued work on the integration of smart cards within the VB IDE will smooth over these bumps and make the creation of custom smart cards a task that any application programmer can tackle without having to learn arcane facts about microcontrollers, ROM masks, and chip production.

THE ZEITCONTROL BASIC CARD

The ZeitControl Basic card was and still is the first programmable smart card to offer an integrated application development environment that spans both the off-card and the on-card application simultaneously. You bring up the off-card application in one window, the on-card in an adjacent window, and single-step through the off-card, over to the on-card, and then back to the off-card. At the time they were introduced in 1996, the card and its IDE were light-years ahead of the competition. In a number of ways, they still are. The IDE is free and can be downloaded from *www.zeitcontrol.de*.

ZeitControl Basic (ZC-Basic) contains most of the usual Basic language constructs including strings and string functions, arrays, and user-defined data types. Like the Microsoft card, the Basic card sports a DOS-like FAT file system with the familiar Basic programming interface.

The ZeitControl Basic Card Virtual Machine

The Compact version of the ZeitControl Basic card virtual machine supports 1-, 2-, and 4-byte signed integer and string data types. The Extended version also supports floats. It is the only virtual machine that supports floats. The 116 byte codes in the Compact ZeitControl virtual machine are shown in Table 5.7.

Table 5.7 Byte Codes for Basic Card Virtual Machine

Mnemonic	Description
ABSL	Pop slX ; push Abs(slX)
ABSW	Pop swX ; push Abs(swX)
ADD$	Pop X$; pop Z$; pop Y$; X$ = Y$ + Z$
ADDL	Pop slY ; pop slX ; push slX + slY
ADDSP	SP += scDelta (if scDelta > 0, 'pushed' bytes are initialized to zero)

Table 5.7 Byte Codes for Basic Card Virtual Machine (Continued)

Mnemonic	Description
ADDW	Pop swY ; pop swX ; push swX + swY
ALLOCA	Pop A ; pop bounds word uwBr for each dimension r, in reverse order; allocate data area of A and initialize all elements to 0
ANDL	Pop ulY ; pop ulX ; push ulX And ulY
ANDW	Pop uwY ; pop uwX ; push uwX And uwY
ARRAY	Pop A ; pop subscript swIr for each dimension r, in reverse order ; push address of array element A (swI1, swI2, . . . , swIn)
ASC$	Pop X$; push Asc(X$) as CHAR
BOUNDA	Pop swHi ; pop swLo ; push 400*swLo + (swHi – swLo) as WORD
CALL	Procedure call or GoSub: push PC+3 as WORD ; PC = uwAddr
CHKDIM	Pop A ; push A ; if Dim(A) <> ucNdims then execute ERROR 0C
COMP$	Pop Y$; pop X$; compare ; push for WORD comparison
COMPL	Pop slY ; pop slX ; compare ; push for WORD comparison
COPY$	Pop X$; pop Y$; X$ = Y$
CVTCW	Pop ucX ; swY = ucX ; push swY
CVTLW	Pop slX ; swY = slX ; push swY
CVTWC	Pop swX ; ucY = swX ; push ucY
CVTWL	Pop swX ; slY = swX ; push slY
DIVL	Pop slY ; pop slX ; push slX / slY
DIVW	Pop swY ; pop swX ; push swX / swY
DUP	Push the top ucLen stack bytes
ENTER	Push FP ; push SP + ucFrmSiz + F ; FP = SP ; SP = SP + ucFrmSiz
ERROR	Generate a P-Code error condition

Table 5.7 Byte Codes for Basic Card Virtual Machine (Continued)

Mnemonic	Description
EXIT	Exit the Virtual Machine
FDATA	Copy data (ucLen bytes) to address FP + scAddr
FREE$	Pop 2-byte handle to variable-length string X$; X$ = empty string
FREEA	Pop A ; if Dynamic then deallocate A, else set all elements of A to 0
FREEA$	Pop string array A ; free all strings in A ; if Dynamic then deallocate A
HEX$	Pop X$; pop slX ; X$ = Hex$(slX)
INCL	Pop slX ; push slX + 1
INCW	Pop swX ; push swX + 1
JEQWB	Pop swY ; pop swX ; if swX = swY then PC = PC + scDisp + 2
JGEWB	Pop swY ; pop swX ; if swX >= swY then PC = PC + scDisp + 2
JGTWB	Pop swY ; pop swX ; if swX > swY then PC = PC + scDisp + 2
JLEWB	Pop swY ; pop swX ; if swX <= swY then PC = PC + scDisp + 2
JLTWB	Pop swY ; pop swX ; if swX < swY then PC = PC + scDisp + 2
JNEWB	Pop swY ; pop swX ; if swX <> swY then PC = PC + scDisp + 2
JNZWB	Pop swX ; if swX <> 0 then PC = PC + scDisp + 2
JUMPB	PC = PC + scDisp + 2
JUMPW	PC = uwAddr
JZRWB	Pop swX ; if swX = 0 then PC = PC + scDisp + 2
LBOUND	Pop A ; pop ucDim ; push lower bound of subscript ucDim as WORD
LCASE$	Pop X$; pop Y$; X$ = LCase$(Y$)
LEAVE	Return from procedure: SP = FP – F ; pop FP ; pop PC
LEFT$	Pop swLen ; pop X$; push Left$(X$, swLen)

Table 5.7 Byte Codes for Basic Card Virtual Machine (Continued)

Mnemonic	Description
LEN$	Pop X$; push Len(X$) as CHAR
LOOP	Pop swX ; if swX >= 0 then execute JLEWB else execute JGEWB
LTRIM$	Pop X$; push LTrim$(X$)
MID$	Pop swLen ; pop swStart ; pop X$; push Mid$(X$, swStart, swLen)
MODL	Pop slY ; pop slX ; push slX Mod slY
MODW	Pop swY ; pop swX ; push swX Mod swY
MULL	Pop slY ; pop slX ; push slX * slY
MULW	Pop swY ; pop swX ; push swX * swY
NEGL	Pop slX ; push –slX
NEGW	Pop swX ; push –swX
NOP	No operation
NOTL	Pop ulX ; push Not(ulX)
NOTW	Pop uwX ; push Not(uwX)
ORL	Pop ulY ; pop ulX ; push ulX Or ulY
ORW	Pop uwY ; pop uwX ; push uwX Or uwY
POECW	Pop CHAR at address uwAddr
POELW	Pop LONG at address uwAddr
POEWW	Pop WORD at address uwAddr
POFCB	Pop CHAR at address FP + scAddr
POFLB	Pop LONG at address FP + scAddr
POFWB	Pop WORD at address FP + scAddr
POINC	Pop uwAddr ; pop CHAR at address uwAddr

Table 5.7 Byte Codes for Basic Card Virtual Machine (Continued)

Mnemonic	Description
POINL	Pop uwAddr ; pop LONG at address uwAddr
POINW	Pop uwAddr ; pop WORD at address uwAddr
PORCB	Pop CHAR at address ucAddr
PORLB	Pop LONG at address ucAddr
PORWB	Pop WORD at address ucAddr
PUCCB	Push constant CHAR ucConst
PUCWB	Push constant scConst sign-extended to WORD
PUCWC	Push constant ucConst zero-extended to WORD
PUCWW	Push constant WORD swConst
PUECW	Push CHAR at address uwAddr
PUELW	Push LONG at address uwAddr
PUESW	Push STRING at address uwAddr
PUEWW	Push WORD at address uwAddr
PUFAB	Push FP + scAddr as WORD
PUFCB	Push CHAR at address FP + scAddr
PUFLB	Push LONG at address FP + scAddr
PUFSB	Push STRING at address FP + scAddr
PUFWB	Push WORD at address FP + scAddr
PUINC	Pop uwAddr ; push CHAR at address uwAddr
PUINL	Pop uwAddr ; push LONG at address uwAddr
PUINW	Pop uwAddr ; push WORD at address uwAddr
PUPSB	Push 3-byte STRING parameter at address FP + scAddr

Table 5.7 Byte Codes for Basic Card Virtual Machine (Continued)

Mnemonic	Description
PURCB	Push CHAR at address ucAddr
PURLB	Push LONG at address ucAddr
PURSB	Push STRING at address ucAddr
PURWB	Push WORD at address ucAddr
PUSAB	Push SP – ucAddr as WORD
RAND	Push a LONG random number
RDATA	Copy data (ucLen bytes) to address ucAddr
RETURN	Return from GoSub: pop PC
RIGHT$	Pop swLen ; pop X$; push Right$(X$, swLen)
RTRIM$	Pop X$; push RTrim$(X$)
STRING$	Pop X$; pop ucChar ; pop swLen ; X$ = String$(swLen, ucChar)
STRL$	Pop X$; pop slX ; X$ = Str$(slX)
SUBL	Pop slY ; pop slX ; push slX – slY
SUBW	Pop swY ; pop swX ; push swX – swY
SYSTEM	Operating system call
UBOUND	Pop A ; pop ucDim ; push upper bound of subscript ucDim as WORD
UCASE$	Pop X$; pop Y$; X$ = UCase$(Y$)
VALHL$	Pop X$; slVal = ValH(X$, ucLen) ; push slVal ; push ucLen
VALL$	Pop X$; slVal = Val&(X$, ucLen) ; push slVal ; push ucLen
WTX	Send a Waiting Time Extension request
XORL	Pop ulY ; pop ulX ; push ulX Xor ulY
XORW	Pop uwY ; pop uwX ; push uwX Xor uwY

The ZeitControl Programming Model

ZeitControl Basic extends the Subroutine and Function procedure types of regular Basic with a new type called `Command`. You create `Command` procedures on the card and then simply call them as functions from the off-card application. All the smart card communication and APDU handling is taken care of by the ZeitControl runtime system. Data is passed into the card from the host and back to the host from the card in the arguments to the `Command` procedure.

For example, in the on-card application, you might include the code

```
Command &HC0 &H10 MyAPDU(in As Long, out As String)

    if in <> 0 then
        out = "Not Zero"
    else
        out = "Zero"
End Command
```

You would call this `Command` from the off-card application by writing

```
Declare Command &HC0 &H10 MyAPDU(in As Long, out As String)
Dim S As String
...
Call MyApdu(0, S)
...
```

The P1 and P2 parameters of the APDU can be used but they are optional.

The ZeitControl development environment encourages tight integration of the off-card and on-card application. The tools, language features, and runtime support provided for Basic card applications are most effective when both sides of the application are written in ZC Basic. But this is not a necessity. A Basic card running a ZC Basic application will field ISO 7816-4 APDUs coming from any off-card program and will return ISO 7816-4–compliant responses. The details of the APDU formats used to communicate with a Basic card are given in the Basic Card User's Guide.

The SCADA Online Application for the ZeitControl Card

Code for Online SCADA Application for Basic Card

```
Const NEWRECORD = &H1

Const TABERROR = &H6F00

Eeprom recs, rows As Byte

Command &HC0 &H10 AccumulateData(d as Long)

    Dim n As Integer
```

```
    Dim v, v2 As Long

    If recs = 0 Or P2 = NEWRECORD Then
        recs = recs + 1
    End If

    Open "data" For Binary Access Read Write As #1

    Seek #1, (recs-1)*10

    Get #1, , n
    Get #1, , v
    Get #1, , v2

    n = n + 1
    v = v + d
    v2 = v2 + d * d

    Seek #1, (recs-1)*10

    Put #1, , n
    Put #1, , v
    Put #1, , v2

    Close #1

End Command

Command &HC0 &H20 ProvideCommand(d as Long, c1 as Long, c2 as
Long)
    Dim i as Byte
    Dim lb, ub as Integer
    Dim row(0 to 11) as Byte

    Open Chr$(P1) For Binary Access Read As #1

    For i = 0 To rows
        Get #1, , lb
        Get #1, , ub
        Get #1, , c1
        Get #1, , c2

        If d > lb And d <= ub Then
            Exit Command
        End If
    Next

    SW1SW2 = TABERROR

End Command
```

The SCADA online application compiles into a mere 260 bytes of executable byte codes for the ZeitControl Basic card.

Direct reading and writing of variables from files is a big win for ZC –Basic, as is treating nonvolatile memory as both a variable store and a file system. APDU handling, which introduces so much unnecessary complexity into Java card and WfSC programs, is totally absent from ZC Basic programs. The simple command-as-subroutine metaphor turns terminal communication into a simple remote procedure call.

THE BASIC CARD APPLICATION DEVELOPMENT CYCLE

The Basic card has by far and away the most tightly integrated, most efficient, and easiest to use application development cycle. The ZeitControl "Double Debugger" is identical to the Microsoft Visual Basic environment but the integration of the card and the off-card application is much tighter and more seamless than in the Visual Basic IDE.

Within single running instance of the Double Debugger, you create and edit both sides of the application. Each side can be compiled by itself or the two sides can be compiled simultaneously. After successful compilation, the source code for each side can be loaded into side-by-side windows and you can single-step through the off-card application, follow an APDU to the on-card application, single-step through the on-card code, follow a response back to the off-card application, and continue single-stepping through the host code. All communication between the off-card and the on-card application is visible as are current variable values on both sides. The usual debugging features, such as breakpoints and watch points in each window, are available.

Next, the on-card application can be downloaded to a Basic card. Single-stepping through the off-card application proceeds as previously. Communication between the host and the card is visible but response from the card is immediate.

DATA ACCESS CONTROL

You may have six applications on your smart card but you only have one home address. Clearly, you want the six applications and any new ones that might be loaded onto your card to share this information but you may want only one, the personal information management application, for example, to be able to change it. The video store application and the pizza parlor application on your card may want to share a loyalty points purse but they don't want the ice cream store to figure out how much time you're spending at the other end of Main Street by reading the number of video-pizza loyalty points you have accumulated.

There can be 5, 10, or even 20 different entities that have one or more rights to access various pieces of data on a multiapplication smart card. The cardholder is an obvious example of one of these entities. The issuer of the electronic purse on the card is another example. The capacity to enforce data access control policies—ensuring that each entity can do what it is allowed to do and not do what it is not allowed to do—is in fact the defining characteristic of a smart card.

Data access control is more comprehensive than data security. Data security typically means making sure that unauthorized entities can't access a piece of data. It is focused primarily on locking people out, not on selectively letting some people do some things and other people do other things. Data access control certainly includes data security in this sense but goes on to ensure that, for example, entities that are only allowed to read the data can't change it or entities that are only allowed to add data to a file can't delete data from it.

The four programmable cards as described previously are functionally identical—write an application in a high-level language, compile it to byte codes, load the byte codes onto the card, place them in execution, and talk to the running application with APDUs. The approach taken by one is preferred by some and the approach taken by another preferred by others. But they are basically the same with respect to the broad outlines of creating, loading, and running an on-card application.

Given then that data access control is the defining property of smart cards, it is perhaps surprising where these four cards differ as much as they do in this aspect of their operation. You might have thought that the users and the makers of smart cards would long ago have come to a consensus on the right way to do data access control and that all the cards would simply implement this given wisdom. Actually, it can be argued that they did; however, the resulting mechanisms don't fit well into a multiapplication environment where applications want to share data.

The problem of on-card data sharing and access control in its full generality is actually relatively new to smart cards. In the pre-multiapplication card era, there were only a few entities on a card (the cardholder, the issuer, the generic point of use), the number of data items was static, and the access rights of each entity were frozen when the card was created. It didn't take much in the way of on-card software to meet these modest data access control requirements. It wasn't until the advent of serious commercial interest in the multiapplication card in the late 1990s that the realization dawned that existing smart card data access control machinery was not up to the challenges of these new kinds of cards. The number of entities a card had to keep track of multiplied many times over. The entities could come and go with the applications. The complexity of the trust relationships between the entities and the data on the card multiplied.

Application-Centric versus Data-Centric Access Control

There are two general approaches to data access control. One way—the *application-centric* approach—associates the data with an application and lets the application control access to the data. The other way—the *data-centric* approach—associates access control policies with the data and lets the operating system mediate between the data and its accessors using these policies. As we will see, the Java card and the Multos card implement the application-centric approach and the Microsoft card and the ZeitControl card implement the data-centric approach. Each approach has its supporters and detractors; each can find preferred utility in certain classes of problems.

The application-centric approach has the advantage that more fine-grain data access control policies can be implemented because the application knows the semantics of the data. The disadvantage is that these fine-grain policies are embedded in application code so that the code has to be changed if the policies are changed. There is the additional disadvantage that if the application goes away, so does the access control to the data it is responsible for.

The data-centric approach has the advantage that data access control policies are externalized and have a common representation across all data. Applications can concentrate on processing data, not administering outside access to it. Furthermore, because applications and access control have been separated, each can come and go independently of the other. Obviously, this is also a disadvantage if the two evolve independently without significant regard for the other. Another disadvantage is that the access control policy language, by definition, has to be very general and of a one-size-fits-all nature and thus typically can't key off of data semantics or even data values.

Recently in updating the standard smart card command set of standards, ISO 7816, the worldwide smart card standards community, also put in place a very general standard for data access control on smart cards. It is a data-centric (and file system-oriented) approach called Security Attributes and it is included in ISO 7816-9 that was ratified as an ISO standard on May 9, 2000.

ISO 7816-9 Data Access Control

ISO 7816-9 lets you associate one or more security attributes with any operation on any file. A security attribute is simply an assertion about the current security status of the card. For example, you might associate the security attribute "Cardholder has been authenticated" with the UPDATE operation on the PIN file. This means that the operating system will allow an UPDATE operation on the PIN file to proceed only if the PIN contained the file that had already been presented to the card. In everyday language, you have to know the PIN in order to change the PIN.

How the security status of the card is described is covered in ISO 7816-8. These descriptions can become quite complex and so security attributes themselves can become quite complex. Furthermore, if more than one security attribute is associated with a particular operation on a particular file, they can be ANDed together or ORed together. In the first case, they all have to be true if the operation is to proceed. In the latter case, at least one has to be true if the operation is to proceed. The ISO 7816-9 Security Attributes Task Force has tried and largely succeeded in preserving the advantages of data-centric access control while reaching for some of the fine-grain capabilities of application-centric data access control.

Of the four cards discussed in this chapter, the Microsoft card comes the closest to the ISO 7816-9 Security Attributes standard. As we will see, it allows arbitrary Boolean expressions in card authentications to be associated with each possible operation on a file. Card authentications are one type of security status and Boolean expressions generalize the simple ANDing and ORing defined by ISO 7816-9.

Application-Centric Access Control Using Data Ownership and Interapplication Communication

The Multos card and the Java card take basically the same approach to data access control. They both begin by positing that each piece of data on the card is owned by the application that created it. To access data owned by an application, you send the owning application a message asking for the data and, if the owning application wishes, it returns what you asked for. The challenge, of course, is for the called application to figure out if it wishes or not. This usually turns on identifying the requesting application somehow. Both the Java card and the Multos card leave this as an exercise for the card issuer and application providers and only provide the basic interapplication communication services. The basic problem is the extension of "identity" from the off-card to the on-card environment and the ability to simultaneously treat multiple identities within the smart card itself.

Interapplication communication can obviously be used for purposes above and beyond simply sharing data between applications. Request-receiving applications can be created to provide a wide range of general-purpose utility services to other on-card applications. We will confine our attention in this section to the use of this general-purpose capability to the task of data access control and data sharing.

For small, relatively fixed populations of applications, the notion of data ownership and the use of interapplication communication to share data among applications works well. When applications can come and go, however, the notion of ownership and application-based access control can quickly become problematic. All too often, we want to get rid of the application but not the data that it has created. This means we have to either leave behind a shadow of the application simply to administer the access to the data or pass ownership of the data and the administration of access to another application. Neither of these alternatives is particularly attractive.

Data Sharing on a Java Card

All on-card Java card applications share a common namespace; hence, the framework can use the namespace to move data between requesting applications and owning applications. Owning applications export function names to the framework that provide access to the data they are willing to share. Requesting applications ask the framework for access to shared data by calling out the owning application's AID. The framework then passes back to the requesting applications the access functions registered by the owning application. It is still up to the owning application to determine if it wants to provide its data to the requesting application.

The downside of this approach is that an application has to know the AIDs of all the applications it wants to acquire data from and what data is associated with each AID. This can work fine in small, stable, predefined sets of applications, but it doesn't seem to scale well. As the number of applications grows and as applications are loaded onto and deleted from individual cards, the task of managing the AID-based connection between pairs of applications on each card gets exponentially harder.

Data Sharing on the Multos Card

Like the Java card, each Multos application owns the data it creates and shares this data with other applications according to is own preferences. Unlike the Java card, there is no *capo de capo* framework with root privileges on the Multos card that mediates interapplication communication. There is no registry of the data applications willing to share data nor a central directory of shared data. Instead, Multos applications communicate with one another by sending each other APDUs. This unifies interapplication and host communication and allows the smart card designer to migrate functionality between the terminal and the card without rewriting all the applications on the card. Making the APDU the *de facto* intra-on-card messaging format, does involve a fairly heavy-weight mechanism in the process.

Interapplication communication on the Multos card is called *delegation*. The sender of the APDU is the delegator and the receiver of the APDU is the delegate. The delegator addresses the delegate using the delegate's AID and the delegate program is responsible for determining if the delegator is who it says it is and if it should be served.

Data-Centric Access Control Using File Attributes and Access Control Lists

The Windows card and the Basic card take a wholly different approach to data access control and sharing. It is the approach found in almost all big iron operating systems and it is the approach underpinning the smart card standard for data access control, ISO 7816-9. Rather than associating data with an application and then forcing that application to administer access to it, the approach used is to associate access privilege descriptions directly with the data and let the operating system administer access for all applications using these descriptions. In this scheme, access controls exist for the lifetime of the data rather than for the lifetime of the application that created the data. Furthermore, data access can be represented and administered uniformly across all data in a way that access policies are visible rather than embedded down inside application code. The flip side of this, of course, is that access policies have to be defined and implemented across an entire application structure (off-card and on-card), which can raise a number of coordination issues in its own right.

Data Sharing on the Basic Card

The ZeitControl Compact Basic card does not support any file access conditions. All applications on the card can open, read, write, and update all the files on the card as long as they know the name of the file. The Enhanced Basic card supports the association of a read lock, a write lock, and a read-and-write lock with any file or directory, but this is a lock from the point of view of the off-card application, not a lock between applications on the card.

Data Sharing on the Microsoft Card

The access control subsystem of the Microsoft card is the most comprehensive and the most general of the four cards discussed in this chapter; that is, of any mechanisms specified as part of the basic system for the various cards. It is based on the access control list concepts invented for the Multics operating system and is compatible with and extends the security attribute recommendations of ISO 7816-9.

The WfSC scheme associates an access control list with every file and every directory. The access control list consists of a sequence of pairs, (Op, Bool), where Op is an operation that can be performed on the file or directory such as read, write, or create and Bool is a Boolean expression over authentication status of the entities that might want to perform the Op operation on the file or directory. An authentication status is TRUE if the entity has been authenticated by the card during the current session and the authentication status is FALSE if the entity has not been authenticated by the card in the current session.

The Boolean expression is evaluated any time any application attempts to perform the Op operation on the file or directory. If the Boolean expression evaluates to TRUE, then the operation is allowed to proceed. If the Boolean expression evaluates to FALSE, the operation is not allowed to proceed.

Access control lists are themselves stored in files and, therefore, in turn have access control lists guarding them. Clearly, the access control list describing access to an access control list will, in all likelihood, be quite different than the access control list it guards.

SUMMARY OF THE FOUR PROGRAMMABLE SMART CARDS

In this chapter, we have discussed on-card programming and compared and contrasted the four major multiapplication, programmable smart cards on the market. Each card, together with its application development environment, has its strengths and weaknesses. They are certainly all different and there are undoubtedly practical smart card applications where any one of them would outshine all of the others.

The Multos card and the Windows card are minimalist RISC type cards that provide maximum freedom to the application programmer. Java card and Basic card are CISC type cards with richer programming models but more application programmer creature comforts once you learn how to navigate them.

Our discussions of the four cards can be summarized in the following five property tables (Tables 5.8 through 5.12):

Table 5.8 Virtual Machine Type

RISC	CISC
Multos, Microsoft	Java, ZeitControl

Table 5.9 On-Card API Complexity

Simple	Complex
Multos, Microsoft	Java, ZeitControl

Table 5.10 Program Development Environment Complexity

Simple	Complex
Multos, ZeitControl	Java, Microsoft

Table 5.11 Access Control Style

Data-Centric	Application-Centric
Microsoft, ZeitControl	Java, Multos

Table 5.12 Terminal Communication Complexity

Simple	Complicated
Multos, ZeitControl	Java, Microsoft

Finally, Table 5.13 gives some descriptive information about each card as of the writing of this book.

Table 5.13 Characteristics of the Major Programmable Smart Cards

	Multos Card 4.0	Java Card 2.1.2	Windows Card 1.0	Basic Card 3.1
Implementations	2	6	1	1
Suppliers	2	5	7	1
Programming Languages	C, Java, MEL	Java Card	Visual Basic, C	ZC Basic
Virtual Machine Byte Codes				
Core	31	108	27	116
Extended	—	—	23	61
On-Card API Functions				
Core	24	119	45	42
Extended	1151	472	—	29
Application Selection	AID, Name	AID	Application APDU	APDU Procedure Call
Data Access Control	Delegated Commands	Exported Methods	Access Control Lists	File Locks
Byte Code Image Size in Bytes				
SCADA Online Example	4591	6802	1753	260
Dhrystones Benchmark	18781	23522	4461	977
Performance in Dhrystones/Second	1.27	1.37		

SUMMARY

While it may be hard to conclude from the preceding discussion, things are actually getting better for the smart card application developer. Most, if not all of the Java cards are being brought into cross-compatibility. The ETSI SCP series of smart card standards yield interoperable cards—not just standards-compliance marketing claims. And smart cards with multitasking operating systems on 32-bit chips have been announced. Whether or not card issuers turn to the third-party application development community for applications is solely a function of how compelling and innovative the applications created by that community are. This is progress.

6

Commercial Smart Card Commands

A s we've seen in previous chapters, there are two distinct styles of smart cards found in widespread deployment today:

- fixed command set cards built around the ISO/IEC 7816-4 command set
- post-issuance programmable smart cards

With the first style, the card is designed with a command set that is applicable to a particular application area. As you remember from Chapter 4, the International Standards Organization (ISO) command set is aimed at provision of an on-card file system for storing and retrieving data, and with a security model through which the on-card and off-card elements of applications can authenticate themselves to each other. This security model also allows the cardholder to authenticate himself or herself to the card in order to validate that the card is operating on behalf of the correct person. With the second style of card, a command set can be custom designed for an application to be loaded onto the smart card. By adding more and more such applications, a single smart card can be used in a wide variety of application areas. To understand these two card styles in more detail, we're going to review the specifics of two cards, one of each style. These are cards currently offered by Schlumberger and are in widespread commercial use today: the Cryptoflex 32K eGate® card and the Cyberflex Access 32K eGate® card.

You'll notice that both cards have the term *eGate* in their names. This is the name that Schlumberger has given to a technology added into the integrated circuit chip (ICC) of both of these cards that enables the chip to communicate using Universal Serial Bus (USB) protocols in addition to the usual smart card communication protocols defined in ISO 7816-3. As we'll see later in this chapter, the USB signaling makes use of two of the unused connections through the smart card connection face plate.

The Cryptoflex smart card is a *cryptographic services* smart card. That is, it includes an auxiliary processor that accelerates the integer arithmetic necessary when performing public key cryptography. This card is intended to provide a token component to general security systems, including Public Key Infrastructures (PKIs). As we examine the command set, we'll see that many of the commands are derived from the ISO/IEC 7816-4 command set; several new commands round out the capabilities required to service the off-card security environment. Because it uses an eGate chip, with the correct drivers on the host computer, the Cryptoflex 32K eGate smart card can communicate with the host either through a standard smart card reader or through a USB port.

Following the evolution of smart cards to the current state of the art, we'll next review the command set of a multiapplication smart card; in this case, the Cyberflex Access 32K eGate (Java Card), also from Schlumberger. This card also includes a cryptographic coprocessor, which allows the card to do efficient public key cryptography. We'll see in this case, however, that the base capability of the card is less than the basic command set provided by, for example, the Cryptoflex card. Rather, the Cyberflex Access card is a general platform that can be used to provide highly specialized tokens for off-card security environments, as well as components for other application systems.

The Cyberflex Access smart card, in addition to being a Java Card-compliant smart card, is also a GlobalPlatform (GP)-compliant card. That is, it provides features for communicating between the off-card and the on-card environments that conform to protocols defined by the GlobalPlatform specification, which is supported by the GlobalPlatform consortium. GP defines a security infrastructure that can be used to load new applications onto the smart card and also for invoking and communicating with distinct applications on the card. As part of our review, we'll look (at least architecturally) at the on-card application(s) required to use the Cyberflex Access card in much the same fashion as the Cryptoflex card would be used.

CRYPTOFLEX 32K EGATE

The Cryptoflex 32K eGate smart card (or, for purposes of our discussion, just the Cryptoflex smart card) is a fixed-command set type of smart card. From the commands that it offers, it is clear that the card was designed to be primarily aimed at supporting the operations of host (off-card) security infrastructures. It offers a command set that is based on the command set defined in the ISO/IEC 7816-4 standard along with some additional commands. It has, for example, a complete set of commands aimed at secure manipulation of on-card files and for selected transaction operations with information stored in these files. These additional commands are particularly adept at supporting on-card purse operations via the card's file system. As we'll see in a more detailed example application in Chapter 9, the command set is quite adequate for interesting variations on the security infrastructure theme.

The discussion of the Cryptoflex commands found in the remainder of this chapter does not constitute a complete technical specification for the Cryptoflex card or its command set. We're examining many (most) of the commands in some detail in an effort to give you a sense of what the commands are attempting to accomplish. However, you may find it necessary to consult the technical specification of the card provided by Schlumberger, the card vendor, in order to answer all of your detailed questions aimed at actually programming with the Cryptoflex card.

Commands

The Cryptoflex card provides four classes of commands:

- *Administrative commands* are used to prepare the card for distribution to the individual cardholders. These commands are used only during the manufacturing process and are typically disabled prior to card issuance.
- *Security commands* are used to authenticate identities of the various entities that will be participating in smart card operations and transactions.
- *Operational commands* are used to manipulate information stored on the card.
- *Auxiliary commands* are used primarily for housekeeping operations needed during the course of a smart card application.

Administrative Commands

The Administrative commands provided by the Cryptoflex card are used in two distinct ways in the preparation and personalization of the card: for soft-mask additions to the card and for construction of a file hierarchy to be used by the applications supported by the card. All of these commands are controlled by access conditions that must be fulfilled prior to the individual commands being used. Through these access conditions, the commands can be made unusable outside of the manufacturing operation. In certain instances, the CREATE FILE, CREATE RECORD, and DELETE FILE commands are controlled by access conditions that allow manipulation of the file hierarchy during the personalization operation, which may actually occur after cards have been provided to the card issuer by the card manufacturer.

CREATE FILE. The CREATE FILE command is used to create each of the files found in the on-card file structure of a Cryptoflex card. This is a very complex command due to the many attributes that must be established in creating a file and recognizing that, for security's sake, all of the many attributes need to be established during one atomic operation. The CLA and INS bytes for the command are $F0_{16}$ and $E0_{16}$, respectively. The P1 argument defines how the file is to be initialized. If P1 is 00_{16}, then each byte of the file is initialized to a value of 00_{16}. If P1 is FF_{16}, then the file body is not initialized; rather, each byte is left as it was at the CREATE FILE time.

The parameter P2 defines the number of records in the file, if it is a record-oriented file type (i.e., if the file being created is a linear file with fixed-length records or if the file is a cyclic file). The P3 parameter defines the length of the data field that is to be transmitted (to the card) as part of this CREATE FILE command. This data field has a complex structure through which the remaining attributes of the file (being created) are defined. If the Access condition for the CREATE FILE command happens to be PROtected, then we know that a cryptogram is going to be added onto the end of the command (i.e., as an extension to the data field, see Figure 6.1). This will alter the value of the P3 parameter, depending on the type of file being created. The amount by which P3 is increased (due to the AC being PRO) is shown in Table 6.1.

Table 6.1 Data Field Lengths for CREATE FILE Command

P3 Value	File Type
10_{16}	Dedicated file
10_{16}	Transparent
10_{16}	Linear file with variable record structure
11_{16}	Linear file with fixed record structure
11_{16}	Cyclic

The data field can have two distinct structures, depending on whether a dedicated file or an elementary file is being created. The two structures are shown in Table 6.2.

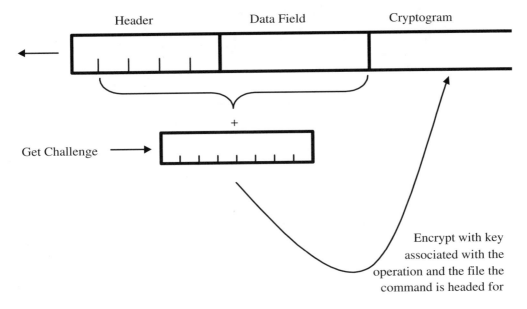

Header   Data Field   Cryptogram

Get Challenge ⟶ +

Encrypt with key
associated with the
operation and the file the
command is headed for

▶ **Figure 6.1**   PROtected mode command.

Table 6.2 Data Field Format for CREATE FILE Command

Bytes	DATA FIELD Description		Length
	For an elementary file	**For a dedicated file**	
1-2	RFU	RFU	2 bytes
3-4	File size (2)	File size	2 bytes
5-6	File ID	File ID	2 bytes
7	File Type (see next table)	File Type (see next table)	1 byte
8-11	Access Condition levels	Access Condition levels	4 bytes
12	File status	File status	1 byte
13	Length of the following data (14-end)	Length of the following data (14-end)	1 byte
14-16	Access keys	Access keys	3 bytes
17	Record length (If EF = LF or CY)		1 byte

The File Type parameter is given in Table 6.3.

Table 6.3 File Type Parameter for CREATE FILE Command Data Field

File Type	File Type Byte
Transparent elementary file	01_{16}
Linear fixed elementary file	02_{16}
Linear variable elementary file	04_{16}
Cyclic elementary file	06_{16}
Dedicated file	38_{16}

Now, a very interesting attribute of the CREATE FILE command (in fact, of the on-card file system itself) is found buried in the middle of this Data field (i.e., the specification of Access Conditions to be associated with commands that can subsequently act on the file being created). If you remember from our discussion in Chapter 4, a number of Access Conditions can be defined such that they must be fulfilled before a command can be issued. For the Cryptoflex card, the set of Access Conditions is shown in Table 6.4.

Table 6.4 Access Conditions

Access Condition Level Number	Access Condition Name
0	ALW(ays)
1	CHV1
2	CHV2
3	PRO
4	AUT
5	RFU
6	CHV1/PRO
7	CHV2/PRO
8	CHV1/AUT

Table 6.4 Access Conditions (Continued)

Access Condition Level Number	Access Condition Name
9	CHV2/AUT
10	RFU
11	RFU
12	RFU
13	RFU
14	RFU
15	NEV(er)

We note that we can specify this complete set of Access Conditions with three bits. Looking back at the data field, we see that 4 bytes (32 bits) are reserved in the field for specifying Access Conditions. One of these bytes (byte 8) will be used to set limits on what an INCREASE or DECREASE command can do when operating on a file and the other three bytes will be used to allow us to establish six different sets of Access Conditions for various commands. We use one "nibble" (4 bits) to convey each definition of Access Conditions. The commands to which the Access Conditions apply are shown in Table 6.5.

Table 6.5 Access Conditions for File Commands

Byte Number	Most Significant Nibble	Least Significant Nibble
9	• READ • READ RECORD • SEEK	• UPDATE • UPDATE RECORD • DECREASE
10	• INCREASE • READ BIN ENCIPHERED	• CREATE RECORD • UPDATE BIN ENCIPHERED
11	• REHABILITATE	• INVALIDATE

Thus, we see that commands that have similar effects (e.g., READ and READ RECORD) have the same Access Condition to be fulfilled before either command can be executed. Conversely, we see that complementary instructions can have different Access Conditions. For example, a different Access Condition can be required to write into a file versus what's required to read from a file. One Access Condition can be required to INCREASE a value stored in a file while a different Access Condition can be required in order to DECREASE a value stored in a file. A bank identity is required to add value (money) to a purse stored on the card while a cardholder's identity is required to decrease value (spend money) from a purse stored on the card.

We should get a good idea in the following sections about what each of these commands is going to do; in most cases, it is fairly self-evident. In particular, if we store the bit pattern "0100" in the most significant byte nibble of byte number 9, it means that we could have to have achieved an AUT Access Condition before we could issue a READ command to the particular file being created by the CREATE FILE command.

So, a moderately typical CREATE FILE command, when reduced to its constituent byte string (APDU, or application protocol data unit), might look like the following:

CLA	INS	P1	P2	Lc	Data
$F0_{16}$	$E0_{16}$	00_{16}	10_{16}	10_{16}	Variable Data Field

Remember that in dealing with the on-card file system, there's a logical pointer running around that, at any particular instant of program execution, points at a specific "target file." We position this logical pointer to point at a specific file by doing a SELECT command and selecting that file. Another way to position the pointer is as the result of a command. So, for example, on the successful completion of a CREATE FILE command, the pointer is aimed at the file just created.

This is perhaps a good point to note that there are several files that have special significance indicated by the name of the file. Specifically, there are a number of elementary files that contain the keys to be validated through the various security commands. These files (and their names) are shown in Table 6.6.

Note that the relevant key file (in Table 6.6) is the one that is either in the same dedicated file as the file to which the logical pointer is pointing, or is contained in a parent dedicated file of the immediate dedicated file if no key files are present in the current dedicated file. As an example then, an elementary file with a name (ID) of "0001" contains a key that represents an identity that can be authenticated by the successful execution of an INTERNAL AUTHENTICATE command. This key file would be used for an authentication command any time the logical file pointer was pointed at a file descended from the dedicated file that contains this key file. We'll look at the internal structure of these files a bit later.

Table 6.6 Key Files Used for Access Condition Establishment

Type	Data Field	ID	Level
Key files	CHV1	0000	(Relevant)
	CHV2	0100	(Relevant)
	EF Key INT	0001	(Relevant)
	EF Key EXT	0011	(Relevant)
	EF RSA pri	0012	
	EF RSA pub	1012	
ATR file	EF ATR	2F01	Root
Root	Root	3F00	

CREATE RECORD. The CREATE RECORD command is used, as the name implies, to create an individual record in a record-oriented file structure. There are two such record-oriented filed types: linear fixed (with fixed-length records) and linear variable (with variable-length records); both are obviously elementary file types. A dedicated file has no internal structure accessible through READ or WRITE commands.

The APDU structure for the CREATE RECORD command does not make use of parameters P1 and P2. The P3 parameter specifies the length of the data field, which then contains the contents to be written into the record that is created by the command. If an Access Condition of PRO(tected) is specified for the command, then a cryptogram is appended to the end of the command. This allows integrity checking on the command as it is executed.

A typical APDU for the CREATE RECORD command might look like the following:

CLA	INS	P1	P2	Lc	Data
$C0_{16}$	$E2_{16}$	00_{16}	00_{16}	Length	Data Field (Record Contents)

DELETE FILE. The DELETE FILE command is used to both logically and physically delete a file from the on-card file system. That is, the internal file system indicator for the file is removed from the dedicated file that the (deleted)

file belongs to and the contents of the file space is zeroed out. There is a requirement that files in any dedicated file get deleted in the inverse order in which they were created if you want to be able to reuse the space freed up by the deleted file. If you delete a file in the wrong order, it will get deleted; but you won't be able to reuse the freed space.

A typical APDU for the DELETE FILE command looks like the following:

CLA	INS	P1	P2	Lc	Data
$F0_{16}$	$E4_{16}$	00_{16}	00_{16}	Length	File ID + cryptogram (PRO)

There are a few other Administrative commands, but their use is somewhat esoteric. You can find them in the technical specification document for the Cryptoflex card, but we won't cover them here. Rather, we want to emphasize the fact that the three commands that we've discussed are typically used to prepare (prepersonalize or personalize) a specific card prior to its being issued to a cardholder. As with most commands, the use of the Administrative commands can be limited through the Access Conditions attached to the commands. Quite often, Access Conditions are set such that *none* of these Administrative commands can be issued after the card is in the hands of the cardholder. This means that the file structure on a card is established and access to it (the file structure) is tested before a card is released into the hands of a cardholder.

Security Commands

Another set of commands offered by the Cryptoflex card is a set of Security commands, many of whose definitions closely match those found in the ISO 7816-4 specifications. Beyond the ISO command set, however, are a number of commands aimed at supporting public key cryptography or, more appropriately, public key infrastructures. We reviewed the elements of public key cryptography in Chapter 4, so the utility of the various Cryptoflex commands should be rather evident.

First, then, we'll review the commands that are derivative of the ISO 7816-4 command set and that are closely tailored to the various aspects of the transaction environment in which smart cards typically participate.

Key Files. Within any dedicated file, a number of elementary files can be created to hold keys to be used by the following Security commands. The Security commands will be used to establish Access Condition states to control commands operating on files contained within this dedicated file, down to a level where another key file (or set of key files) is found in the file hierarchy. We listed these files previously and here, we'll look at the internal structure of these files. The first is the CHV file. This is the file that holds PIN values to be verified through the VERIFY CHV command. There are two CHV files possible in every dedicated file: CHV1, which has file ID "0000," holds PIN1 and CHV2, which has file ID "0100," holds PIN2. This allows the specification of 16 levels of Access Condition coding on various commands that are descendants from this particular dedicated file. The CHV file structure is shown in Table 6.7.

Table 6.7 CHV (PIN) File Structure

Bytes	Description	Length
1	Activation Byte	1 byte
2	RFU	1 byte
3	RFU	1 byte
4-11	CHV (the PIN)	8 bytes
12	VERIFY CHV attempts—preset value	1 byte
13	Remaining VERIFY CHV attempts counter	1 byte
14-21	Unblock CHV (PIN to allow unblocking a blocked CHV file)	8 bytes
22	Remaining Unblock CHV attempt counter	1 byte
23	Number of remaining times the UNBLOCK mechanism can be used	1 byte

To establish a PIN for a dedicated file and the files structure descended from it, we first use the CREATE FILE command to create its CHV file. To do this, we have to satisfy the Access Condition necessary to use the CREATE FILE command. Having created the CHV file, we then must satisfy the Access Condition to use a file input command, such as the UPDATE BINARY. With the UPDATE BINARY command, then, we write a 23-byte string into the CHV file with the preceding information (from Table 6.7).

Another type of key file is used to store cryptographic keys that are used by the INTERNAL AUTHENTICATION and the EXTERNAL AUTHENTICATION commands that allow the off-card application and the card to authenticate themselves to each other. The external key file, which has a file ID of "0011," has the structure indicated in Table 6.8.

Table 6.8 External Key File Structure

Bytes	Description	Length
1	RFU	1 byte
2	Key length of key 0 (X)	1 byte
3	Algorithm ID for key 0	1 byte
4-3+X	Key 0	X bytes
5+X	Key 0 Attempt Preset Value	1 byte
6+X	Key 0 Remaining Attempt Counter	1 byte
7+X	Key length of key 1	1 byte
...	...	...

Both the external key file and the internal key file have chained segments, each defining a single key; so, the file itself can hold many keys. The set of chained keys is terminated by setting the key length of the final key to zero. Thus, through these key files, many different off-card identities can authenticate themselves to the card and many on-card identities can authenticate themselves to the off-card application for any specific dedicated file structure. By defining different key files within different dedicated file structures, we can enable the use of a large number of identities to restrict access to information or operations on the card; the card can truly work for a large number of masters.

Before a Cryptoflex card is released from the manufacturing process, a master file with ID "3F00" is created on the card. Under this dedicated file, an elementary file for external keys with ID "0011" is created with two keys in it. Key 0 is termed the Application Transport Key (ATK) and Key 1 is termed the Application Activation Key. Key 0 is used to limit access to commands to create an application file structure and Key 1 is used to limit access to commands that enable transactions using this file structure.

For use with public key cryptography, two RSA key file structures can be defined on the card as well: one for the private key (of an RSA key pair) and the other for the public key (of an RSA key pair). The structure of the private key files is defined in Table 6.9.

Table 6.9 RSA Private Key File Structure

Bytes	Description	M / O[*]	Length
1	Length of the key block (MSB)	M	1
2	Length of the key block (LSB)	M	1
3	Key number	M	1
4 - …	Factor of the public module (P)	M	32/48/64/128
	Factor of the public module (Q)	M	32/48/64/128
	Reverse of the factor P ($a = Q^{-1} \bmod P$)	M	32/48/64/128
	Subsecret exponent ($c = Ks \bmod (P\text{-}1)$)	M	32/48/64/128
	Subsecret exponent ($f = Ks \bmod (Q\text{-}1)$)	M	32/48/64/128
	Length of the key block (MSB)	M	1
	Length of the key block (LSB)	M	1
	Key number	M	1
	Factor of the public module (P)	M	32/48/64/128
…	…	…	…
Last 3 bytes	00 00 00h	M	3

* M stands for Mandatory and O stands for Optional.

Note that the private key file can hold keys of 512 bits, 768 bits, 1024 bits, or 2048 bits.

The public key (of an RSA key pair) can take one of three formats as shown in Table 6.10.

This particular file structure stores all public components of the RSA key. This structure is backward compatible with previous versions of the Cryptoflex card. The second type of structure deletes storing the Montgomery constants (J0 and H) in order to save space. This file structure is as shown in Table 6.11.

Table 6.10 RSA Public Key File Structure—Type 1

Bytes	Description	M / O*	Length
1	Length of the key block (MSB)	M	1
2	Length of the key block (LSB)	M	1
3	Key number	M	1
4 - ...	Public module (N)	M	64/96/128/256
	J0	M	32/48/64/128
	H	M	64/96/128/256
	Public exponent (e)	M	4
	Length of the key block (MSB)	M	1
	Length of the key block (LSB)	M	1
	Key number	M	1
	Public module (N)	M	64/96/128/256
...	...	...	...
Last 3 bytes	00 00 00h	M	3

* M stands for Mandatory and O stands for Optional.

Table 6.11 RSA Public Key File Structure—Type 2

Bytes	Description	M / O*	Length
1	Length of the key block (MSB)	M	1
2	Length of the key block (LSB)	M	1
3	Key number	M	1
4 - ...	Public module (N)	M	64/96/128/256

Table 6.11 RSA Public Key File Structure—Type 2 (Continued)

Bytes	Description	M / O*	Length
	Public exponent (e)	M	4
	Length of the key block (MSB)	M	1
	Length of the key block (LSB)	M	1
	Key number	M	1
...	...	...	...
Last 3 bytes	00 00 00h	M	3

* M stands for Mandatory and O stands for Optional.

The last file structure provides for only storing the public exponent of the RSA key. This is the minimum required by the RSA signature operation, which we'll examine in the following section. This file format, then, is described in Table 6.12.

Table 6.12 RSA Public Key File Structure—Type 3

Bytes	Description	M / O*	Length
1	Length of the key block (MSB)	M	1
2	Length of the key block (LSB)	M	1
3	Key number	M	1
4	Public exponent (e)	M	4
	Length of the key block (MSB)	M	1
	Length of the key block (LSB)	M	1
	Key number	M	1
	Public exponent (e)	M	4
	Length of the key block (MSB)	M	1
...	...	...	...
Last 3 bytes	00 00 00h	M	3

* M stands for Mandatory and O stands for Optional.

VERIFY KEY. Smart cards interact with both computers and people. In the course of various transactions, a smart card must worry about authenticating the identity of either type of entity. Moreover, the smart card must establish its identity as a trusted computer among other computers that may be involved in a transaction. How the card authenticates itself to the cardholder is left as an exercise for the reader.

Computers typically authenticate their identities to each other by proving that they share a common secret. The shared secret is most typically a key that is used in cryptographic operations. This is an advantageous secret to share because each side can tell whether or not the other side shares the secret without ever passing the secret between them. Rather, an example of the use of the shared secret can be passed between the two sides; specifically, a bit of text is encrypted by one side and then decrypted by the other side.

All that said, the first command we'll look at is one that really doesn't do an identity authentication in the best way (i.e., the VERIFY KEY command. With the VERIFY KEY command, a copy of a key is transferred onto the card and the position of a stored key (on the card) is specified (in the command). In the execution of the command, the "transported key" is compared to the stored key. If they match, then the AUT Access Condition is established; other commands that require an AUT Access Condition are now able to function.

The number of failed attempts at validating a key through the VERIFY KEY command is strictly limited. If the number of allowed failed attempts is exceeded, then the key is blocked and no further attempts can be made until the key is unblocked. The following table illustrates a typical APDU for the VERIFY KEY command.

CLA	INS	P1	P2	Lc	Data
$F0_{16}$	$2A_{16}$	00_{16}	Key #	Length	The Key Itself

VERIFY CHV. The other type of identity that smart cards need to worry about is the identity of people—specifically, the identity of the owner/bearer of the smart card. When a smart card is introduced into some type of transaction, it is necessary for the card and the card acceptance device (e.g., personal computer) to authenticate each other's identity. Before proceeding with the intended transaction, however, it is also good security design for the cardholder to authenticate his or her identity to the card. In this way, simply having possession of a smart card (perhaps a stolen smart card) does not give the person in possession of the card unfettered access to any transaction the smart card is capable of supporting. Instead, the card must be assured that the cardholder is the person authorized to use the card. Then, when this identity is authenticated, the smart card can act in a transaction on behalf of the cardholder.

The typical authentication approach is to store a secret number on the card and then allow the cardholder to prove that he or she knows what this number is. The number stored on the card is typically referred to as a *personal identification number* (PIN) and the command used to prove knowledge of the PIN is the VERIFY CHV command.

In a system that uses the VERIFY CHV command (or any system that checks a PIN), the security of the PIN pad and the communication pathway from the PIN pad to the card is often suspect. In many (most) instances, the PIN is captured by an off-card component (keyboard) and shipped across the communication channel from the reader to the smart card. The PIN is usually transferred in the clear, so an eavesdropper on this line can often steal the PIN code. Simply encrypting the PIN in some fashion is a good guard against this type of attack.

A more common attack, and one in which the VERIFY CHV command is well designed to thwart, is simply trying to guess the PIN. When a PIN is stored in a file on the smart card, a counter is set with the number of allowed (incorrect) guesses on the PIN. If this many successive VERIFY CHV commands are performed without the correct PIN being presented, then the PIN is "blocked" until such time as a card administrator is able to issue an UNBLOCK CHV command. If a VERIFY CHV command completes successfully, then an Access Condition of CHV (Card Holder Verified) is achieved. Following is a typical APDU string for the VERIFY CHV command.

CLA	INS	P1	P2	Lc	Data
$C0_{16}$	20_{16}	00_{16}	CHV #	Length	CHV PIN

CHANGE CHV. The CHANGE CHV command is used, as might be expected given the name, to change the value of the PIN stored in a PIN file on the smart card. It's interesting to note that this command does not have any Access Condition attached to it. Rather, you are required to pass along the "old" (current) PIN along with the new PIN. If the "old" PIN matches what is stored in the PIN file, then the "new" PIN is stored into the PIN file. If the "old" PIN doesn't match, then the "incorrect try" counter is incremented, on its way to blocking the PIN if the cardholder doesn't ultimately remember it.

A typical APDU string for the CHANGE CHV command is as follows:

CLA	INS	P1	P2	Lc	Data
$F0_{16}$	24_{16}	00_{16}	CHV #	10_{16}	Old PIN and New PIN

UNBLOCK CHV.   The CHV mechanism is superior over a routine specification of an account and password combination (usually) because the number of wild guesses (i.e., an attack on the security mechanism) can be strictly limited to a small number. This being the case, an eight-character PIN is relatively secure against such an attack. However, it would be unfortunate if issuing a small number of wild guesses allowed an attacker to completely invalidate any further use of the card. This form of "denial of service" attack would be an easy harassment to be made on users of such a card system. So, the whole CHV mechanism has a nice backup, which allows a PIN that is blocked by too many incorrect entries of a PIN to be unblocked if a separate "Unblock CHV PIN" can be presented. This is done through the UNBLOCK CHV command.

If the correct "Unblock CHV PIN" is presented through this command, the counter that limits the number of successive incorrect PIN entries is reset to a predefined value. In addition, a new PIN, provided in the UNBLOCK CHV command parameter list, is installed as the new CHV PIN. If the original counter was set to a limit of five successive incorrect PIN entries, then the counter is now reset to 5. It's rather easy to see that if you could make a large number of tries at entering (guessing) the "Unblock CHV PIN" then this would make a good attack mechanism in its own right. So, there is a similar mechanism that actually limits the number of times that the UNBLOCK CHV command can be issued. For each time (the command is issued) a counter is decremented. When the counter goes to 0, the unblock mechanism (command) can no longer be used.

A typical APDU string for the UNBLOCK CHV command is as follows:

CLA	INS	P1	P2	Lc	Data
$F0_{16}$	$2C_{16}$	00_{16}	CHV #	10_{16}	Unblock CHV PIN and new PIN

LOGOUT AC.   The LOGOUT AC command allows an off-card application to remove or destroy the current Access Condition state that has been achieved on a card. There are essentially three Access Condition states on the card: CHV1, CHV2, and AUT. The first two are achieved by providing a valid PIN via a VERIFY CHV command and either matching the first or second PIN in the CHV file. The third state is achieved when an EXTERNAL AUTHENTICA-

TION command is successfully executed. Through the LOGOUT AC command, any or all of these Access Condition states can be reset (to an invalidated state). Commands dependent on having acquired the specific Access Condition state would no longer be able to successfully execute.

The specific Access Condition(s) to reset are determined by a bit-mask conveyed in a single parameter of the APDU string. Only three bits of the parameter byte are used (for the three currently defined Access Condition states); the other five bits are reserved for future use.

A typical APDU string for the LOGOUT AC command is as follows:

CLA	INS	P1	P2	Lc	Data
$F0_{16}$	22_{16}	AC bit mask	00_{16}	00_{16}	None

GET CHALLENGE. The GET CHALLENGE command is part of a two-command process through which the off-card (i.e., PC-side) application proves (authenticates) its identity to the card so that the card will then allow the off-card application to issue commands (which the card will successfully execute) that are guarded by an AUT Access Condition. The GET CHALLENGE command is used in conjunction with an EXTERNAL AUTHENTICATION or with any other command that requires an Access Condition of PRO. In the latter case, an Access Condition of PRO on a command requires that the authentication operation be done at the same time as the command.

The GET CHALLENGE command has response information that is returned to the off-card application along with the usual SW1 and SW2 status words. The incoming command can specify the length of the challenge to be returned. The card then, on executing the command, generates a random string of bits of the prescribed length. This string is returned to the off-card calling program in the command response.

This random number will now be "remembered" by the card and, if the next command contains a cryptogram (i.e., the random number encrypted with a specified key) the card will be able to decrypt the cryptogram with the specified key and validate that the random number extracted is the challenge number that was previously sent by the card. This result can then be used either to establish an AUT Access Condition (if the command is an EXTERNAL AUTHENTICATION) or to accept the operation of a command that is executed under a PRO Access Condition.

The APDU string for the GET CHALLENGE command will typically look like:

CLA	INS	P1	P2	Lc	Data
$C0_{16}$	84_{16}	00_{16}	00_{16}	Length of challenge	None

INTERNAL AUTHENTICATION. The INTERNAL AUTHENTICA-TION command is used to establish the identity of the card to the off-card application. Successful execution of the INTERNAL AUTHENTICATION means that the off-card application and the card share a common (secret) key. This command allows the card to prove that it knows this secret key, but without ever exposing the key to the outside world. The card does this by encrypting (creating a cryptogram) the challenge (a random number) with the specified key. To complete the authentication process, the off-card application then must issue a GET RESPONSE command through which it retrieves part of the cryptogram; that is, enough of the cryptogram to confirm that the card does have the correct key. Only a portion of the computed cryptogram is returned by the card to the off-card application so that this command cannot be used as a general-purpose encryption mechanism. Thus, the card can be used as an identity authentication mechanism, but not necessarily as a general, bulk encryption engine.

CLA	INS	P1	P2	Lc	Data
$C0_{16}$	88_{16}	00_{16}	Key #	08_{16}	Challenge

EXTERNAL AUTHENTICATION. The EXTERNAL AUTHENTICA-TION allows the off-card application to authenticate itself to the card. In so doing, it (the off-card application) establishes an AUT Access Condition on the card and can subsequently send commands that require an AUT Access Condition before the card will execute them. The EXTERNAL AUTHENTICATION command must directly follow a GET CHALLENGE command that provides the random number used to build the EXTERNAL AUTHENTICATION cryptogram.

As part of the EXTERNAL AUTHENTICATION command, the off-card application encrypts (computes a cryptogram of) the random number provided by the card, using a key that the off-card application and the card share knowledge of. With the EXTERNAL AUTHENTICATION command, the off-card application provides this cryptogram to the card, along with a pointer to the specific key used to create the cryptogram. If the card can decrypt this cryptogram with the stored key and then verify that the random number found in the cryptogram is the same one that the card remembers from the GET CHALLENGE command, then the command has been successfully executed and the AUT Access Condition state is achieved.

A typical APDU string for the EXTERNAL AUTHENTICATION command is as follows:

CLA	INS	P1	P2	Lc	Data
$C0_{16}$	82_{16}	00_{16}	00_{16}	07_{16}	Key # and Cryptogram

INVALIDATE.   The INVALIDATE command is used to make a file inaccessible to most commands. Specifically, when a file is INVALIDATEd, data can no longer be read from or written to the file by the normal I/O commands. The INVALIDATEd file cannot be accessed by any commands except for the SELECT, DELETE, and REHABILITATE commands. There typically is no data associated with this command unless an Access Condition of PROtected is specified; then, the data field contains any required fill characters in addition to the cryptogram used to authenticate the command.

A typical APDU string for the INVALIDATE command is:

CLA	INS	P1	P2	Lc	Data
$F0_{16}$	04_{16}	00_{16}	00_{16}	Length	Fill block + cryptogram

REHABILITATE.   An INVALIDATEd file can be restored to full functionality by using a REHABILITATE command. As with the INVALIDATE command, there is typically no data field associated with the command unless a PROtected Access Condition is used to control the command.

A typical APDU string for the REHABILITATE command is:

CLA	INS	P1	P2	Lc	Data
$F0_{16}$	44_{16}	00_{16}	00_{16}	Length	Fill block + cryptogram

Public Key Cryptography Support

The Cryptoflex card provides a platform especially designed to fit into a cryptographic services infrastructure, based on public key cryptography. In such an environment, as we discussed in Chapter 4, it is particularly useful to be able to perform certain operations on a secure token (a smart card). In this section, we will review a number of commands that facilitate such operations.

SHA_1 INTERMEDIATE.   One of the characteristics of security, from the standpoint of computers or computer networks, is the concept of information or data integrity—having assurance that data has not been changed as it winds its way through various systems and transactions. The most generally used technique for assuring data integrity, short of doing a bit-by-bit comparison of the data at different points, is to capture a relatively short string of bits that is uniquely associated with a full set of data for which integrity is sought. A useful mechanism for generating such a "short string" is a one-way hash function; SHA-1 is one such hash function.

With a one-way hash function, a long string of bytes is processed through the hashing algorithm to generate a unique code for the specific byte string. This unique code, also known as the *hash code*, can be used in a digital signature mechanism to validate the integrity of the information to be digitally signed.

To perform an SHA_1 algorithm on a smart card, the information to be hashed must be moved onto the card a segment at a time. Because only a relatively short string of bytes can be moved onto the card at any one time, two commands are defined through which the hash code of an arbitrary byte string can be calculated. The SHA_1INTERMEDIATE command is used to hash a data block of exactly 64 bytes. An arbitrary byte string is processed 64 bytes at a time until a last block that is equal to or less than 64 bytes remains.

The APDU string for a typical SHA_1INTERMEDIATE command is as follows:

CLA	INS	P1	P2	Lc	Data
10_{16}	40_{16}	00_{16}	00_{16}	40_{16}	64 bytes of data to be hashed

SHA_1 LAST.   If a block of information is equal to or less than 64 bytes, then it can be hashed with a single command—the SHA_1 LAST command. In addition, if the byte string to be hashed is greater than 64 bytes, then it is processed 64 bytes at a time with the SHA_1 INTERMEDIATE command and then the last block of 64 or fewer bytes is processed with the SHA_1 LAST command.

After the SHA_1 LAST command is executed, the resulting hash code for the entire sequence of hashing commands is available through a GET RESPONSE command. The typical APDU string for the SHA_1 LAST command is as follows:

CLA	INS	P1	P2	Lc	Data
00_{16}	40_{16}	00_{16}	00_{16}	Length	64 or fewer bytes of data to be hashed

GENERATE DES KEY.   As we have seen, the INTERNAL AUTHENTICATION command confirms identities by allowing proof that a specific secret (key) is known by both the off-card and the on-card application components. The GENERATE DES KEY command can be used to generate such a key (on-card) and store the key in the appropriate position of the key file on the card. The APDU string for this command is as follows:

CLA	INS	P1	P2	Lc	Data
$F0_{16}$	50_{16}	00_{16}	Key #	00_{16}	None

The GENERATE DES KEY is an interesting command if one wants to use the card for encryption of information. The internal key file, in addition to being used for authentication, can be used as the key for encryption with commands discussed in the following section.

DES BLOCK INIT. As with the SHA_1 operation, if one is going to do DES encryption of a large amount of data, the data must be passed to the card a small amount at a time. The DES BLOCK INIT command is used to prepare the card for just such an operation. The first "length" bytes are encrypted with the specified key and using the algorithm associated with that key in the key file. The mode parameter tells whether to encrypt ("00_{16}") or to decrypt ("01_{16}").

CLA	INS	P1	P2	Lc	Data
$F0_{16}$	56_{16}	mode	Key #	Length	Byte string to be encrypted

The encrypted ciphertext is stored in RAM in the card. A GET RESPONSE command must follow to retrieve the ciphertext. Encryption or decryption of the remaining data is done with a DES BLOCK command.

DES BLOCK. The DES BLOCK command continues the encryption or decryption operation initiated with the DES BLOCK INIT command. Each command must be followed by a GET RESPONSE command to retrieve the results for the operation.

CLA	INS	P1	P2	Lc	Data
$F0_{16}$	58_{16}	Mode	Key #	Length	Length bytes of data

The cipher block chaining (CBC) mode is used in the encryption or decryption operation.

RSA SIGNATURE. Three commands are available through which an arbitrary byte string of up to 256 bytes can be encrypted with the RSA algorithm using a private key stored in the currently selected RSA private key file. This encryption operation is termed a digital signature. The byte string to be digitally signed is typically a hash code of a long byte string such as a financial transaction of some sort.

If the byte string is 128 bytes or less, then the command RSA SIGNATURE can be used to encrypt it. A key of 512, 768, or 1024 bits can be used. The byte string to be signed is conveyed as the data field of the APDU string. The resulting signature is retrieved from the card through a GET RESPONSE command.

The status word response from the RSA SIGNATURE command specifies the number of bytes to be retrieved by the GET RESPONSE command.

CLA	INS	P1	P2	Lc	Data
$C0_{16}$	88_{16}	00_{16}	Key #	Data length	Byte string to be signed

After the signing operation is completed in the card, but before the status is returned, the inverse (verification) operation is performed using the complementary (to the private signing key) public key stored in the card. Only if the reciprocal operation is consistent with the original byte string does the command response occur; otherwise, an error indication is returned. This confirmation operation defeats what is termed the *Bellcore attack*, through which an attacker attempts to gain knowledge about an RSA key by intercepting repeated results in which the encryption (signing) operation is interrupted through some external means.

RSA SIGNATURE INTERMEDIATE.   If the byte string to be signed is longer than 128 bytes and/or if a signing key of 2048 bits is to be used, then the signing operation requires two (or more) successive commands. The first part of the byte string is signed with the RSA SIGNATURE INTERMEDIATE command. The partial results are stored on the card. The last part of the byte string is then encrypted using the RSA SIGNATURE LAST command, after which the results are fetched from the card using a GET RESPONSE command.

CLA	INS	P1	P2	Lc	Data
10_{16}	88_{16}	00_{16}	Key #	Data Length	Partial byte string

RSA SIGNATURE LAST.   After one or more calls to the RSA SIGNATURE INTERMEDIATE command have been made, the last part of the byte string is encrypted with the RSA SIGNATURE LAST. Then, if the signature operation has completed correctly, the resulting ciphertext is retrieved from the card with the GET RESPONSE command.

CLA	INS	P1	P2	Lc	Data
00_{16}	88_{16}	00_{16}	Key #	Data Length	Final part of byte string

RSA KEY GENERATION.   The digital signature is a way to protect in a secure fashion the identity represented by the private key of an RSA key pair outside of the card. The private key that actually authenticates the identity is stored on the card and never has to leave the card in order to be authenticated. Rather, just the public key associated with the private key needs to be exported from the card in order to test the signature operation.

The RSA KEY GENERATION command is provided to generate a public/private key pair inside the Cryptoflex card. Here's the format of this command:

CLA	INS	P1	P2	Lc	Data
$F0_{16}$	46_{16}	Key #	Modulus length	04	Public exponent

The low-order nibble of P1 is used to set the key number of the generated key. Table 6.13 defines how the high-order nibble is interpreted.

Table 6.13 Public Key File Structure Specification

Parameter P1	Effect on the Public Components	Stored in Public Key File
"0000xxxx" = 0Xh	All components of public key generated in public key file.	Public module, J0, H, and public exponent
"1000xxxx" = 8Xh	All components of public key generated in public key file. Public module is ready to be output.	Public module, J0, H, and public exponent
"0100xxxx" = 4Xh	Only public module and exponent generated in public key file.	Public module and public exponent
"1100xxxx" = CXh	Only public module and exponent generated in public key file. Public module is ready to be output.	Public module and public exponent
"1010xxxx" = AXh	Only public exponent in public key file. Public module is ready to be output.	Public exponent
"1001xxxx" = 9Xh	Public module is ready to be output.	Nothing

File System Commands

In the previous sections, we've examined the commands of the Cryptoflex card that provide for a security infrastructure in which the card operates and a number of operations through which the card can provide services to an off-card security infrastructure, particularly to a public key infrastructure. We now want to look at a series of commands through which the on-card file system is utilized in an application. These will be a series of commands that allow us to store and retrieve information to or from a file on a card and will allow us to manipulate information in a file.

SELECT.   The SELECT command is used to position a logical pointer at a specific file. This will then determine which file subsequent commands will act on, or which key files are to be used for establishing Access Conditions. A SELECT command can only move this logical pointer to point to:

- Any file which is an immediate child of the current dedicated file

- The parent (dedicated file of the current file)

- The master file of the file system

The APDU for the SELECT command is as follows:

CLA	INS	P1	P2	Lc	Data
$C0_{16}$	$A4_{16}$	00_{16}	00_{16}	02_{16}	A 2-byte file ID

UPDATE BINARY.   The UPDATE BINARY command allows an application to write a byte string into a transparent file. The byte string is conveyed in the Data field of the command with the number of bytes to be written being determined by the Length argument. The P1 and P2 parameters form a 16-bit offset pointer into the file. This pointer determines the first byte location in the file in which to write the first byte of the new data field. An UPDATE BINARY command causes the exact input byte string to be deposited into the specified position of the current selected file.

CLA	INS	P1	P2	Lc	Data
$C0_{16}$	$D6_{16}$	Offset/High	Offset/Low	Length+X	Byte string

UPDATE BINARY ENCIPHERED.   The UPDATE BINARY ENCI-PHERED command functions much as the UPDATE BINARY command, with the additional capability that the Data field is encrypted. The encryption is done with the key corresponding to the key stored in the current external key file. The input data is decrypted with this key and the data stored in the file in the clear. Again, the P1 and P2 parameters form a 15-bit offset pointer into the file showing where the first new data byte is to be deposited. For this command, the input byte string must be a multiple of 8 bytes and must be equal or less than 232 bytes.

CLA	INS	P1	P2	Lc	Data
04_{16}	$D6_{16}$	Offset/High	Offset/Low	Length	Encrypted byte string

UPDATE RECORD.   The UPDATE RECORD command allows an application to write a new record into a record-oriented file structure. The new record is conveyed in the form of a byte string carried as the Data field of the command. The position (record) into which the new data is written is determined by the mode according to Table 6.14.

Table 6.14 Write Position Indicator

P2	Mode
00	First record
01	Last record
02	Next record
03	Previous record
04	If P1=00, current mode or absolute mode with record number in P1

The APDU string for the command is as follows:

CLA	INS	P1	P2	Lc	Data
$C0_{16}$	DC_{16}	Rec #	Mode	length+X	New record byte string

READ BINARY.   The READ BINARY command allows a byte string to be read from the selected file. The P1 and P2 parameters together form a 16-bit offset into the file, which must be a transparent file type. Then, according to Lc, a maximum of 256 bytes may be read from the file and returned in the status response return for the command. To specify reading 256 bytes, the Lc parameter is set to 00_{16}.

CLA	INS	P1	P2	Lc	Data
$C0_{16}$	$B0_{16}$	Offset/High	Offset/Low	Length	None

READ BINARY ENCIPHERED.   To avoid moving the contents of a file across the off-card to on-card interface in the clear, the data from the on-card file may be read and then encrypted before movement to the off-card application. The data is encrypted with the key in the current external key file. The file segment read must be a multiple of 8 bytes and must be equal to or less than 232 bytes.

CLA	INS	P1	P2	Lc	Data
04_{16}	$B0_{16}$	Offset/High	Offset/Low	Length	None

READ RECORD.   A record-oriented file can be read using the READ RECORD command. The record read is determined by the mode parameter according to Table 6.15.

Table 6.15 Record Selector

P2	Mode
00_{16}	First record
01_{16}	Last record
02_{16}	Next record
03_{16}	Previous record
04_{16}	If P1=00, current mode or absolute mode with record number in P1

An internal record pointer is maintained as the file is read. If the mode indicated in P2 is 04_{16} and P1 is 00_{16}, then the contents of the record pointed at by the internal record pointer is read. Following the read operation, this internal record pointer is incremented to point at the next record in the file. The record is returned in the status response to the command. The APDU string is as follows:

CLA	INS	P1	P2	Lc	Data
$C0_{16}$	$B2_{16}$	Rec #	Mode	Length	None

SEEK.   The SEEK command is used to search for a particular sequence of bytes within a record of a file. If the pattern is found, then the internal record pointer is set to the record where the pattern was found. The record could then be read with a READ BINARY command. Where the search starts (within the file) is determined by the P1 parameter, which is record offset into the file, and by the P2 parameter, which is a mode designation according to Table 6.16.

Table 6.16 Read Offset Selector

P2	Mode
00	From the beginning forward
02	From the next location forward

The APDU string for a SEEK command is as follows:

CLA	INS	P1	P2	Lc	Data
$F0_{16}$	$A2_{16}$	Offset	Mode	Length	Search pattern data

DECREASE.   The DECREASE command is used to decrease the content of the last updated record in the current selected cyclic file. This command is typically used in the implementation of a purse of some type. It allows for decrementing the purse, which is maintained in a cyclic file. Using a cyclic file allows for maintaining a transaction log a few transactions deep and for a rollback operation in the event of an error.

CLA	INS	P1	P2	Lc	Data
$F0_{16}$	30_{16}	00_{16}	00_{16}	03_{16}+X	The value to be deducted+crypto if AC = PRO

INCREASE.   This INCREASE command is used to increase the contents of the last updated record in the current selected cyclic file. This instruction will not be performed if the result exceeds the maximum value of the record (all bytes set to FFh). It also will not be performed if the record length of the cyclic file is not between 3 and 252.

CLA	INS	P1	P2	Lc	Data
$F0_{16}$	32_{16}	00_{16}	00_{16}	03+X	The value to be added+crypto if AC = PRO

DIR NEXT. The DIR NEXT command, another very useful non-ISO 7816-4 command, is used to retrieve a set of file descriptor information from the "next" file in the current dedicated file. The returned information is of the form as shown in Table 6.17.

Table 6.17 Directory Command Response

DATA	Description
1-2	File Size Modulo 4 (see note 1)
3-4	File Identifier
5	File Type
6	FSI: for transparent, linear-fixed, linear-variable, directory INST-FSI: for cyclic
7-9	Access Condition level
10	Status
11	RFU
12-14	Access Condition key number
15	RFU: for transparent RL: for linear-fixed, linear-variable, cyclic NSD: for directory
16	RFU: for transparent NR: for linear-fixed, linear-variable, cyclic, directory

By using the SELECT command to point to specific dedicated files, a complete mapping of all the files in a card's file structure can be mapped with the DIR NEXT command. The file descriptor information is returned with the status response of the command.

The typical APDU byte string for the DIR NEXT command is as follows:

CLA	INS	P1	P2	Lc	Data
$F0_{16}$	$A8_{16}$	00_{16}	00_{16}	Length	None

GET AC KEYS. This GET AC KEYS command is used to give information about the access conditions applicable to the currently selected file. It returns the three key index bytes corresponding to the three access conditions defined for the current file. The GET AC KEYS command is needed because the access condition information is not included in the file control information returned by the SELECT command.

CLA	INS	P1	P2	Lc	Data
$F0_{16}$	$C4_{16}$	00_{16}	00_{16}	03_{16}	None

GET RESPONSE. This GET RESPONSE command is used by the off-card application to retrieve (from the card) data calculated by the immediately preceding command executed in the Cryptoflex card. The data is returned in the status response for the command.

The typical APDU string for this command is as follows:

CLA	INS	P1	P2	Lc	Data
00_{16}	$C0_{16}$	00_{16}	00_{16}	Length	None

Cryptoflex Summary

The Cryptoflex card is a fixed, command-set card. The Cryptoflex card can:

- Protect itself through a number of smart card security mechanisms.
- Provide cryptographic services to off-card security infrastructures—specifically, to store cryptographic keys and perform cryptographic operations on a secure processor.
- Provide a standard card file system that can be used to securely store information and allow access to it by very explicitly identified entities.

We'll look at some specific implementations in Chapter 9, which make use of the Cryptoflex card.

CYBERFLEX 32K EGATE

The Cyberflex Access 32K eGate smart card is a Java Card 2.1.1-compliant smart card. It is also compliant with the GP 2.0 specification and it incorporates a USB interface in the on-card ICC. Thus, the Cyberflex Access eGate card can be physically interfaced to a host computer system through a standard smart card reader or directly through a USB port on the host computer. This card is a post-issuance programmable smart card with 32 kilobytes of electrically erasable and programmable read-only memory (EEPROM) in the ICC that can be used for storing either data or Java Card applet code that can be loaded onto the card even after it has been issued to the individual cardholders. The Cyberflex Access eGate smart card is based on the STMicroelectronics ST19XT34® ICC.

Java Card is a specific language variant of Java and is defined through a specification issued by Sun Microsystems. Java Card 2.1.1 identifies a specific version of the Java Card specification. It also defines a set of APIs that are mandated to be present (on the smart card) for on-card applets to access. Among the APIs supported on the Cyberflex Access card are javacard.security and javacard.crypto. These APIs allow an applet to access cryptographic services provided by the base operating system on the card. An excellent general reference on Java Card programming is the book *Java Card™ Technology for Smart Cards* by Zhiqun Chen (ISBN 0-201-70329-7, Addison-Wesley, 2000). Figure 6.2 illustrates the basic Java Card architecture of the Cyberflex Access smart card. A general operating system insulates applications from the hardware architecture of the ICC and its connection to off-card application com-

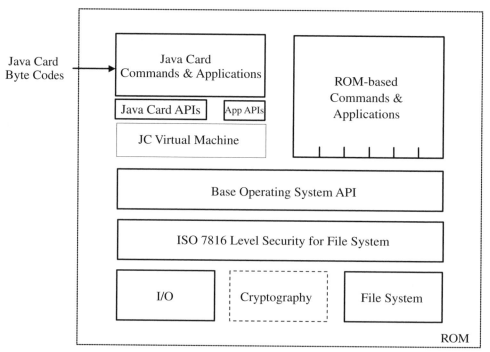

▶ **Figure 6.2**   Java Card smart card general architecture.

ponents. Layered on top of this base operating system is a Java Card virtual machine, which facilitates the execution of on-card applets by an interpretation process. Java Card APIs are available to the on-card applets and provide (to the on-card applets) a variety of access and services to the underlying operating system.

The Java Card specification alone does not provide a comprehensive security infrastructure for administering and using on-card applets. Because such an infrastructure is required for real-world use of Java Card smart cards and, to support an open marketplace, it is very desirable that such an infrastructure adhere to well-defined (and open) specifications; various attempts at defining infrastructures have been made. The most successful is the GlobalPlatform specification, developed initially by Visa International and now under the control of the GlobalPlatform consortium.

Although neutral with regard to the specific operating system found on a smart card, GP provides an infrastructure definition that is very well suited for the Java Card world. GP provides specifications in three distinct areas, which allow exploitation of the Java Card architecture for real-world applications. These areas are:

- an identity authentication infrastructure
- a secure messaging methodology
- an (on-card) applet loading and control infrastructure

Within the GP architecture, these capabilities are enabled through the presence of a controlling application on the card, an application called the "Card Manager." When a Java Card smart card is introduced to a PC or terminal application system, the default application first contacted is the Card Manager. Further communication with and control of the smart card are accomplished through the Card Manager. This GP plus Java Card architecture is illustrated in Figure 6.3. In the following section, we'll look at the GP specifications in a bit more detail.

GlobalPlatform Architecture

GlobalPlatform (GP) comprises a security infrastructure for smart cards. It is neutral with respect to the on-card operating system. However, for purposes of our discussion in this chapter, we will present GP in the context of Java Card smart cards, recognizing, of course, that other varieties of smart card operating systems could be used and still fit within the GP framework.

GP operates in terms of a well-defined life cycle for its cards. This life cycle can be illustrated as five distinct states that support well-defined and well-controlled transitions among each other as illustrated in Figure 6.4.

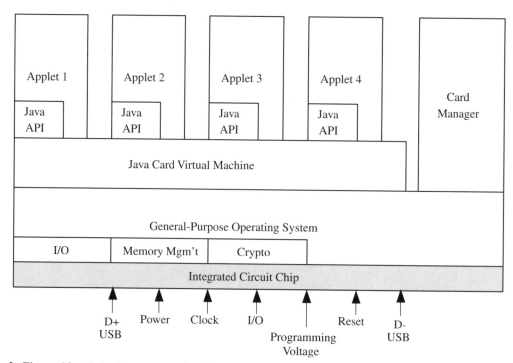

▶ **Figure 6.3**   Cyberflex access card architecture.

Life Cycle

The GlobalPlatform card life cycle covers the period from when a card becomes fully compliant with the GP specifications during the manufacturing process until the card is retired from use. In fact, a card spends the vast majority of its life span in a single state (as long as it's working correctly), that of "Secured." Figure 6.4 illustrates the various states and the transitions that occur to move the card from one state to another. In this section, we'll examine the definition of each life cycle state and discuss the characteristics of the transitions that take the card from one state to the next. Central to understanding the various GP mechanisms is understanding how a variety of identities are established within the GP framework. This is done through a series of "key sets" which can be stored on the GP compliant card and subsequently used, through a series of security commands, to establish a specific identity. The first key set installed on the card is used to establish the identity of the owner/controller of the card; that is, typically the card issuer. This first key set is used to establish a secure channel between the off-card application and the on-card Card Manager application. Thus, the Card Manager is the on-card representative of the card issuer.

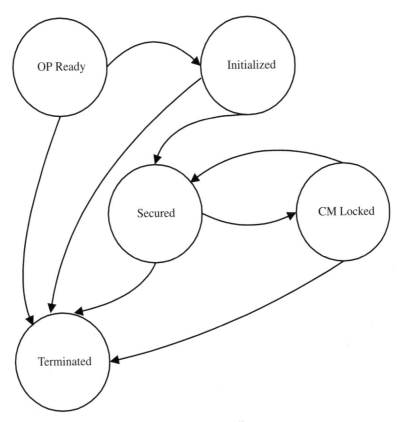

▶ **Figure 6.4** GlobalPlatform life cycle state diagram.

The specific life cycle state that a card is in is stored within the card. A STA-TUS command, supplied by the Card Manager, is used to transition from one state to the next. So, let's first examine these key sets and then examine the use of them to move the card through its various life cycle states.

Key Sets. A GP-compliant smart card makes use of a set of three crypto-graphic keys through which it establishes identity, maintains privacy of data transfer between the off-card application and the on-card applet, and ensures the integrity of data transferred between these two environments. The three keys in a set are labeled:

- *AUTH key*—used for authentication of identity and for general encryption: $K_{(ENC,AUTH)}$
- *MAC key*—used for a MAC computation to ensure data integrity: $K_{(MAC)}$
- *KEK key*—used for key encryption: $K_{(KEK)}$

The AUTH key is key #1 of the set, the MAC key is key #2 of the set, and the KEK key is key #3 of the set. Each key is a 16-byte, triple DES (TDES) key. When a cryptographic operation is to be performed with a certain key, the key is identified by its key set version number and by its position (index) within the key set.

The first key set establishes the identity of the Card Issuer and allows the off-card application of the Card Issuer to communicate with the Card Manager application on the card. Further, through the Card Manager application the Card Issuer's off-card application can effect control of other aspects of the card. Subsequent key sets (after the first) are used to establish the identities of Security Domains on the card. These applications on the card are used by application providers, who may be other than the Card Issuer, to invoke and run various applications on the card.

OP_Ready. The card enters the OP_Ready state whenever it is compliant with the Java Card and the GP specifications and when it has an initial key set stored on the card. At this point, the base operating system is complete from a Java Card standpoint. The characteristics of the Java Card virtual machine are well established and the APIs present on the card for applets to access are well defined. Further, the card contains a Card Manager application, which acts as the overall controlling entity on the card.

A basic key set is present on the card, which allows the identity of the card issuer to be established and for a secure communication channel to be established between the off-card application and the Card Manager on the card. In this state, a single key is actually used for all three purposes; that is, $K_{(ENC,AUTH)}$, $K_{(MAC)}$, and $K_{(KEK)}$.

From this state, a full set of keys can be stored on the card in order to provide a more robust security environment. When this is done, the card passes to the next life-cycle state.

Initialized. The Initialized state is entered when at least one full set (of three keys) is stored on the card. That is $K_{(ENC,AUTH)}$, $K_{(MAC)}$, and $K_{(KEK)}$ are each unique, independent keys. This key set identifies the Card Issuer. If additional Security Domains are to be present on the card, then the key sets to establish their identities are loaded while the card is in this state of its life cycle.

The card generally passes through the Initialized state of its life cycle while it is still under direct physical control of the card manufacturer or the card issuer.

Secured. Once key sets have been loaded onto the card and it is in its Initialized state, it is possible to invoke a secure channel between the off-card application component and the on-card Card Manager application. This is done by issuing the SELECT, the INITIALIZE/UPDATE, and the EXTERNAL AUTHENTICATE commands in sequence. These commands will cause the two ends of the communication channel to perform a mutual identity authenticate operation and then create a session key to be used to encrypt the channel between the off-card application and the on-card Card Manager.

Once the card has entered its Secured state, all communication with the Card Manager must be by way of a secured channel. Open channels may be used in communicating with individual applications on the card other than the Card Manager.

CM_Locked. The Card Manager maintains a "Global PIN," which can be used by all applications for cardholder verification. If an application wants to use the Global PIN, it must provide its own equivalent of a VERIFY CHV command because this command is not provided by the Card Manager. In case of any error condition encountered in the use of the card, the card can be placed into a CM Locked state. While in this state, only the Card Manager application on the card can be accessed.

The Card Manager must be contacted through a secure channel. In general, the only operations that the Card Manager can perform while in this state are to correct the error condition and put the card back into a Secure state.

Terminated. When the card reaches the end of its life, it is placed in a Terminated state. In this state, the card can no longer be used.

Card Manager

The Card Manager is an apparently standard Java Card applet found on a GP-compliant smart card. By "apparently standard," we mean simply that the Card Manager conforms to the same rules of construction and use as any other Java Card applet; from outward appearances it is much like other applets. However, the fact is, the Card Manager is a very special animal; in fact, it doesn't really have to be a Java Card applet at all. Indeed, native mode Card Manager applications can be built. What's really important about the Card Manager is that it's the "first among equals" of all the applets stored on a card; it is the application that is automatically selected to run when a Java Card is inserted into a "card acceptance device." It is the responsibility of the Card Manager to establish and enforce the security infrastructure of the card. To this end, it provides for the establishment of identity on the card, in the form of what are called *security domains*.

The identities that can be established via the Card Manager derive from a set of three keys to define each identity; we'll look at the use of these keys in more detail a little later. The Card Manager can store and control eight sets of such keys, essentially allowing the definition of seven identities (security domains) in addition to that of the Card Manager itself. In general, one thinks of the Card Manager identity as being that of the card issuer (i.e., the entity responsible, in the end, for all that goes in and on the card).

Security Domain

Security domains are established on behalf of an application provider when the provider requires the use of keys on the card that are completely separate and isolated from the card issuer's keys. Because the card issuer owns applications on the card as well, the Card Manager includes the card issuer's security domain as a subcomponent.

In the current implementation, security domains do not allow delegated management but support DAP verification.

The card is not limited in terms of creation of security domains (as many as we want) that can be installed at any time during the life of the card.

Applications can access security domain services by first obtaining a handle to their security domain through the GP API. With this handle, the application can rely on cryptographic support from the security domain to ensure confidentiality and integrity during personalization, and optionally, during runtime as well.

In the current implementation, the cryptographic services offered by security domains through the GP API are identical to the Card Manager services, and are not customizable. Consequently, a security domain can be viewed as a key repository with cryptographic services identical to those of the Card Manager.

Commands

Perhaps the first thing you'll notice about the command set supported by the basic Cyberflex Access card is that there are no file system commands; indeed, Cyberflex Access, as a typical Java Card smart card, does not include an on-card file system conforming to the ISO 7816-4 command set. Rather, the assumption is that information stored on the Cyberflex Access card will be stored within "objects" defined within the Java Card applets stored on the card. Access to this information must then be provided through a command or set of commands supported by the applet (in which the "objects" are defined) as a means of communicating between the on-card applet and the off-card application.

Card Manager Exclusive Commands

DELETE. The DELETE command is used by the Card Manager to delete a load file (package) or an application (applet instance). Deleting an application consists in deleting only the instance (objects) of the applet without deleting the applet itself or package. A load file cannot be deleted as long as an instance of one of its applet(s) still exists within the card. If an instance is linked to a package, it is not possible to delete this package without deleting all the instances linked to it. A security domain can never be deleted.

The APDU string for the DELETE command is as follows:

CLA	INS	P1	P2	Lc	Data
80_{16}	$E4_{16}$	00_{16}	00_{16}	Length	TLV AID

INSTALL. Installing an application or security domain requires the invocation of several different on-card functions. The INSTALL command is used to instruct a security domain or the Card Manager as to which installation step it shall perform during an application installation process. If the INSTALL/LOAD command is not immediately followed by a LOAD command, then it is void and the allocated space is recovered. The INSTALL (Make Selectable) command can be issued on an application that is already selectable to set or unset the Default Selection privilege. The INSTALL command can also be used to install and/or make a security domain selectable.

The APDU string for the INSTALL command is as follows:

CLA	INS	P1	P2	Lc	Data
80_{16}	$E6_{16}$	Ref Ctrl	00_{16}	Length	Data field as defined next

The parameter values for the INSTALL command are shown in Table 6.18.

Table 6.18 INSTALL Command Parameter Values

Field	Length	Description
P1	1 byte	Reference Control Parameter: 02 : Load 04 : Install (& Register) 08 : Make Selectable 0C : Install (& Register) + Make Selectable
P2	1 byte	Security Control Parameter (RFU) = 00
Lc	1 byte	Length of the following data
DATA	Lc bytes	Data + Cryptogram
Le	None 1 byte	No data Length of the data response

Depending on the P1 parameter, the data field may have a number of different structures. The LOAD data field is defined as shown in Table 6.19.

Table 6.19 LOAD Command Data Field

Bytes	Description	Length
1	Length of Load File AID (05 to 10)	1 byte
2 – X	Load File AID	5 to 16 bytes
	Length of Security Domain AID (00 or 05 to 10)	1 byte
	Card Manager (implicit AID)	0 byte
	Security Domain AID	5 to 16 bytes
	Length of Load File Hash (00 or 14)	1 byte
	No Load File Hash Present	0 byte
	Load File Hash (SHA-1)	20 bytes
	Length of Load Parameters Field = 06	1 byte
	Load Parameters	6 bytes
	Length of Load Token = 00 (Delegate Management)	1 byte

For an INSTALL and then Make Selectable command, the data field is defined in Table 6.20.

Table 6.20 INSTALL Command Data Field

Bytes	Description	Length
1	Length of Load File AID (05 to 10)	1 byte
2 – X	Load File AID (Package AID)	5 to 16 bytes
	Length of AID within Load File (05 to 10)	1 byte
	AID within Load File	5 to 16 bytes
	Length of Application Instance AID (00 or 05 to 10)	1 byte
	Empty field	0 byte
	Application Instance AID	5 to 16 bytes
	Length of Application Properties = 01	1 byte
	Application Properties (Application Privilege Byte)	1 byte
	Length of Install Parameter Field	1 byte
	Install Parameter Field	X bytes
	Length of Install Token = 00 (Delegate Management)	1 byte

The Application Privilege byte is defined in Table 6.21.

Table 6.21 Application Privilege Byte Definition

b8	b7	b6	b5	b4	b3	b2	b1	Description (If Bit Is Set)
X								Security Domain
	X							DAP DES Verification
		0						RFU (Always 0)
			X					Card Manager Lock Privilege
				X				Card Terminate Privilege
					X			Default Selected Applet (Only If P1 = 0C)
						X		PIN CHANGE Privilege
							0	RFU (Always 0)

The data field for the `INSTALL` and `Make Selectable` command is shown in Table 6.22.

Table 6.22 INSTALL Data Field Definition

Bytes	Description	Length
1	Length of Load File AID = 00	1 byte
2	Length of AID within Load File = 00	1 byte
3	Length of Application Instance AID (05 to 10)	1 byte
4 – X	Application Instance AID	5 to 16 bytes
	Length of Application Properties = 01	1 byte
	Application Properties (Application Privilege Byte) (00 or 04)	1 byte
	Length of Install Parameter Field = 00	1 byte
	Length of Install Token = 00 (Delegate Management)	1 byte

LOAD. The `LOAD` command is used to load the byte codes of the load file defined in the previously issued `INSTALL` command. The command loads one load file block at a time. Load file blocks are numbered. The first load file block must be numbered "00." The block numbering must be strictly sequential and increment by one ("FF" to "00" rollover possible). The card must be informed of the last block. After receiving the last block, the card must perform the necessary functions to link the applet. The card does not invoke the install() method of the applet at this point. The size of the data field in the command data must not exceed the maximum block length returned by the card upon selecting the Card Manager. A previous successful execution of the INSTALL command with P1 = "02" (Load) is required prior to processing the first LOAD command. A previous successful execution of the LOAD command with P1 = "00" (more blocks) is required prior to processing the LOAD LAST command with P1 = "80." If any problem occurs during a LOAD command, the process is aborted and the space is recovered. It is required then to restart the full sequence again including the INSTALL/INSTALL command.

CLA	INS	P1	P2	Lc	Data
80_{16}	$E8_{16}$	00_{16}	Block #	Length	Data field as defined next

The parameter fields of the APDU are defined in Table 6.23.

Table 6.23 LOAD Command Parameter Fields

Field	Length	Description
P1	1 byte	00 more block(s) to load
		80 last block (must have at least 1 byte of data)
P2	1 byte	Block number (sequential from 00 to FF with rollover possible if more than 256 blocks)
Lc	1 byte	Length of the following data
DATA	Lc bytes	Data (see Table 6.24) + Cryptogram
Le	None	No data
	1 byte	Length of the data response (only for last block)

The data field for a simple load (first block) is defined in Table 6.24.

Table 6.24 LOAD Data Field (First Block)

Bytes	Description	Length
1	Tag of the CAP file = C4	1 byte
2 – X	CAP file length	1 to 3 bytes
X+1 – Lc	CAP file block	Lc-X bytes

And, for subsequent blocks, the data field is defined as in Table 6.25.

Table 6.25 LOAD Data Field (Subsequent Blocks)

Bytes	Description	Length
1 – Lc	CAP file block	Lc bytes

Establishing Secure Channels

GP defines a comprehensive secure channel mechanism through which commands and information may be transferred between an off-card application and an on-card applet. This mechanism is reminiscent of the standard ISO 7816-4 secure messaging mechanism but is incompatible with it. A secure channel can provide several distinct levels of security:

- *Clear*—No security; data is passed across the communication channel as clear text with no integrity checking done. This security level cannot be used with a card that has progressed to a "secured" or "locked" life cycle state.
- *MAC*—Integrity checking security level. Command sequence integrity at this security level is enforced by chaining the APDU MACs; the MAC of one APDU becomes the initialization chaining vector (ICV) in the MAC calculation for the next APDU.
- *MAC + ENC*—Private, integrity checking security level. Privacy is ensured by encrypting the APDU data and integrity checking is done by performing a MAC operation on the APDU data.

A secure channel is established by invoking three of the default Card Manager commands in sequence. First, a SELECT command is issued to define the application that is to be connected to. Then an INITALIZE UPDATE command is issued to take the first steps in establishing a secure channel. Finally, an EXTERNAL AUTHENTICATE command is called to force mutual authentication of the off-card and the on-card application elements. We will go through this sequence in a bit more detail later on.

Card Manager and Security Domain Commands

The Card Manager application on the Cyberflex Access card supports several standard commands that are used to provide administration and operational support for the applets on the card. These commands are typically not used within specific applications, although there's no real prohibition from doing so. Like the Global-

Platform version of secure messaging, some of these commands have the same names as ISO 7816-4 commands but they are not compatible with this standard.

EXTERNAL AUTHENTICATE. The EXTERNAL AUTHENTICATE command is used by the card to authenticate the host, to establish the secure channel, and to determine the level of security required for all subsequent commands within the secure channel. A previous and successful execution of the INITIALIZE UPDATE command is required prior to processing this command.

The APDU string for the EXTERNAL AUTHENTICATE command is shown below:

CLA	INS	P1	P2	Lc	Data
84_{16}	82_{16}	Var	00_{16}	Length	Data field as defined in Table 6.26

The parameter set definitions are shown in Table 6.26.

Table 6.26 EXTERNAL AUTHENTICATE Command Parameter Values

Field	Length	Description
P1	1 byte	00: No security (pre-issuance) 01: MAC 03: MAC and ENC
P2	1 byte	00
Lc	1 byte	10
DATA	8 bytes	Data (see Table 6.27)

The data field is defined in Table 6.27.

Table 6.27 Data Field Values

Bytes	Description	Length
1 – 8	Host cryptogram	8 bytes
9 – 16	Certificate (MAC)	8 bytes

The host cryptogram is calculated according to the following algorithm in Figure 6.5.

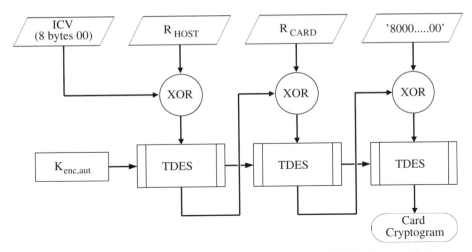

GET DATA.   The GET DATA command is used to retrieve a single data object from the card. It can be used to retrieve any data that has been loaded to the Card Manager using the PUT DATA command.

This command is available outside of a secure channel. However, if issued within a secure channel, it must follow the same security level as defined in EXTERNAL AUTHENTICATE.

The APDU string for the GET DATA command is as follows:

CLA	INS	P1	P2	Lc	Data
84_{16}	CA_{16}	$9F_{16}$	$7F_{16}$	08_{16}	None

GET STATUS.   If the Card Manager is the current application, the GET STATUS command is used to retrieve Card Manager and application-related life-cycle status information according to given search criteria. Because the Card Manager has access to the card registry, it can respond with information related to its own life cycle as well as package and application life cycles. It can also report on the privileges of an application. This command is not allowed in a security domain.

The APDU string for the GET STATUS command is as follows:

CLA	INS	P1	P2	Lc	Data
84_{16}	$F2_{16}$	Var	00_{16}	08_{16}	None

GET RESPONSE. The GET RESPONSE command is restricted to CASE 4 commands in T=0 protocol. In T=1 for a CASE 4 command, the card response is sent directly after the command execution, so this command is not supported. In T=0 for an incoming command that has data to send back (indicated by the status word "61_{16}" "XX_{16}" with "XX_{16}" corresponding to the number of bytes), the data is received with the GET RESPONSE command sent immediately after the command to which it is related.

The APDU string for the GET RESPONSE command is as follows:

CLA	INS	P1	P2	Lc	Data
00_{16}	$C0_{16}$	00_{16}	00_{16}	Length	None

INITIALIZE UPDATE. The INITIALIZE UPDATE command is used to initiate a secure channel for the Card Manager. Card and host session data are exchanged, and the card upon completion of this command generates session keys. However, the secure channel is considered open upon completion of a successful EXTERNAL AUTHENTICATE command that must immediately follow the INITIALIZE UPDATE command. This two-step process ensures mutual authentication of the host/card and is a prerequisite to any Card Manager command. Therefore, INITIALIZE UPDATE must be the very first command issued to the card following the selection of the Card Manager.

At any time within a current secure channel, the command can be issued to the card to close the current secure channel and initiate a new one. If a security domain has not been initialized with a valid key set yet, then the default Card Manager key set is used to initiate the secure channel instead. As soon as the security domain has a valid key set, the Card Manager keys are never used by the security domain again.

The APDU string for the INITIALIZE UPDATE command is as follows:

CLA	INS	P1	P2	Lc	Data
80_{16}	50_{16}	Var	$00_{16}/01_{16}$	08_{16}	None

PIN CHANGE/UNBLOCK. The PIN CHANGE/UNBLOCK command is used by the Card Manager/security domain to store, replace, or unblock the Global PIN, and reset the associated PIN Try Counter to the value of the PIN Try Limit. The security domain can process the command only if authorized by the Card Manager (i.e., application privileges byte properly set when installing the security domain with the INSTALL for Install command). When the PIN is changed, it is loaded encrypted using the static key K_{KEK} and so whatever the security level required by the secure channel. If the secure channel requires both MAC and ENC then the secure channel encryption using the diversified key $K_{ENC,AUTH}$ comes on top of the key encryption using K_{KEK}. This is a case of double key encryption.

The APDU string for the `PIN CHANGE/UNBLOCK` command is as follows:

CLA	INS	P1	P2	Lc	Data
80_{16}	24_{16}	00_{16}	Var	Var	None

PUT DATA. The `PUT DATA` command is used to store or replace one tagged data object provided in the command data field. When already existing in the ICC, the current data object shall be replaced. The new data object shall be presented with the same format and length as it exists within the card (except AID).

The APDU string for the `PUT DATA` command is as follows:

CLA	INS	P1	P2	Lc	Data
80_{16}	DA_{16}	00_{16}	$4F_{16}$	Length	None

PUT KEY. The `PUT KEY` command is used to

- replace a single or multiple (consecutive) key(s) within an existing key set version
- replace an existing key set version with a new key set version (and update at least one key)
- add a new key set version containing exactly three keys

Its key set version and its position (index) within the key set identify a key. Each key set contains exactly three static keys (i.e., $K_{ENC,AUTH}$, K_{MAC}, K_{KEK}) with index 1 to 3, but the Card Manager/security domain can have multiple key sets. Loading or updating key(s) must be done atomically. Keys are loaded encrypted (using the static key K_{KEK}) and so whatever the security level required by the secure channel. If the Secure Channel requires both MAC and ENC then the Secure Channel encryption using the diversified key $K_{ENC,AUTH}$ comes on top of the key encryption using K_{KEK}. This is a case of double key encryption.

When replacing existing keys, the new keys must be presented with the same length for each key as it exists within the card. If the card does not support the algorithm identified in the Algorithm ID, an error condition is returned. If any problem happens while processing the data field, all new keys must be discarded (key set not created or not updated).

If a new key set is being loaded and the initialization key is still present on the card, the initialization key must be disabled upon successful completion of the command. In addition, the first key set loaded becomes the default key set and stays so during the life of the card. This first key set is loaded using the Card Manager default key set.

The APDU string for the PUT KEY command is as follows:

CLA	INS	P1	P2	Lc	Data
80_{16}	$D8_{16}$	Var	Var	Length	None

The key encryption mechanism used with the PUT KEY command is illustrated in Figure 6.6.

SELECT.   The SELECT command is used for selecting an application, or a file within an application's file system. The Card Manager may be selected either for the loading of a load file or for installing a previously loaded application. This command is not required to select the Card Manager when there is no default-selected application. The Card Manager is the ultimate default-selected application.

It is possible to use a truncated AID in the command. When searching for the AID given in the command, the number of characters compared between the command data and the AID stored internally within the card registry is the number of characters in the command data field.

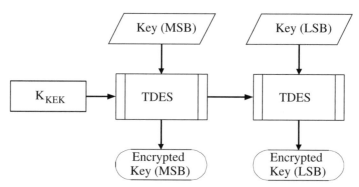

▶ **Figure 6.6**   Key encryption mechanism. (Reprinted by permission of Schlumberger. All rights reserved.)

Only applications in a selectable state (i.e., SELECTABLE, PERSONAL-IZED, or BLOCKED) are included in the select process.

The APDU string for the SELECT command is as follows:

CLA	INS	P1	P2	Lc	Data
00_{16}	$A4_{16}$	04_{16}	$00_{16}/02_{16}$	Length	None

SET STATUS. The SET STATUS command is used by the Card Manager to modify the life-cycle state of the card (Card Manager Life Cycle, or CMLC) or the life-cycle state of an application (Application Life Cycle, or ALC). This command is used by the security domain to modify the CMLC to CM_LOCKED or TERMINATED if authorized in application privileges byte of security domain) or its own ALC.

The APDU string for the SET STATUS command is as follows:

CLA	INS	P1	P2	Lc	Data
80_{16}	$F0_{16}$	$40_{16}/80_{16}$	Var	Length	None

Applet APIs

Applets on a Cyberflex Access card have can use the standard Java Card APIs defined in the Java Card 2.2.1 specification. This includes the following packages:

- java.lang
- javacard.framework
- javacard.security
- javacardx.crypto
- visa.openplatform

The specific classes provided by these packages were reviewed briefly in Chapter 5.

SUMMARY

This chapter has reviewed in some detail two commercially available smart cards. The Cryptoflex card is a fixed command set card aimed at providing cryptographic services in general security infrastructures. The Cyberflex Access card is a post-issuance programmable smart card based on the Java Card specification and the GlobalPlatform specification. Much of the material found in this chapter was gleaned from the technical specifications of these two smart cards as it is provided by Schlumberger. The authors gratefully acknowledge the generosity of Schlumberger in allowing us to present a view of this material in the context of this book.

7

Smart Card Infrastructure

Previous chapters have dealt primarily with the various aspects of smart cards that govern their construction, their communications, and the functions that they perform. As anyone well versed with personal computer (PC) architectures knows, this is obviously only part of the story. The manner in which smart card readers are integrated into PC systems and the manner in which, through them, PC applications communicate with smart cards in order to accomplish some higher level application, has been a fertile ground for standardization efforts as well.

The problem is one of providing data interchange between two applications running on two different computer systems, which are physically connected by a communication channel. In Figure 7.1, we illustrate the generic connection that needs to be supported. The smart card constitutes one independent computer system. We have software running on this computer which performs some set of functions needed by an application running on a second computer; in the case shown in Figure 7.1, it is a laptop computer. The physical channel connecting the two computers is supported by a smart card reader that connects to an I/O channel from the laptop; perhaps a serial port. The smart card, when inserted into the smart card reader, then completes the two computer interconnect.

We've alluded to the fact that this interconnect between two computers fits the OSI reference model for communication protocols. This model is a guiding factor in establishing the architecture of a "smart card stack" within the PC system software. By way of this protocol stack, an application at the top of the stack can send to and receive information from the smart card computer. The architecture doesn't resolve to the perfect seven-layer model, but then real-world implementations rarely exactly match our idealized models. So, in this chapter,

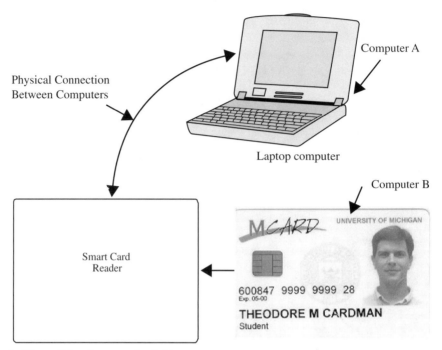

▶ **Figure 7.1**   Smart card to PC interconnect.

we're going to examine the establishment of a variety of smart card stacks for various computer systems into which we want to introduce smart cards.

As with any large-scale system these days, the goals of standardization are in the eye of the beholder. That is, if representatives from a number of different technical areas address the problem, they'll each typically try to relegate the other technologies to "commodity stuff." Such is the way it is with smart cards in large-scale application systems. In the case of PC systems, the standardization efforts have the implicit goal of arriving at an architecture as illustrated in Figure 7.2. Further, the goal is that the standardization then:

- Make all smart card readers be vendor neutral—an application should be able to work with any vendor's smart card reader.
- Make all smart cards be vendor neutral—an application should be able to make use of smart cards provided by different vendors.

We see in Figure 7.2 that we'd like to support many applications running on the PC, each of which wants to independently access a smart card. We'd like for each application to be able to use an API to establish a connection to a specific

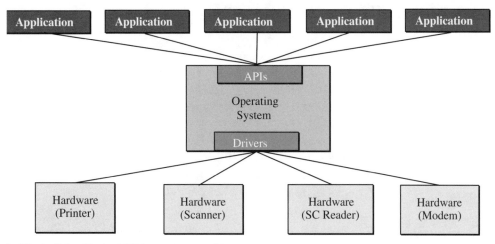

▶ **Figure 7.2**   Desired PC interconnect architecture.

smart card. The API for each smart card should have the services of the general operating system at its disposal in order to effect the desired connection with a specific smart card that is plugged into a specific smart card reader. We don't want to have to deal (at the application level) with any eccentricities of this specific smart card reader; we'd like the smart card protocol stack to make all the readers look the same.

Smart card readers are not standard elements of PC architectures. Rather, we have varieties of smart card readers that interface to PCs through standard I/O ports into the PC system; perhaps a serial port, perhaps a parallel port, perhaps some other. We expect the differences between the specific I/O port used and the specific smart card reader connected to that port, to be "normalized" by a standard device driver architecture within the operating system. Thus, again looking at Figure 7.2, a specific application connects to a specific smart card by using the intervening PC system as a general switch.

If one happens to manufacture smart card readers, or smart cards for that matter, and standardization washes out all prospects for product innovation to distinguish competitors from each other, then you have a pretty poor reason for being in the business. So, the trick is to establish standards to stabilize the marketplace and avoid application systems being forced into single source situations. However, the standards must allow sufficient space for product differentiation. These are the guiding principles of most standardization efforts, be they driven by international standards bodies, industry consortia, or even individual companies. Of course, it's the continued efforts of a wide range of participants that keeps the process (in some fashion) "honest."

SMART CARD PROTOCOL STACKS

Every smart card vendor, for many years now, has provided a proprietary software package that will allow its smart cards and smart card readers to be used on general-purpose computer systems. Over the last several years, however, a number of efforts have been initiated to develop "standard" smart card software stacks on a variety of general computer platforms. The best known and most successful of these efforts are the

- Personal Computer/Smart Card (PC/SC) Workgroup
- Open Card Framework (OCF)
- Small Terminal Interoperability Platform (STIP)

In Chapter 5, we discussed another specification called EMV. EMV is a specification for both off-card and on-card environments developed as a joint effort by Europay, MasterCard, and Visa. The specification is aimed at infrastructures for large-scale deployment of multiapplication cards based around financial transaction systems. EMV finds its way into all of the general PC-based infrastructures that we've mentioned here through the manner in which applications are named (on multiapplication cards), the way that they are accessed on multiapplication cards, and in electrical characteristics. We won't cover the EMV terminal specifications further in this book, choosing rather to concentrate on the more general smart card stacks that you'll likely encounter in smart card applications developed for general purpose computing platforms. The EMV application access methods were discussed in Chapter 5.

The OCF effort has evolved into an excellent open source platform for supporting smart cards on full-scale Java-oriented computing platforms. A quite good description of OCF is found in the book, *Smart Card Application Development Using Java* (Hansmann et al. 2000).

The PC/SC effort has evolved a smart card stack that has proven applicable to a variety of general computer platforms, and it will be the focus of our considerations in this chapter.

The STIP effort is aimed (as the name implies) at small terminal platforms, developed in Java; it is gaining popularity among terminal manufacturers. This specification is being developed through close cooperation between the STIP group and the Global Platform consortium. In the following sections, we'll primarily consider the PC/SC architecture along with a brief overview of the STIP architecture.

PC/SC

Led by Microsoft, a team of PC and smart card manufacturers including CP8 Transarc, Hewlett-Packard, Schlumberger, and Siemens-Nixdorf defined a general-purpose architecture for including smart card support in PC systems. The specification for this architecture was first published in December 1996 and is called the Interoperability Specification for ICCs and Personal Computer Systems. It has come to be known as simply PC/SC.

A primary purpose of the PC/SC architecture and specification is to enable card reader manufacturers and smart card manufacturers to develop products independently but have the results of their efforts work together smoothly. As a result of this effort, application programmers can build smart card applications that aren't tied to particular readers or cards, and system builders can mix and match readers and cards freely.

The approach used, as illustrated in Figure 7.3, involves three distinct software layers within the PC operating system. First, a series of modules each provides an API that closely corresponds to the command set supported by a specific smart card. At its simplest, each module presents a method through which an application program can send a specific APDU to a smart card where it will be executed and the results conveyed back to the application. These API modules are termed "smart card service providers" (SSP, where smart card is treated as one word, not two). We might expect to find one SSP for each smart card to be used by a PC system.

When an application accesses an SSP, the SSP provides services to generate an APDU to convey a specific command to a specific smart card. These APDUs are conveyed, by way of a well-defined API, to a second software layer within the smart card stack called the smart card resource manager. The resource manager is a broker, or a traffic cop if you will, which serves to route APDUs from an SSP to the device driver for a smart card reader into which the desired smart card is inserted. SSPs talk to the resource manager through a standard API and the resource manager talks to the device drivers for the smart card readers through a standard API. Consequently, the resource manager can connect an SSP to a smart card inserted into any available smart card reader. The readers are interchangeable.

The third layer of this smart card stack is then a set of device drivers for each smart card reader. The device drivers have to normalize away any differences between the specific I/O channels being used by the smart card reader and then be able to communicate directly with the smart card reader.

Figure 7.3 illustrates the fundamental structure of the PC/SC smart card architecture.

The PC/SC architecture defines the interface between smart card readers and the resource manager so that, from the application's point of view "looking through" the resource manager, all smart card readers look and behave the same. A smart card reader manufacturer provides along with its smart card reader hardware a PC/SC driver that connects the reader hardware to the resource manager. Thus, a smart card reader is treated by the system just like a floppy disk

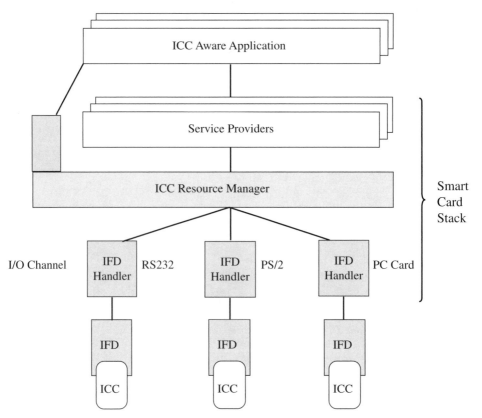

▶ **Figure 7.3**   The PC/SC architecture.

reader or a CD-ROM reader. The only difference is that you put a smart card into it rather than a floppy disk or a CD-ROM.

Because smart card readers vary more widely and can contain more functionality than a simple floppy disk reader, there is a provision in the PC/SC architecture for the application program to communicate directly with the smart card reader in addition to communicating with the smart card that it contains. This capability is indicated by the line (in Figure 7.3) directly between the application and the resource manager. This interface could be of use when, for example, the smart card reader is an automatic teller machine (ATM) or a point-of-sale (POS) terminal.

The actual application programming interface (API) seen by the smart card application is provided by the smart card service provider (SSP). This interface can be card specific, domain specific, or completely general purpose. The PC/SC specification includes a description of the general-purpose interface, which includes card authorization, PIN verification, file access, and cryptographic services. The goal of the SSP is to make it appear that a PC application is talking directly to a smart card, as illustrated in Figure 7.4.

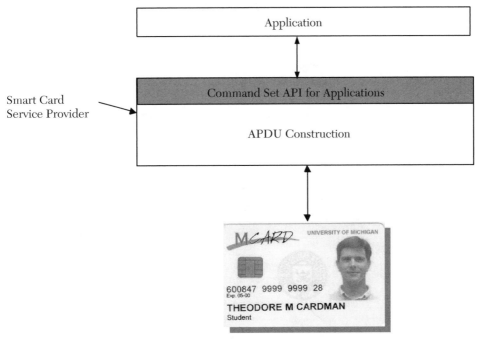

▶ **Figure 7.4**   Functional goal of a smart card service provider.

Card-specific PC/SC smart card service providers are typically written by smart card manufacturers and included with the cards themselves. Thus, for example, Gemplus provides an SSP for each of its off-the-shelf cards, as do Schlumberger and Oberthur. Minimally, these card-specific SSPs make each command supported by the card available to the application in an easy-to-use manner. Some also support some higher level functionalities that can be built from the basic commands.

As smart card application domains become more well defined through various standards and specification efforts, SSPs that support these standards and specifications have appeared. Thus, for example, we now have Java Card SSPs along with digital signature SSPs. These domain-specific SSPs not only support the processing and procedures that are characteristic of the domain, but they assume cards that contain the data structures and computing capabilities that are specified for the domain. Domain-specific SSPs are prime business opportunities for third-party smart card software companies.

A Simple SSP API

For purposes of looking at an SSP in a bit more detail, let's assume that we have a smart card which essentially supports an ISO 7816-4 command set, such as we discussed back in Chapter 4 or perhaps even the Cryptoflex card we considered in Chapter 6. This command set supports a number of security commands as well as an on-card file system and a command set to access this file system. This simple SSP API serves more as an example of how to build SSPs than it does as a commercially available and widely used smart card API. Figure 7.5 illustrates the general layout of this API. An SSP can be oriented at a specific smart card or a specific class of smart card. This class of smart card is comprised of a fixed command set with typical commands for providing smart card security functions and file access functions. In addition, the Cryptoflex smart card provides cryptographic services and these are generally available through the API as well. As we'll see a bit later in this chapter, there are at least two well-defined software modules for using tokens (smart cards) in support of general cryptographic operations. These modules require a more specific API than is considered here.

SCARD connects to the card and maintains a context in which the other functions can operate. It has two functions, `AttachByHandle` and `AttachBy-IFD`, that let the application specify a card to access and two more functions, `Detach` and `Reconnect`, to administer this connection.

The CARDAUTH interface provides functions to enable the card to authenticate the application and the application to authenticate the card. Included on this very generic interface are `GetChallenge`, `ICC_Auth`, `APP_Auth`, and `User_Auth`. `GetChallenge` returns a random data string from the card that is to be encrypted by the application and returned in the `APP_Auth` call. `ICC_Auth` sends a random string to the card that is to encrypt it and return it.

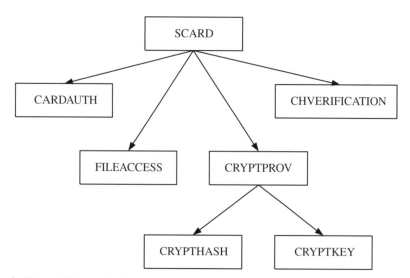

▶ **Figure 7.5**   A simple smart card service provider API architecture.

Finally, `User_Auth` is a general interface to vendor-specific routines for user authentication.

CHVERIFICATION is a collection of functions that connect to PIN functionality on a smart card. The functions on the interface are `Verify`, `ChangeCode`, `Unblock`, and `ResetSecurityState`. `Verify` presents a PIN to the card and returns success or failure. `ChangeCode` allows the cardholder by way of the application to change the card's PIN. `Unblock` lets the card's issuer unblock a PIN that has become blocked through too many unsuccessful attempts to present a PIN. Finally, `ResetSecurityState` causes a vendor-specific resetting of the PIN security on the card.

The FILEACCESS routines present the expected set of functions for manipulating files on the card. They are

- `ChangeDir`—Changes to a different directory.
- `GetCurrentDir`—Returns the name of the current directory.
- `Directory`—Returns a list of the files in the current directory.
- `GetProperties`—Returns the properties of the current file.
- `SetProperties`—Sets the properties of the current file.
- `GetFileCapabilities`—Gets capabilities of the current file.
- `Open`—Opens a file for access and makes it the current file.
- `Close`—Closes the current file.
- `Seek`—Files a data pattern in the current file.
- `Write`—Writes data into the current file.
- `Read`—Reads data from the current file.
- `Create`—Creates a file in the current directory.
- `Delete`—Deletes a file in the current directory.
- `Invalidate`—Marks a file as unavailable.
- `Rehabilitate`—Marks a file as available.

Finally, *CRYPTPROV* supports some basic routines for accessing cryptographic services on a smart card. It is not the full-fledged Microsoft Cryptographic Services API (CAPI), but rather is a smart card–centric subset of CAPI that is nonetheless quite useful for adding smart card–provided cryptographic services to an application. Functions on the *CRYPTPROV* interfaces are

- `Decrypt`—Decodes an encrypted data block using a specified key.
- `DeriveKey`—Creates keys from fixed data.
- `Encrypt`—Encodes a data block using a specified key.
- `Export`—Returns a key stored on the smart card.
- `GenKey`—Creates keys from random data.
- `GetParm`—Returns parameters being used by the routines.

- `GetRandom`—Returns random bytes.
- `GetUserKey`—Returns the public key.
- `HashData`—Computes the cryptographic hash of a stream of data.
- `HashSessionKey`—Computes the cryptographic hash of a key.
- `ImportKey`—Provides a key to the smart card.
- `SetParam`—Sets the parameters being used by the routines.
- `SignHash`—Computes the signature on a hash using an asymmetric key.
- `VerifySignature`—Verifies the signature of a hash using an asymmetric key.

The Smart Card Protocol Stack

The SSP that we considered in the previous section will prepare a set of APDUs to be conveyed to the smart card. In terms of the OSI reference model, we will think of the SSP API as an application level interface and the APDUs as the presentation layer interface. Let's now consider the rest of the smart card protocol stack from the bottom up.

In Figure 7.6, we see the elements of the PC/SC smart card protocol stack, which corresponds to the link-level layer of the OSI Reference Model. The PC I/O channel, the smart card reader, and its connection to the contact faceplate on the smart card establishes the physical layer of the stack. TPDU packets constructed within the smart card reader driver as part of its support of the T=0 or T=1 protocol are passed across this physical layer to the T=0 or T=1 software within the smart card ICC.

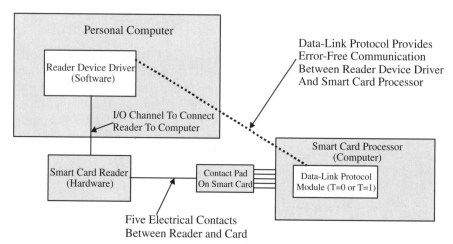

▶ **Figure 7.6**   Link and physical layers of the smart card protocol stack.

As we mentioned earlier, the smart card resource manager acts much like a traffic cop in the smart card protocol stack. Through commands from the application, the resource manager seeks to establish a link between itself and a specific smart card reader device driver, and hence on to the specific smart card. So, in terms of the OSI reference model, the connection between the resource manager and the APDU dispatcher (if you refer all the way back to Figure 3.6) is essentially a session layer connection, which is illustrated in Figure 7.7. Our ability to effect a switched network connection is found in the fact that we can extract a smart card from one reader and insert it into another reader and then have the resource manager select the smart card reader device driver for that reader. Thus, the transport and network layers of our protocol really degenerate into an essentially fixed pathway.

In Figure 7.7, we see the illustration of this session layer connection. APDUs (the presentation layer protocol) are passed from the smart card resource manager to the APDU dispatch code on the smart card. On the smart card at that point, the APDU is interpreted and the information passed to the command processor for the command corresponding to that APDU. The command is executed on the smart card by application-level code. The results of the command execution are then repacked into a response APDU structure and returned through the smart card protocol stack to the application code on the PC. This is all illustrated in Figure 7.8.

The end result from the PC/SC architecture is very much what was originally desired. We can indeed write PC smart card applications that don't have to

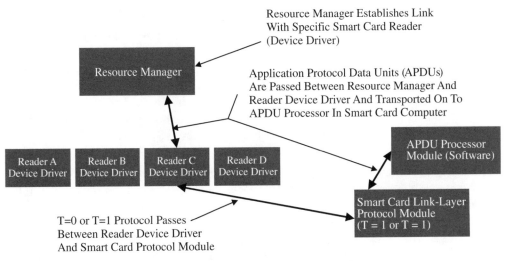

▶ **Figure 7.7**   Session layer interconnect of the smart card protocol stack.

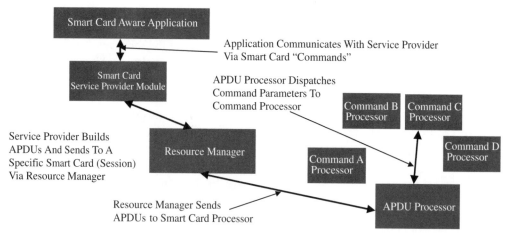

Application layer interconnect of the smart card protocol stack.

worry about the details of which smart card reader is going to be used. Further, by swapping out SSPs, it is possible to move a PC application from using one specific smart card to then use a different smart card. We'll see this explicitly in a later section when we look at cryptographic services provided through the smart card stack.

Unix PC/SC Architecture

The reference implementation for the PC/SC Specifications was built for Windows™ platforms and is now shipped with most Windows™ based systems. The wide introduction of smart cards into the personal computer and workstation arena has posed the issue of support for a number of platforms that are not as widely used as standard Windows™ systems; platforms such as the Macintosh™, Solaris™, Linux™, and other operating systems. Many corporations have a large number of these platforms that are used for specific applications, and support for these platforms is highly desirable. At first, most solutions for these platforms were proprietary and included vertical stacks that worked only with the solution providers' hardware provided.

As a work product of the PC/SC Workgroup, documentation was provided to describe the behavior of how a resource manager for smart cards and cryptographic devices should behave, independent of the PC operating system. Initial developers' packages for PC/SC included API documentation of actual function calls that applications could make to access anonymous smart card reader devices in an abstract fashion. The PC/SC standard provided an opportunity for other platforms to support smart cards in a way that would be compatible on

Windows™ platforms. In one non-Windows environment, a PC/SC stack was created by the Movement for the Use of Smart Cards in a Linux Environment (MUSCLE) group (*www.linuxnet.com*) initially to work on the Linux platform. Subsequently, a number of manufacturers and universities have adopted the MUSCLE PC/SC stack (called *PC/SC Lite*), making it available for numerous platforms, free of charge with source code included. Currently, PC/SC Lite implementations can be found on Linux, Solaris, Mac OS X, BSD, and HP-UX. The initial PC/SC Lite implementation went through many iterations while determining the best way to provide smart card services to multiple applications, cope with platform dependencies, and continue to follow the PC/SC behavior guidelines. Early versions of PC/SC Lite envisioned smart card resource managers as abstract objects in a network environment where smart card services could be accessed either in a local or a remote fashion. In Unix environments, services such as telnet, ftp, and others would require authentication for these services. Because the card and reader would generally be located in a different location than the authentication requesting host, a need for virtualization of smart card services was envisioned. A novel idea it was, yet it provided many security concerns. However, perhaps the cut was too low level. Consider the risks involved in this approach:

- Because raw application protocol data units (APDUs) could be sent anonymously to the smart card, an anonymous user could connect to a user's card remotely and call invalid `VERIFY KEY` commands blocking the user's key or PIN on the card. This would create quite a problematic denial of service attack.

- Consider an application that connects in shared mode, verifies a PIN, and waits for user input. Meanwhile a remote user connects and has complete control of the card because PIN authentication has already been met. Perhaps the remote user has just briefly stolen your identity and you never knew it.

Several measures could be taken to avoid these scenarios, including authenticating the remote host to the local machine. While attractive in theory, the mechanism is undesireable because it tends to position identity authentication outside the realm of the smart card where the security of the platforms can be questioned.

Perhaps the best way to provide remote services to a smart card is to make the cut at a higher level. Above the card or crypto service provider for the card is aware of the card's capabilities and its ability to tolerate invalid PINs. By providing a limited set of functions to the remote application, you invalidate many scenarios where remote users can engage in probing attacks.

PC/SC Lite Implementation

To develop a smart card stack on various computer O/S platforms, a local smart card resource manager was needed, and support for remote services would need to be a layered service on top of this, if desired (perhaps through ssh or gss-api). Users could choose to accept the security risk of a remote service provider instead of having it by default. To provide a cross-platform means of interprocess communication, POSIX-style domain sockets were chosen as the best means of providing this service. Sockets have novel ways of providing a queuing mechanism for application ordering. Also, with their tight kernel integration, the resource manager can detect when a client dies from a segmentation violation or even when it exits normally. This is important because a client could connect to the resource manager in shared mode, validate a PIN, and then segmentation fault or exit without closing its sessions. It may be possible for another application to connect to the card and use this validated PIN for access to other card services. With client exit detection, PC/SC Lite has a mechanism in which it will automatically reset all cards associated with a dead client immediately to deny the possibility of an inherent security risk associated with open sessions.

PC/SC Lite is written with most of the well-known GNU tools allowing it to build on most any platform where GNU tools are present. It was written in ANSI C calling conventions with little interaction with external libraries. Its core service pcscd is a daemon that runs in a privileged mode so that it can access hardware responsible for being an arbiter to multiple

- applications
- readers with multiple slots
- users
- smart card types

The pcscd daemon can be started from the command-line mode or it can be instantiated to run on startup as a background process. Its sole purpose is to make decisions. When instantiated, it follows these steps:

- allocates memory for readers and public share
- gathers information about static readers, such as serial readers
- probes the hotplug plug-in mechanism for hot pluggable readers, such as USB or PCMCIA devices
- sets up its common channel for applications to make initial requests
- listens for common channel requests

Applications connect to pcscd by linking with a small client-side library called libpcsclite.so (on Macintosh platforms by adding PCSC.framework in Project Builder). Their initial call to SCardEstablishContext will send a packet to the common channel and the server will set up a unique port for the application. This will initiate a communication channel that the application holds privately with the resource manager. Each application holds its own communication channel that the resource manager blocks on in a bit mask using a select system call. Each call to the resource manager is serialized and then executed, with the result being passed to the application. PC/SC Lite currently supports up to 16 simultaneous readers with up to 4 slots per reader. It can handle 16 applications and even manage to track the insertion and removal of new devices.

Linux Implementation

Since Unix evolved over many years, different services arose from the platform to allow functionality either locally or remotely. Most of these services would utilize the standard /etc/passwd file and perform an authentication based on passwords. Many corporations struggled with the fact that each Unix system might require different passwords for users and a particular user might need access to many Unix workstations. Some services such as NIS were introduced to help alleviate this lack of single sign-on by mapping the /etc/passwd file from a network file share. Recently, single sign-on has been introduced in Unix systems to allow pluggable authentication through the use of Pluggable Authentication Modules (PAM). PAM allows the system administrator to choose its means of authentication for a particular service. Administrators may choose to "stack" PAM modules so that multiple forms of authentication must be met in order for successful login. In order for PAM to be successful, application writers must use the PAM interface to write software to in order to accommodate this. Currently, PAM has been adopted for most Unix services including login, ftp, telnet, ssh, chfn, and xdm. Each application can have its own authentication method. An administrator may choose that login require strong authentication and ftp not as strong. In this scenario, it would be possible to have login use Kerberos for authentication and passwords for the ftp daemon. Smart card authentication can be provided through PAM in the same mechanism. The following shows an example PAM module, which for simplicity, looks for the presence of a smart card:

```
#define PAM_SM_SESSION

#include <security/pam_modules.h>
#include <winscard.h>

PAM_EXTERN int pam_sm_authenticate(pam_handle_t *pamh, int flags,
                        int argc, const char **argv) {
  LONG rv;
```

```
SCARDCONTEXT hContext;
SCARDHANDLE hCard;
SCARD_READERSTATE_A rgReaderStates;

pam_get_user( pamh, &sUser, "Login: " );

/* Connect to the smartcard subsystem */
  SCardEstablishContext(SCARD_SCOPE_SYSTEM, 0, 0, &hContext);

mszGroups = 0;
SCardListReaders( hContext, mszGroups, 0, &dwReaders );
mszReaders = (char *)malloc(sizeof(char)*dwReaders);
SCardListReaders( hContext, mszGroups, mszReaders, &dwReaders
);

rgReaderStates.szReader          = mszReaders;
rgReaderStates.dwCurrentState = SCARD_STATE_EMPTY;

/* Wait for a card to be inserted */
printf("Please insert your smartcard - ");
fflush(stdout);
SCardGetStatusChange( hContext, INFINITE, &rgReaderStates, 1 );

rv = SCardReleaseContext( hContext );

return PAM_SUCCESS;
}
```

The following is an example configuration file for using the PAM module with the login service:

```
auth      required      /lib/security/pam_smartcard.so

...
```

Many Unix applications could make use of the smart card for authentication purposes. The GSS API is used in many instances to authenticate applications that reside on different hosts. Kerberos is currently used as a means of authentication in hundreds of institutions, schools, and businesses. PAM is used on most Unix systems today as an abstract means of authentication. Smart cards will creep into these infrastructures and play a vast role in the Unix environment as the middleware and drivers mature and become available for these platforms.

Mac OS Implementation

In 2000, Apple Computer joined the PC/SC Workgroup as a core member and adopted the PC/SC Lite framework for its core smart card services. Apple's PC/SC stack would exist in its revolutionary Unix-based operating system, Mac OS X. It was necessary to provide smart card services in a way that would benefit the average Macintosh user. To do this, Apple chose widely adopted standards to support in its operating system, including CCID-based readers and Java

Card–compliant cards. OS X consists of a security framework called CDSA™, which was developed by Intel's Architecture Labs (IAL) in the mid 1990s. CDSA provides a high-level API for most security services, including certificate management, cryptographic service providers, trust policies managers, authorization policies, directory service management, and more. It was released into the open source to provide a totally open security middleware for the development of security-aware applications. By using a pluggable architecture, an application can request security services in an abstract manner and not have to worry about specific technologies. Apple's core security-aware applications make use of the high-level CDSA API, allowing vendors to plug support for their devices without modifying existing applications. One notable example is the Apple Keychain. The Keychain is an application that stores passwords from programs to ease the memories of the user. Because most users are cluttered with remembering many passwords, these are stored encrypted with a master password. By adding smart card support to the CDSA cryptographic service provider (CSP), these applications and new applications can make use of the smart card for cryptographic services. Apple also has a means of pluggable authentication to allow a user to write a pluggable module, in which a smart card can be used to authenticate to system services available under Mac OS X.

Drivers for Mac OS X follow the same guidelines, as do drivers for other Unix platforms. Because the Macintosh has deprecated the serial port for quite some time, hot pluggable USB readers are the standard reader for the Macintosh platform. Because the drivers are written in user space and not as kernel modules, it is possible to abstract much of the USB communication and have one driver code base that works on multiple platforms. The bundle architecture allows you to provide separate subdirectories for each driver library and distribute one package that works on multiple platforms for USB readers.

SSP

Above the communication layer in libpcsclite exists the application provider interface, which applications call to use the functionality of the smart card resource manager. This API, which also exists on Windows-based platforms, provides the lowest level application usable set of functions in the PC/SC stack.

Applications or service providers use the following API:

```
long SCardEstablishContext(    unsigned long   dwScope,
               const void *pvReserved1,
               const void *pvReserved2,
               long *phContext );

long SCardReleaseContext(       long hContext );

long SCardSetTimeout(             long hContext,
```

```
                                              unsigned long dwTimeout );

long SCardConnect(                              long hContext,
                const char   *szReader,
                unsigned long  dwShareMode,
                unsigned long  dwPreferredProtocols,
                long *phCard,
                unsigned long *pdwActiveProtocol );

long SCardReconnect(                       long hCard,
                                    unsigned long dwShareMode,
                unsigned long dwPreferredProtocols,
                unsigned long dwInitialization,
                unsigned long *pdwActiveProtocol );

long SCardDisconnect(                      long hCard,
                unsigned long dwDisposition );

long SCardBeginTransaction(   long hCard );

long SCardEndTransaction(      long hCard,
                               unsigned long dwDisposition);

long SCardCancelTransaction(   long hCard );


long SCardStatus(                          long hCard,
                char *mszReaderNames,
                unsigned long *pcchReaderLen,
                unsigned long *pdwState,
                unsigned long *pdwProtocol,
                unsigned char *pbAtr,
                unsigned long *pcbAtrLen );

long SCardGetStatusChange(     long hContext,
                               unsigned long dwTimeout,
                               LPSCARD_READERSTATE_A rgReader-
States,
                               unsigned long cReaders );

long SCardControl(                         long hCard,
                const unsigned char *pbSendBuffer,
                unsigned long       cbSendLength,
                unsigned char       *pbRecvBuffer,
                unsigned long       *pcbRecvLength );

long SCardTransmit(                        long hCard,
                LPSCARD_IO_REQUEST  pioSendPci,
                const unsigned char *pbSendBuffer,
                unsigned long       cbSendLength,
                LPSCARD_IO_REQUEST  pioRecvPci,
                unsigned char       *pbRecvBuffer,
                unsigned long       *pcbRecvLength );

long SCardListReaderGroups(    long hContext,
```

```
                                                          char   *msz-
Groups,
                                      unsigned long *pcchGroups );

   long SCardListReaders(              long hContext,
              const char *mszGroups,
              char *mszReaders,
              unsigned long *pcchReaders);

   long SCardCancel(                   long hContext );
```

This level of abstraction provides a clean API to communicate to a card without knowing anything about the reader. It provides a means of multiple application communication to a particular card by providing sharing and locking mechanisms so that each application can hold a transaction to a particular card for a period of time.

Reader Device Driver

Drivers for Unix follow a simple user space API. User space drivers are easy to port, easy to debug, and have equal security as kernel drivers when written properly. PC/SC Lite became popular because driver writing was a quick and easy procedure even if the programmer had no driver writing experience whatsoever. IFD Handler developer's kits are provided on the MUSCLE site with skeleton code to allow quick addition of support for other readers. All drivers can be easily written using a few functions. The following is a list of the functions used for PC/SC Lite drivers:

```
RESPONSECODE IFDHCreateChannel (  DWORD, DWORD );
  RESPONSECODE IFDHCloseChannel (   DWORD );
  RESPONSECODE IFDHGetCapabilities ( DWORD, DWORD, PDWORD,
                                          PUCHAR );
  RESPONSECODE IFDHSetCapabilities (  DWORD, DWORD, DWORD,
                  PUCHAR );
  RESPONSECODE IFDHSetProtocolParameters ( DWORD, DWORD, UCHAR,
                                          UCHAR,
UCHAR, UCHAR );
  RESPONSECODE IFDHPowerICC (         DWORD, DWORD, PUCHAR,
PDWORD );
  RESPONSECODE IFDHTransmitToICC ( DWORD, SCARD_IO_HEADER,
PUCHAR,
                                          DWORD, PUCHAR,
PDWORD,
                                          PSCARD_IO_HEADER
);
  RESPONSECODE IFDHControl (             DWORD, PUCHAR, DWORD,
                      PUCHAR, PDWORD );
  RESPONSECODE IFDHICCPresence(      DWORD );
```

These functions provide a simple, yet robust API for establishing communication to a smart card or cryptographic device. The device may even not exist as a smart card, yet it could adhere to this API and be made available in the PC/SC framework. It is important that non–smart card functionality be provided by which this API provides the IFDHControl function. This function accepts a string of bytes that the driver interprets as commands. Drivers adhere to the MCT specifications for extended services such as LCD and PIN pads.

In most Unix platforms, plug-and-play exists only for PCI, USB, and PCMCIA devices. On Windows, it is possible to have a plug-and-play serial device. Unix provides no means of plug-and-play for serial devices and, therefore, pcscd does not allow hotplugging of serial devices. These "static" devices must be specified in a configuration file called /etc/reader.conf. A typical configuration file might look like the following:

```
# reader.conf by David Corcoran

FRIENDLYNAME      "Generic Reader"
DEVICENAME        GEN_SMART_RDR
LIBPATH                  /usr/lib/readers/libgen_ifd.so
CHANNELID             0x0103F8
```

FRIENDLYNAME is the name of the reader, DEVICENAME is reserved for future use, LIBPATH is the path to the driver, and CHANNELID specifies the channel. In this example, COM1 is stated "3F8". In many instances, this mechanism for identifying readers can become cumbersome, especially if your reader is a hotpluggable reader such as a USB reader. In this case, the driver is placed in a drop folder, typically /usr/local/pcsc/drivers/. This folder includes drivers for hotpluggable readers and they are in "bundle" form. The NSBundle came from Apple's OS X as a means of providing a driver and obtaining information in an abstract manner.

The pcscd daemon uses a bundle parsing library to provide functions to bundles that would be in the general OS X distribution to provide cross-platform support for bundles. Hotpluggable drivers in the form of a bundle contain a file Info.plist, which contains XML information about the driver itself, including its name, library path, and other parameters. A typical short Info.plist file might look like the following:

```
<?xml version="1.0" encoding="UTF-8"?>
<!DOCTYPE plist SYSTEM "file://localhost/Sys-
tem/Library/DTDs/PropertyList.dtd">
<plist version="0.9">
<dict>
        <key>CFBundleDevelopmentRegion</key>
        <string>English</string>
        <key>CFBundleExecutable</key>
```

```
            <string>slbReflexUSB</string>

            <key>ifdVendorID</key>
            <string>0x04E6</string>
            <key>ifdProductID</key>
            <string>0x2004</string>
            <key>ifdFriendlyName</key>
            <string>SLB Reflex USB</string>

            <key>CFBundleInfoDictionaryVersion</key>
            <string>6.0</string>
            <key>CFBundlePackageType</key>
            <string>BNDL</string>
            <key>CFBundleSignature</key>
            <string>????</string>
            <key>CFBundleVersion</key>
            <string>0.0.1d1</string>
         <key>CSResourcesFileMapped</key>
            <true/>
  </dict>
  </plist>
```

The pcscd daemon looks at the specified vendor and product IDs in the bundle and scans for the devices on the bus to determine whether they need to be loaded or unloaded. The bundle style also allows you to distribute multiple OS drivers in the same package just by changing the Info.plist. Supporting OEM devices is as simple as changing the Info.plist. As you can see from the preceding code, there are four items necessary to inform pcscd of the reader: `ifdVendorID`, `ifd-ProductID`, `ifdFriendlyName`, and `CFBundleExecutable`.

CryptoAPI

A major use of smart cards in any general computer system, as has been intimated throughout the course of this book, is the provision of cryptographic services in support of general security infrastructures. In particular, the smart card is the best place to store a private key (of a public/private key pair) through which an individual's identity is established in a public key infrastructure. Also, the smart card, as a secure computing platform, is the best place to actually perform the digital signature operation that makes use of the private key. Today, two major cryptographic modules exist to provide application-level cryptographic services:

- CryptoAPI on Windows platforms
- PKCS-11 on Windows and other platforms

Both of these software packages can provide cryptographic services independent of any use of smart cards. However, both can also allow the use of smart cards as personalized security tokens within these systems. Let's first look at the CryptoAPI (or CAPI) architecture that is found as an integral part of the Windows systems.

Architecture. There are two levels to the CAPI architecture. The CryptoAPI itself, which offers an API comprised of a number of functions that applications can use to perform cryptographic operations. These functions allow for bulk encryption of information as well as for computation of digital signatures on bulk data structures. Many general Windows applications such as Web browsers and email readers make use of CAPI services for security. Figure 7.9 illustrates the general CAPI architecture.

API. The CAPI is a general-purpose API through which applications can gain access to cryptographic services. Just as with other standardized APIs that we've considered, this one seeks to isolate the application from any of the differences that can occur within the actual implementation of the API. In the case of cryptographic services, there are a number of ways that system services can vary.

First of all, cryptography is often subject to export restrictions in a number of countries. In some instances, cryptography can't be used at all while in others the quality of the cryptographic operaion is limited. In these instances, it is useful to be able to support what we call "strong cryptography" in some instances

Microsoft defined - Windows component

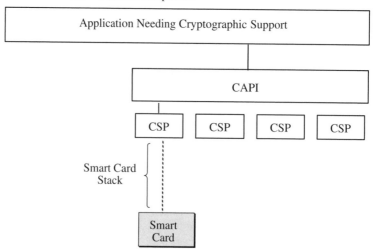

▶ **Figure 7.9**   CryptoAPI architecture.

while supporting "weak" or "exportable cryptography" in other instances. In both cases, we prefer that the application not have to know about the differences. The CAPI architecture allows us to achieve this.

Within the CAPI architecture is a layer labeled the Cryptographic Services Provider or CSP layer. The CAPI itself can actually go to any CSP for its actual cryptographic operations. So, by providing a variety of CSPs, one can wash out the differences (in cryptographic operations) from the viewpoint of the application. This mechanism allows us to use a number of different smart cards for cryptographic operations as well.

As we've learned in previous chapters, smart cards are good, secure platforms on which to store keys and do limited encryption and decryption operations. Of course, we want to be able to use smart cards from a variety of vendors. We can do this within the CAPI architecture by having a different CSP for each smart card we want to use.

CSP. The CAPI model allows for a variety of token devices to be integrated with CAPI-based applications. As you'll note in Figure 7.9, the CAPI architecture allows for a variety of CSPs to be integrated into the CAPI package. Each of these CSPs can support a single token (smart card). When an application makes a reference to the CAPI interface for some cryptographic operation, if that operation can be performed via some token, the CAPI module makes a further reference to the CSP interface for a specific token. The result is that applications can be built that make use of a token, but that token can actually be provided by a number of different vendors, without requiring any change on the part of the application.

PKCS-11

An alternative cryptographic module exists in the form of PKCS-11. Above the service to plug in a smart card or cryptographic token resides a layer for abstracting simple cryptographic operations into methods of use with public key systems. In the early 1990s, RSA Laboratories announced a new specification targeted at cryptographic devices known as PKCS-11, or Cryptoki. This standardized API gives cryptographic token abstraction, service sharing, and management of keys and data while treating the device like an object. Since the introduction of PKCS-11, it has become a widely accepted cryptographic plug-in interface and has been implemented in applications and frameworks such as Netscape and CDSA, as well as many others. It also is responsible for event notification, such as if a card or token is removed from its slot. It must convey a device's capabilities to the above application or framework so that it is known whether the currently selected device supports a particular cryptographic algorithm. It must manage PIN numbers or CHVs that are commonly used to link a key to a person with "something he or she knows." It offers cryptographic services such as digital signing, hashing, encryption/decryption, signature verification, key generation, and certification management.

Architecture. Figure 7.10 illustrates the general architecture of the PKCS-11 model. As with the CAPI model, many different applications can make use of the PKCS-11 API and therefore be insulated from differences in many aspects of how cryptographic operations are actually performed. A single PKCS-11 module can support many smart card readers and many different smart cards.

In Figure 7.10, two slightly different PKCS-11 stacks are represented. In the first, on the left of the figure, a PKCS-11 module is built on top of a standard PC/SC smart card stack. The top of the smart card stack in this case is the SSP for the specific smart card being used. By providing different SSPs, each of which actually presents the same API to the PKCS-11 package, a variety of smart cards can be used. Notice in this case that the SSP API is not a standard specification. Thus, a single PKCS-11 module provider might adopt a home-grown SSP API, but a different smart card vendor would have to gain access to that API definition if a new smart card was to be introduced. The point is that PKCS-11 doesn't have quite the same API layer definition that the CSP API represents in the CAPI arena. This is, it didn't until the definition (relatively recently) of the PKCS #15 API.

PKCS #15. PKCS #15 is a specification of a general storage facility for the objects used within PKCS #11. This storage facility can simply be a software implementation on the PC, much like the PKCS #11 module is. However, a PKCS #15 module can also make use of a token, such as a smart card, for storage of the PKCS #11 objects. So, cryptographic keys, for example, can be stored on a smart card and access a standard PKCS #15 API. This makes it fairly straightforward to build a general PKCS #11 module that can, in turn, make use of a variety of different smart cards for key storage.

The parallel between PKCS #15 and the CSP is not quite exact in that through the CSP interface one can also access cryptographic operations on the smart card.

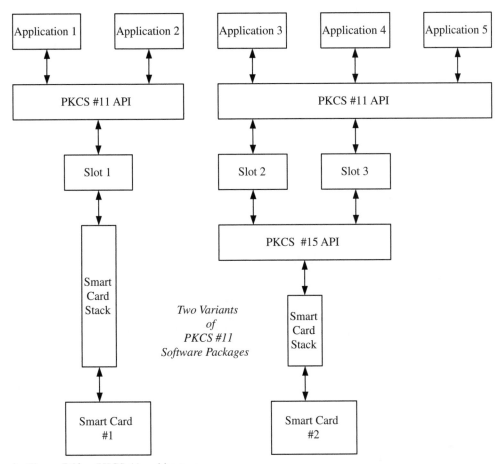

▶ **Figure 7.10** PKCS-11 architecture.

Standardizing on a Smart Card Application (Applet)

An alternative to PC side APIs is to define a portable application that provides cryptographic services. Such an applet could be written for Java Card smart cards and then loaded onto Java Card-compliant smart cards from various vendors. If an SSP is written to talk to this applet, then a true card edge interface for smart card support for cryptographic operations should be achieved. The MUS-CLE group has moved in this direction by releasing an open, card-independent specification and implementation of a Java Card applet for easy use of a smart card called the MuscleCard Cryptographic Card Edge Interface (CCEI). The idea was to provide most of the user's needs and create an applet that could be widely deployed by following the Java Card specification, thus allowing an application provider to use any (Java Card-compliant) card that follows this standard.

The applet is split into four major sections:

- key management and use
- PIN management and use
- object management and use
- utility functions

Key management and use includes all functions that would make use of cryptographic keys. These functions include, `Import`, `Export`, `GenerateKeyPair`, `Crypt`, and `ExtAuthenticate`. RSA, DSA, DES, and 3DES are currently supported.

PIN management and use includes all functions that would make use of PIN or cardholder verification (CHV). These functions include `CreatePIN`, `ChangePIN`, `VerifyPIN`, and `UnblockPIN`. Eight PIN numbers are currently supported on the card.

Object management and use includes all functions that would make use of data objects to be stored or retrieved on the card. These functions include `CreateObject`, `DeleteObject`, `ReadObject`, and `WriteObject`.

Utility functions include all functions that convey information or provide utility to the calling application. These functions include `ListKeys`, `ListPINs`, `ListObjects`, `GetRandom`, and `LogoutAll`.

STIP–SMALL TERMINAL INTEROPERABILITY PLATFORM

Another significant effort to provide a standard smart card stack comes for a group creating the STIP specification. STIP (small terminal interoperability platform) is aimed at small terminal systems, and is written in Java. The STIP architecture is illustrated in Figure 7.11.

STIP assumes a general Java environment for a terminal. It allows various applications to be written and loaded onto the terminal in a standard fashion. These applications will be portable across a variety of hardware platforms that support STIP. The STIP APIs and various hardware elements connected to the terminal can be utilized by the terminal.

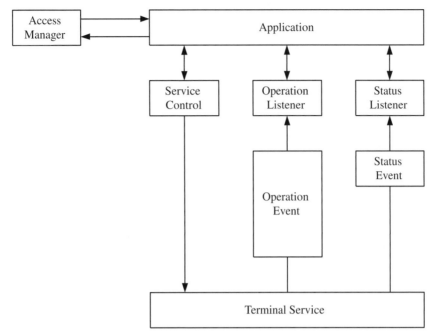

▶ **Figure 7.11**   STIP architecture.

SUMMARY

In this chapter, we've considered some aspects of smart card middleware on a variety of computer platforms. We've concentrated on the PC/SC architecture as it has been applied to both Windows platforms as well as a variety of other general computer platforms. This has provided a means of making applications independent of specific smart card readers and, to a large extent, provided for the prospect of obtaining smart cards (for a particular application) from a variety of vendors. We've looked at the use of the PC/SC specifications to build smart card stacks on many PC configurations besides Windows. In addition, we've looked at the use of smart cards to support cryptographic services in the context of a PC/SC-based smart card stack.

8

GSM and Smart Cards

INTRODUCTION

A *subscriber identification module* is a smart card that is used in a communication device. It is usually known by its acronym, SIM. There were approximately 600 million SIMs in GSM and 3G mobile phones and 70 million SIMs in DTH TV set-top boxes as of the end of 2001. SIM smart cards are being added to TDMA and CDMA mobile phones and to PDAs such as the Palm Pilot™ and the Handspring Visor™; their use as general-purpose network identity tokens is being actively explored. SIMs are by far the leading application of smart cards and the big-ticket items from most smart card manufacturers.

The SIM has two primary purposes. The first is to enable access to a particular communication network by the device (telephone handset) in which it, the SIM, has been inserted. The second is to undeniably and contractually associate the subsequent use of that network with a payment account. The first purpose is authorization and the second purpose is authentication, non-repudiation and accounting. The SIM often provides other services such as the creation of session keys for encryption and the storage of personal information such as telephone numbers.

Historically, the SIM was owned, issued, and managed by the operator of the network to which it authorized access. In particular, it was not owned by the person paying the bills for network use or by the person using the communication device. In this regard, SIM is like a bank card that is owned by the bank. But also like a bank card, as the SIM evolves to become an application platform that can contain multiple accounts and provide access to multiple (and possibly competing) networks, this is changing.

In this new model, what used to be the purpose-built SIM smart card is a bag of bits on a multiapplication and multi-issuer smart card. Not surprisingly, this has set off a scramble for who is the card's super user and has root privileges. Telecom operators are convinced that you should put your banking applications on their SIM cards. Banks are of the view that you should put your telecommunications applications on their bank cards. About the only thing they see eye-to-eye on is that person paying the piper—you—doesn't call the tune. The cardholder owned and operated "white card" is an anathema to both of them. This too is slowly changing.

Besides being a tamper-resistant place to store keys and perform cryptographic operations, the easy portability of the SIM card lets both the issuer and the subscriber move the SIM's data, including payment account information from one communication device to another and even to use this payment data in non-network settings. There is no technical reason, for example, that the same keys that protect your bits on a 3G network couldn't protect your bits on a WiFi network. In fact, there are some European GSM network operators that are doing exactly this. Pop the SIM out of your Nokia 5190® GSM handset, pop it into your Nokia C110® WiFi card, and carry on. It's all digital communications and it's always you.

The portability story of the SIM is given lie somewhat by some cellular network operators who don't want you to use another operator's SIM in the handset that comes with the packages they sell. Handsets that only work with one operator's SIM are called *locked*, or *latched*, phones because they will only work with (are locked to) SIMs from the network operator that sold you the handset. If you buy a phone from VoiceStream, for example, it will likely (as of this writing) only work with a SIM provided by VoiceStream. The cost of the handsets in these packages is heavily subsidized by the operator selling the package and they understandably want to recoup this subsidy through your use of their network. Of course, you can buy unsubsidized handsets that are not locked and can be used with any operator's SIM. Just don't typically expect to buy one from an operator.

SIMs are becoming application platforms. This seems strange at first blush for a smart card that has such a highly focused purpose and has been so financially successful fulfilling this purpose. Why add applications with dubious business models and risk upsetting the authorization applecart?

Note

The reason the SIM is programmable at all is due in no small part to the locking behavior discussed previously. In the early 1990s, a European Telecommunications Standards Institute (ETSI) technical working group was drafting specifications for a standard way to unlatch phones over the air. When wind of this activity got to the market-oversighted

Eurocrats, they saw what was essentially anticompetitive behavior being enshrined in European telecommunications standards. This caused no small amount of very official "harrumphing" in Brussels. As a result, the ETSI committee, promulgating the unlatching standards in a particularly deft piece of field reversal running, promptly rewrote the specifications as a general-purpose way of administering the SIM over the air and called the result the SIM Application Toolkit. A technique to make the phone less useful led to a technique that makes it more useful. James Burke is taking notes.

Because they protect two very valuable assets—a network and a payment obligation—SIMs are highly secure and carefully guarded computers. It may therefore seem strange that we are devoting a whole chapter of this book to building applications for them. But it is exactly because they do hold the keys—literally and figuratively—to valuable assets that make SIMs such attractive platforms for mobile applications. After all, how many other application platforms can you name that come with a worldwide communication capability, secure user identification, and microbilling; all for only about $10?

Primarily because they been around longer and because there are more of them in actual daily use, the GSM and 3G SIM currently are the most advanced of the SIMs from an application development point of view. As a result, we will focus on building applications on the GSM and 3G SIMs in this chapter. But while the details of the discussion in the chapter will pertain to these particular SIMs, the application designs, security considerations, and application development opportunities that we discuss apply by and large to SIMs wherever they are and will be found.

It is an ongoing quest of the telecommunications network operators—the current owners of SIM populations—to figure out a way to provide the services of the SIM to non-network applications without in any way compromising the SIM's network security responsibilities. The Holy Grail at the end of this quest is filled with the gold they will charge to provide these services. Initially, the operators imagined that they and only they would build these services. The success of NTT DoCoMo that flowed from energizing the independent application development community has, however, started to change this view. Applications developed by independents are now not only considered but are actively sought by the more forward-thinking network operators.

What differentiates SIM applications from handset applications based on the Wireless Application Protocol (WAP) or BREW framework is that they can be trusted. Mobile computing is about transactions, which to be of any use, must be able to be trusted and acted upon. The handset is an untrusted platform. It's fine for surfing the Web or catching the Joke–of–the–Day, but when it comes to sending a message that makes a difference—one that buys a book or boots a mail server, for example—it is more likely that the message will be trusted if it came from a SIM than if it came from the handset. Such mobile transaction applications for the SIM are the topic of this chapter.

SIM STANDARDS AND THEIR EVOLUTION

While the ISO 7816 series of smart card standards leave many points of ambiguity, the SIM standards tend to be much more complete and are implemented to the letter by the smart card manufacturers. The International Standards Organization (ISO) standards are really more conceptual than practical. There are no ISO 7816 cards because there are no ISO 7816 compliance tests. A SIM, on the other hand, is compliance-tested each time the mobile telephone is turned on. If it doesn't follow the standards, the subscriber doesn't get on the network. This makes for grumpy subscribers and even grumpier network operators. And all these grumps end up at the doorstep of the smart card manufacturer. As a result, unlike the ISO standards, interoperable applications can be built on top of the SIM standards with considerable hope that they will work when they get into the field and, what's more, work on SIMs from any smart card manufacturer.

SIM standards were originally part and parcel of the overall GSM standards set that is administered by the ETSI. Again, unlike the ISO standards, these standards are available for free download from the ETSI Web site at *www.etsi.org*. In the late 1990s, these standards were turned over to the Third Generation Partnership Program (3GPP) when GSM itself began its evolution to higher data rates and more universal usage. The 3GPP versions of these standards are also available for download from *ftp.3gpp.org*. On these Web sites, you can not only get all the current and past versions of the standards, but you also can monitor the standards meetings that are held to correct, update, and evolve them.

In early 2000, ETSI started a new project called the Smart Card Platform (SCP) to consider the use of the SIM in all telecommunications settings—not just GSM and 3G networks. The theory is that SCP will create a foundation of generic standards for the SIM and SIM applications on which the GSM and 3GPP standards for the mobile telephone can rest. The not-so-secret agenda of SCP is to build a set of standards for all smart cards that can actually be built and that will deliver on the promise of interoperability that the ISO 7816 standard really hasn't achieved. The latest versions of the SCP standards are available at *www.docbox.etsi.org/tech-org/scp/Document/scp/*.

The formation of the SCP project has led to a certain amount of confusion as the tried-and-true GSM standards were split into three parts; those being

- specific to the GSM phone and staying within ETSI
- applicable to all 3GPP phones, but not to all network devices and going to 3GPP
- common to all network devices and going to back the ETSI, but in the SCP project

No one ever said evolution with backward compatibility was either pretty or elegant.

Table 8.1 gives a snapshot of the state of a small part of evolution as of late 2001.

Table 8.1 The Evolution of Some SIM Standards

Description	GSM	3GPP	SCP
(U)SIM and IC Card Requirements		21.111	
Physical and Logical Characteristics	11.11	51.011	102.221
Characteristics of the SIM Application		31.102	
Security Mechanisms for the SAT-Stage 1	02.48		
Security Mechanisms for the SAT-Stage 2	03.48	33.102	102.225
Administrative Commands			102.222
Numbering System for Card Applications		31.110	101.220
(U)SIM Application Toolkit	11.14	31.111	102.223
UICC Application Programming Interface			102.240
SIM API for Java	03.19		102.241
SIM API for C		31.131	
USAT Interpreter		31.113	

As of 2002, this evolution is still very much underway and new entries are being made in this table on an almost-monthly basis. The reader is well advised to check with the Web sites mentioned previously for the latest version of the current standards and the arrival of new ones.

The Core Standards for Secure Mobile Applications

The seminal SIM standards are GSM 11.11 and GSM 11.14. You will hear these standards referred to frequently in discussions of the SIM. The SCP evolutions of these two oldies but goodies are ETSI TS 102.221 and ETSI TS 101.223, respectively.

GSM 11.11 is the original SIM standard and covers the SIM data files and application protocol data units (APDUs) that are sent by the handset to the SIM in establishing network access and subscriber account authentication. GSM 11.11 is based on ISO 7816-4 and certainly credits this standard to be its genesis, at least in public. As you read GSM 11.11, you will find all of your old APDU friends from ISO 7816-4. Where ISO 7816-4 is vague or provides wiggle room for proprietary implementations or hollow claims of standards compliance, GSM 11.11 is specific and says exactly how it shall be.

GSM 11.14 describes a quiet smart card revolution that took place in the mid-1990s. You will recall that from the dawn of smart card time, the smart card was the slave and the terminal was the master. The card spoke only when spoken to and did only what it was bid to do. GSM 11.14 turns history on its head and describes commands that the SIM can send to the handset. It was this document, GSM 11.14, that transformed the smart card in the GSM mobile telephone from a simple data store and session key computer to a full-fledged network-aware application platform. Two business necessities and two elegant insights into their solution provided the explosive power for this revolution.

First, when the network operator wanted to perform some administrative functions on the SIM, he couldn't very well just tell the subscriber to drop by network headquarters at an appointed time. The SIM was connected to a network device—the handset—so why couldn't the administration be done over the air? The instructions to be followed by the SIM had to go through the network and the handset right to the SIM, untouched and uninterpreted by these intermediate nodes. This brought the SIM itself onto the network. It was no longer just a peripheral on the handset, but a network node engaging in direct, end-to-end communication with network central.

Second, if the SIM was going to be a viable network node, it had to be able to initiate activity and not just be a slave to duty. Up to this time, a basic tenet of smart cards was that code running inside the smart card only needed to respond to commands from outside. GSM 11.14 introduced the radical notion that on-card code could initiate calls on services outside the card. In one flourish of the standard writer's pen, the GSM handset was transformed from a demanding master to a mere docking station.

The two technical innovations that converted these standards requirements to street realities were called *event download* and *proactive commands*. Event download requires the handset to tell the SIM about events that are taking place on the handset itself and on the network. Proactive commands let the SIM tell the handset what to do. Event download was invented by Swisscom and proactive commands were invented by BT Cellnet. For a detailed description of their discoveries, see *Mobile Application Development with SMS and the SIM Toolkit* (Guthery and Cronin, 2001).

These two new smart card usage conventions—event download and proactive commands—form the foundation of the SIM Application Toolkit, which we discuss in detail a bit later. The first convention governs the flow of information and control from the mobile equipment to the card and the second governs the flow of information and control from the card to the mobile handset. Both were simple straightforward elaborations of existing practice, but when used together, caused a revolution in the use of the GSM mobile phone.

SIM APDUs

A SIM is just a smart card with the plastic cut away so that it snuggles down inside the tiniest mobile handset. The handset reads and writes information on the SIM using the same basic ISO 7816-4 commands that we discussed in previous chapters. These APDUs are documented in detail in ETSI TS 102.221 and listed in Table 8.2.

Table 8.2 Smart Card Commands
Recognized by SIMs

CHANGE PIN

DISABLE PIN

ENABLE PIN

GET RESPONSE

INCREASE

INVALIDATE

READ BINARY

READ RECORD

REHABILITATE

SEEK

SELECT FILE

UNBLOCK PIN

UPDATE BINARY

UPDATE RECORD

VERIFY PIN

The software on the handset uses these commands in its interactions with the SIM in the process of performing various telecommunications functions. For example, it would use the READ BINARY command to read telephone numbers from the phone book on the SIM and VERIFY PIN to authenticate the warmware at the keypad.

There are five additional APDU commands that are unique to any ETSI TS 102.221 SIM. These are the APDUs that implement event download and proactive commands. They are listed in Table 8.3.

Table 8.3 Commands for Event Download
and Proactive Commands

FETCH
STATUS
TERMINAL RESPONSE
TERMINAL PROFILE
ENVELOPE

What differentiates one SIM from another, what separates the GSM SIM from the 3G SIM, or the 3G SIM from the CDMA SIM, for example, is not these everyday APDUs, but the one used for INTERNAL AUTHENTICATION. This is because each network has its own authentication protocols and cryptographic algorithms. Table 8.4 lists the authentication APDUs for some popular networks.

Table 8.4 Subscriber Authentication Commands for Various Networks

Network Technology	Authentication APDU
GSM	*RUN GSM ALGORITHM*
3G	*AUTHENTICATE*
TDMA	*INTERNAL AUTHENTICATE*
WAP	*AUTHENTICATE*

These are all variants of the INTERNAL AUTHENTICATE APDU because they are all used by the network to determine if the SIM is a SIM with which the network wants to do business. The commands are used by the network to authenticate the SIM. The details of these APDUs are particular to each network and beyond the scope of this book.

What about EXTERNAL AUTHENTICATION? How does the SIM make sure that it is dealing with a network with which it wants to do business? Recall that was what the EXTERNAL AUTHENTICATION APDU was all about. There was no provision for this in GSM networks and this turned out to be a minor problem. The situation has been addressed in 3G, but it is handled as an integral part of the internal authentication protocol so no additional external authentication APDU is needed. Interestingly enough, a very similar approach was introduced in the OP specifications and the Cyberflex Access command set we looked at in Chapter 6. That is, the authentication operation has become a mutual authentication operation. As SIMs come into use outside of strictly telecommunication settings, these APDUs will probably have to be added. So will the DECREASE APDU, but that's another story.

In this chapter, we will concentrate on the APDUs in Table 8.3 that are specific to ETSI TS 102.221 SIMs. These are the APDUs that bring applications on a SIM to life.

TERMINAL PROFILE and the SIM Service Table

How can five simple APDUs create an application platform where none existed before? There are hundreds of calls on the Windows or Linux application programming interface (API), for example. Are these guys just making heavy water?

We will discover that these five simple ETSI TS 102.221 APDUs aren't really so simple after all and that they pack a lot of information and functionality into their little frames. What is simple, however, is the model of computation for the use of these APDUs.

First, early in the initial interaction between a handset and a SIM, the handset sends the SIM the first of the five platform APDUs, the TERMINAL PROFILE APDU. The data field of this APDU tells the SIM exactly what the terminal can do. The implicit semantics of the APDU are "Here's what I, the handset, am capable of. If you ask me to do anything else, you'll get an error return." Table 8.5 is a list of the capabilities the handset can tell the SIM about in the TERMINAL PROFILE APDU. The handset sends up to 160 bits (20 bytes) to the SIM in the data field of the TERMINAL PROFILE APDU and sets a bit to 1 if it (the handset) has the associated capability and to 0 if it doesn't. This makes for a lot of information packed into a little package.

Table 8.5 Data Field of the TERMINAL PROFILE APDU

First Byte (Download):

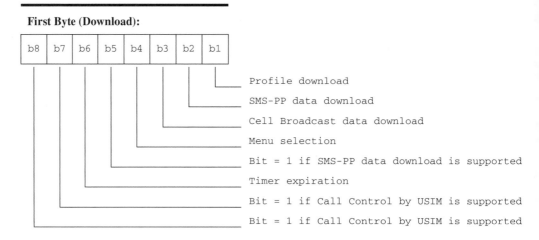

| b8 | b7 | b6 | b5 | b4 | b3 | b2 | b1 |

- Profile download
- SMS-PP data download
- Cell Broadcast data download
- Menu selection
- Bit = 1 if SMS-PP data download is supported
- Timer expiration
- Bit = 1 if Call Control by USIM is supported
- Bit = 1 if Call Control by USIM is supported

Second Byte (Other):

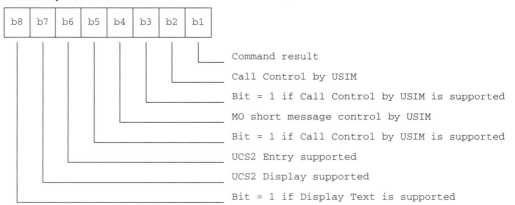

| b8 | b7 | b6 | b5 | b4 | b3 | b2 | b1 |

- Command result
- Call Control by USIM
- Bit = 1 if Call Control by USIM is supported
- MO short message control by USIM
- Bit = 1 if Call Control by USIM is supported
- UCS2 Entry supported
- UCS2 Display supported
- Bit = 1 if Display Text is supported

Third Byte (Proactive UICC):

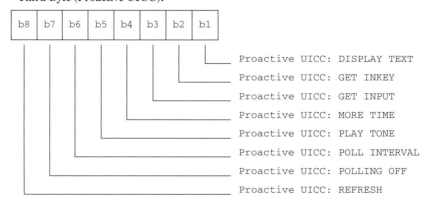

| b8 | b7 | b6 | b5 | b4 | b3 | b2 | b1 |

- Proactive UICC: DISPLAY TEXT
- Proactive UICC: GET INKEY
- Proactive UICC: GET INPUT
- Proactive UICC: MORE TIME
- Proactive UICC: PLAY TONE
- Proactive UICC: POLL INTERVAL
- Proactive UICC: POLLING OFF
- Proactive UICC: REFRESH

Table 8.5 Data Field of the TERMINAL PROFILE APDU (Continued)

Fourth Byte (Proactive UICC):

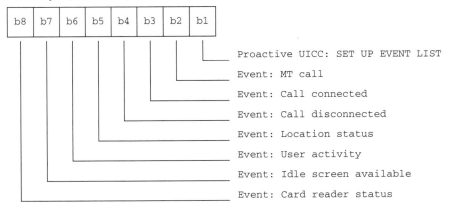

b8	b7	b6	b5	b4	b3	b2	b1

Proactive UICC: SELECT ITEM

Proactive UICC: SEND SHORT MESSAGE

Proactive UICC: SEND SS

Proactive UICC: SEND USSD

Proactive UICC: SET UP CALL

Proactive UICC: SET UP MENU

Proactive UICC: PROVIDE LOCAL INFORMATION (MCC, MNC, LAC, Cell ID & IMEI)

Proactive UICC: PROVIDE LOCAL INFORMATION (NMR)

Fifth Byte (Event-Driven Information):

b8	b7	b6	b5	b4	b3	b2	b1

Proactive UICC: SET UP EVENT LIST

Event: MT call

Event: Call connected

Event: Call disconnected

Event: Location status

Event: User activity

Event: Idle screen available

Event: Card reader status

Table 8.5 Data Field of the TERMINAL PROFILE APDU (Continued)

Sixth Byte (Event-Driven Information Extensions):

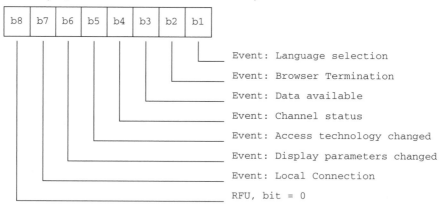

Event: Language selection
Event: Browser Termination
Event: Data available
Event: Channel status
Event: Access technology changed
Event: Display parameters changed
Event: Local Connection
RFU, bit = 0

Seventh Byte (Multiple Card Proactive Commands) for Class "A":

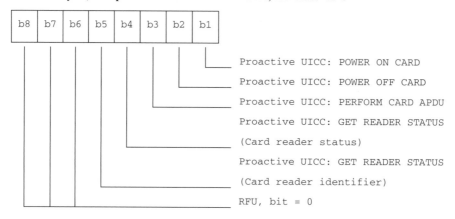

Proactive UICC: POWER ON CARD

Proactive UICC: POWER OFF CARD

Proactive UICC: PERFORM CARD APDU

Proactive UICC: GET READER STATUS
(Card reader status)

Proactive UICC: GET READER STATUS
(Card reader identifier)

RFU, bit = 0

Table 8.5 Data Field of the TERMINAL PROFILE APDU (Continued)

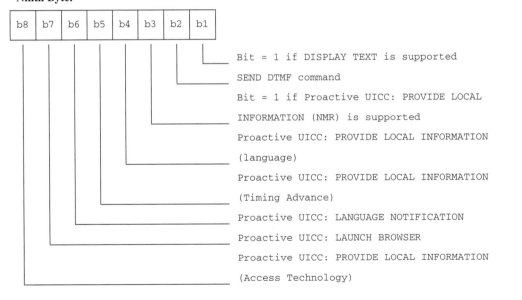

Eighth Byte (Proactive UICC):

b8	b7	b6	b5	b4	b3	b2	b1

Proactive UICC: TIMER MANAGEMENT (start, stop)

Proactive UICC: TIMER MANAGEMENT (get current value)

Proactive UICC: PROVIDE LOCAL INFORMATION (date, time and time zone)

Bit = 1 if GET INKEY is supported

SET UP IDLE MODE TEXT

RUN AT COMMAND (i.e. class "b" is supported)

Bit = 1 if SETUP CALL by USIM is supported

Bit = 1 if Call Control by USIM is supported

Ninth Byte:

b8	b7	b6	b5	b4	b3	b2	b1

Bit = 1 if DISPLAY TEXT is supported

SEND DTMF command

Bit = 1 if Proactive UICC: PROVIDE LOCAL INFORMATION (NMR) is supported

Proactive UICC: PROVIDE LOCAL INFORMATION (language)

Proactive UICC: PROVIDE LOCAL INFORMATION (Timing Advance)

Proactive UICC: LANGUAGE NOTIFICATION

Proactive UICC: LAUNCH BROWSER

Proactive UICC: PROVIDE LOCAL INFORMATION (Access Technology)

Table 8.5 Data Field of the TERMINAL PROFILE APDU (Continued)

Tenth Byte (Soft Keys Support) for Class "D":

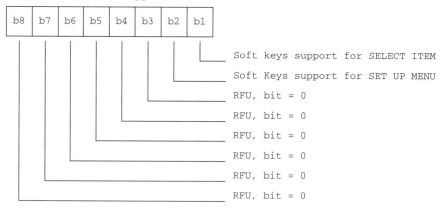

Soft keys support for SELECT ITEM

Soft Keys support for SET UP MENU

RFU, bit = 0

RFU, bit = 0

RFU, bit = 0

RFU, bit = 0

RFU, bit = 0

RFU, bit = 0

Eleventh Byte (Soft Keys Information):

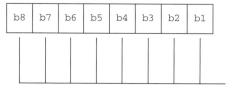

Maximum number of soft keys available
'FF' value is reserved for future use

Twelfth Byte:

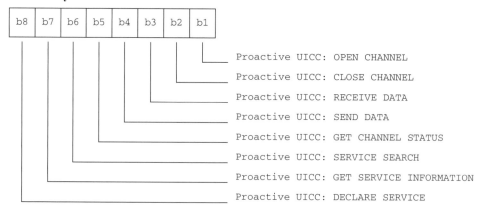

Proactive UICC: OPEN CHANNEL

Proactive UICC: CLOSE CHANNEL

Proactive UICC: RECEIVE DATA

Proactive UICC: SEND DATA

Proactive UICC: GET CHANNEL STATUS

Proactive UICC: SERVICE SEARCH

Proactive UICC: GET SERVICE INFORMATION

Proactive UICC: DECLARE SERVICE

Table 8.5 Data Field of the TERMINAL PROFILE APDU (Continued)

Thirteenth Byte:

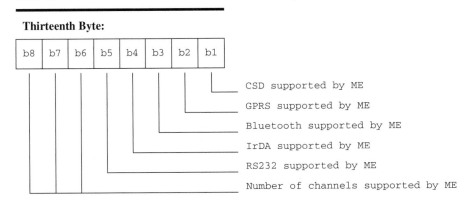

Fourteenth Byte (Screen Height):

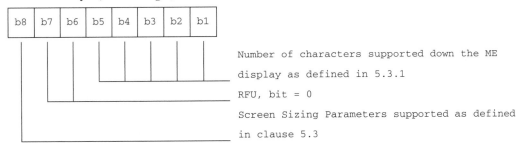

Fifteenth byte (Screen Width):

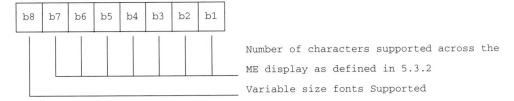

Table 8.5 Data Field of the TERMINAL PROFILE APDU (Continued)

Sixteenth Byte (Screen Effects):

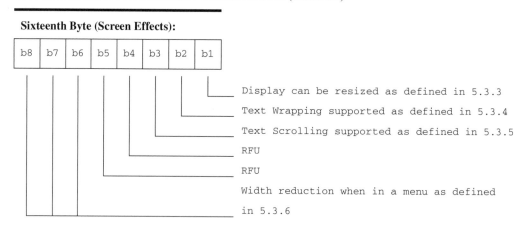

Display can be resized as defined in 5.3.3

Text Wrapping supported as defined in 5.3.4

Text Scrolling supported as defined in 5.3.5

RFU

RFU

Width reduction when in a menu as defined in 5.3.6

Seventeenth Byte:

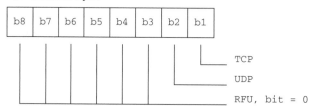

TCP

UDP

RFU, bit = 0

Eighteenth Byte:

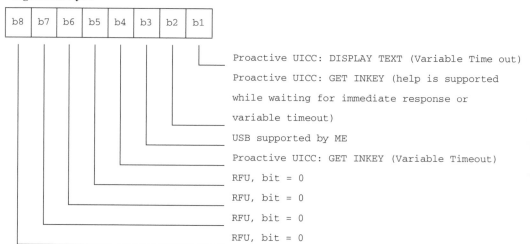

Proactive UICC: DISPLAY TEXT (Variable Time out)

Proactive UICC: GET INKEY (help is supported while waiting for immediate response or variable timeout)

USB supported by ME

Proactive UICC: GET INKEY (Variable Timeout)

RFU, bit = 0

RFU, bit = 0

RFU, bit = 0

RFU, bit = 0

Table 8.5 Data Field of the TERMINAL PROFILE APDU (Continued)

Nineteenth Byte (Reserved for TIA/EIA-136 Facilities):

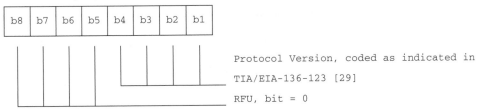

Twentieth Byte (Reserved for TIA/EIA/IS-820 Facilities):

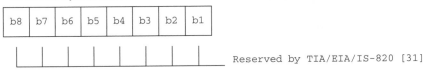

The TERMINAL PROFILE APDU is half of the getting-to-know-you protocol. The other half is the terminal finding out what the SIM can do. The terminal accomplishes this by using a plain old READ BINARY APDU to read the contents of a file called the SIM service table. This is file "6F38" in the SIM ADF. Table 8.6 lists the format of this file. Just like the TERMINAL PROFILE data field, the SIM sets a bit to 1 in this file if it can perform a particular function and to 0 if it can't. Table 8.7 gives the services.

Table 8.6 Format of the SIM Service Table Transparent File (from 3GPP TS 31.102)

Nth Byte:

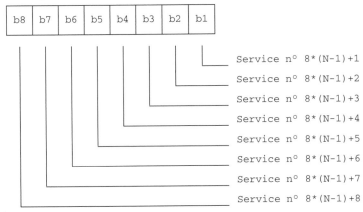

Table 8.7 Services Indicated in the SIM Service Table

Services
Services
Service n°1:   Local Phone Book
Contents:
Service n°2:   Fixed Dialing Numbers (FDN)
Service n°3:   Extension 2
Service n°4:   Service Dialing Numbers (SDN)
Service n°5:   Extension 3
Service n°6:   Barred Dialing Numbers (BDN)
Service n°7:   Extension 4
Service n°8:   Outgoing Call Information (OCI and OCT)
Service n°9:   Incoming Call Information (ICI and ICT)
Service n°10:   Short Message Storage (SMS)
Service n°11:   Short Message Status Reports (SMSR)
Service n°12:   Short Message Service Parameters (SMSP)
Service n°13:   Advice of Charge (AoC)
Service n°14:   Capability Configuration Parameters (CCP)
Service n°15:   Cell Broadcast Message Identifier
Service n°16:   Cell Broadcast Message Identifier Ranges
Service n°17:   Group Identifier Level 1
Service n°18:   Group Identifier Level 2
Service n°19:   Service Provider Name
Service n°20:   User-Controlled PLMN Selector with Access Technology
Service n°21:   MSISDN

Table 8.7 Services Indicated in the SIM Service Table (Continued)

Service n°22:	Image (IMG)
Service n°23:	Not Used (Reserved for SoLSA)
Service n°24:	Enhanced Multilevel Precedence and Pre-emption Service
Service n°25:	Automatic Answer for eMLPP
Service n°26:	RFU
Service n°27:	GSM Access
Service n°28:	Data Download via SMS-PP
Service n°29:	Data Download via SMS-CB
Service n°30:	Call Control by USIM
Service n°31:	MO-SMS Control by USIM
Service n°32:	RUN AT COMMAND Command
Service n°33:	Shall Be Set to "1"
Service n°34:	Enabled Services Table
Service n°35:	APN Control List (ACL)
Service n°36:	Depersonalization Control Keys
Service n°37:	Cooperative Network List
Service n°38:	GSM Security Context
Service n°39:	CPBCCH Information
Service n°40:	Investigation Scan
Service n°41:	MExE
Service n°42:	Operator-Controlled PLMN Selector with Access Technology
Service n°43:	HPLMN Selector with Access Technology

Table 8.7 Services Indicated in the SIM Service Table (Continued)

Service n°44:	Extension 5
Service n°45:	PLMN Network Name
Service n°46:	Operator PLMN List
Service n°47:	Mailbox Dialing Numbers
Service n°48:	Message Waiting Indication Status
Service n°49:	Call Forwarding Indication Status
Service n°50:	RPLMN Last-Used Access Technology
Service n°51:	Service Provider Display Information

At the end of this mutual introduction phase of the SIM Toolkit model of computation, the handset and the SIM each know what the other can do and will avoid asking the other to do something that it knows it can't do. Now they can get down to work.

Recall that the two technical capabilities that we are creating are event download and proactive commands. Event download is where the terminal tells the SIM about something that happened—an event of some sort. Proactive commands are where the SIM tells the handset to do something. The ENVELOPE APDU implements event download and the FETCH, TERMINAL RESPONSE, and STATUS APDUs implement proactive commands. Let's look at event download first because that's the easy one.

Event Download

The ISO 7816-3 T=0 and T=1 communication protocols between the handset and the SIM let the handset talk to the SIM just about anytime it wants to. It just sends the SIM an APDU. In order to tell the SIM about an event, it uses the escape APDU from ISO 7816-4, the ENVELOPE APDU. The ENVELOPE APDU was first defined as a way to overcome deficiencies in the secure messaging mechanisms of ISO 7816-4; however, it is a way to send a random undifferentiated blob of data to a smart card. Unlike UPDATE RECORD or VERIFY PIN, which carry data intended for a specific use, namely the use defined by the APDU, the semantics of ENVELOPE are more like "Here's a blob of data. I assume you know what to do." What GSM 11.14 and ETSI 102.223 do is organize and give meaning to the data field of the ENVELOPE APDU when it is sent to a SIM smart card.

As you recall, ISO 7816-4 establishes, roughly speaking, a one-to-one relationship between what you want the card to do and a command to ask it to do it.

READ BINARY reads from a file, VERIFY PIN checks a PIN value, and so forth. But the folks that wrote ISO 7816-4 understood well that they couldn't imagine all possible uses of a smart card, so they built themselves and all the rest of us an escape hatch to the future: the ENVELOPE command. The design intent of ENVELOPE was to be able to put proprietary and special-purpose information and commands inside a standard ISO 7816 command "envelope" in order to transmit them to the card.

In keeping with the over-arching policy of being as compatible as possible with existing smart card standards, the authors of GSM 11.14 chose the ENVE-LOPE command to get all sorts of non-APDU–based information to the SIM. Thus, whether it is message traffic coming from the user, the handset, or somewhere out on the network, it is moved to the SIM tucked inside an ENVELOPE command. There are a number of different variants of the SIM ENVELOPE command, but the three primary ones correspond to these three sources of message traffic for the SIM. We discuss these immediately after we look at the ENVELOPE command itself.

The syntax of the ISO 7816-4 ENVELOPE APDU is simplicity itself:

Command	Class	INS	P1	P2	P3	Data Field
ENVELOPE	$A0_{16}$	$C2_{16}$	00_{16}	00_{16}	n	Blob of n bytes of undifferentiated data

There is no P1 or P2—just a CLA and an INS, a length, and a data field. The entire message to be loaded into the smart card—in the case at hand, the SIM—is put into the data field. The thinking was that if you wanted to dream up a new smart card command, you could still use all the smart card readers in the field by encapsulating or tunneling your command in the ENVELOPE command.

The first type of SIM event download ENVELOPE APDU is for messages from the user and is called ENVELOPE (MENU SELECTION). The data field contains an index of the menu item that was selected and assumes that the SIM kept track of the list of choices that were offered to the user.

The second type of event comes from the handset itself and consists of the handset informing the card of events that are taking place upstairs. Examples of such events are pressing a key or initiating a call. An ENVELOPE APDU that contains such event notifications is called ENVELOPE (EVENT DOWNLOAD).

The final type of the ENVELOPE APDU for events originating in the network (e.g., the host-side or off-card component of your application sitting on a server somewhere) is called ENVELOPE (SMS-PP DOWNLOAD).

Of the three event types, SMS-PP DOWNLOAD is the most useful and the most powerful from the point of view of application construction. Using this event download, the off-card application communicates with the on-card application by sending it a short message using the network's short message system

(SMS). Coding in the SMS message tells the handset to pack the entire SMS message into an ENVELOPE command and pass it onto the SIM. SMS-PP DOWNLOAD can also be used to load new applications onto the SIM.

Table 8.8 is a list of the all the event download ENVELOPEs defined in 3GPP TS 31.111. There are 13 for event notification, 2 for short message reception, 2 for call control, and 1 each for menu selection and timer expiration.

Table 8.8 ENVELOPE *Commands* in 3GPP TS 31.111

ENVELOPE (SMS-PP DOWNLOAD)
ENVELOPE (CELL BROADCAST DOWNLOAD)
ENVELOPE (OUTGOING CALL CONTROL)
ENVELOPE (OUTGOING SHORT MESSAGE CONTROL)
ENVELOPE (TIMER EXPIRATION)
ENVELOPE (MENU SELECTION)
ENVELOPE (EVENT DOWNLOAD – Incoming Call)
ENVELOPE (EVENT DOWNLOAD – Call Connected)
ENVELOPE (EVENT DOWNLOAD – Call Disconnected)
ENVELOPE (EVENT DOWNLOAD – Location Status)
ENVELOPE (EVENT DOWNLOAD – User Activity)
ENVELOPE (EVENT DOWNLOAD – Idle Screen Available)
ENVELOPE (EVENT DOWNLOAD – Card Reader Status)
ENVELOPE (EVENT DOWNLOAD – Language Selection)
ENVELOPE (EVENT DOWNLOAD – Browser Termination)
ENVELOPE (EVENT DOWNLOAD – Data Available)
ENVELOPE (EVENT DOWNLOAD – Channel Status)
ENVELOPE (EVENT DOWNLOAD – Access Technology Change)
ENVELOPE (EVENT DOWNLOAD – Display Parameters Change)

The innovation in event download wasn't in the invention of new technique or the promulgation of a new standard. It was using a piece of existing smart card technology, the ENVELOPE APDU, for a revolutionary purpose: to carry information from outside the SIM to inside the SIM to enable the SIM to respond to this information based on the policies it contained. The original use for which Swisscom invented event download was to silently let the SIM redirect calls being placed on the handset in order to use the network more efficiently. When combined with proactive commands that we describe next, event download turns the SIM from a passive data store into an integral and interactive part of the mobile application framework.

The "91 XX" Status Word

Even with event download, the SIM is still reactive rather than proactive. It can react to the events that it is told about but it can't create an event. You can easily imagine tinkering with the communication protocol between the handset and the SIM to let the SIM initiate communication, but any changes had to be a graceful evolution of the existing SIM because new SIMs had to work in all the old handsets. In particular, a proactive SIM had to live within the ISO 7816-4 framework on which the existing SIMs were built. This meant that at the lower levels of the communication protocol, the handset had to be the master and the card was still the slave.

In order to turn the tables at the higher levels, Colin Hamling of BT Cellnet, then vice-chairman of SMG9, the ETSI committee charged with solving the over-the-air unlatching problem, proposed something very modest and innocent but with far-reaching consequences: a new status word.

Here are the words taken directly from GSM 11.14 version 5.9.0 Release 1996 that gave the SIM a voice:

> *"The response code '91 XX' shall indicate to the ME that the previous command has been successfully executed by the SIM in the same way as '90 00' (i.e., "OK"), but additionally it shall indicate response data which contains a command from the SIM for a particular ME procedure (defined in subclause 6.4)."*

In other words, upon receiving a "0x91xx" status code, the handset is now obliged to respond with a FETCH APDU to find out what the card wants it, the handset, to do... and, what's more, it was obliged to do it. Gasp! The slave presumes to issue commands to the master.

Thus, at the lower levels of the T=0 protocol, the handset was still the master, but at the upper levels, the smart card was now in charge. This modest and yet elegant addition to the set of ISO 7816-4 status words transformed the SIM from a floppy disk with an attitude to a secure mobile computer with a perfectly useable human interface and some truly awesome communication capabilities. But one more conceptual leap had to be taken before this would be an application platform. Kristian Woodsend, who worked for Colin Hamling at the time, took this leap.

What had to happen was that the commands the SIM could give to the handset had to be standardized. This standardization, together with the standardization of event downloads, would mean that any SIM with applications could work with any handset. This was where we started when the SIM was just a data store and this had to be where we ended when the SIM became an application platform.

The Birth of the SIM Application Toolkit

The recognition of the need for a general way to build mobile applications using the SIM was in the air in the middle of 1994. Up to that time, each new SIM application required application-specific and often operator-specific modifications to the handset; this was obviously a very large impediment to rolling out new applications. A general-purpose way to control the phone from the SIM had been discussed briefly at SMG9 #2 of that year and a work item titled "Proactive SIM" approved at the SMG9 #12 plenary meeting.

At the same time, discussions were being held within SMG9 on a general-purpose and standardized way to extend Swisscom's "SicapNATEL" technique for the data on the SIM. This work item was called "SIM Data Download." The synergy between these two work items was quickly realized—applications needed to be able to catch data and downloaded data needed someone to catch it. These two tasks were combined in early 1995 into the SIM Application Toolkit work item, which was approved at the SMG9 #14 plenary meeting.

The description of the SIM Application Toolkit work item was:

> "A set of facilities which allow the SIM to interact with external entities (e.g., the network, the mobile equipment, or the user) to enable value-added applications to exist in the SIM."

Colin Hamling was the rapporteur of the original SIM Application Toolkit work item but this duty was passed to Kristian Woodsend, also of BT Cellnet, at SMG9 #6 in September 1995. Kristian set to work to create the first draft of GSM 11.14, which was to combine the ideas of Swiss Telecom PTT for data download, the need for standardized unlatching, and above all else, a standard way for the SIM to give commands to the handset. The first draft of GSM 11.14 was presented to SMG9 #7 at the end of November 1995, a mere two months later.

A GSM handset was already obliged to send a STATUS APDU to the SIM every 30 seconds. The primary purpose of the STATUS command was to make sure the SIM was still there. If it wasn't, the call that was in progress was immediately terminated and the handset dropped off the network. With this new status word, if the card had a command waiting for the handset, it would respond to the STATUS command with a "91xx" as previously. Otherwise, it would just respond with "9000" as before.

So that's the story of five little APDUs and how they turned the SIM smart card from a data store into an application platform: TERMINAL PROFILE, to tell the SIM about the capabilities of the docking station it has been plugged into; the event download ENVELOPE, to tell it what is going on; a new status word with two new APDUs, FETCH and TERMINAL RESPONSE, to let it initiate action; and finally, an update of the STATUS APDU to let it get a word in edgewise. This is a motley set of technical bits and pieces to be sure, but when working together, they create what could turn out to be the salvation of many a network operator's business: a mobile application platform. The remainder of this chapter is about putting this motley crew to work for your applications.

The Card Application Toolkit

Things have moved on since GSM 11.14. The proactive command set is now called the Card Application Toolkit and the commands themselves are codified in ETSI TS 102.223, which is under the care of ETSI's Smart Card Platform project.

Table 8.9 contains a list of the 32 proactive commands defined in the latest version of ETSI TS 102.223.

Table 8.9 The 32-Card Application Toolkit Proactive Commands

CLOSE CHANNEL
DECLARE SERVICE
DISPLAY TEXT
GET CHANNEL STATUS
GET INKEY
GET INPUT
GET READER STATUS
GET SERVICE INFORMATION
LANGUAGE NOTIFICATION

Table 8.9 The 32-Card Application Toolkit
Proactive Commands (Continued)

LAUNCH BROWSER

MORE TIME

OPEN CHANNEL

PERFORM CARD APDU

PLAY TONE

POLL INTERVAL

POLLING OFF

POWER OFF CARD

POWER ON CARD

PROVIDE LOCAL INFORMATION

RECEIVE DATA

REFRESH

RUN AT COMMAND

SELECT ITEM

SEND DATA

SEND DTMF

SEND SHORT MESSAGE

SERVICE SEARCH

SET UP CALL

SET UP EVENT LIST

SET UP IDLE MODE TEXT

SET UP MENU

TIMER MANAGEMENT

Even without knowing the details of these commands, you can see that there is a lot that your mobile application can do. The Card Application Toolkit is a very rich application development environment, far richer, for example, than the WAP application environment. You can find all the grisly details in ETSI TS 102.223, but a couple of these commands deserve a brief description here so you can get a sense of what is possible.

The POLLING INTERVAL command lets you set how frequently the handset polls the SIM with the STATUS command. You can't set it to a value less than the 30 seconds called for in other GSM standards, but if you have a lot of work for the handset to do, you can set the interval to less than 30 seconds. An issue that hasn't yet been fully resolved is: Who is ultimately in charge here? The handset? The 11.11 part of the SIM? The SIM application? The WAP browser? The network? The user? The PC to which the handset is connected? The server sending commands to the SIM? There are a lot of entities demanding space on the screen and the user's attention and virtually no machinery in place for them to coordinate or cooperate their activities.

The POWER ON CARD, PERFORM CARD APDU, and POWER OFF CARD commands are all meant to let the application on the SIM control and communicate with another smart card plugged into the handset. POWER ON and POWER OFF obviously tell the handset to provide power to the second card and to remove power from the second card, respectively. The PERFORM CARD APDU lets the SIM send an APDU to the second card by way of the handset.

The TERMINAL RESPONSE to this command is the reply of the second card. The vision was that the second card could be a credit card or an e-cash card of some sort that could be used in conjunction with SIM applications to conduct e-commerce. Unfortunately, dual-slot handsets haven't become widely available, so this vision is still more of a dream than a reality.

The PROVIDE LOCAL INFORMATION command lets the SIM application acquire data about the current environment from the handset. Included in the data available is information about the current location of the handset so that the SIM application can be sensitive to the geography in which it finds itself. These are called location-based applications, and there is a lot of work going on in this area. The resolution of the mobile's location available to the SIM is not as good as, say, GPS or even what is available to the network operator, but it is a beginning and certainly sufficient to get the creative juices flowing.

DISPLAY TEXT, GET INKEY, GET INPUT, PLAY TONE, SELECT ITEM, SETUP IDLE MODE TEXT, and SETUP MENU are all human interface commands that access the screen and the keypad on the handset. While there are certainly standards for handsets as well as for the SIM card, they aren't so tight that you can write fully handset-independent applications. There is still enough variation in screen size, display capability, and keypad layout that you will want to test your SIM application with a number of different handsets before you send it out into the world.

OPEN CHANNEL, RECEIVE DATA, SEND DATA, GET CHANNEL STA-TUS, and CLOSE CHANNEL enable your SIM application to communicate with servers out on the Internet. There is not yet a full TCP/IP stack on the SIM but this is coming.

Finally, SEND DTMF, SEND SHORT MESSAGE, SEND SS, SEND USSD, and SETUP CALL provide the means for your application to communicate with the outside world using the telephone network as opposed to the Internet. Of particular note is SEND SHORT MESSAGE, which enables your application to send a text message of up to 140 characters to any other GSM phone. SETUP CALL opens a voice channel to any other telephone number and SEND DTMF sends the touch pad tones down the wire. You can doubtless imagine some creative uses of this capability.

The Card Application Toolkit is a very capable application platform that provides some unique and very useful services to your mobile application. It is understandable why network operators don't let just anybody download applications to their SIMs. In fact, getting your applications into use—and thus turning them into money—will loom as just as big a challenge as creating the applications in the first place.

PROGRAMMING LANGUAGE BINDINGS FOR THE CARD APPLICATION TOOLKIT

From a technical perspective, there are two kinds of SIM applications: ones that are translated into the hardware instructions of the SIM microprocessor and ones that are translated into byte codes that are interpreted by an interpreter program installed on the SIM. Interpreted applications can be loaded onto and deleted from the SIM more easily than native code applications, but they run up to an order of magnitude slower than native code applications, depending on how much of the application is done by underlying "system code," which is invoked from the interpreted application.

Whether it is translated into microprocessor instructions or interpreted byte codes, an application is written in a programming language against an API. The generic programming API for applications on the Card Application Toolkit is codified in ETSI TS 102.240 "UICC Application Programming Interface (API)." Language-specific bindings of this generic API have been produced for a number of procedural programming languages, including Visual Basic, C, Java, and Modula.

Recently, however, what may ultimately be the winning programming paradigm for creating and deploying SIM-based mobile applications, has emerged. It is called the USAT Interpreter. Rather than supporting procedural programming languages such as Visual Basic or Java, the USAT Interpreter takes a cue from the success of the World Wide Web and focuses on markup languages that have been designed specifically for mobile applications such as HDML, cHTML, WML, and XHTML. A USAT Interpreter application is a series of pages that are sent to the mobile phone in SMS messages. The USAT Interpreter interprets each page just like your desktop browser interprets HTLM pages it retrieves from the Web. (This is why the USAT Interpreter is sometimes called a SIM microbrowser.) After the USAT Interpreter has processed a page, the page is thrown away and another page of the application is retrieved from the network.

The USAT Interpreter approach to mobile applications has a number of very attractive characteristics from the point of view of the network operators. It may also more closely model the intrinsic nature of mobile applications than a procedural language program.

There are three things that make USAT Interpreter applications an attractive alternative to procedural language applications to a network operator:

- *The administration costs of USAT Interpreter programs are much lower than those of procedural language programs.* The USAT Interpreter's "fire and forget" model of computation means that applications don't have to be installed on the SIM and linked into the SIM Toolkit framework. Loading and installing SIM Application Toolkit programs understandably involves a lot of fancy cryptography and procedural safeguards because live code is being added to the SIM. The cost of these administrative procedures is avoided with USAT Interpreter programs because an interpreter page is just held in a temporary buffer while it is being processed. Of course, if you turn off the phone, the pages go away. For a network operator, this is a feature, not a bug.
- *A USAT Interpreter program doesn't take up any of the precious EEPROM space on the SIM because it isn't installed permanently.* This means that there is plenty of room for telephony data such as phonebooks, dialing policies, and routing and roaming data. It also means that the subscriber can change his or her mind about what mobile applications he or she wants to use without contacting the operator's SIM administration system. This is much more convenient for the subscriber and much more efficient for the operator.
- *A USAT Interpreter program has regularization and control of the user interface.* Customer care centers are expensive to operate. They are a

necessary part of doing business, but each call to a customer care center is money down the tubes. If a subscriber has problems with a mobile application, they aren't going to call the provider of the program. They are going to call the operator's customer care center.

It is hard to tell by analyzing a procedural language program what the user experience with the program will be. It's even harder to build a procedural language program that adapts itself to the human interface style policies of different operators. Exactly the opposite is true of markup language programs. A markup language page in a sense *is* the human interface to the page. And each operator can publish markup language style templates that describe and enforce the user experience with that particular operator's applications. Applications just add data to these templates. The human interface stays consistent, just the application context and task change. The requirements of the network operators are exactly why markup languages were invented. The operator controls the presentation and the application provider controls the content.

Table 8.10 lists the standards documents that define the USAT Interpreter. Full-text markup language pages are converted to USAT Interpreter byte codes for efficient transmission and execution but this is purely a behind-the-scenes process as far as the application provider is concerned. All the application provider has to do is put the pages for his or her application on an Internet server. The network operator takes it from there.

Table 8.10 3GPP Standards Describing the USAT Interpreter

Number	Title
3GPP TS 22.112	USAT Interpreter Stage 1
3GPP TS 31.112	USAT Interpreter Stage 2
3GPP TS 31.113	USAT Interpreter Byte Codes
3GPP TS 31.114	USAT Interpreter Transmission Protocol and Administration

That's just like WAP, you say. Yes, but there is one very big difference. A SIM-originated transaction is secured and can be trusted and acted upon. A handset-originated transaction is not secure because the handset is not a trusted computing platform. You trust it at your own risk. There's a reason the WIM card was added to WAP after all. USAT Interpreter transactions are WIM transactions without the overhead of WAP.

EXAMPLE: THE RAPID REORDER APPLICATION

To make the building of SIM Application Toolkit applications concrete, we will develop a simple example.

Imagine that you are the proprietor of a small convenience store or even a street vendor. You have a small inventory of items to sell and, within that small inventory, there are items that move very quickly. For a number of reasons, not the least of which is that you can't afford to, you don't keep a lot of inventory on the shelf or in your cart. When you start to run short of an item, you want to call the distributor of the item and get delivery quickly.

You've got a 3G mobile phone and, of course, you could place a voice call, but the person you'd speak with is a significant added expense for the distributor and really only listens to what you are saying and fills out a form on a screen. The screen contents then get translated into a transaction on an inventory and delivery scheduling system.

Why not just move that screen from the distributor to your mobile phone and do away with the slow, error-prone mouth-to-ear communication link? You can fill out the form right on the phone and then have the application on the phone send the transaction directly into the inventory and delivery system. This works because the number of items is small and the list of items is relatively fixed. We will call this the *Rapid Reorder application* and we will develop both the part that sits on the SIM in the mobile phone and the part that sits on the servers of the various distributors from whom inventory is ordered.

In the world of our example, the distributors have trucks with inventory in them, always on the move in the field. Transactions that you send in from your mobile phone are immediately sent to the drivers of these trucks after being run through the billing department, of course. The truck closest to you is on its way to you with your order as soon as you press the Send key.

Interaction with the on-card (mobile phone) Rapid Reorder application looks like this:

1. Pick the Rapid Reorder application from the list of applications on the SIM chip.
2. Scroll down the list of presented product categories (Dairy Products, Cold Drinks, Cold Cuts, Chip Products, etc.) and pick the category from which you are ordering.
3. Within the product category chosen, pick the product you are ordering (2% Milk/Quart, Skim Milk/Quart, Cottage Cheese).
4. Answer the pop-up question "Usual amount?" If your answer is "No," use the keypad to enter the number of units you want in the pop-up box provided.
5. Review the complete order displayed on the screen and press OK if it is correct and should be sent.

It is up to the SIM application to know the phone number of the distributor of each of the product categories, to format the message sent to the distributor, and to keep trying to send the message until it gets through and an acknowledgement is received. When an acknowledgement is received, the application may pop up a "Hot Dogs on the Way" message on the phone and, depending on the IT maturity of the distributor, could even give an estimated arrival time.

The off-card application is running on a machine that can communicate with the distributor's order entry system. A GSM phone is connected to the machine as a kind of wireless modem. When an SMS message from the SIM arrives at the phone, it is retrieved from the phone by the off-card application, translated into the format needed by the order entry system, and passed off to the order entry system. The off-card application then goes back to polling the air modem, looking for the next incoming message.

Before starting to write the on-card application, we have to say a little about what the programming environment on the SIM card looks like.

Overview of the Rapid Reorder Use of the SIM Toolkit

There is a main menu on the SIM that displays a pick list of all of the available applications. When the Rapid Reorder selection is made from this menu, an ENVELOPE (MENU SELECTION) APDU is sent from the handset to the SIM containing the index of the menu item selected. The SIM card operating system knows that the index selected is Rapid Reorder and activates our application.

Rapid Reorder uses the list of product categories to build a SELECT ITEM proactive command and passes this command back to the operating system. The operating system returns a "91xx" to the handset in response to its ENVELOPE command and the handset turns around and issues a FETCH command to retrieve our SELECT ITEM command.

After presenting the category list to the user and getting a pick, the handset issues a TERMINAL RESPONSE command to the SIM containing the list index of the item picked. The operating system remembers that it was the Rapid Reorder application that sent the proactive command and calls Rapid Reorder with the reply from the handset.

Rapid Reorder goes around this loop once more using the list of products in the chosen category to get a selection of the exact product that is being reordered. The Rapid Reorder application uses the GET INKEY proactive command to get a "Y" or "N" response to the question about whether the usual quantity of items should be ordered.

After acquiring the quantity either from an internal table ("Y") or asking for a numeric input using GET INPUT ("N"), the Rapid Reorder application uses the GET INKEY proactive command again to display the entire transaction and get back another "Y" or "N" response. Assuming all the information is correct and that "Y" is chosen, Rapid Reorder formats the transaction, retrieves the phone number of the distributor associated with the category, and uses the SEND SHORT MESSAGE proactive command to send the transaction to the distributor.

When the transaction gets to the off-card application and is entered into the distributor's order entry system, the off-card Rapid Reorder application sends an SMS back to the mobile that sent it the transaction containing whatever information had been given to it by the order entry system. This short message is received by the handset and passed to the SIM in an ENVELOPE (SMS-PP DOWN-LOAD) APDU. The operating system hands the SMS to each of the applications on the card that indicated they might be receiving SMS messages. In due time, it is handed to Rapid Reorder, which recognizes it as a message from its off-card application and uses a DISPLAY TEXT proactive command to pop up a window that contains whatever information that had been passed along from the order entry system. It also informs the operating system that it handled the message.

Very abbreviated, here's what the on-card Rapid Reorder application looks like:

1. SELECT ITEM proactive command to get the product category.
2. SELECT ITEM proactive command to get the product within the category.
3. GET INKEY proactive command to inquire about the amount.
4. Optional: GET INPUT proactive command to get the amount from the user.
5. SEND SHORT MESSAGE proactive command to send the transaction to the distributor.
6. SMS-PP DOWNLOAD to receive acknowledgement of the transaction from the distributor.
7. DISPLAY TEXT to display status of order.

To say the least, this is not top-down, fastback, fully recursive compiler programming. The challenge in SIM Toolkit programming isn't writing wads of code, but rather working efficiently and elegantly within a rich but very complex and highly constrained environment. In other words, the challenge is to get the environment to do the work, not your code.

The C Code for Rapid Reorder

To build our example Rapid Reorder SIM Toolkit application, we used the Microsoft Smart Card for Windows Visual Studio development environment coupled with Rowley's SmartWorks C® compiler. This lets us program in C and run on the Microsoft Smart Card for Windows SIM card.

Whatever SIM Application Toolkit development environment you use, start by configuring a main menu on the SIM card. In the case at hand, we add a "Rapid Reorder" entry to the main menu and connect it to the compiled code we download onto the card. When this menu entry is selected on the handset, an

ENVELOPE (MENU SELECTION) APDU is sent to the card. The SIM operating system notes which menu item has been selected, starts the corresponding application, and passes the entire ENVELOPE APDU to it.

Here's the entire ENVELOPE APDU that the Rapid Reorder application gets from the operating system (see Table 8.11):

Table 8.11 ENVELOPE (MENU SELECTION) APDU

CLA	INS	P1	P2	Lc	Menu Select Tag	Length	Device Tag	Length	ME	SIM	Item Tag	Length	Item No.
A0	C2	00	00	09	D3	07	82	02	83	82	90	01	01

The data field of the ENVELOPE APDU is a compound TLV. The tag of this TLV, D3, is the Toolkit tag for the Menu Selection. The value field of the Menu Selection TLV consists of two simple TLVs: Device Identifier (tag 82) and Item Identifier (tag 90). The Device Identifier TLV says that the command is going from the ME (83) to the SIM (81). The Item Identifier TLV says that Item #1 was selected.

Because there are two events that can cause our Rapid Reorder application to be placed into execution, the first thing that the application does is check to see which of the two events has occurred this time. If it is the Menu Selection event, then it sends a SELECT ITEM proactive command menu back to the handset to get the category of the product to be reordered.

Under the covers, the SIM operating system returns the status code 0x9134 to the handset in response to the ENVELOPE APDU. This says, "The ENVELOPE command was executed successfully and I have 0x34 bytes of proactive command for you." The handset sends a FETCH APDU to the card

CAL	INS	P1	P2	Lc	Le
A0	12	00	00	00	34

to retrieve the 0x34 bytes of the proactive command. The SIM operating system responds with

```
D0 32                             // Proactive Command of 0x32 bytes
     81 03 02 24 01               // Command Details
     82 02 81 82                  // Device Identifier
     05 07 43 61 74 65 67 6F 72   // Alpha Identifier "Category"
     8F 06 01 44 61 69 72 79      // Item #1 "Dairy"
     8F 06 02 44 72 69 6E 6B      // Item #2 "Drink"
     8F 06 03 4D 65 61 74 73      // Item #3 "Meats"
     8F 06 04 43 68 69 70 73      // Item #4 "Chips"
```

The handset collects a choice from the user and sends a TERMINAL RESPONSE APDU back to the SIM:

CLA	INS	P1	P1	Lc	Data Field
A0	14	00	00	0F	81 03 06 24 01 82 02 82 81 83 01 00 90 01 01

This particular TERMINAL RESPONSE says that Item #1 was selected. The SIM operating system feeds the final 01 back to the Rapid Reorder application in the variable passed to the GsmEndSelectItem call that sent the menu to the handset.

This fundamental Card Application Toolkit protocol continues through the selection of a product from the category, an answer to the "Usual Amount?" question and terminates in the sending of an SMS message to the distributor that contains the order.

In actual fact, the display of the status message back from the distributor could have been left to the handset because it is nothing but a normal SMS message, but we've included its handling in the application to demonstrate how you might catch and process normal incoming SMS messages in a SAT application as follows.

C Source Code for the Rapid Reorder Application

```
/*
** Rapid Reorder SIM Toolkit Application
*/
#include <scw.h>
#include <string.h>
#include <gsm.h>

typedef const unsigned char *STR;

#define CLA_GSM        0xA0
#define INS_ENVELOPE   0xC2

#define SW_BADCLA   0x6402
#define SW_BADINS   0x6404
#define SW_BADTAG   0x6406

#define TAG_SMS_PP_DOWNLOAD   0xD1
#define TAG_MENU_SELECTION    0xD3

#define CATEGORY_DAIRY   0x01
#define CATEGORY_DRINK   0x02
#define CATEGORY_MEATS   0x03
#define CATEGORY_CHIPS   0x04

char *sms_title = "Rapid Reorder";
```

```
char *distributor_number="16179256888";

char *product[4][4] = {
{{"020 Skim Milk/Pt"},
{"020 Whole Milk/Pt"},
{"010 Skim Milk/Qt"},
{"010 Whole Milk/Qt"}},
{{"050 Coke/6Pack"},
{"030 Coke/2Lt"},
{"050 Pepsi/6Pack"},
{"030 Pepsi/2Lt"}},
{{"035 Hot Dogs"},
{"020 Bologna"},
{"040 Salami"},
{"010 Liverwurst"}},
{{"100 Potato Chips"},
{"050 Fritos"},
{"025 Pringles"},
{"040 Pretzels"}}
};

void main(void)
{
  BYTE dlTag, dlLen, category, pick, answer[4], anslen;
  BYTE data[36];
  GsmDCSValue dcsValue;

  /*
  ** Make sure it's an ENVELOPE command
  */
  if (ScwGetOSParam(CURRENT_CLA) != CLA_GSM)
    ScwExitSW(SW_BADCLA);

  if (ScwGetOSParam(CURRENT_INS) != INS_ENVELOPE)
    ScwExitSW(SW_BADINS);

  /*
  ** Get the download tag and total length of the download
  */
  dlTag = ScwGetCommByte();
  dlLen = ScwGetCommByte();

  /* Branch on the download tag */
  switch (dlTag)
    {
      /*
      ** MENU_SELECTION
**
** The Rapid Reorder Application has been selected to place an
order
      **     - get a selection from the list of product categories
      **     - get a subselection from the products in that cate-
gory
**     - if not usual amount, get the amount desired
      **     - send an SMS message to the distributor to place the
order
      */
      case TAG_MENU_SELECTION:
          GsmSelectItem(7, (STR)"Category",
PRESENT_AS_DATA_VALUES_NO_HELP);
```

```
            GsmAddItem(5, (STR)"Dairy", CATEGORY_DAIRY);
            GsmAddItem(5, (STR)"Drink", CATEGORY_DRINK);
            GsmAddItem(5, (STR)"Meats", CATEGORY_MEATS);
            GsmAddItem(5, (STR)"Chips", CATEGORY_CHIPS);
            GsmEndSelectItem(&category);

            switch(category) {
              case CATEGORY_DAIRY:
              GsmSelectItem(14, (STR)"Dairy Products",
                                 PRESENT_AS_DATA_VALUES_NO_HELP);
              GsmAddItem(5, (STR)"Skim Milk/Pt", 1);
              GsmAddItem(5, (STR)"Whole Milk/Pt", 2);
              GsmAddItem(5, (STR)"Skim Milk/Qt", 3);
              GsmAddItem(5, (STR)"Whole Milk/Qt", 4);
              GsmEndSelectItem(&pick);
                    break;

                case CATEGORY_DRINK:
              GsmSelectItem(12, (STR)"Cold Drinks",
                                 PRESENT_AS_DATA_VALUES_NO_HELP);
              GsmAddItem(5, (STR)"Coke/6Pack", 1);
              GsmAddItem(5, (STR)"Coke/2Lt", 2);
              GsmAddItem(5, (STR)"Pepsi/6Pack", 3);
              GsmAddItem(5, (STR)"Pepsi/2Lt", 4);
              GsmEndSelectItem(&pick);
                    break;

                case CATEGORY_MEATS:
              GsmSelectItem(7, (STR)"Cold Cuts",
                                 PRESENT_AS_DATA_VALUES_NO_HELP);
              GsmAddItem(8, (STR)"Hot Dogs", 1);
              GsmAddItem(7, (STR)"Bologna", 2);
              GsmAddItem(6, (STR)"Salami", 3);
              GsmAddItem(11, (STR)"Liverwurst", 4);
              GsmEndSelectItem(&pick);
                    break;

                case CATEGORY_CHIPS:
              GsmSelectItem(7, (STR)"Snack Food",
                                 PRESENT_AS_DATA_VALUES_NO_HELP);
              GsmAddItem(12, (STR)"Potato Chips", 1);
              GsmAddItem(6, (STR)"Fritos", 2);
              GsmAddItem(8, (STR)"Pringles", 3);
              GsmAddItem(8, (STR)"Pretzels", 4);
              GsmEndSelectItem(&pick);
                    break;
        }

    /* See if the usual amount is to be ordered */
            GsmGetInKey(DCS_SMS_UNPACKED, 14, (STR)"Usual Amount?",
                        YES_NO_OPTION_NO_HELP, &dcsValue,
&answer[0]);
    /* If not, get the amount to be ordered */
        if(!answer) {
            GsmGetInput(DCS_SMS_UNPACKED, 9, (STR)"How Many?",
                UNPACKED_DIGITS_ONLY_NO_HELP,
                DCS_SMS_UNPACKED, 4, (STR)"10",
                3, 3, &dcsValue, answer, &anslen);
        memcpy(product[category][pick], answer, 3);
    }
```

```
    /* Send the order off to the distributor */
        GsmSendSMS(13, (STR)sms_title,
TON_INTERNATIONAL_AND_NPI_TELEPHONE,
                    sizeof(distributor_number),
(STR)distributor_number,
                    14, (STR)(&product[category][pick][0]),
PACKING_NOT_REQUIRED);
            break;

    /*
    ** SMS_PP_DOWNLOAD
    **
    ** If it's an order status message from the distributor, display
    it
    **
    */
        case TAG_SMS_PP_DOWNLOAD:
      ScwGetCommBytes(data, 2);
      ScwGetCommBytes(data, data[1]); // Fan the device TLV
      ScwGetCommBytes(data, 2);
      ScwGetCommBytes(data, data[1]); // Fan the address of the SMSC
      ScwGetCommBytes(data, 2);
      ScwGetCommBytes(data, data[1]); // Get the Originating Address
      if(memcmp(data, distributor_number, data[1]) != 0)
      break;
      ScwGetCommBytes(data, 10);
      anslen = data[9];
      ScwGetCommBytes(data, anslen); // Get the message from the dis-
    tributor
            GsmDisplayText(DCS_SMS_UNPACKED, anslen, (STR)data,

HIGH_PRIORITY_USER_CLEAR, 0);
            break;

        default:
          ScwExitSW(SW_BADTAG);
        }

      /* Add standard success SW. */
      ScwExitSW(GSM_S_COMMAND_SUCCESSFUL);
    }
```

EVOLUTION OF THE SIM AND THE CARD APPLICATION TOOLKIT

There is no shortage of ideas from application developers to evolve the Card Application Toolkit and also plenty of financial incentive for the SIM manufacturers and system software providers to do so. At the same time, there are 600 million SIM-packin' handsets in the field that have to be kept whole. Even large-scale changes in the mobile network such as those envisioned by 3GPP and UMTS don't include a process step titled "SIM Recall and Reissuing." This is why engineering elegance such as that exhibited by Colin Hamling when he made that slight change to the smart card status word is the greatest challenge in the years to come. Small evolutionary changes with complete backward compatibility that open broad new possibilities is an excellent model for standards extension.

A question often asked is, "Will the SIM go away?" The authors don't think so. Some tamper-resistant way of controlling access to the network is required as much in the future as it was in the past. An alternative to the SIM would be to put the keys and such into a tamper-resistant part of the chip that runs the handset. This is essentially what AMPS phones did. The cost and hassle of moving keys from one handset to another throttled the introduction of new handsets and thereby the growth of mobile applications. Furthermore, making part or all of a handset processor tamper-resistant adds noticeable cost to the handset, and blurs what is the user's property and what is the network operator's property. Separating the keys and the handset is a compelling architectural decision on both technical and business grounds and one that may well find its way into other computing domains.

A follow-up question is, "Do SIM applications really make any sense?" Positive answers to this question usually involve a lot of abstract heavy breathing about security. While the security contribution of the SIM is real and an integral part of the security offer of GSM, telephone operators (except NTT DoCoMo) have been very slow to extend the application of their key infrastructure beyond their own networks (i.e., to provide security to non-network applications). What is more compelling about the SIM as an application environment is that it is a controlled environment. A side effect of the operator's security concerns is that the operator is able to control which applications get on the SIM. This provides an opportunity to coordinate the applications (e.g., imposing a common human interface style on all of them). Bottom line? SIM applications can make sense if the operators want them to, which means they can figure out how to make money in the process.

SUMMARY

The SIM Application Toolkit is a highly specialized smart card programming environment and a very powerful one. The raw technology is in place today to build a wide range of compelling mobile applications. What is not in place is a business model to fund them. The SIM Application Toolkit is being used creatively by some telecom operators, Radiomobil in the Czech Republic, for example, but its potential hasn't begun to be tapped. Whether it ever will be is up to the owners of the SIM, the mobile network operators.

9

Authorization: Public Keys Without the Infrastructure

INTRODUCTION

Public key smart cards are most often found in public key infrastructures (PKIs) and typically are associated with authentication (i.e., with the certified identification of an individual). A lot of conferences have been held and a lot of venture capital burned pursuing the commercial viability of authentication services based on PKIs with, to date, relatively little net effect. Stefan Brand and Bruce Schneier and Carl Ellison have raised a number of cautions and concerns regarding the use of public key smart cards as identity tokens. At the same time, events have stimulated the consideration of public keys, along with biometric smart cards, as more general identity tokens.

Interestingly enough, public key smart cards are not limited to a supporting role in PKIs. In fact, when you strip away all the servers, software, and certificates, you are left with what is really valuable about public key cryptography on a smart card: a tamper-resistant binding between the single copy of some useful cryptographic material (the private key) and a physical thing (the smart card). In effect, you have a software equivalent of a physical key, such as a key to a safe or key to a drawer.

At first blush, a tamper-resistant binding between a unique digital object and a unique physical object doesn't seem like a very big deal. There are two direct consequences of this binding that are quite useful in IT architectures, however. First, the card must be present for the key to be used. Second, if there is evidence that the key was used, then the card must have been present. In addition, there is the rather nice effect that the key can act "at a distance"; it can be presented at one point in a network and act up a lock at some widely separated other point within the network.

In this chapter, we will explore through examples the use of a public key smart card as a bearer instrument in use as an authorization token rather than as an authentication or identity token.

MAKING THE INTANGIBLE TANGIBLE

To bring into sharp focus the difference between a card used for authorization and a card used for authentication, let's start with a personal example: access to your medical records. Suppose that the database holding your medical records only provides access to those records from a network address that demonstrates that your medical records access card is present. You could keep your card under your pillow at home and access your records whenever you wanted to via your DSL line. Or, you could carry your card with you so that emergency medical personnel could access your records from the ambulance if they found you unconscious. Or, you could leave it with your doctor to study your medical history if you came down with a strange affliction. Or, you could give it to the hospital when you checked in.

Your medical records card authorizes access to your records. It does not identify either you or the person accessing the records. It is a bearer instrument. Anyone possessing it can access your records anonymously. The only thing that is authenticated is the card itself.

The authorization protocol executed by the medical records database to authenticate the card is straightforward. As a matter of fact, it looks very much like the standard smart card security commands for identity authentication. The public key associated with the private key in the card is filed away with your medical records. When a request for access comes in, a random number is sent back to the card for encryption by the private key. The encrypted random number is sent back to the access point and if it decrypts with the public key in your records, the IP address, cell phone number, or whatever communication channel the request came in on is noted and access is granted to that channel.

Binding a Right to a Physical Object

The right to access to your medical records is hard-wired to possession of the smart card. Anyone possessing the card gets in. Anyone without the card doesn't. When you have it in your possession, no one else can access your records. You can give someone else permission to access your records by giving him or her the card. And, you can rescind this permission by taking back the card. This probably seems incredibly intuitive to us because this is the way that we use a key to the front door of our houses or the key to our automobiles.

Anyway, it is this latter property of an authorization card that differentiates it from a password and makes it more like a key (not a cryptographic key, but a physical key). A password can't be rescinded. In order to rescind the right that went with the password, the right has to be disconnected from the password and attached to a new password. You have to change, not the person to whom you loaned the right.

Another difference is that passwords can be easily duplicated. Sometimes this is not a problem. But in situations where you want to control the total number of people exercising a right or the number of people exercising the right simultaneously, the ease with which passwords can be passed along makes administering the right more difficult and more expensive. The ease with which passwords can be duplicated also makes selectively rescinding them more difficult.

The tight binding of a right to a physical object is something that is familiar and is something everyone can understand. As we shall see, it also makes managing the right more certain and less expensive and, in the end, makes the right itself more useful. From the point of view of the grantor of the right, it means the right can't be cloned and that it can be rescinded with certainty. From the point of view of the user of the right, it means that his or her identity is not associated with the use of the right and that he or she can, pending other rules, transfer use of the right to others.

In a climate of heightened sensitivity about personal privacy and the use of individual identities, it makes sense to resort to authentication when it is absolutely necessary and to not use it needlessly when only authorization is required.

The next four sections describe IT situations where public key smart card authorization could be employed. The settings are all different, but the role of the card is the same—namely, a binding of a private key to a physical object. We follow these four scenarios with two detailed practical examples of building and using an authorization card based on public key cryptography.

SHARED RIGHTS

Suppose that your employer wants to provide access to an online service to the employees of your company. Because not all employees will be using the service at the same time, it makes no sense to buy a subscription for each employee. Rather, your employer works out a deal with the service that allows no more than ten employees to access the service at any one time.

Both the service and your employer want to make certain—with a minimum of administrative overhead—that their agreement is enforced. What they have done is create ten public key smart cards and given them to the librarian or the receptionist, or they've just hung them on the wall in the kitchen. In order to access the service, an employee gets a card, sticks it in the card reader on his or her desktop, and surfs away. When done, he or she returns the card so that other employees can use the service.

At the service, a list is kept of all the public keys that are authorized to use the service. When a request comes in, a random number is sent back out to the origin of the request. What is expected back is an encryption of the random number with the private key on the access card along with the public key stored on the card that goes with the private key on the card. If the returned public key is on the approved list and if the random number decrypts with the public key, then access to the service is granted. This protocol is rerun every five or ten minutes to make sure the card is still there.

The service access card is a bearer token. A right to access the service is bound to the key and the key is bound to the card. If you possess the card, you possess the right. You can't clone the card, so you can't clone the key or the right.

GROUP MEMBERSHIP

You can be identified as being a member of a group without revealing your individual identity. Suppose, for example, that all the engineers assigned to a particular project are allowed to access the project's files, but engineers in other projects are not. If access is administered on the basis of individual authentication, then as engineers come and go, there has to be constant administration of the access control lists for the project files.

If, on the other hand, the project manager creates a batch of public key cards that permit access to the project files—just like the online service or medical record card previously—the manager can give an access card to project engineers when they are assigned to the project and collect them back when they leave the project.

In this case, because the number of cards is small, we are essentially performing a remote INTERNAL AUTHENTICATION command on the card when we verify it. An advantage of the use of public key cryptography over secret key INTERNAL AUTHENTICATION is that there is no sensitive key material in the computer room. There is only the list of public keys that can access the project files. It does no good to steal this list, and making unauthorized additions to it are easily detected.

DIGITAL RIGHTS MANAGEMENT (DRM)

A *digital right*—the right to listen to a song or to view a video—is an everyday case of authorization without authentication. The possession of a CD carries with it the right to listen to the songs that the CD contains. In the rapidly fading era where intellectual property was tightly bound to one physical media or another—songs to vinyl, words to paper, video to cellulose, pictures to silver halide or color emulsions—it rarely occurred to people that the right and the media were separable. That is probably why we never talked much about *analog rights*.

A public key smart card can play the role of the CD in the post-Napster era (i.e., a physical object whose presence is necessary in order for a right to be exercised). In fact, the digital rights management smart card may not only have to be present, but it will probably contain rules or policies for the digital rights it is managing (e.g., "can only be exercised ten times" or "can only be exercised when an allied right is present" or "when right manifested by this card is exercised increment a frequent listener counter on the card by one").

Digital rights are not just about Britney Spears or The Academy of Ancient Music. Digital rights management also applies to corporate communications and personal correspondence. The number of start-ups that have failed trying to provide DRM to bit streams other than songs and video is roughly equal to the number of start-ups that thought they had a way to defeat the digital pirates in Hong Kong.

A subject that always comes up in talking about the use of smart cards for DRM is difficulty of running an entire book, record, or film through a smart card. Of course, you can't—and you don't need to. The seminal paper showing how to use a smart card for DRM is Matt Blaze's "High-Bandwidth Encryption for Low-Bandwidth Smartcards" [*Cambridge Workshop on Fast Software Encryption*, February 1996]. There is a lot of additional published and patented work in this area, almost all of which cite Matt's paper as their wellspring.

REMOTE CONTROL

The bits generated by the card can be used to simply demonstrate possession of the card as in the preceding cases or they can cause something to happen at a remote location. Suppose, for example, that you want to send a Short Message Storage (SMS) message from your mobile phone to reset a printer queue at work. You send the reset message to the remote control gateway server, it verifies your authorization to reset the queue, and forwards a reset SNMP message to the printer. This is all standard stuff except for the authorization step.

The authorization gateway can use the telephone number on the incoming SMS message as an authorizer, but this has a number of shortcomings. First, you have to use a different authorizer for each mode of communication with the gateway. Some will provide good assurance and some will provide less-than-good assurance, but they will certainly all be different, which adds complexity to the gateway. Second, there is the issue of liability and due diligence. Using the telephone number as an authenticator to reset the printer queue essentially means you are using the telephone company's key infrastructure to control access to your company's computer center. This is definitely not the intended use of these keys and, if something goes wrong, you won't have much of a case against the telecom.

An approach that addresses both of these shortcomings is to use a public key smart card. (You may have seen that coming.) The authorization gateway sends a random number back down the same line that the message came in on and waits for the return of an encrypted version along with a public key. When the encrypted random number and the public key come back, the gateway makes sure the provided key decrypts the provided encryption and also checks to see if the public key is allowed to perform the operation in the message. If so, it fires off the SNMP message to the printer or to the network management system that will, in turn, send it to the printer.

If the number of remote sysops is small, it doesn't even need the public key. It can decrypt the random number with each key on the authorized list until it finds one that works.

Figure 9.1 is a general diagram of using a public key smart card for remote control.

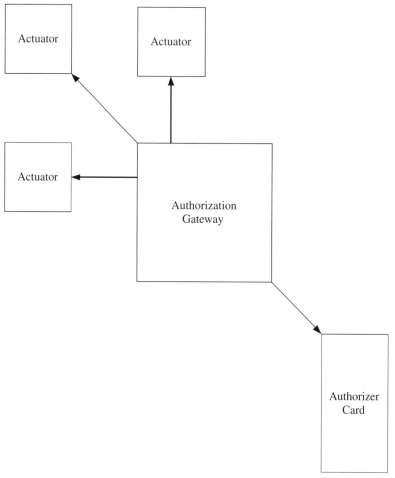

▶ **Figure 9.1**   Remote control using a public key smart card.

Whether or not you need to use an authorization gateway depends on a number of factors, including the complexity of the cryptography used, the capabilities of the actuators, and the number of people sending commands. There are situations in which the actuator itself can perform the authorization function.

Review

Authentication is too often used as a proxy for authorization. Not only does this introduce additional costs that provide no benefit, but it involves handling information that is more sensitive than is necessary for the task at hand. All you get for the higher price is more risk and more liability exposure.

Public key smart cards used as authorization tokens (i.e., without a PKI) can be tailored to the authorization task or tasks at hand. The tight binding of the authorization (the private key) to a physical object (the smart card) is easy to understand and easy to manage.

We will conclude this chapter with two programming examples. The first, the WCLA Auction Card, uses the Schlumberger Cryptoflex public key smart card and a simple Windows program to create a card that can be used for anonymous bidding. The second programming example uses a Wireless Application Protocol (WAP) phone, a simple WML script, and an ISO 7816-8 WIM card to do remote control authorization.

EXAMPLE 1: THE WCLA AUCTION CARD

The local classical radio station, WCLA, gives an auction to raise money once every year. Some listeners have expressed some reluctance to bid on the high-ticket items on privacy grounds. For a number of reasons, they don't want to identify themselves to unknown WCLA auction volunteers as either being interested in such items or able to pay for such items.

The IT manager of WCLA understands this reluctance and is highly motivated to address these concerns so that these preferred bidders won't abandon the auction. So, she has created the WCLA Auction Card. Here's how it works.

Auction Card Initialization

Bidders can drop by the radio station and pick up an auction card from a great big bowl full of Auction Cards—no questions asked. Or, if the bidder has a mustard seed's worth of trust in WCLA, he can call and ask to have someone draw a card out for him and have an Auction Card Kit sent to him.

In either case, what he gets is a Schlumberger Cryptoflex card—the WCLA Auction Card—and a CD-ROM containing the WCLA Auction Advisor program that we will discuss at length in the next few sections. The Auction Card had been pre-personalized to contain a public key pair and nothing else. In other words, there is no association between the bidder and the card. The card is a bearer instrument.

Making a Bid

When an item comes up for bid on which the listener wants to bid, he once again fires up the Auction Advisor, enters the item number and bid into the appropriate windows, has these two numbers encrypted by the freshly generated private key, and cuts-and-pastes the text blob that appears in the output window into a bid form on the WCLA Web site. The text blob contains the item number, the bid amount, the encrypted item number and bid, and the public key that goes with the private key that does the encrypting.

The WCLA Web server decrypts the encrypted item number and bid using the public key and checks them against the plain-text item number and bid. If they are the same, the server enters the bid on the item on behalf of the cardholder.

Redeeming a Winning Bid

At the end of the auction, the winning public keys that match the items won are posted on the WCLA Web site. In order to claim an item, an anonymous someone with the card containing the private key that goes with a posted public key goes to the WCLA studios. WCLA gives the presented card the item number and the winning bid for the item that is being claimed. If the card produces the same text blob that was the original bid sent into the Web site, WCLA accepts the satchel of unmarked $20s and the anonymous someone walks away with the Ming vase.

Of course, at this point, the bidder is no longer dealing with auction volunteers but with WCLA staff, so he might be willing to actually write a check—but you get the idea.

THE AUCTION ADVISOR PROGRAM

As obtained from WCLA, the Auction Card contains the files in Table 9.1. This is the simplest of all possible public key cards.

The PIN for the card is the PIN that is found in the majority of smart cards in use: 1234. The bidder doesn't really need a PIN for this use of a public key card, but the Schlumberger Cryptoflex card requires that there be one.

Table 9.1 Files on the WCLA Auction Card

Directory	File	Contents
0x3F00	0x0000	User PIN
	0x0002	Card Identifier
	0x0011	Administration Keys
0x4F01	0x0012	Private Key
	0x1012	Public Key

Figure 9.2 is a screenshot of the Auction Advisor in action. The bidder now just cuts the text in the Cut-and-Paste Window into the WCLA Bid Form and he has entered his bid.

When the program is started, the WCLA Auction Card is initialized and the public key is extracted:

```
hResult = SCardEstablishContext(
                  SCARD_SCOPE_SYSTEM, NULL, NULL, &hContext);
    hResult = SCardListReaders(hContext, NULL, Reader,
                                              &ReaderLength);
hResult = SCardConnect(hContext, Reader, SCARD_SHARE_EXCLUSIVE,
                  SCARD_PROTOCOL_T0, &hCard, &dwActiveProtocol);

cbAtrLen = sizeof(Atr);
hResult = SCardState(hCard, &dwState, &dwProtocol, Atr,
                                              &cbAtrLen);

DO(select_mf);
DO(verify_pin);
DO(select_4F01);
DO(select_1012);
DO(get_public_key);
memcpy(PublicKey, bpRecvBuffer, sizeof(PublicKey));
```

The DO macro just sends an APDU to the card and retrieves the response

```
#define DO(command) \
        cbRecvLength=sizeof(bpRecvBuffer); \
    memset(bpRecvBuffer, 0, sizeof(bpRecvBuffer)); \
        hResult = SCardTransmit(hCard, SCARD_PCI_T0, command, \
          sizeof(command), NULL, bpRecvBuffer, &cbRecvLength);
```

where, for example, `select_mf` is just

```
BYTE select_mf[] = {0xC0, 0xA4, 0x00, 0x00, 0x02, 0x3F, 0x00};
```

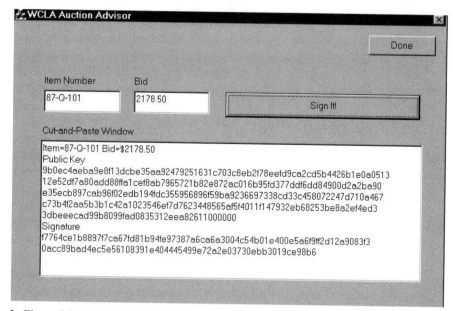

▶ **Figure 9.2**   The WCLA Auction Advisor Window.

The code for the Sign It! Button, in the grimmest detail, looks like this:

```
void CWcla1Dlg::OnSignIt()
{
int i, j;

m_ItemNumber.GetWindowText(ItemNumber, sizeof(ItemNumber));

m_BidAmount.GetWindowText(BidAmount, sizeof(BidAmount));

memset(&sign_data[5], ' ', sizeof(sign_data)-5);

    memcpy(&sign_data[5], ItemNumber, strlen(ItemNumber));

memcpy(&sign_data[10], BidAmount, strlen(BidAmount));

DO(sign_data);

DO(get_signature);

memcpy(Signature, bpRecvBuffer, sizeof(Signature));

sprintf(CutAndPasteBuffer, "Item=%s Bid=$%s\r\nPublic Key\r\n",
                               ItemNumber, BidAmount);

for(i=3, j=strlen(CutAndPasteBuffer); i < sizeof(PublicKey); i++)
  {
    sprintf(&CutAndPasteBuffer[j], "%02x", PublicKey[i]);
    j += 2;
    if(((i-3)+1)%36 == 0) {
```

```
            CutAndPasteBuffer[j++] = '\r';
            CutAndPasteBuffer[j++] = '\n';
            CutAndPasteBuffer[j] = '\0';
        }

    }

    sprintf(&CutAndPasteBuffer[j], "\r\nSignature\r\n");

    for(i=0, j=strlen(CutAndPasteBuffer); i < sizeof(Signature); i++)
      {
        sprintf(&CutAndPasteBuffer[j], "%02x", Signature[i]);
        j += 2;
        if((i+1)%36 == 0) {
            CutAndPasteBuffer[j++] = '\r';
            CutAndPasteBuffer[j++] = '\n';
            CutAndPasteBuffer[j] = '\0';
        }

    }

    m_CutAndPaste.SetWindowText(CutAndPasteBuffer);
}
```

EXAMPLE 2: MOBILE AUTHORIZATION USING A WIM

In Chapter 8, we described the SIM smart card and the SIM Application Toolkit. SIM is an acronym for subscriber identification module and it is the smart card that is in GSM and 3G mobile telephones. The SIM is an authorization smart card, just like a public key smart card except that it uses symmetric (secret) key cryptography rather than the asymmetric (public) key cryptography. When you get a new account with a GSM mobile operator, you are given a SIM that contains the secret key associated with your account. A copy of the key is in the operator's network operations center.

What a SIM authorizes the bearer to do is use a mobile network. The network operator performs a slightly more complicated version of the authorization protocol we have seen previously with the SIM when you turn on the phone. The operator doesn't know or care who is actually using the phone. All the operator really cares about is who is going to pay for the usage. It is the contract you signed when you opened the account that links the key on the SIM to a payment obligation. This contractual binding to pay for network use is over and above the binding of the secret key in the SIM and the physical SIM itself. This latter binding makes it hard for you to claim that it wasn't your SIM that made the call, but it also lets you argue that the call that was made in Eastern Slovenia wasn't you. The binding of a physical object and a digital object cuts both ways.

There is another smart card that is used in mobile applications called the WIM. WIM is an acronym for WAP identification module. Details of the WIM and the application programming interfaces (APIs) to it can be found on the WAP Forum Web site at *www.wapforum.org.*

The WIM is a public key smart card just like the ones we've been describing. Originally, it was designed to be part of a PKI; this may still happen some day. In the meantime, we can use it for mobile authorization without a PKI.

Figure 9.3 shows the flow of the authorization protocol to the WIM and back to the mobile authorization gateway.

The WML script that the mobile authorization gatewaysends to the WAP phone to ask for an authorization might look like this:

```
<wml>
    <card id="Query"
    <select name="YESorNO" title="Reset BLUE Printer?">
        <option value="YES">YES</option>
        <option value="NO">NO</option>
    </select>
    <do type="Accept">
        <go href="SignIt.wmls#signIt($(YESorNO))"/
        </go>
    </do>
    </card>
    <card id="Return"
    <do type="Accept" title="Send authorization?">
     <go href="http://www.sguthery.com/gateway.asp" method="post">
        <postfield name="Signature" value="$(Signature)"/>
     </go>
    </do>
    </card>
</wml>
```

The WMLScript function `signIt` looks like this:

```
extern function signIt(data)
{
    WMLBrowser.setVar("Signature", Crypto.signText(data, 1, 0,
"\x00"));

    WMLBrowser.go("WMLScriptExample.wml#Return");
};
```

The `Crypto.signText` function is an element of the WMLScript Crypto library. The execution of the `signIt` function by the WAP browser on the handset causes five ISO 7816-8 APDUs to be sent to the WIM smart card. The

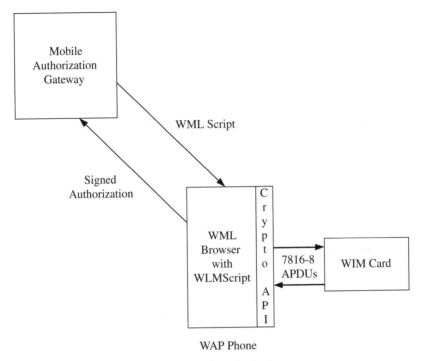

▶ Figure 9.3 WIM card used for mobile authorization.

first one is a `Manage Security Environment` command that establishes the WIM security environment on the card:

CLA	INS	P1	P2	Lc	Data
80_{16}	22_{16}	$F3_{16}$	06_{16}	01_{16}	00_{16}

The second one is a `VERIFY PIN` APDU that provides access to the private key:

CLA	INS	P1	P2	Lc	Data
80_{16}	20_{16}	00_{16}	01_{16}	04_{16}	$31_{16}\,32_{16}\,33_{16}\,34_{16}$

The third one is another MANAGE SECURITY ENVIRONMENT command that says what private key file and what key in that file to use:

CLA	INS	P1	P2	Lc	Data
80_{16}	22_{16}	41_{16}	$B6_{16}$	07_{16}	$81_{16}\,02_{16}\,00_{16}\,12_{16}\,84_{16}\,01_{16}\,01$

In our case, we are using key #1 in the file 0x0012.

The fourth APDU is the PERFORM SECURITY OPERATION APDU that actually sends the data into the WIM for signing:

CLA	INS	P1	P2	Lc	Data
80_{16}	$2A_{16}$	$9E_{16}$	$9A_{16}$	03_{16}	'Y' 'E' 'S'

And the final APDU is a GET RESPONSE APDU that retrieves the 64-byte signature:

CLA	INS	P1	P2	Lc	Data
00_{16}	$C0_{16}$	00_{16}	00_{16}	40_{16}	

SWIMs, WIBs, and the USAT Interpreter

As fate would have it, WAP has not been one of the world's great successes. Not only are there few WAP handsets out there, there were even fewer WIM cards. Nevertheless, the idea of adding additional keys and the ISO 7816-8 APDUs to the mobile environment is compelling. Thus was born the SWIM card. A SWIM card is a SIM with WIM capabilities; namely, it supports the ISO 7816-8 needed to implement the WIM signing and verification protocols. To be sure, network operators aren't thrilled by having keys other than their own on the SIM, but the alternative of having a second smart card on the scene is even more distasteful. At least with the SWIM, they still own the platform.

Additional keys are fine, but what about the WMLScript and interacting with the mobile cardholder? How do we accomplish this without a WAP phone? The answer is to install a nanobrowser on the SIM itself.

This was first accomplished by Across Wireless in 1998. The SIM-based browser was called the Wireless Internet Browser, or WIB for short. The Across Wireless (now SmartTrust) WIB was very well received in the GSM and 3G marketplace and has proved to be a more manageable and less costly way to roll out mobile applications than downloading Java applets to the SIM. The Across Wireless WIB supports a public key cryptography plug-in, just like the browser on your desktop; this plug-in can be used for mobile authorization just like the WML Crypto library was previously. The WML that you send to the Across Wireless WIB is almost identical to the WML that you would have sent to a WAP handset.

Telecom operators are adamant about standardization and while, they liked the approach of the Across WIB, they were uncomfortable with installing essentially proprietary technology on their SIMs. In early 2000, they launched an effort in 3GPP to standardize the SIM-based microbrowser. The result is the USAT (for UICC SIM Application Toolkit) Interpreter that we discussed in Chapter 8.

SUMMARY

A public key smart card creates a tamper-resistant binding between a digital object (a private key) and a physical object (the smart card). In order to use the key, the card must be present. If the key is used, then the card is present. If the key is a right, then the right is bound to the card and can be transferred by transferring possession of the card. The act of encrypting a piece of data with a private key generated on a smart card associates the piece of data bound to the possession of the card. It does not associate the data with any particular person.

10

Smart Card System Management

As we have discussed throughout this book, a smart card can be a valuable addition to a variety of applications, many based in wide area computer systems and networks. A smart card is an excellent security token for large-scale security infrastructures. Its ability to store information in a tamper-resistant and tamper-evident package and to provide secure computation on the same platform makes it an excellent facility to store cryptographic keys through which the identity of the cardholder can be authenticated. Further, a wide variety of personal information about the cardholder can be stored on the card and carried on his or her person.

As we've looked at the various aspects of smart cards, we've touched on many if not all of the elements of large-scale smart card systems: the participants in developing, deploying and using the systems; the constituent elements of the systems; and many of the mechanisms used within the systems. In this chapter, we'd like to bring all of these into focus and, with this in mind, look at the characteristics that will guide why and how we want to manage the system. This will hopefully give you a basis on which to ground your understanding of the issues involved in fielding a smart card system and the aspects of card management that you'll need to consider as you field that smart card system.

CONVERGING SYSTEMS

Using smart cards in an application involving individuals (cardholders) and a wide area infrastructure such as a banking system or mobile telephone system involves the intersection of two large-scale systems. If the smart card is capable of supporting multiple applications, and even more so if the card is post-issuance programmable, then the convergce of three large-scale systems is involved:

- *Card system*—Smart card development, manufacturing, and deployment
- *Operating Infrastructure*—Application Operations System infrastructure development, deployment, and operations
- *Application system*—Application development

Figure 10.1 is a simplified illustration of the convergence of these large-scale systems, portraying them by showing many of their constituent activities and the interconnection of these activities. At the top of the figure we see the principle operations involved in developing and deploying the smart card system; below are shown the steps involved in developing and deploying the applications that will make use of the smart cards. Finally, at the bottom and down the right-hand side of the figure are shown the primary elements of the operational and management system for families of applications. As illustrated in Figure 10.1, each of these systems represents a significant administrative and support load in its

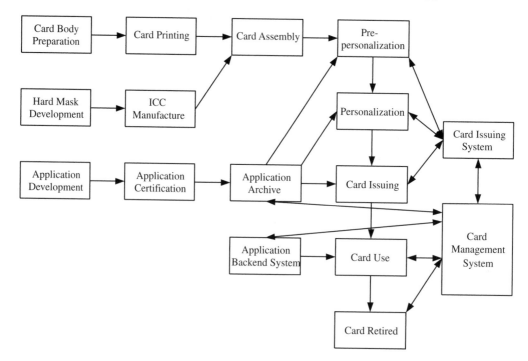

▶ **Figure 10.1**   Converging systems.

own right. Making all three types of systems work together is a particularly daunting task. To accomplish it well, a coherent management approach and an integrated management system are desirable, if not mandatory.

THE ACTORS

Within large-scale, smart card–based application systems, there are a number of distinct roles played out in the development, deployment, and ongoing operations of the complete system infrastructure. Some of these roles are consistent with those found in typical IT systems. Some are perhaps a bit unique to the smart card arena. In the course of this book, we've mentioned most of these principals from time to time; now, in the following sections, we'll examine some of them in a more coherent fashion. In a couple of areas, we'll provide the names of some organizations that are well known in these particular arenas. Theirs aren't the only groups in these areas, but serve as examples of the types of groups you'll seek out if you become involved in considering the deployment of a smart card-based system.

The Card Issuer

The central entity in any commercial smart card application venture is the *card issuer*. This is the control point for the application system—the owner of it, if you will. More to the point, the card issuer is usually the ultimate risk taker/holder in the system. If there is a breakdown in the overall integrity (security) of the system, it is the card issuer's nickel at stake.

Historically, smart card systems started with the card issuer. The card issuer would develop the concept for the application or application system and would approach the smart card manufacturer, and others, to develop on-card and off-card components of the system. In many instances, particularly with financial systems, the card issuer would be responsible for the long-term operation of the system. With current systems, we are at a bit of a transition point insofar as system development goes. Today, significant parts of an application infrastructure either exist or are off-the-shelf components, ready to be integrated into a final system.

With the current style of system deployment, smart cards themselves are often off-the-shelf items. The card's integrated circuit chip (ICC) architecture is developed as a moderately general-purpose computing platform and the installation of the final application software on it typically involves either soft-mask or application installation at prepersonalization time (a concept we'll look at in more detail a little later on in this chapter).

The card is typically given to the cardholder by a card issuer. In the case of financial cards, the issuer is generally a bank or other financial institution. The card issuer generally is responsible for providing the system in which the card can be used to perform its security-related functions. One aspect of this system is typically the linking of salient information about the cardholder to the functional characteristics of the card. In this area, the issuer functions as a certification authority or as a "trust broker." It is through the actions of the issuer that various parties of a subsequent transaction can achieve some level of trust in the transaction even though they do not know each other prior to the initiation of the transaction.

In the financial environment, very well-defined protocols have been put in place by associations of financial organizations and buttressed by binding national and international laws and agreements. In the emerging world of computer networks, the existence of equivalent certification authorities is only now being legitimized by evolving system deployment.

A significant impediment to the deployment of smart card-based systems in the IT world has been the lack of card issuer experience in the area. The degree of liability assumed by the card issuer in this situation can be difficult to assess. In a corporate environment, it is a natural assumption that the corporate entity assume the role of card issuer, and, in fact, this is the most common model for successful systems. Given that a common role for smart cards in any system, but particularly in IT systems, is to establish an authenticated identity, the corporate HR function is perhaps the most logical card issuer of choice. As a matter of fact, the identity that can be established through a corporate HR office is probably the "best" identity that can be established short of a government ID based on a comprehensive security check.

The ICC Manufacturer

As we saw in Chapter 2, the ICC contained in a smart card is a complete computer assembly contained within a single chip. The various elements of the ICC (i.e., the central processing unit, the various types of memory, and the other components) are quite comparable to those components as housed for general-purpose computer systems. The *ICC manufacturers* for smart cards are general silicon vendors who also design and manufacture components for more general-purpose computer systems. Some of the well-known ICC manufacturers are:

- Infineon (www.infineon.com)
- ST Microelectronics (www.stm.com)
- Atmel (www.atmel.com)
- Philips Semiconductors (www.philips.com)
- Fujitsu (www.fujitsu.com)
- Hitachi (www.hitachi.com)

The relationship among card issuers, ICC manufacturers, and smart card manufacturers is complex. Each has evolved a degree of control in developing and deploying smart card systems; in many instances, these entities are complementary while in some areas they appear competitive.

The product delivered by the ICC manufacturer is typically a smart card chip delivered in one of two forms: either as a wafer with many ICCs on it or as a module comprised of a single ICC and its associated contact faceplate. Smart card manufacturers can typically work with either variant.

The Smart Card Manufacturer

The *smart card manufacturer*, as the name implies, is the entity that builds the smart card. The manufacturer typically develops the base operating system software for the card and perhaps the application-level software as well. The card manufacturer creates the card body from raw PVC and installs the ICC into it. The manufacturer will typically be responsible for card printing and system personalization (or the ICC), although these functions are sometimes assumed by the issuer or perhaps even a service bureau function. We'll look at the manufacturing process for a smart card a little later in this chapter.

Some of the prevalent smart card manufacturers are:

- Gemplus (www.gemplus.com)
- SchlumbergerSema (www.schlumbergersema.com)
- Giesicke & Devrient (www.gdm.de)
- Oberthur (www.oberthur.com)

These companies provide a significant fraction of the smart cards produced in the world today.

The Application Developer

The *application developer* in today's system environment is part developer and part integrator. Many components of the overall application are built as standard modules, ready to be specialized for inclusion into a specific application system.

In today's marketplace, application developers are generally recruited by the card issuers or they are in the (speculative) business of building systems and recruiting card issuers to deploy them. What does not exist today is a significant population of application developers who can develop a product to sell into deployed systems. Thus, smart card systems are not yet like PC systems where applications can be independently marketed. It is, in fact, one small goal of this book to help facilitate such developers.

The POS Manufacturer

In the world of financial applications, a very significant role is played by the developer of the point-of-sale terminal. While smart cards provide a significant security environment for the component of the system that resides with the cardholder, a standard personal computer that might be found in the office or store of a vendor does not provide an equivalent security level. This is the realm of the POS terminal. These terminals can contain most or all of the off-card application necessary to interact with the cardholder's smart card.

The POS often contains a smart card in its own right. This *security authentication module* (SAM) will be contained within a POS and it serves (at least) two purposes: to authenticate the identity of the POS and to contain a purse on behalf of the POS owner/vendor to record transactions and their values.

POS manufacturers have a variety of associations, but one of the more active at the moment is the STIP group, which we discussed in Chapter 7.

The Cardholder

A smart card can represent the *cardholder* in an electronic environment. Further, the card can be programmed to require some type of identity authentication from the cardholder before it will provide such electronic representation for the cardholder. That is, the smart card can use a variety of mechanisms in a transaction with the cardholder through which the cardholder convinces the card that it should act on the cardholder's behalf. Some of the mechanisms used by the card to authenticate the identity of the bearer include requiring

- the bearer to enter a personal identification number (PIN)
- the bearer to enter some known personal information stored on the card
- some biometrical characteristic of the bearer, such as a fingerprint or a facial image, to be measured by a sensor or collection of sensors and then matched against a benchmark of this characteristic stored on the card
- the bearer to properly perform a series of operations leading to a specific state known to the card

The identity authentication transaction that occurs between the card and the cardholder is a rather complete, specific example of the transaction that one wants to occur generally through the enabling actions of the card. That is, both sides of the transaction (i.e., the card and the cardholder) must be concerned with

- authenticating the identity of the other (party to the transaction)
- being authorized with the appropriate privileges once identity is authenticated
- being assured of the integrity of the transaction
- being assured of the privacy of the transaction
- being able to confirm that the transaction took place in a proper fashion

THE INFRASTRUCTURE

We've examined the main actors in a large-scale smart card system. Now let's look at the infrastructure of the system itself. The infrastructure for smart card-based systems is, today, probably best represented by the Internet. That is, the infrastructure is comprised of many platforms and their network connections through which specific elements of smart card-based systems can be interconnected.

Essentially none of the platforms and none of the communication channels used in a widespread smart card application can be assumed to be secure in and of themselves. Consequently, the smart card (as a security platform itself) must be vigilant as to what other entities it is talking to. The designers and developers of systems have to guard against nonsecure elements of the infrastructure from being able to authenticate an identity to which the smart card will free to talk.

The Card

Smart cards use a computer platform on which information can be stored such that access to it can be strictly controlled by the cardholder, the card issuer, or the provider of any specific applications on the card. Further, software can be executed on the card under strict control of either the cardholder, the card issuer, or the provider of specific applications on the card. Given these characteristics, the smart card provides a variety of useful security characteristics, including

- storage of passwords for access to computer systems, networks, information stores, and so forth
- storage of keys, public and private, for authenticating identity
- storage of keys, public and private, for encrypting information to ensure its privacy
- storage of information to be conveyed to various access points for a system (e.g., a financial system) without the cardholder being able to access or change that information in any way
- performance of encryption algorithms for authenticating identity
- performance of encryption algorithms for ensuring the privacy of information

The InterFace Device

The access point of any smart card with any electronic system is typically referred to *in the ISO specifications as an InterFace Device (IFD);* most of the time, the terms *terminal, smart card reader* or *smart card interface device* are used. Terminals can vary significantly in complexity and capability and, hence, in the level of security that they support. At the most capable level, a terminal is a secure computing platform on a par with the smart card itself, although typically not nearly so small, inexpensive, and portable. In such a configuration, a terminal might contain a comparatively powerful computer processor, memory, telecommunications interfaces to local and wide area computer networks, display screens, and input devices (e.g., a keypad or keyboard) through which a user can enter information (to the terminal's processor and then perhaps on to the smart card), and perhaps even biometric sensors that the terminal can use to ascertain personal characteristics of the cardholder. For example, fingerprint readers and facial characteristics scanners are beginning to emerge within the security marketplace as viable elements of terminals.

A highly integrated configuration, including a tamper-resistant computer, memory and secondary storage, and a secure cardholder verification entry facility, typically would be provided by a card issuer to a merchant. This terminal provides a secure point of presence (from the standpoint of the card system issuer) in the merchant's environment through which the issuer system can communicate with the cardholder's smart card.

Simple Readers

The most basic job of the reader is to provide a physical connection to the eight contact pins on the face plate of a smart card. Because the smart card is a serial device, some of the first smart card readers merely extended the serial port to contacts that would touch the plates on the smart card. These readers eventually gained the name *dumb* or *pass-thru* readers because they relied on the host to implement the low-level communications and timing issues involved with the communication. Typical dumb readers have a crystal to drive a clock and a means of powering the chip with possibly some rudimentary protocol negotiating capabilities with the card. On the other end of the spectrum exist readers that implement the entire protocol in their firmware. Such readers may accept up to a 260-byte APDU, reset the card, examine the atr, set the protocol parameters, and perform the low-level T=0/1 protocol automatically just returning the result of the command. Typically, this type of behavior is implemented in a reader that is hoping to achieve EMV certification.

Simple smart card readers come in a variety of shapes and sizes and also can connect to your computer in a variety of ways. Some of the more common readers include:

- *Keyboard*—Built into the keyboard so no extra cords exist. A PIN pad exists in the keyboard. High convenience; high cost ($30–80).
- *PCMCIA*—Able to fit into a PCMCIA socket. This is useful for mobile applications such as a laptop or a handheld portable. Moderate cost ($30–60).

- *Serial port*—Connects to a serial port. This is the most common reader, although USB is becoming more popular. Lowest cost ($10–40).

- *Floppy*—Fits into something that looks like a floppy disk. This has been used as a means to have a cross-platform reader. Not common; high cost ($80+).

- *USB*—Low-cost reader of the future. Many can be on the bus at a time, hardware is cheap, and standards exist for communication to it. Low cost ($15–50).

- *Contactless*—Has no contacts but uses inductance to communicate. Mostly used for physical access systems. High cost ($150+).

Each of these readers can also have a variety of capabilities with them such as an embedded LCD display so the user can be prompted to do a particular action. They may also have an embedded PIN pad so the user can authenticate to the card. There might be a biometric, such as a fingerprint panel; we'll consider this a bit more in a later section of this chapter.

The reader may have multiple slots so that two cards can be required to perform a particular transaction. PC/SC has a manufacturer-specific `SCardControl` function such that applications or service providers can send commands to the driver to trigger some of these extended capabilities. An abstract way to do this was not done in the first draft of PC/SC, but the 2.0 draft outlines how this might be done.

The "ultimate" smart card reader would perhaps do three-factor authentication without communicating to an external device. It would contain a smart card reader for "something you have," a PIN pad for "something you know," and a biometric sensor for "something you are." It would also contain an LCD display to give feedback to the user about his or her status or position of biometric.

The PC

In emerging computer network environments, the terminal component from earlier smart card–based systems is separated into a computer component (i.e., a PC, a network computer, a workstation, or some similar designation) to which is attached a relatively simple smart card reader. This particular configuration raises some security concerns with respect to the use of smart cards. In particular, the cardholder should always understand the security risks in providing verification of identity to the card through a computer system of unknown control. Obviously, this same concern can be raised for all levels of systems; Trojan horse ATMs reportedly have been deployed to fraudulently gain account numbers and PINs from unsuspecting users. For home computer-type systems, however, the risks of the system being in a position to capture sensitive information are significantly greater.

The point then is that the cardholder should be reasonably cautious of the computer systems through which the card is used. If it's the personal computer system of the cardholder, then the risks are greatly minimized because the cardholder has control over the system's security environment. If it's a personal computer system being used in a commercial environment, then the cardholder should be concerned with the general security environment presented; for example, with the manner in which a PIN is entered.

If a personal computer configuration makes use of a simple smart card reader and the cardholder is expected to enter a PIN through the computer's keyboard, then it's a relatively simple procedure for the system manager of the personal computer configuration to be able to capture the keystrokes and hence to know the PIN for the cardholder's card. If the computer belongs to the cardholder and is under the direct control of the cardholder, then the security risks (of having the PIN captured) are greatly minimized. For public environments, it is possible to obtain more sophisticated smart card readers that have integrated keypads through which a PIN can be entered and passed on to the card, not to the computer system to which this terminal is connected.

The Network

The network through which computer systems are connected should always be treated as a completely unsecure environment. The application developer, the card issuer, and the cardholder should all view the communication channel as completely open to the world. Information that passes through these channels can be monitored, captured, and manipulated by unknown persons and/or systems.

The Application

The *application* is the particular system or system component that is provided through the auspices of the card issuer (or at least with the concurrence of the card issuer) and is intended to provide some type of service to be accessed by the cardholder. The application may make use of an infrastructure within the network or within the end computer system through which the cardholder gains access to it. In these cases, however, the application must be concerned with the security of this infrastructure.

In many existing smart card–enabled systems, all the players operate within an environment provided by the card issuer. In the Internet environment, it is more difficult to provide a well-controlled infrastructure for all these players. They must each understand the security limits of the components that they deal with.

THE CARD SYSTEM

We've had an overview of the actors and the infrastructure for a large scale smart card system; now let's look at some aspects of the convergent systems that were introduced in Figure 10.1. From its design inception to its widespread deployment, a smart card typically goes through a rather consistent life cycle. This life cycle may vary a bit from card manufacturer to card manufacturer and from application system to application system, but for the most part, it goes through a consistent series of phases.

Life Cycle

A smart card typically involves two distinct development phases:

- development of the smart card operating system and application software
- manufacturing of the smart cards

In Figure 10.1, these two phases are illustrated in the two top rows of tasks shown. Consider first the development of software for the card. Throughout the course of this book we've examined a variety of approaches for providing software, both systems and applications on a smart card. We'll do a succinct review in the following section. Then, we will consider the manufacturing, deployment, and operation of a smart card system.

Smart Card Operating System Software Development

Applications that make use of smart cards typically comprise software that runs on an off-card computer (a PC or PC-class computer), on the smart card itself, and perhaps even on other computers widely distributed within a local area or wide area network. Software to run on the card itself (i.e., within the ICC embedded in the card), comes in a spectrum of flavors as illustrated in Figure 10.2.

Hard-mask software is developed in advance of the manufacture of the ICC, which is embedded in a smart card plastic body. The hard-mask software is provided to the chip manufacturer and it is created as a bit pattern in the read-only memory (ROM) of the ICC. Hard-mask software comprises the base operating system of the smart card. Historically, all of the application and operating system software of the card was built into ROM. As an evolutionary measure, however, some of the base operating system and application software came to be stored in electrically erasable and programmable read-only memory (EEPROM).

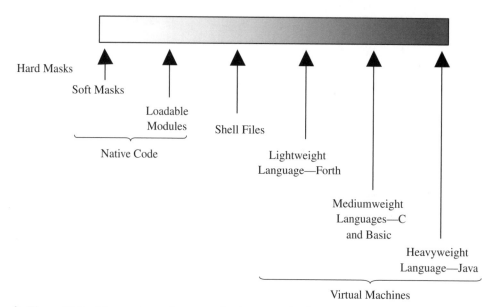

▶ **Figure 10.2**   The spectrum of smart card software mechanisms.

In developing hard-mask software, it is difficult to debug and test the software completely prior to its being built into ROM during the ICC manufacturing process. Because of this, in some instances, the hard mask would have errors in it following the manufacturing process—not manufacturing errors, mind you, but rather design and coding errors in the operating system software. It was found that by designing appropriately positioned "jump tables" in the ROM software (we considered this in Chapter 6), it was possible to make use of software loaded into EEPROM after the ICC manufacturing was completed.

The software loaded into EEPROM came to be known as soft-mask software (soft, because it could actually be modified after ICC manufacturing). This mechanism then allowed two distinct types of software to be added after manufacturing:

- bug fixes for the base operating system

- additional commands for supporting application systems

Now, if an error in the hard mask prevented its being used, there was a chance to correct the error through a soft mask. This was a great time saver over having to redo the manufacture of the ICC. With judicious design, it even became feasible to develop new commands to be loaded into (and executed from) EEPROM. This meant that a more generic smart card could be tailored for a specific application without completely redesigning the ICC software. Thus, the turnaround time for deploying a smart card application was decreased.

Finally, with the advent of the addition of a virtual machine on the card, it became possible to develop new application code in an interpreted language. Such programs could then be loaded onto the card even after the card had been issued to the cardholder.

Mask Development

Programs to be stored into the chip on a smart card are often referred to as *masks*. The term derives from the fact that the software is actually reduced to a bit pattern, which is actually masked onto the silicon components (the ROM) of the chip during the fabrication process. If the program is to be stored into ROM as part of the fabrication process of the chip itself, then this is generally referred to as a *hard mask*.

On a chip, software can also be stored in, and executed from, EEPROM. In this case, the software can actually be written to the chip after the card manufacturing process is completed. This type of software is often referred to as a *soft mask* in the smart card domain. For other domains—that is, in other areas where embedded microprocessor units are used—this would often be referred to as *firmware*.

Code Development

As we have seen through the course of this book, the form of software on a smart card can take a variety of forms. The two cards that we examined in some detail in Chapter 6, the Cryptoflex and the Cyberflex Access cards, contain variants of most of the known forms. The Cryptoflex card makes use of a hard mask to contain the base operating system and a fixed command set to which the card responds. The hard mask was developed in a high-level programming language, probably C or C++, and the compiled and linked machine language form was masked into the ROM of the ICC embedded in the smart card plastic body. The Cryptoflex card includes several administrative commands that allow additional base operating system or additional fixed commands to be stored in EEPROM during the final phases of the card manufacturing operation (i.e., using a soft-mask approach). Prior to the cards being issued to the cardholder, the administrative commands that support soft-mask development were permanently disabled on the card.

The Cyberflex Access card also makes use of hard mask for the base operating system and the Card Manager application. This card also includes administrative commands that allow the addition of soft-mask software prior to releasing the card to the cardholder. The primary way to add software (commands) to the Cyberflex Access card is through Java Card applets, which are loaded onto the card either as part of the prepersonalization phase of manufacturing or after the card has been issued to the cardholder.

All of these various mechanisms for adding software to a card have their own sets of benefits and liabilities. Each requires a specialized software development environment as well. Included in most of these environments are various types of specialized equipment or software support infrastructures.

Chip Simulators

For (hard-mask) software loaded onto the chip during the manufacturing process, the process for writing and then checking the software (debugging) can be very long and involved. In particular, supporting a debugging environment in which checkpoints can be set with code and a dynamic debugger used to isolate errors is difficult to provide on an isolated ICC meant for a smart card. In order to mitigate this difficult situation somewhat, most chip manufacturers provide software simulators for their chips. This allows the software developer to create a full complement of software for a chip and check it out via the simulator prior to actually fabricating a set of chips with the software included.

While a chip simulator improves the software development process, it still leaves many aspects of the software unchecked. For example, it is very difficult to check the timing of various operations through a simulator. As seen in Chapter 3, many aspects of the communication between the off-card and the on-card application are critically depending on the timing of various transactions between the reader and the card. These aspects of the software's execution can usually not be tested with the simulators provided for most chips. Instead, development tools called *chip emulators* are available that allow the actual ICC hardware to be used, but augmented by external memory and other debugging aids.

Chip Emulators

To improve the testing environment, but without requiring the actual fabrication of chips with embedded application software, most chip manufacturers provide hardware emulators for their chips. With an emulator, a variant of memory is provided that can be accessed both by a computer being used for the software development environment and by the processor of a chip of the form to be deployed on the smart card. This emulator allows the software developer to write code and load it into this sharable memory. The code, thus loaded, can then be executed by the processor in the emulator. In this way, the code is being run in an environment much like that in the final smart card; the timing of operations is much closer to that found on the smart card itself.

Protocol Analyzers

The communication between the reader and the smart card occurs through a half-duplex communication channel, much like is found with a typical PC connection to a local or wide area network. In this environment, it is very useful to be able to monitor the bits traveling across the interface lines between the reader and the card. Just as in the case with a local or wide area network connection, this can be accomplished with a protocol analyzer.

CARD MANUFACTURING

The manufacturing of smart cards comprises a number of distinct steps:

1. *Fabrication of the chip, or many chips in the form of a wafer.* Several thousand ICCs are manufactured at a time in the form of silicon wafers. An individual chip for a smart card is approximately 25 square mm, or about 5 mm on a side. The template for the circuitry on a chip is repeated many thousands of times to overlay a silicon wafer approximately 4 inches in diameter. Such a wafer might routinely contain 3,000 to 4,000 chips when completed. The actual fabrication of the chips on the silicon wafer (illustrated in Figure 10.3) is done through a highly refined process of vacuum deposition of extremely pure semiconductor material on the silicon substrate.

2. *Packaging of individual chips for insertion into a card.* Once a wafer is completed, each individual chip on the wafer must be tested to make sure that it is operable. Each good chip is identified by a physical marking in preparation for sawing the wafer into many thousands of pieces (i.e., one chip in each piece). Once the chips are segmented, an electrical connector, which is larger than the chip itself, is attached. Very tiny electrical connectors (wires) link various areas on this connector with specific pins on the chip itself. The various steps involved in getting to this point were shown in Figure 10.3. The resulting configuration is referred to as a *module*. Figure 10.4 illustrates the components of a module, including the microelectronic connections between the connector and the chip.

3. *Fabrication of the card.* The card itself is constructed out of polyvinyl chloride (PVC) or some similar material. Both the chemical characteristics

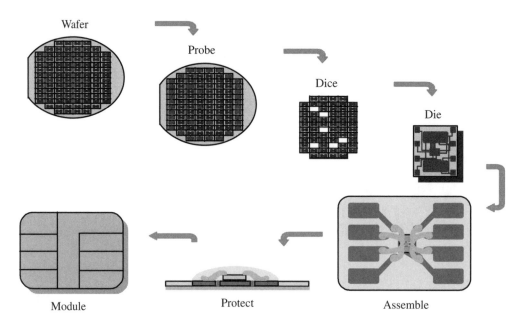

and the dimensions of the card and its associated tolerances are stringently
regulated by international standards (further discussed in Chapter 3). The
card material is produced in a large, flat sheet of the prescribed thickness.
For many types of mass-produced cards, these sheets are then printed.
Individual cards are then punched from this flat sheet and the edges of
each card are ground to a smooth finish.

4. *Insertion of the chip into the card*. Once the module and card are prepared,
the two are brought together during an insertion operation. A hole is made
in the card, and the module is glued into it. This hole is typically produced
either through a milling operation or by melting the material and pushing
the module directly into it as illustrated in Figure 10.5.

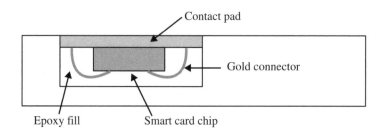

▶ **Figure 10.4**   Elements of a smart card module.

5. *Prepersonalization*. Once the module is inserted into the card, most smart card applications require that certain programs and/or data files be installed on each chip (card) before the card can be personalized and given to a specific cardholder. This general preparation of software or files on the card is done through an operation called *prepersonalization*, which is done through the I/O connectors on the surface of the card and, hence, can proceed only at the speed supported by that interface. Prepersonalization of the card generally entails loading information onto each individual card that pertains to a large collection of cards. Historically, this information might involve a file structure to be present on the card to hold information about the cardholder and about applications in which the cardholder could be involved. With more recent card developments, such as post-issuance programmable smart cards, the prepersonalization activity might involve loading application software directly onto the card.

6. *Personalization*. The personalization procedure involves putting information such as names and account numbers into the chip on the card. This

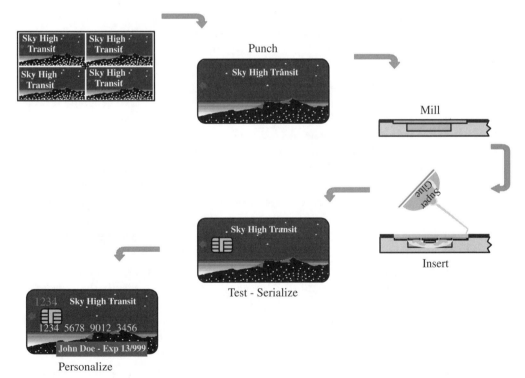

also usually entails writing a PIN on the card that the cardholder can then use to confirm his or her identity to the card. The personalization procedure usually involves physical manipulation of the card as well (i.e., pictures, names, and address information often are printed on the card). In addition, some information, such as account numbers, may be embossed on the card to allow physical transference of that information onto other media (e.g., printing a paper receipt of a credit card transaction).

Card personalization is typically the last step in preparing the card before it is issued to the cardholder and put into the cardholder's possession. This final personalization step may involve physical preparation of the card's body and/or preparation of information stored in the ICC of the card. This final personalization step has at least two distinct purposes, both of which help define the physical requirements on the personalization operation itself. First, the card will likely contain information through which the card can authenticate its identity to the (one or more) application system(s) in which it may operate and keys through which the cardholder can authenticate his or her identity to the card. This information must be prepared and loaded into the card in a secure fashion, which generally means in a secure environment as well as through secure procedures. Second, the card must be placed directly into the possession of the cardholder and then activated for use by the cardholder.

7. *Printing of the card.* The printing of graphics and text on a smart card is an extremely important feature. The appearance of the card generally reflects both aesthetically and financially on the issuer of the card. Branding information, such as corporate symbols and logos, builds name recognition for the issuer and has significant advertising value. When a card is used as a personal identification card, a person's picture, along with name and address information, often is printed on the card. For many cards supporting financial transactions, issuers often are concerned with the threat of counterfeiting of their cards and will sometimes make use of anti-counterfeiting mechanisms such as holograms printed on the face of the card as a safeguard, much as is found in thwarting the counterfeiting of currency (Figure 10.5).

Depending on the information to be placed on a card, a variety of printing processes can be utilized. For cards that will have exactly the same graphics on every card (e.g., telephone cards, transit tokens, and the like), the printing step is often done prior to the insertion of the ICC in the card. In this case, the cards are formed from large plastic sheets. The printing is done on the sheet, prior to cutting the individual cards from the sheet. Following the printing operation, the individual cards are stamped from the sheet and their edges are smoothed to conform to ISO specifications, which are examined in a bit more detail in Chapter 3.

8. *Card activation—initialization of the program and program information on the chip in the card.* Distinct from prepersonalization activities, these

initialization activities involve actually activating the applications on the card. This is typically the last act in issuing the card to the cardholder and, in some instances, may actually be done after the card is in the hands of the cardholder. In such cases, the activation activity has more to do with backend processing systems than with the card itself.

CHARACTERISTICS TO BE MANAGED

Having looked at the actors, infrastructure, and some of the operational elements of a large-scale smart card-based system, let's now see if we can identify the aspects of the system that we need to manage through a comprehensive card management system. In addition, we'll examine some of the mechanisms that we'll use for our management activities.

In Figure 10.6, we illustrate the four major components of a general smart card system. Our goal is to make sure that each of these components is operating in a well-defined manner, which is capable of being measured and hence managed. By measured, we mean that we will consider each of these components in terms of a finite state machine and that through a comprehensive management system we will be able to monitor and hopefully control the state of each component and the state transitions that will occur as our system functions. If we can do this, then we can maximize the probability that the functioning system will achieve the business goals that we've established. In other words, we want to build our level of trust in the functioning system.

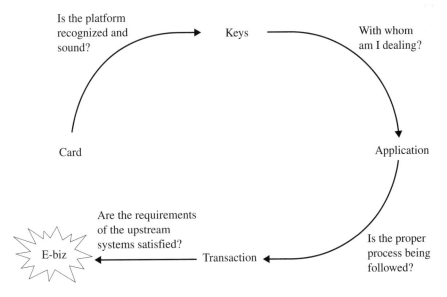

Figure 10.6 Major system components.

Data Model

The components that will form the basis of our management activities are related to each other in a predictable fashion. We will establish this relationship in the form of a data model, which we can graphically represent in terms of an entity-relationship diagram as shown in Figure 10.7. Hopefully, the E-R diagram is self-explanatory, but let's browse through it just to be sure. We can pick any of the entities as our starting point, but let's focus first on the main topic of this book: the smart card.

The smart card is the personal token to be carried by and used by the card-holder in this system. The card has a number of well-defined states that it moves through as it progresses through the manufacturing to deployment to use phases. We'll look at the various card states and the transitions among them in the next section. A card has two main purposes as indicated by the E-R diagram: it contains some aspect of an application and it participates in the general application by virtue of this aspect and also the keys that the card contains. The E-R diagram says that the card has a "one-to-many" relationship with each of these other entities: one card can contain many keys and one card can contain many applications, or elements of applications.

Working our way around the diagram then, let's now consider the key. As the diagram indicates, a key (or keys) controls access to a card and also controls execu-

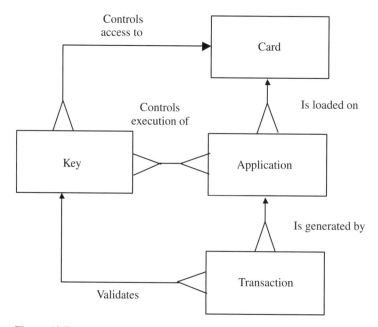

Figure 10.7   Data model for smart card management system.

tion of (or access to the execution of) applications. There can be many keys associated with one card and there can be many keys associated with many applications.

Continuing on, let's examine the application. Many applications can be related to many keys and many applications can be related to (loaded onto) one card. The application is essentially the specific business goal of our system. It is effected by its generating a number of transactions; actually, it may create from one to many transactions. The transaction is a specific mechanism by which our business goal (our application's purpose) is achieved. An application generates a transaction if so controlled by a key(s) and the key itself is the validation of the transaction.

So, our management system is going to be a mechanism that allows us to monitor the state of these four main entities and to at least monitor, and perhaps control, the transitions between the various states of these entities. As we've illustrated in Figure 10.8, a state transition itself is a well-defined thing. So, let's now look at the state diagrams and transition tables for each of these entities.

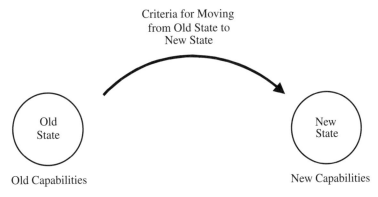

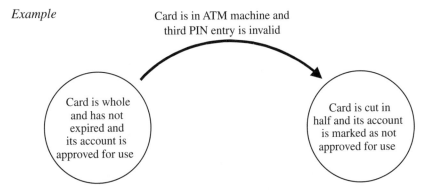

Figure 10.8   Some definitions for state diagrams and state transitions.

Card

In Chapter 6, we briefly considered the life-cycle states of a card as defined within the GlobalPlatform specifications. We're going to adopt a slightly different set of states in an attempt to consider a bit more general application architecture. The life-cycle states of a card are then defined in Figure 10.9.

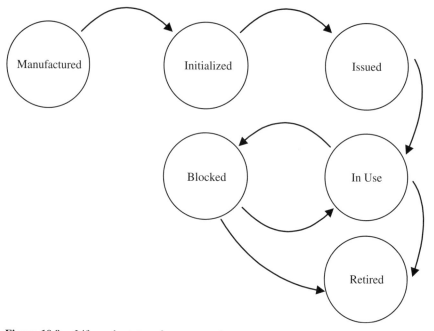

Figure 10.9   Life-cycle states of a smart card.

A card moves through these states in a series of well-defined, atomic transitions. These are indicated in Table 10.1.

Table 10.1 State Transitions for a Card

Old State	New State	Transition Criteria
Manufactured	Initialized	Add card and issuer data to card
Initialized	Issued	Add cardholder to card and get into possession of cardholder
Issued	In Use	Cardholder acknowledges possession of card
In Use	Blocked	Excessive unsuccessful PIN entries

Table 10.1 State Transitions for a Card (Continued)

Old State	New State	Transition Criteria
Blocked	In Use	Successful entry of Unblock PIN
Blocked	Retired	No more Unblock PIN entries possible
In Use	Retired	Passage of expiration date

Keys

Through the use of public key cryptography mechanisms, it is possible to address the concepts of authentication and integrity in a highly dispersed security infrastructure. In fact, many of the same techniques can be used to address authorization and privacy as well, and those points are discussed in Chapter 4.

In smart card–based systems, *keys* are used to establish identities. As we've seen in a number of cases, we typically need to establish the identities of computers talking to computers, people talking to computers, and people talking (communicating with) other people. The establishing of keys through which we can authenticate identities is one of the most critical, security-related tasks in preparing and issuing smart cards.

Both private key and public key cryptography can be used to establish identity. In the security commands of the two smart cards we examined in Chapter 6, we noted that we can use either cryptographic system with the same set of commands. The real difference between the systems comes from their respective difficulties in preparing and distributing the keys.

If we have a large number of smart cards in a system and a large number of terminals that provide the computer interfaces into which smart cards are inserted, we can either have a large number of unique keys establishing the various identities or we can have a few keys to essentially identify the boundary of the system (i.e., we can identify participants in the system). If we use a lot of unique keys, then we have a difficult key distribution problem in creating all those keys in the first place, associating them with various identities, and then distributing them to the platforms encompassed by those identities.

If we make use of a small number of keys and use them to establish participation in the system, then we increase the risk to the entire system if a key is compromised in any way. Given the philosophy we're to use for key management, we then have the problem of generating the keys, confirming that they're "good" keys, and distributing them to the relevant platforms. That said, let's now define the life-cycle states of the keys to be used in our system; this is done in Figure 10.10.

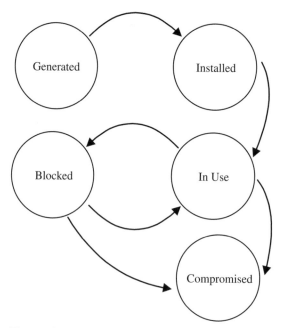

Figure 10.10   Key life-cycle states.

The state transition criteria for movement among these states is indicated in the transition table shown in Table 10.2.

Table 10.2 Key State Transitions

Old State	New State	Transition Criteria
Generated	Installed	Key successfully generated on card or injected onto card from off-card
Installed	In Use	Passing of key quality and installation tests
In Use	Blocked	Excessive, unsuccessful attempts to use the key
Blocked	Compromised	Declaration that key is no longer valid
Blocked	In Use	Reinstatement of key by holder of master key
In Use	Compromised	Expiration of lifetime for key

Personal Identification Number (PIN)

Another variant of a key is a PIN. Authenticating the identity of a person to a computer (smart card) typically involves the use of a *PIN*. A PIN can either be assigned by the card management system, or it can be chosen by the cardholder so that it's a number that is easy to remember. In either case, the point at which we store the PIN on the card, and activate it as the means of doing cardholder verification, is the point at which we've actually issued the card.

If we use a mechanism of allowing the cardholder to select the PIN, then we must provide to the cardholder a secure computing platform on which to enter the selected PIN. If we allow the card management system to select the PIN, then we'll typically use a different (physical) pathway to load the PIN onto the card versus the pathway we use to tell the cardholder what the PIN is.

Private

Private keys can refer either to the keys used in symmetric algorithms or it can refer to the private key portion of a public/private key pair in a public key cryptographic system. In either case, generating the key involves generation of a test random number string, and then performing a variety of "goodness" tests to determine whether the key has good cryptographic qualities.

Perhaps the most important aspect of generating a key is to start with a sufficiently randomized process for the initial key generation. Most instances of compromised security systems that we see in the literature arise from not using adequately randomized key generation procedures. If the generation of a particular key can be anticipated (guessed), then the entire security infrastructure is compromised.

Given an appropriately random key to start with, there are a variety of tests for either symmetric or asymmetric cryptographic systems to determine how "good" a particular key is. For asymmetric cryptographic systems, the tests are generally aimed at determining whether the seed for the key is truly a prime number (with large prime numbers being the basis for good asymmetric key pairs).

Private keys are typically stored on smart cards and are always used on the card. They are never removed from the card once stored there. When made possible by the card, it is very attractive to actually generate the key on the smart card itself. This is perhaps the most secure form of key generation. It does require, however, that key "goodness" tests be available on the smart card.

Public

Public keys generally refer to one of the keys in an asymmetric cryptographic system. It is the key that is incorporated into a digital certificate and then widely circulated within the PKI. At smart card personalization time, a public/private key pair is generated on the card. They are put through a series of "goodness" tests. Then, the private key is stored in a key file on the card while the public key is exported off of the card and used in a request for a signed digital certificate. The certificate is stored back onto the card and is also typically stored in a network directory server.

Applications

We defined the starting point of a card to be when it is considered to be "manufactured." For an application, we'll consider the starting point of its lifetime to be when it is "archived" following the development process. From this point on, it is ready to be loaded onto a card and put into general use. The life-cycle states for an application are shown in Figure 10.11.

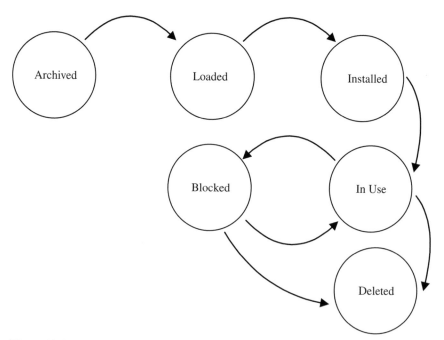

Figure 10.11   Application life-cycle states.

The state transitions for an application are shown in Table 10.3.

Table 10.3 Application State Transitions

Old State	New State	Transition Criteria
Archived	Loaded	Writing of code from server to EEPROM
Loaded	Installed	Link application into card application selection mechanism
Installed	In Use	Initial activation of program to set up application context
In Use	Blocked	Detection of attempt of unauthorized or inappropriate use
Blocked	In Use	Reception of valid application unblock message
Blocked	Deleted	Erasure of EEPROM holding application
In Use	Deleted	Removal of program from application selection mechanism on card

Transaction

The transaction is the basic building block of the functioning application; the real work of the system is done during transactions. Remember, a transaction is an atomic operation; either it all gets completed successfully or none of it is completed. The states of a transaction are illustrated in Figure 10.12.

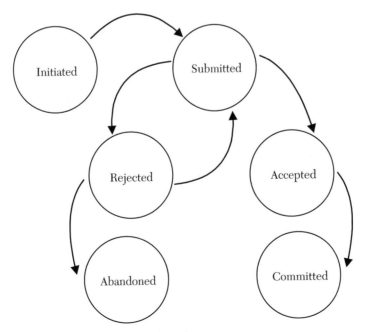

Figure 10.12   Transaction life-cycle states.

The transition criteria for transaction state changes are listed in Table 10.4.

Table 10.4 Transaction State Transactions

Old State	New State	Transition Criteria
Initiated	Submitted	Transaction has been formatted and sent to transaction processing center
Submitted	Rejected	Rejection message received back from transaction processing center
Rejected	Submitted	Corrective action taken on rejected transaction and it is resent to transaction processing center
Submitted	Accepted	Acceptance message received back from transaction processing center
Rejected	Abandoned	Data contained in transaction declared to be invalid and log entry is made
Accepted	Committed	All data used to build transaction is updated to reflect transaction

It is worth noting that many transactions that smart cards are involved with occur in terminals or back-end processing systems. In these instances, the terminals or back-end systems can archive the transaction processing and make it available to the card management system, or actually be part of the card management system. In some instances, however, the card itself can log the transactions that it takes part in. In these cases, it is interesting to consider how to feed these transaction logs (stored on many smart cards) back into a card management system.

ELEMENTS OF A CARD MANAGEMENT SYSTEM

We now have some idea of the information that we need to track within a card management system. That is, the information involved in creating and using the four major characteristics of our system. This will entail capturing, storing, and providing general access to a great deal of information. There are a number of general management system components that can be combined in a number of ways to achieve the management capabilities that we're after.

We'll view our card management system as being comprised of two major subsystems, which are tightly related to (connected to) each other. In general, we might actually consider the second to be a subsystem of the first. These are:

- card management system
- card issuing system

Each of these subsystems in turn is comprised of a number of elements.

Card Management System Components

We'll think of the card management system as being comprised of four general elements as indicated in Figure 10.13.

Certification Authority

Most trust models in this emerging infrastructure are based on the concept of a certificate that ties real-world identification information for an entity together with a public key component of a public/private key pair to be used to authenticate identity in an electronic environment. A certificate is to be issued by a *certification authority* (CA), which is some person or entity that will attest to some degree to the connection of identity information to a public key.

One variant of this model makes use of the trust between individuals who know each other to build a chain of trust from one individual to another when the two may not actually know each other. In this model, one receives a public key and associated identity information from a person he or she knows and who will vouch for the information received. This model could be seen to work for

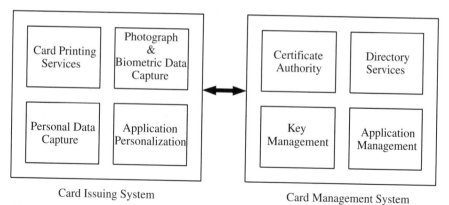

Card Issuing System   Card Management System

Figure 10.13   Components of a card management system.

relatively small numbers of individuals, but its applicability for handling very large numbers of individuals is still being explored.

Large-scale trust models are currently rooted in the concept of a CA or even hierarchies of CAs (i.e., organizational entities known as CAs perform the service of validating identity information, associating that information with a specific entity [person or organization], and associating all this with a public key). This attestation is provided in the form of a document (a certificate) that is digitally signed by the CA. The intent is that the CA forms a trusted third party to all two-way transactions. If two different parties can each trust the CA, then they can trust the information received from the CA (certificates) and, hence, can trust each other if each has received a certificate from the CA.

Registration Authorities

Issuing a signed digital certificate requires a two-stage operation. As we've seen, the purpose of the certificate is to tie together physical identity (of a person) with a private key, which can be used to authenticate their identity or to project their identity over a distant network. The act of ensuring that the physical information actually corresponds to the identity in question becomes a task for a *registration authority* (RA). Once the RA approves the issuance of a certificate, it can then be signed by a certifying authority.

Certificate Format

A *certificate* is a set of information that connects a physical identity (for example, a name, an address, a telephone number, a Social Security number, a driver license number) with the logical identity represented by a public/private key pair. Here's an example:

```
Serial Number = 889fba340000000000010000000000
X.509 Certificate Signature Algorithm ID:
   { 1 3 14 3 2 13 } == SHA-WITH-DSA-SIGNATURE
X.509 Certificate Signature Algorithm parameters:
30 5a 02 20 c2 0a 28 7b f5 7e ce 13 c2 a3 6e 72 92 c7 13 67
d9 8f 15 73 e2 ea 19 b1 67 8f 80 f8 8a d4 c2 a3 02 14 ff 9a
ff a2 7b 05 01 2e 99 a8 49 a8 cb 7f d6 ab fd 68 2f 1d 02 20
c0 c9 2d 97 f5 28 11 f5 3b 8d 81 8c 02 59 67 2a 54 25 4b 81
ae 91 c3 70 f9 9b 90 cb de f3 2b 9e
Issuer Name: /C=USA/O=SmartCommerceCorp
Not Valid Before:   12:39:16, 08/30/2000 GMT
Not Valid After:    12:39:16, 11/28/2002 GMT
Subject Name: /C=USA/S=NY/L=Albany/O=SmartCommerceCorp/
OU=Sales/CN=Jane Doe/T=Sales Manager
Subject Public Key Algorithm:   { 1 2 840 113549 1 3 1 } ==
Diffie-Hellman
Subject Public Key Algorithm parameters:
Diffie-Hellman Modulus (p):
575e67ece4e0a0b76fd457621dca50b3fd631c7d622105a3461865da39a42ffb
Diffie-Hellman Generator (g): 6b4b0d3255bfef95601890afd8070994
Subject Public Key: Diffie-Hellman public value =
3bf531a6602de246927003d0121d57d9cf089dbafcc99e65524d40adf73b12aa
```

There are a variety of recognized standards associated with such certificates. The information content is defined in the X.509 specification. Actual formats for conveying certificates are defined in the Public Key Cryptography Specifications (PKCSs). The specification PKCS #10 defines the format for requesting a certificate from a CA and the specification PKCS #7 defines the format for the certificate issued by the CA.

Key Management

The key management component of the card management system is distinct from the CA in that it involves itself with the generation and (private/secret) archiving of keys used throughout the smart card system. The key management system must be able to create or generate keys as needed and securely distribute them to where they are needed. A significant aspect of key management is the escrowing of keys such that, with proper authorization, keys can be retrieved in order to access secret (encrypted) information.

The key management system must be involved with the initial preparation of cards as well as their ongoing use.

Directory Services

In a network infrastructure supporting the use of smart cards within a PKI, a general directory service is a useful backup mechanism to the card itself. That is, information from digital certificates and, in fact, the certificates themselves, can be stored on a directory server accessible by applications in a wide area network. Such directory servers are typically built along the lines of X.500 servers. These servers can be accessed from various applications through the *lightweight directory access protocol* or LDAP mechanism. Such directory services are often referred to as LDAP services.

Real-Time Confirmation. As indicated previously, signed digital certificates are an effective way to build a chain of trust from a central authentication authority to widely distributed access points. The signature on the certificate is easily authenticated and subsequently provides an excellent mechanism through which a trusted environment can be extended from a trusted third party to other participants in transactions around the network.

A digital certificate typically contains a time interval during which it is valid. If a certificate is presented during the period when it is indicated to be valid, then a receiving entity should be able to trust the authentication information presented in the certificate. The certificate allows use of the authentication (and other) information from the certificate in *off-line* as well as *online* transactions. An off-line transaction is one in which there is no real-time communication link extending beyond the systems directly involved in the transaction. This is an arena of significant opportunity for smart card–based transactions.

In some cases, however, a real-time check on the authenticity of a certificate is required. In this case, a database of invalidated certificates can be maintained.

Certificate Revocation Lists. A *certificate revocation list* (CRL) is such a list of invalidated certificates. To be used in confirming the authenticity of certificates during a transaction, the list must be continuously available online and its address must be known and authenticated in its own right. The contents of such a CRL are essentially a digital certificate. It is issued by the card management system in response to some action that serves to invalidate the certificate.

During the course of a transaction, when a certificate is obtained from a card, if a general network connection is available, it is a straightforward operation to access a CRL to confirm that the certificate is still valid. Should the certificate be found to have been revoked, it is useful if a command can be issued to the card to lock it and prevent it from being used for further services. If possible, cards should be physically confiscated at this point; but if not, locking the card will at least prevent its being used again. Further, it is possible to report the locking operation to the card management system to indicate that a card has been deactivated and to prevent the card from being presented for reactivation.

Application Management

The application management component is concerned with the applications found on cards or the applications that cards participate in. This is where transaction archiving and/or monitoring would come into play. The element of the management system would need to keep track of all the applications in the system, who can use them, who has used them, what has been done with them, and the current state of their being. Obviously there is a lot of latitude for such a component.

Locked Cards. A typical approach through which smart card systems are programmed to react in the event of a detected attack on the smart card itself is by locking down the card and not allowing it to communicate with the outside world in other than a highly restricted way. For example, if a PIN code is used to authenticate the identity of the cardholder to the card, and if a PIN is incorrectly entered several times, a card is often programmed to go mute as a response to this perceived attack. When this happens, the only thing the card will respond to is a command sequence from the off-card application through which an UNBLOCK PIN command is issued to the card. This command contains a second order PIN which, if the card identifies it as the correct such PIN, causes the card to reset the counter, which determines the number of incorrect PIN entries that can be entered. This command can typically also redefine the PIN to some new value.

Such an operation is typically done only at some administrative center staffed by the card issuer. The cardholder is required to bring the card to the center, reprove his or her identity is the one actually associated with the card, and then allow an administrator to reset the PIN code.

The protocol for blocking a card when a card contains a number of applications, each from potentially different application developers, might be more involved. However, most card issuers tend to enforce very strict responses to perceived attacks.

Lost Cards. One of the very common occurrences that a card management system must accommodate is lost cards. A mechanism for replacing lost cards with a new replacement card must be supported, but the security and integrity of the system must be maintained in so doing.

Replacing an identity card can be as simple as reprinting and activating a new card based on information stored within the card management system during the card issuing process. In concert with this operation, however, is a need to invalidate the old card in order to subvert attempts to surreptitiously obtain additional (perhaps fraudulent) cards. The CRL we discussed previously is a good mechanism to achieve this end.

Card Issuing System Components

Using smart cards within an application system is only possible if you can handle the logistical problem of preparing the cards for the individual cardholder. In virtually all systems, a card issuing system is an integral part of overall card management. This system is the point where the cardholder meets the card and both meet the system management or administration. Let's look at the four components of this (sub)system.

Personal Data Capture

In the very first chapter of this book, we discussed the "Big 4" applications in the IT world for which smart cards were particularly applicable. In these applications, it was obvious that cards would be issued to individual cardholders and the card personalization would involve both printing and electronic preparation of the card. This being the case, an important aspect of the issuing system is to capture the required personal information about each individual cardholder. Capturing the information implies that we can validate the information as well as fetch other related information from a variety of sources. The usual result of the component will be a database of information about the cardholders in the system.

Card Printing Services

If a card is personalized for each cardholder and includes a photograph or other biometric information, then the issuing system will have to be equipped to actually print the card. Properly sizing the printing services to the loading (number of cardholders to be served) is a very important aspect of overall system architecture. In particular, whether to do printing in widely dispersed locations in real-time or to do it in centralized locations in a service-bureau style of operation is part of this architectural puzzle.

In general, the printing services will require a printer capable of 4-color printing of a card, application of anti-counterfeiting mechanisms, writing of magnetic stripes, and personalization of the on-card ICC.

Application Personalization

The application personalization component can be through of as the application management system presence at the card issuance operation. This component will deal with directly connecting the individual cardholders to each application found on the card.

Biometric Information and Photograph Capture

Smart cards are just beginning to use authentication mechanisms that rely on biometric (from the Greek, roughly translated as *life measurement*) information to uniquely identify the cardholder. Several types of biometric information are currently in use, although not always with smart cards.

- *Fingerprint recognition*—Relies on unique fingerprint ridges.
- *Voice pattern*—Relies on our unique voice patterns.
- *DNA sampling*—Relies on our unique patterns of DNA.
- *Facial recognition*—Relies on facial and bone structure of individuals.
- *Keystroke recognition*—Relies on unique typing style of individuals.
- *Handwriting recognition*—Relies on unique handwriting styles of individuals.
- *Iris/Retinal recognition*—Takes a snapshot of the blood vessels in the retina or pattern of coloration in the cornea of the eye.

Each of these techniques ties the authentication of the cardholder to measurable characteristics of the cardholder's person. In using this type of information to establish the identity of the cardholder, a number of security criteria must be met in issuing the card:

- The measurement of the biometric information must be performed on a secure (trusted) platform where it can be loaded onto the card as well as stored in a card management system.
- The identity of the cardholder (name, address, etc.) must be firmly established before the biometric information is gathered.
- The information must be recorded on the card without external copies being made, which might subsequently be used to impersonate the cardholder.

The oldest and most widely used biometric is fingerprint recognition. Each finger contains a characteristic known as *friction ridges*. While many are similar, no two friction ridges are the same. By imaging these ridges, we get a fingerprint.

Combination smart card and fingerprint readers come in several styles but, most notable are the image and capacitance types. Image style readers take a picture of the finger and then image the print based on the picture. Capacitance array readers contain millions of capacitors where ridges of a fingerprint will make a bridge between their endpoints, enabling a more accurate representation of the ridges and valleys of the print.

Most implementations of fingerprint biometrics create a template from the original image, which is a fraction of the size of the original fingerprint image. This template can be used only to compare the fingerprint against other templates. Think of it like a one-way function: A gets squashed down to B. If we want to see if C is equal to A, we must squash C down to D and compare B and D. In this manner, the template cannot be used to re-create the original print but rather a simple mathematical representation of it.

Because these templates are fairly small in size, they can easily be stored onto a smart card. This provides two benefits:

- The user walks away with his or her identity, which is stored on the card.
- To perform the authentication operation, there is a 1-to-1 match instead of a 1-to-many match.

There are two terms to describe the functionality of biometrics: *FAR* and *FRR*. FAR is the False Acceptance Rate or the probability that an intruder is accepted with a measurement that does not belong to the enrolled user. FRR is the False Rejection Rate, which is the probability that a valid user is not recognized. Good biometrics have a low FAR and low FRR, but sometimes it is necessary to tweak them so that user convenience is not hindered.

SUMMARY

This chapter has offered a broad overview of the characteristics of card management systems that are necessary in deploying smart cards in large-scale systems. Such systems are available from a number of sources. Our goal has been to identify some of the characteristics that you need to be aware of in selecting such a system for use in deploying a large-scale smart card–based infrastructure.

11

Current Trends and Future Directions

THE FRONTIER OF IT NETWORKS

A smart card is a tiny outpost on the frontier of an IT network. It provides a secure place to store information and a secure platform for performing a modest amount of processing. It is able to sense and record what happens out there and communicate in a secure manner back to other nodes of the network. And, on its own, it can enable or disable functionality at its point of use based on policies installed by its issuer.

The success of smart cards in the GSM network has been based on their use as authentication tokens, but their value is by no means limited to this application. Indeed, even in the GSM network, the value of a secure computing platform at the edge of the network is being recognized by a number of applications that are independent of the original authentication function of the SIM.

Like most of the other elements of an IT architecture, a smart card cannot justify its existence if it serves only one purpose or is hardwired to only one application. It must be configurable and programmable and it must be able to adapt to new situations and new requirements. If it is purpose-built and static, it will likely be left behind, doomed by the infrastructure demands we have discussed throughout the course of this book. In this final chapter, we will don our borrowed wizards' hats, gaze into our cloudy crystal balls, and seek to review the current trends and future directions in smart card standardization and smart card development.

When it comes to real-life standardization, the efforts of Dr. Klaus Vedder in the European Telecommunications Standards Institute (ETSI) Smart Card Platform (SCP) project are setting the pace. As generalizations of the core of GSM and 3G SIM standards, the SCP standards build on a field-proven and market-tested base. There are other smart card standardization efforts both under the umbrella of recognized standards development organizations such as the International Standards Organization (ISO) and within industry organizations such as the GlobalPlatform consortium and the Java Card Forum organization. The SCP effort is interesting in that while it, like the other organizations mentioned, is driven by representatives of both the smart card industry as well as the issuer and application communities, the SCP is perhaps a bit more focused on creating practical standards that can be verified through stringent interoperability testing.

Pressures driving smart card development over the last decade or so involved standardization of the infrastructure (software stack and hardware) of PC and terminal systems along with requirements for improved efficiency by letting smart cards work in more than one application area simultaneously. When it comes to future trends and directions in smart card operating systems and the smart card as an application platform, there are two relatively new driving forces at play: *concurrent execution* and *network access*. These forces are evolving smart card operating systems from simple command dispatch loops into real operating systems and they are enabling applications to cooperate with each other rather than having to be worlds unto themselves.

The notion of context switching among applications on a smart card was introduced by Java Card in support of the Shareable Interface Object (SIO). SIO is essentially a remote procedure call (RPC) from one card application to another. The calling application is blocked until the called application returns the answer. This mechanism allows for the on-card extension of multiple applications that may well have been developed and deployed in isolation. Such mechanisms do not, however, push us to the state of multiprocessing and multithreading, which we see on mainstream operating systems. Rather, it is the efficiency demand of multiapplication cards being able to interact with many transactions throughout a widespread network in a near simultaneous fashion that drives the need for multiprogramming mechanisms.

Work on operating systems for smart cards that is more comparable to the operating systems on general computing platforms is going on in a number of quarters. One of the first ones out of the gate is Fujitsu's HIPERSIM smart card operating system. Because one of the authors of this book designed HIPERSIM, this "next generation" smart card operating system will be discussed as representative of work in this area. It is probably safe to assume that others will follow.

THE ETSI SMART CARD PLATFORM PROJECT

The ETSI Smart Card Platform (SCP) project was a direct descendant of the ETSI SMG9 working group that had been so successful in specifying and standardizing the most successful smart card rollout, the GSM SIM. In fact, during its birthing process, SCP was known as "newSMG9."

The terms of reference of the ETSI Project Smart Card Platform (EP SCP) are given in the following sections.

Responsibilities

The main responsibilities of EP SCP are:

- development and maintenance of a common integrated circuit chip (ICC) platform for all mobile telecommunication systems
- development and maintenance of application-independent specifications for the ICC/Terminal Equipment interface of those telecommunication systems under the responsibility of ETSI
- development and maintenance of application-independent ICC standards for general telecommunication purposes
- development and maintenance of ICC standards employing advanced security methods for telecommunications applications, such as financial transactions over Mobile Telecommunication Networks ("mobile commerce")

Tasks

The main tasks of EP SCP are:

- maintenance of the common platform standards developed by the committee
- specification of enhancements to the common platform to allow the addition of innovative features and functions
- specification of generic items for ICC for telecommunications, including, but not restricted to
  - interface enhancements, such as new commands and improved transmission efficiency
  - application management, including download and load mechanisms
  - electrical/physical parameters and protocol issues

- advanced security mechanisms and related protocols
- advanced functionality for use by applications supported by the common platform standards
- specifications for the use of low-voltage technology for telecommunications cards
- elaboration and maintenance of ICC-related test specifications for the common platform in collaboration with the respective groups of 3GPP and other smart card specification bodies

Organization

The committee meets at least three times a year in plenary. These meetings would normally be co-located with the meeting of at least one of the participating committees using the common platform specifications. To facilitate a truly international participation, the chairman of EP SCP is invited to exercise the chairman's rights to invite participation in the initial stage from companies involved in the standardization work for mobile communication systems in 3GPP, 3GPP2, GAIT, T1P1, TR45, and others to be identified. To facilitate its smooth functioning the committee elects in plenary a chair and two vice-chairs. To facilitate the progression of work, working parties are established and closed as (and when) necessary. EP SCP will reflect on its work and its future organizational structure (e.g., a partnership project) after the first meetings have been held.

Liaisons

To facilitate its work, EP SCP identifies relevant bodies and sets up liaisons to these bodies. EP SCP has direct communications with the relevant bodies of all committees involved in elaborating the common platform, in particular, with those bodies involved in the specification of security matters such as ETSI TC SEC and AHAG. In addition, EP SCP has a liaison with CEN TC224 and other regional/national bodies to be identified. Some informal liaisons are handled by delegates attending international standardization meetings and forums; for example, ISO TC68 SC6, ISO/IEC JTC1/SC17, the Java Card Forum, and the WAP Forum.

The approach of SCP is to define a core set of smart card standards and to imagine that entities using those standards will adapt the core set to their particular situation by defining, if need be, deltas or modifications on the core set for the specific situation. Thus, for example, there are 3GPP and GSM deltas on top of the SCP core standards that say how the core specifications are constrained or applied to become the specifications for 3G and GSM SIMs, respectively.

ACHIEVING SMART CARD INTEROPERABILITY

The SIM standards for smart cards come as close as the smart card industry has ever come to delivering on the promise of card interoperability, arguably for four very practical reasons:

- The standards are written to be implemented.
- The standards include test suites.
- Hardware is built that is predicated on compliance to the standards.
- SIM issuers are serious about and test for interoperability.

It is worthwhile discussing each of these points briefly because standardization and interoperability are quite difficult to achieve in practice, yet are so enticing in theory. First, SIM standards were and are written to actually be implemented. They include the intersection and "consensus-ized" version of all the good ideas about smart cards. They avoid the inclusion of a lot of variants and options, and phrases like "left to the implementation." ISO standards, on the other hand, end up being the union of everybody's ideas of how smart cards are supposed to be so that everyone can claim compliance but with no resulting interoperability. Second, SIM standards include test suite standards. Perhaps the most famous (in a very rarefied domain of fame, to be sure) smart card test suite standard is GSM 11.17, "Subscriber Identity Module (SIM) conformance test specification." A test suite standard converts the statements of the standard (for with it is the test suite) into defined behavior. For example, Section 8.8 of GSM 11.11 defines the INCREASE command as follows:

INCREASE

This function adds the value given by the ME to the value of the last increased/updated record of the current cyclic EF, and stores the result into the oldest record. The record pointer is set to this record and this becomes record number 1. This function shall be used only if this EF has an INCREASE access condition assigned and this condition is fulfilled (see bytes 8 and 10 in the response parameters/data of the current EF, clause 9). The SIM shall not perform the increase if the result will exceed the maximum value of the record (represented by all bytes set to "FF").

Input:

- value to be added

Output:

- value of the increased record
- value that has been added

The test for this GSM 11.11 command in GSM 11.17 is described as follows:

INCREASE *Function*

Definition and Applicability

It shall be mandatory for all cards complying with GSM 11.11 and containing EF_{ACM} and EF_{ACMMAX} to support all functions described therein.

Conformance Requirement

- CR1—This function shall add the value given to the value of the last increased/updated record of the current cyclic EF and store the result into the oldest record.
- CR2—The record pointer shall be set to this record and this record becomes the first record.
- CR3—The function shall only be used if the INCREASE access condition is fulfilled.
- CR4—The function shall accept as an input, the value to be added.
- CR5—The function shall output the value of the increased record and the value that has been added.
- CR6—The SIM shall not perform the INCREASE if the result would exceed the maximum value of the record (represented by all bytes set to "FF").

Test Purpose

To verify that the INCREASE function conforms to the preceding requirements.

Method of Test

Initial conditions:

- The SIM is connected to an ME simulator.
- Each record in EF_{ACM} contains the data "00 00 01."

Test procedure:

- The ME simulator resets the SIM.
- The ME simulator sends SELECT commands to the SIM to select EF_{ACM} under DF_{GSM}.
- The ME simulator sends an INCREASE command with value "00 00 02" to the SIM.
  - The status condition returned by the SIM shall be SW1='98_{16}', SW2='04_{16}' - access condition not fulfilled [CR3].
- The ME simulator sends a VERIFY CHV command to the SIM.
- The ME simulator sends an INCREASE command with value "00_{16} 00_{16} 03_{16}" to the SIM.
  - The status condition returned by the SIM shall be SW1='$9F_{16}$', SW2='06_{16}' [CR4].
- The ME simulator sends a GET RESPONSE command to the SIM.
  - The response data shall be '00_{16} 00_{16} 04_{16} 00_{16} 00_{16} 03_{16}' [CR1,5].
- The ME simulator sends an INCREASE command with value "01_{16} 02_{16} 00_{16}" to the SIM.
- The ME simulator sends a GET RESPONSE command to the SIM.
  - The response data shall be '01_{16} 02_{16} 04_{16} 01_{16} 02_{16} 00_{16}' [CR1].
- The ME simulator sends a READ RECORD command using ABSOLUTE mode with record 1 to the SIM.
  - The data read shall be '01_{16} 02_{16} 04_{16}' [CR2].
- The ME simulator sends an INCREASE command with value "FF_{16} 00_{16} 00_{16}" to the SIM.
  - The status condition returned by the SIM shall be SW1='98_{16}', SW2='50_{16}' - increase cannot be performed - Max value reached [CR6].
- The ME simulator sends an INCREASE command with value "00_{16} FF_{16} FD_{16}" to the SIM.
- The ME simulator sends a GET RESPONSE command to the SIM.
  - The response data shall be '02_{16} 02_{16} 01_{16} 00_{16} FF_{16} FD_{16}' [CR5].

GSM 11.17 goes through the entire GSM 11.11 standard this way, giving detailed "if you do this, then this should happen" instructions. Such a test suite removes all possibility for Monday morning interpretation and marketing spin on the GSM 11.11 standard. A SIM acts like what GSM 11.17 says, or it doesn't. The hardware has to speak for itself.

The third factor that has contributed to the success of GSM smart card standards is that hardware, namely GSM cell phones, is built that is premised on the standards. Nokia doesn't build one phone for Schlumberger SIMs and another phone for Gemplus SIMs. It builds phones that comply with GSM 11.11. The same holds for Ericsson and Motorola and all the other handset manufacturers. If you want to bring a SIM to market, then it must work in all these handsets, which means it must comply with GSM 11.11 down to the very last bit and byte.

The final factor that makes SIM standards work is that network operators who are the live customers for SIMs really care about interoperability. They shop for it, test for it, and get really grumpy if they find they don't have it. When pressed by a strong marketplace, smart card manufacturers will, at the end of the day, respond to customer demands for interoperability.

One of the reasons why smart cards have met more limited success outside the GSM application is that interoperability was promised but often not delivered. Without the strong market driver and knowledgeable customer base, too often interoperability was not achieved because there was no overarching concern for doing all the sometimes painful things necessary to achieve it. As value of smart cards in the GSM setting was recognized and efforts were mounted to create this value in other settings, the contribution of the GSM standards to the success of the SIM also were recognized. SCP is the first step to extend the SIM standardization process to other cards: first, to cards in telecommunication systems and, perhaps later, to cards in all settings. Certainly, the name of the effort—Smart Card Platform—invites card issuers for whatever application to consider these standards.

THE SCP STANDARDS

Table 11.1 is a list of the standards in the SCP series as of the end of 2001.

The first task of the SCP project has been to "core" the GSM and 3GPP SIM standards and to make the result a specification for smart cards in general, not just TDMA SIMs. This task is nearing completion. The next task will be to consider other smart card standards and to determine which parts of them could be included in the SCP core and which parts are truly a function of their application domain. This process has already started with the consideration of the EMV2000 specifications and the GlobalPlatform specifications.

The participation of the banking card community in SCP has been encouraged but has been, at best, lukewarm to date. Unlike the telecommunications industry, which knows it lives or dies on real interoperability, the banking card community still seems to depend on closely held control that closed, proprietary systems provide. As a result, banks and bank card associations do not generate

Table 11.1 SCP Specifications

ID	Name
SCP 101.222	ETSI Numbering System for Telecommunications Application Providers
SCP 102.221	UICC-Terminal Interface; Physical and Logical Characteristics
SCP 102.222	Administrative Commands for Telecommunications Applications
SCP 102.223	Card Application Toolkit (CAT)
SCP 102.224	Security Mechanisms for the Card Application Toolkit
SCP 102.225	Secured Packet Structure for UICC Applications
SCP 102.226	Remote APDU Structure for UICC-Based Applications
SCP 102.230	UICC-Terminal Interface; Physical, Electrical, and Logical Test Specification
SCP 102.240	UICC Application Programming Interface (API)
SCP 102.241	Java Card™ API for the UICC

the level of customer demand for interoperability and standards compliance that is generated by the telecommunications industry and that is necessary to achieve interoperability and standards compliance.

THE UICC PLATFORM

From a card issuer's perspective, what is compelling about the SCP effort is that the smart card platform it is describing, the UICC, is truly multiapplication. Not only can it contain data from multiple application providers, but it can contain executable code from multiple application providers. This is the first set of smart card specifications that acknowledge the reality of the smart card usage. Namely, if smart cards are to succeed in an IT setting, they have to be multipurpose and able to evolve as the system evolves.

Perhaps because there is no printing on the outside and because the card is hidden in the guts of the mobile phone where it is rarely seen, SIM issuers were the first large issuers to get over the need to see their logos and own the physical card. There are not yet SIMs issued by large corporations, and you can't go down to Radio Shack and buy a SIM and expect your local 3G operator to put its bits on it, but the architecture of the SCP platform, the UICC, differentiates cleanly between the owner of the platform and the provider of each of the applications running on the platform. Thus, for example, both the GSM SIM and the 3G USIM are thought of and standardized as applications running on the UICC. There is no technical necessity for the provider of either of these applications to be the provider of the physical card.

Moving from a single-provider to a multi-provider card poses a number of technical and business challenges. The Global Platform security framework that was described in Chapter 6 has addressed some of the technical challenges, particularly in the area of loading and deleting applications. Two challenges that are still the elephants sitting in the middle of the room are *data sharing* and *application cooperation*.

The mechanics of data sharing can be handled by the Boolean expression access control lists (ACLs) that are already in SCP 102.221. What is missing in the SCP specifications currently is a general-purpose framework for doing authentication and a unified way to store cryptographic information. There are candidates on the horizon for both of these needs—namely, IETF's Extensible Authentication Protocol (EAP) for the former and ISO 7816-15 for the latter.

Application cooperation is knottier than data sharing because it involves real-time trust. The Shareable Object Interface of Java Card is a valiant first attempt at application cooperation and the problems it encountered certainly threw light on how knotty a problem this is going to be. Perhaps the Java Card 3.0 specifications will address some of the deficiencies. In any case, from the cardholder's point of view, using multiple card applications in a single transaction is not an abstract notion. Consider, for example, listening to a tune on your cell phone. You will use one application to gain access to the network, a second to pay for the download, a third to do digital rights management on the download, and perhaps a fourth to get some frequent listener points. All of these applications are involved in what—from the cardholder's point of view— is one transaction.

Application cooperation is one of two demands being placed on smart card operating systems that are causing today's operating systems to show their age. The other is network access.

NEXT GENERATION SMART CARD OPERATING SYSTEMS (COSNG)

The vision of a smart card as an application platform rather than a simple security token is a paradigm shift for smart card operating systems. In the simple security token era, smart card operating systems were little more than file systems with a dispatch loop. The dispatch loop was driven by incoming commands and the microtasks were the handlers for each APDU. The model of computing was that of a single threaded remote procedure call (RPC) server.

There will undoubtedly continue to be demand for this type of smart card operating system. But it is also true that this operating system model cannot completely support the needs of the platform vision or the UICC standards. Just as there are hand calculators and computers, so will there be dispatch loop smart cards and smart cards with real operating systems.

There are a number of forces that are working to create a new type of smart card operating system:

- First, a new generation of smart card processors and memory architectures is currently under development. Many of the compromises forced on today's application frameworks by the limitations of today's processors will be removed. While we will undoubtedly evolve into the future, specifying an API that is unconstrained by the past and is designed explicitly for this new generation of machine can provide a beacon to guide that evolution.

- Second, today's smart card operating systems and application frameworks are intrinsically local and monoapplication. Various cosmetic design patches have been applied to make them appear to be network-aware and multiapplication, but these efforts are, as they say in Texas, tantamount to putting lipstick on a pig. The very notion of first- and second-level applications belies the monoapplication architecture of the current generation of SIM operating systems. The future of the smart card is multiapplication and network connected. These are capabilities of an operating system that can't be laid over the top of a simple, purpose-built APDU dispatch loop. They go all the way to the iron.

- Third, and finally, it is becoming abundantly clear that if the suite of everyday smart card applications is going to extend beyond Windows logon and your favorite coffee shop's frequent drinker points, the creativity, innovation, and entrepreneurial drive of the third party application development community will have to be courted and harnessed. The experience and the market orientation to build the full range of applications that will be needed to deliver on the financial and consumer promises of smart cards in corporate or consumer settings may well require input beyond the players in today's market. Outdated, arcane, and overly constrained programming frameworks send the message to the third party application development community, intended or not, to take your application ideas elsewhere.

The Generic Smart Card Application

Necessarily, smart card applications come in two parts: *on* the smart card and *off* the smart card. We will call the former part the *card part* and the latter part the *terminal part* of the application. The two parts of the application are connected by a communication protocol of some sort that we will give the generic name *secure messaging*. Both the card part and the terminal part of the application are necessarily written against an API, which includes access to the secure messaging function so each part can communicate with the other. From 30,000 feet, a smart card application looks like Figure 11.1.

Smart card application developers are concerned as much, if not more, with the programming interface provided to the terminal side of the application as with the programming interface provided to the card side. Smart card APIs have been covered in Chapters 4 and 6.

▶ **Figure 11.1**   Architecture of a smart card application.

Desidirata for COSng

We propose the following three simple requirements as the basis for the design of COSng:

- Requirement #1: The COSng architecture must be based on modern and familiar models of computation in order to attract the widest range of application developers.
- Requirement #2: COSng must enable concurrently running applications to communicate with one another and cooperate in delivering a service.
- Requirement #3: COSng messaging must enable an application to establish a secure end-to-end communication link between the card side (wherever it is) and the terminal side (wherever it is). Either side of the application can initiate the communication.

One way to think about COSng is to define it in terms of existing popular APIs and to do so in a way that the card API is as close as possible to the terminal API. This strategy can be summarized in the following two COSng Design Rules:

- Design Rule #1: COSng shall be a currying of existing general-purpose computing APIs and widely used data communication protocols.
- Design Rule #2: The card side of the COSng shall be a subset of the terminal side of the COSng.

Generic Example of COSng

COSng has five subsystems. Each subsystem serves a specific purpose. The specification for each part is based on existing, general-purpose computing subsystems.

The five component subsystems are:

- File System Including Data Sharing—SCP 101.221 with Boolean ACLs
- Multitasking Including Inter-Application Communication and Synchronization—Mach, uITRON, L4, eCOS
- Cryptography Including Authentication and Authorization—PKCS #11 and ISO 7816-8 and 9
- Communication Including Secure Messaging—IPv6 over T=1
- Human Interface—SCP 102.223 Card Application Toolkit (CAT)

File System Including Data Sharing

Almost any hierarchical file system with file and directory names of arbitrary length and alphabet will do. The open/read/write/close application program interface to file and directory operations is as close to a universal in computing as you can get.

How file systems still differ is in their approach to access control. The multiparty environment of a smart card does not map gracefully, if at all, into the owner/group/world type of access controls found on workstations and personal computers, nor does its reliance on centralized authorization servers. Fortunately, ISO 7816-9 and SCP 101.221 have defined a very flexible and general-purpose access control notation that can easily be grafted onto file systems with names larger than 2 bytes.

Multitasking Including Inter-Application Communication and Synchronization

There are a number of good candidates here that are good because multitasking and interapplication communication are the most significant steps that smart card operating systems have to make. eCOS is an operating system provided by RedHat that is based on uITRON. Fujitsu's HIPERSIM smart card operating system, which is described in the following sections, is based on Mach.

Cryptography Including Authentication and Authorization

The "Cryptoki" interface to cryptographic operations and cryptographic hardware is field-proven and widely used. In fact, many cryptographic smart cards come with Cryptoki interface libraries. The strength of Cryptoki is that it is designed to span a broad range of cryptographic protocols. In a sense, it is more of a general framework than an API to specific algorithms. On the other hand, PKCS #15 also defines how many, if not all, of the popular algorithms are represented within this framework. An alternative would be to use the algorithm identification scheme of ISO 9979 and ISO 10116 underneath the Cryptoki API.

Communication Including Secure Messaging

The number of different types of communication channels that will be available to applications in general continues to grow. This impacts smart card applications particularly because of their inherently distributed nature. Techniques such as ISO 7816-4 logical channels and secure messaging that do nothing more than connect the smart card to the local terminal are of little use in building other than local applications. The GlobalPlatform specifications deliver a secure messaging concept much closer to the true requirements. However, these specifications are still too emeshed in a business model of card issuance and operations than is desirable and secure messaging is (in GP) heavily intertwined with these concepts.

If the smart card is to be network-aware, then it will have to communicate through, not to, the local terminal. In fact, from the point of view of a growing number of applications, the local terminal is an insecure device and certainly not one that can be trusted in the role of a network proxy server. The smart card must be able to participate in secure, end-to-end communication that regards everything between the two end points, including the handset, as a point of attack.

Another aspect of smart card usage, which will benefit from a more general physical interface, is the infrastructure problem associated with smart cards. Today, for a card with physical contacts, a smart card reader is required on a PC or in a terminal to make a physical connection to the card. As we saw in Chapters 6 and 7, there are moves in this direction by using the USB physical interface. This type of smart card (the two we discussed in Chapter 6) don't require a separate reader; they can use a USB port on a PC. Further, the card can make use of the USB protocol with its higher speed. Unfortunately, even this approach still requires layering on top of the ISO link-level protocol layers.

So, in the longer term, a new I/O mechanism, which would remove the need for a special smart card reader, would be extremely attractive. Perhaps the most attractive option would be a high-speed wireless connection directly from the on-card ICC to a PC or terminal. Unfortunately, this is not likely to happen until a reliable on-card power source is developed. A wireless connection with enough range to be very interesting (e.g., Bluetooth) will likely need a direct power source rather than just an RF signal.

As a general framework for communication programming, sockets have proven to be as popular and useful as Cryptoki has been for cryptographic programming. You can plug a wide range of communication protocols into the sockets framework and, thus, the API is stable as new and better channels become available to connect the two sides of the core API. Perhaps a combination of wireless and IP is the desired wave of the future?

Human Interface

At first blush, it seems strange to talk about a human interface API in a smart card. This function has historically been completely delegated to the terminal. But, the utility of enabling smart card applications to communicate directly with the cardholder has been proven by the GSM SIM Application Toolkit and its descendant, the SCP Card Application Toolkit. There are a couple of reasons why this is attractive:

- By embedding the human interface to a card application in the card itself, the cardholder is presented with the same interface to the application regardless of what terminal devices he or she is using to activate the application.
- A card can provide identifying marks on its human interface that are clues to the cardholder that he or she is really communicating with the card and that the card interface is not being "spoofed" by the terminal.

Fujitsu's HIPERSIM Smart Card Operating System

The first next generation smart card operating system on the market is Fujitsu's HIPERSIM smart card operating system. HIPERSIM is based on the Mach microkernel and was designed and built by a team of engineers led by one of the authors (SBG) of this book.

The Mach micro-kernel was chosen primarily because the message-passing metaphor of Mach was a natural fit to the need for efficient and secured communication between the applications on a smart card. Figure 11.2 shows the "wedding cake" overall architecture of HIPERSIM. The operating system is divided into three major components, or sets:

- The Manufacturer's Set is a generic, multitasking operating system kernel consisting of an input/output subsystem, a file system, a cryptographic framework, and the Mach task manager. The only code in the Manufacturer's Set that knows it is a smart card is the code in the input/output subsystem that handles the T=0 and T=1 protocols of SCP 102.221.
- The Developer's Set is the middle layer of the wedding cake. (Some might think of it as the frosting layer.) This is where the generic operating system of the Manufacturer's Set is turned into a smart card operating system. The Developer's Set layer knows all about the ISO standards and the SCP standards. It is a smart card through and through.
- The Application's Set is the collection of applications that are running on the card. The set will be different from application domain to application domain and from card issuer to card issuer. Domain-specific applications available initially include the GSM SIM and 3G USIM applications, the WIM application of the WAP Forum, and the USAT Interpreter of 3GPP.

There generic application is called the UICC application that implements the commands of SCP 102.221 and SCP 102.222. This application can be included on any card. The efficient interapplication communication capabilities enable all the other applications on the card to use the UICC application for the standard smart card commands that the domain-specific application wants to apply to its files.

SUMMARY

Smart card issuers of yesteryear—the financial institutions, the entertainment distributors, and the network operators—believe they have inherited the right to be the keepers of the trust infrastructure that smart cards create and the value that it generates.

Corporate IT managers and security officers, on the other hand, have realized that their guardianship of enterprise IT assets extends to the very edge of their networks and that they are obliged to take charge of the smart card-protected boundary of their domain. If the banks, media moguls, and the telecoms want to play in the corporate arena, it will be as bags of bits on corporate smart cards.

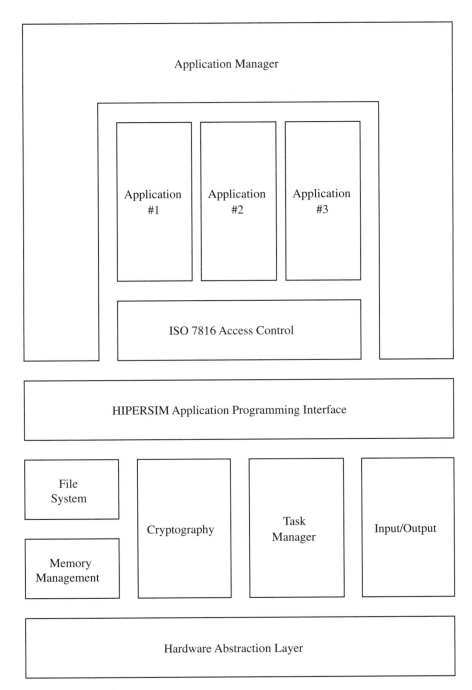

▶ **Figure 11.2**   Architecture overview of HIPERSIM.

For many practical and legal reasons, corporations seem unlikely to cede control of their security infrastructures to either their banks, their ad agencies, or their telecommunications providers. The corporations will own the platform when it involves corporate assets.

A consumer is a corporation of size one, and it is also starting to occur to consumers that they, too, can and should have a say in who their trust brokers will be. They may choose their bank, their phone company, or their classical radio station as the provider of their personal smart card platform. And in the interest of securing and controlling both their privacy and their identity, the consumer will pick and choose their other trust brokers and require them to put their bits on this chosen platform.

Finally, the day of the much-talked-about "white card" is not as unimaginable as it once was. In this not-so-distant smart card era, the customer goes down to Radio Shack and buys a generic smart card—the white card—and is the keeper of his or her own security and privacy. Banks, record companies, movie merchants, phone companies, and perhaps even governments will put their bits on the cardholder's smart card.

Glossary

3GPP (3rd Generation Partnership Project)

A consortium of standards bodies that is writing the standards for the SIM in 3G mobile telephones.

A3 and A8

Two cryptographic algorithms used in GSM cellular telephony and typically implemented in GSM SIM smart cards.

ABS (acrylonitrile butadiene styrene)

A common plastic material used for the manufacture of smart cards.

AC (access condition)

An attribute in a file header that allows or denies execution of certain commands based on certain security conditions, such as authentication of the entity attempting to execute the command.

ADF (application dedicated file)

The directory on a smart card that is the root directory of all the data pertaining to a particular application.

AID (application identifier)

A unique number assigned to smart card applications.

algorithm

A set of detailed instructions for performing a mathematical operation.

alt.technology.smartcards

A Usenet newsgroup devoted to smart cards. The FAQ for the newsgroup is at *www.scdk.com/atsfaq.htm*.

ANSI (American National Standards Institute)

An American technical standards body and the representative of the United States to the International Standards Organization (ISO).

anticollision

When using a contactless smart card, the data being transmitted from the card to the reader doesn't collide or interfere with the data being transmitted from the reader to the card.

APDU (application protocol data unit)

A unit of data transfer between a smart card and an application program; a smart card command or command response.

API (application programming interface)

Contains calls a program can make on routines stored in a function library or implemented in the operating system.

Arimura, Dr. Kunitaka

The Japanese inventor who received a patent on smart cards in 1971.

ASC (application-specific command)

An extension of the basic smart card operating system, often stored in the smart card EEPROM.

ASCII (American Standard Code for Information Interchange)

A method of digitally representing characters in the Latin alphabet using 1 byte or 8 bits. For example, 61_{16} is the ASCII representation of lowercase Latin letter *a. See also* Unicode.

asynchronous protocol

A mode of data transmission in which the transmission start time of a character or block of characters is arbitrary. *See also* synchronous protocol.

ATR (answer to reset)

A data string returned by a smart card when the microprocessor in the card is physically reset. Two types of data strings are standardized: They are described as asynchronous transfer protocols T=0 and T=1.

authenticate

To establish the identity of the origination or originator of a transaction or other data-processing request.

authorize

To grant privileges typically to access data, usually based on successful authentication.

Basic card

A smart card manufactured by ZeitControl that supports on-card applications written in the Basic programming language.

batch card

A smart card that carries a key that enables its holder to unlock a shipment or batch of other smart cards. A batch card carries a transport key. *See also* mother card.

biometrics

The use of a person's physical characteristics such as fingerprints, hand geometry, voice or signature characteristics, eye patterns, and so on for authentication.

black book

A catalog of information used to subvert smart card security systems.

blinding

Taking provisions in a smart card's operation to defeat voltage and timing attacks. Blinding, for example, would ensure that all multiplications take the same amount of time independent of the values of the multiplier and the multiplicand.

Bright, Roy

The French publicist who coined the term smart card.

byte string

A sequence of bytes.

C-SET (Chip-Secured Electronic Transaction)

The French version of SET, which incorporates a smart card in its specification.

CA (certification authority)

An organization or enterprise that issues digital certificates, primarily those attesting to an individual's identity.

CAD (card accepting device)
A smart card reader.

capture
To not return a card to the cardholder if an anomalous condition is encountered before a transaction is complete. A capture reader takes the smart card completely inside its physical security perimeter so that it cannot be extracted by the user before the transaction is completed.

Card Europe
A smart card industry association. See *www.gold.net/users/ct96*.

cardholder
The person carrying and using a smart card. A cardholder does not necessarily own the card or have any rights other than holding and using the card.

CARDIS
An international smart card conference, Smart Card Research and Advanced Applications, held roughly every 18 months that features academic papers on smart card research.

CardTech/Securetech
A North American smart card convention held twice a year.

Carte Bancaire
The smart card issued by Groupement des Cartes Bancaires, a French bank card association.

Cartes
An annual smart card convention held in Paris.

Castrucci, Paul
The American inventor who received U.S. Patent 3,702,464 on a smart card in 1972.

CAT (Card Application Tookit)
The generalization of the APDUs of the SIM Application Toolkit that apply to all telecommunication technologies. These commands support communication between applications on the UICC and human interface and network capabilities of the mobile handset.

CEN (Comité Européen de Normalisation)
A European standards organization located in Brussels.

CEPS (Common Electronic Purse Specification)

The specification for a monetary payment application for smart cards that can handle multiple currencies.

cert

Conversational shorthand for *digital certificate.*

challenge

A random string of bytes sent from a data processing system to another system that it is trying to authenticate. The receiving system must encrypt the challenge with an encryption key in its possession and return the encrypted challenge to the sending system. If the sending system can decrypt the encrypted challenge, it knows the receiving system possesses the key that encrypted it and this authenticates the system to which the challenge was sent.

checksum

A single numeric value computed from a large body of text or data that can be quickly recomputed by the recipient of the text and data to check if any characters in the body have been changed during transmission. Unlike a hash value, similar bodies of text may yield equal checksums. Checksums guard against random transmission errors, not deliberate attempts to alter the content of a message.

CHV (cardholder verification)

A secret number or password, known only to the cardholder, which is required to access certain services on a smart card. Also known as personal identification number (PIN).

CLA

The first data field in an ISO 7816-4 command that gives the class of the command.

CLK

The contact or pad on a smart card module through which clock signals are provided to run the smart card processor.

clock rate

The rate at which the clock signal provided to a smart card processor changes, typically 5 MHz or 5,000,000 pulses per second. Smart card processors divide this by 2 and take on the average of 4 or 5 "clocks" per instruction and so run at about ½ MIP or 500,000 instructions per second.

common criteria

A collection of testing standards for the security aspects of information technology systems, including smart cards.

COMP128

An authentication algorithm popular in telecommunications and often found on GSM SIM cards.

contact card

A smart card that is activated by being inserted into a smart card reader, which presses contacts against the contact pads of the smart card module. *See also* contactless card.

contactless card

A smart card that is activated by being held near the smart card reader rather than being put into the reader, as with contact cards. Power is provided to the card through inductance coils and communication occurs via radio frequency signals and a capacitive plate antenna. *See also* contact card.

core

The instruction set used by a smart card; for example, an 8051 core implements the Intel 8051 instruction set. It is called the core because the integrated circuit that implements the instructions is the core of the smart card integrated circuit.

COS (card operating system)

The program contained in the smart card ROM that is used for communicating with the smart card, managing security, and managing data in the smart card file system.

CPU (central processing unit)

The integrated circuitry on a smart card that executes the program stored on the card.

CRT (Chinese remainder theorem)

A theorem about the unique factorization of integers that is used in some cryptographic algorithms.

cryptographic coprocessor

Special integrated circuits for quickly doing calculations, particularly modular arithmetic and large integer calculations, associated with cryptographic operations and algorithms. These circuits are added to a standard processor core and therefore are called a coprocessor.

cyclic file

A type of file on a smart card that contains records such that the first record is returned when a READ NEXT command is issued on the last record; thus, the records form a ring and cycle from one to the next.

Danmont

A smart card operating system developed in Denmark and used in the VisaCash card. See *www.iccard.dk*.

daughter card

One of a batch or shipment of cards that is unlocked with a mother card.

DEA (data encryption algorithm)

Synonym for DES.

DES (data encryption standard)

A secret key cryptographic algorithm defined and promoted by the U.S. government.

Dethloff, Jürgen

The German co-inventor of the smart card in 1968. *See also* Gröttrupp, Helmut.

DF (dedicated file)

A smart card directory file that holds other files.

digital certificate

A digital message that contains the public key of an individual together with a guarantee from a certificate authority that the public key belongs to the individual.

digital signature

A digital technique that authenticates the user's transaction. A digital signature can, for example, be the encryption of a hash of the transaction with the individual's private key.

diversified key

A smart card key that is computed from a smart card's serial number and a master key. Diversified key techniques let every card in a large set of cards be accessed with a unique key without the necessity of maintaining a record of which key is on which card. Both the master key and the calculation program are kept in a highly secure environment.

DSA (digital signature algorithm)
A cryptographic algorithm approved by the U.S. government for use in creating digital signatures.

DSS (digital signature standard)
The U.S. standard that defines DSA and its use.

E-cash card
A stored-value smart card that contains money in digital form in one or more national currencies such as kroner, francs, yen, marks, or dollars. When you spend money from the card, the host application decrements a currency value; when you add more money to the card, the host application increments a currency value. Don't try this at home.

EEPROM (electrically erasable programmable read-only memory)
Memory in a smart card that holds its contents when power is removed, that is, when the card is removed from the card reader. Unlike with ROM, new values can be written to EEPROM by the smart card CPU. EEPROM is used to store smart card values that are set during personalization, such as account numbers or values that can change, such as the amount of value stored on the card.

EF (elementary file)
An elementary file is part of the smart card file system that contains application data. *See* DF (dedicated file); MF (master file).

EFT (electronic funds transfer)
A funds transfer that is sent electronically, either by telecommunication or written on magnetic media, such as tape, cassette, or disk.

electronic wallet
Similar to an e-purse, with added functions such as credit and debit account access capability. *See also* EP or E-purse.

emulator
A computer program plus special hardware that enables a program developer to run a smart card program on the actual smart card chip but still be able to control and analyze the execution of the program. An emulator, for example, typically allows the developer to single-step the smart card processor and examine the smart card processor's registers and memory.

EMV (Europay, MasterCard, and Visa)
An alliance of bank card associations that generated a smart card standard for payment (credit and debit) smart cards called EMV 2000.

EN 726

A standard for smart cards and terminals for telecommunication use. The standard is the technical basis for smart cards in Europe

EN 742

A standard for the contacts for cards and devices used in Europe. New edition specifies the format used for the GSM subscriber identity module (SIM).

EP or E-purse (electronic purse)

A smart card that stores small amounts of currency, usually less than $1,000. Some electronic purses can be reloaded; some cannot, and are discarded when empty.

ESCAT (European Smart Card Application and Technology)

A smart card convention held regularly at the beginning of September.

ETSI (European Telecommunication Standards Institute)

A European standards body that writes the standards governing the SIM in GSM mobile telephones.

FIPS 140-1

A U.S. federal standard titled "Security Requirements for Cryptographic Modules" that concerns physical security of smart cards when used as cryptographic devices. For more information, go to *www.csrc.ncsl.nist.gov/fips/fips140-1.txt*.

FLASH

A type of nonvolatile memory that can be written much faster than EEPROM memory. Although usually written in all capital letters, FLASH is not an acronym, but rather refers to the fact that the memory can be bulk erased (i.e., electronically "flashed" as PROM memory of yore was flashed with UV light).

FRAM (ferroelectric memory)

A type of nonvolatile memory based on electric field orientation with nearly an infinite write capability as opposed to normal EEPROM memory, which can only be written on the order of 10,000 times.

FSCUG (federal smart card users group)

A U.S. government smart card users group that promulgates standards and specifications for the use of smart cards in government data processing functions.

GlobalPlatform (GP)

A consortium formed to own, support, and further develop the GlobalPlatform specifications for secure smart card application systems, originally developed by Visa International.

GND

The ground contact or pad on a smart card module.

Gröttrupp, Helmut

The German co-inventor of the smart card in 1968. *See also* Dethloff, Jürgen.

GSCAS (Global Smart Card Advisory Service)

A smart card consulting service. For more information, go to *www.gscas.com*.

GSM (Groupe Spécial Mobile or Global Service for Mobile Communications)

A European cellular telephone standard. GSM telephones use smart cards called SIM cards to store subscriber account information.

handshake

A protocol between two devices, such as a smart card and a personal computer, to establish a common dialog.

hard mask

See mask.

hash

A string of bytes of a fixed length that is effectively a unique representation of a longer document. *Effectively unique* means that it is difficult to find another document that produces the same hash value and that any slight change in the long document will produce a different hash value.

HIPERSIM

A smart card operating system created by Fujitsu for its FRAM smart cards.

hybrid card

A smart card that can function as more than one kind of card (e.g., a smart card that can function as both a contact and a contactless card, or a smart card that also has a magnetic stripe or a barcode).

I/O (input/output)

The input/output contact or pad on a smart card module though which messages are passed to and received from the microprocessor in the card.

IC (integrated circuit)

A small electronic device made from metallic and semiconductor materials that contains all the functional components and connections of the circuit, integrated into a single device package.

ICC (integrated circuit card)

Another name for a smart card.

ICMA (International Card Manufacturers Association Suite)

A smart card industry trade association. For more information, go to *www.icma.com*.

IDEA

A cryptographic algorithm commonly thought of as the European equivalent of DES.

IEC (International Electrotechnical Commission)

An international standards body based in Geneva, Switzerland.

IFD (interface device)

Another name for a smart card reader.

induced error attack

An attack on a smart card's security system that causes the CPU to perform erroneous calculations; errors are induced in the smart card's CPU by subjecting the card to unusual environmental conditions such as temperature, voltage, microwaves, radiation, and so on.

initial bit

The first bit of a string of bits presented to an input device. The device will group the series into blocks of, say, 8 bits to make a byte string. It is important to specify if the initial bit is the highest or lowest byte in its byte.

initialization

The process during which the basic data that are common to all chip cards in a manufacturing batch are loaded into the chip.

INS

The second field of an ISO 7816-4 smart card command, which contains the instruction to be executed by the smart card.

intelligent memory card

A memory card that contains some additional features—typically, security features—which limit access to the memory.

inverse convention

A communication convention wherein signal-positive is to be interpreted as 0 and signal-zero is to be interpreted as 1; this is the inverse of the usual translation of these states into binary digits.

ISIM (IMS SIM)

A UICC application that provides digital rights management services for the IP Messaging Service on 3G networks.

ISO (International Standards Organization)

The penultimate technical standards body based in Geneva, Switzerland. With representation on its working committees from almost all countries, the ISO defines technical standards for worldwide interoperability of hardware and software. For more information, go to *www.iso.org*.

ISO/IEC 4909

The ISO standard for magnetic card format for electronic banking data. Some smart cards have magnetic strips on them and others support magnetic stripe communication protocols.

ISO/IEC 7810

The ISO standard for the physical characteristics of an identification card.

ISO/IEC 7811

The ISO standard for identification card recording techniques.

ISO/IEC 7812

The ISO standard encoding for identifying issuers of financial smart cards.

ISO/IEC 7813

The ISO standard that defines the specifics of financial transaction identification cards.

ISO/IEC 7816

The basic set of international standards covering smart cards. There are currently fifteen parts to the ISO 7816 standard:

- **Part 1**—Defines the physical characteristics of the card.
- **Part 2**—Defines the dimensions and location of contacts on the card. It also prescribes the meaning of each contact.
- **Part 3**—Defines the electronic signals and transmission protocols required as specified in Part 2.
- **Part 4**—Defines the commands to read, write, and update data.
- **Part 5**—Defines application identifiers (AIDs).
- **Part 6**—Defines data encoding rules for applications.
- **Part 7**—Defines an SQL interface to smart cards.
- **Part 8**—Defines key management commands.
- **Part 9**—Defines commands for card administration.

- **Part 10**—Defines a synchronous communication protocol.
- **Part 11**—Defines commands and data storage for biometric authentication.
- **Parts 12, 13, 14**—Reserved for future use.
- **Part 15**—Defines a method of organizing cryptographic material on a smart card.

ISO/IEC 8583

The ISO standard for financial transaction messages.

ISO/IEC 9992

The ISO standard that describes the method of communication between card and reader for financial transaction cards.

ISO/IEC 10181-3

The ISO standard for access control.

ISO/IEC 10202

The ISO standard for the architecture of the systems that utilize financial transaction cards.

ISO/IEC 10373

The ISO standard for testing smart cards.

ISO/IEC 10536

The basic ISO standard for contactless smart cards.

ISO/IEC JTC1/SC17

The ISO standing committee responsible for smart card standards. For more information, go to *www.iso.ch/meme/JTC1SC17.html*.

issuer

The institution or organization that creates, provides, and typically owns a smart card.

Java Card

A smart card that includes a Java interpreter in its operating system. For more information, go to *www.javasoft.com*.

Java Card Forum

An organization of smart card manufactures that offer Java smart cards. For more information, go to *www.javacardforum.org*.

KASUMI

A cryptographic algorithm that ensures data confidentiality and integrity in 3G mobile telephone networks.

KLOC

One thousand lines of code.

layout

The organization of dedicated and elementary files in the smart card's EEPROM.

linear file

A type of file in an ISO 7816-4 smart card file system that contains records. The records in a linear file may be fixed length or variable length.

loyalty program

A product marketing scheme that entices customers to purchase the product repeatedly by offering rewards based on the frequency of purchase. Also known as frequent buyer programs or, from its airline origin, frequent flyer programs.

MAC (message authentication code)

A cryptographic checksum used to detect whether text or data in the message has been modified.

MAOS (multiapplication operating system)

A smart card operation system licensed by MAOSCO that is also known as MULTOS. For more information, go to *www.multos.com*.

mask

The program written into a smart card chip's ROM during its manufacture, typically, the smart card's operating system and manufacturer's data.

memory card

A plastic card with a simple memory chip with read and write capability.

memory chipcard

A memory card in which access to the data in the EEPROM is controlled by security logic. *See also* wired logic card.

MF (master file)

The root directory of a smart card's file system. An MF can contain dedicated files (other directories) and elementary files (data files). The master file on an ISO 7816–compliant smart card has the file identifier $3F00_{16}$.

MFC (multifunction card)

A smart card that contains more than one application.

MIP

Million instructions per second.

module

The metal carrier into which a smart card chip is placed before it is embedded into a plastic body to make a smart card. The module provides mechanical protection for the chip and contains the contacts or pads that a smart card reader connects to in order to activate and communicate with the chip.

MONDEX

A smart card operating system developed by NatWest in the U.K. and also an e-cash smart card that supports direct transfer of value from one card to another. For more information, go to *www.mondex.com*.

Montgomery multiplication

An efficient way to do binary multiplication based on shifting and adding. Montgomery multiplication is particularly useful in multiplying the arbitrarily large integers used in some cryptographic algorithms on the 8-bit micro-controller in a smart card.

Moréno, Roland

The French journalist who received a patent on smart cards in 1974.

mother card

A smart card holding a transport key and used to unlock all the cards in a batch or shipment of cards. *See also* daughter card, batch card.

MULTOS

The multiapplication smart card operating system on the MONDEX card and licensable from MAOSCO to be the foundation for any multiapplication smart card. For more information, go to *www.multos.com*.

NACCU (National Association of Campus Card Users)

A North American smart card industry group. For more information, go to *www.naccu.org*.

native code application

An application that is compiled to the instruction set of the smart card's processor rather that to byte codes that are interpreted by an interpreter on the smart card.

NIST (National Institute for Standards and Technology)

An American standards body particularly for the use of information processing technology by the federal government. For more information, go to *www.nist.gov.*

NVM (nonvolatile memory)

A generic term for the memory in a smart card that can be written but still holds its contents after power has been removed; PROM, EPROM, EEPROM, FLASH, and FRAM are examples of NVM.

off-line

The state in which a smart card is not connected to a computer network and must rely on the information stored in its own file system to, for example, approve or deny a transaction.

online

The state in which a smart card is connected to a computer network and can be instructed to, for example, accept or deny a transaction based on information it sends to computers on the network.

Open Platform (OP)

A set of specifications that provide an infrastructure for the secure deployment and operation of post-issuance programmable smart cards, originally developed by Visa International.

optical card

A memory card that can be written once but read many times and can hold between 1 MB and 40 MB of data. Reading and writing uses laser optical technology.

page size

The smallest number of bytes in EEPROM memory that can be written with one write operation. Page sizes in smart cards vary between 1 and 32 bytes.

path

The location of a file with respect to the root directory.

PC/SC (personal computer/smart card)

A group of personal computer and smart card companies founded to work on open specifications to integrate smart cards with personal computers. For more information, go to *www.smartcardsys.com.*

personalization

The process during which individual data are loaded into the smart card chip. Typically performed together with the printing or embossing of personal data (name, ID number, picture, and so on) and an account number onto the face of the card.

phone card

A card that can be used for the payment of telephone calls, typically in a pay phone.

PIN (personal identification number)

Typically a four- or five-digit number used by the operating system on the smart card to authenticate the cardholder.

PKA (public key algorithm)

A cryptographic algorithm that uses a pair of keys, a public key and a private key, that are different from one another. The public key is published and available to anyone wishing to send an encrypted communication to the holder of the private key. *See also* SKA (secret key algorithm).

PKI (public key infrastructure)

A system of storing and distributing public keys together with their current status, typically at scale (that is, millions to billions of keys).

PoS (point of sale)

A type of terminal found, for example, at grocery store check-out stations.

private key

A cryptographic key known only to the owner. Or, the secret component of an asymmetric cryptographic key. *See* PKA (public key algorithm).

processor card

A smart card that contains a microprocessor or microcontroller that can execute a program stored in the card's memory.

processor core

See core.

Proton

A smart card operating system developed by Banksys in Belgium. Used for travel and entertainment by American Express, Hilton Hotels, and American Airlines in the U.S. and for e-cash in Sweden. For more information, go to *www.proton.be*.

public key
The publicly available and distributed component of an asymmetric cryptographic key.

purse file
A type of file in a smart card's file system that is used to implement electronic purses.

PVC (polyvinyl chloride)
Plastic material used for the body of some smart cards.

RAM (random access memory)
Memory used for temporary storage of data by the CPU in a smart card. RAM is volatile; its contents are lost when power is removed from the smart card. *See also* NVM (nonvolatile memory).

Regulation E
A U.S. federal regulation designed to protect users and issuers utilizing electronic financial transfers from fraudulent transactions. It requires users to receive a receipt of financial transactions, puts restrictions on issuance of accessible devices, establishes the conditions of this type of service, and puts limits on consumer liability.

relative path
The location of a file relative to the current file.

retention time
The length of time a smart card will hold data in its nonvolatile memory—typically, 10 years.

RF/DC (radio frequency/direct communication)
A method of communication without physical contact using radio frequency transmission.

RF/ID (radio frequency/identification)
A method identification without physical contact using radio frequency transmission.

ROM (read-only memory)
A permanent memory in a smart card to which the CPU cannot write new information and that cannot be updated or changed. It is written during the manufacturing of the chip and typically contains the smart card operating system and manufacturer keys.

RSA

An asymmetric cryptographic algorithm named after its inventors, Rivest, Shamir, and Adleman. For more information, go to *www.rsa.com*.

RST

The contact or pad on the smart card module that, when activated, causes a physical reset of the microprocessor in the smart card.

SCP (Smart Card Platform)

A standards committee of the European Telecommunications Standards Institute that is creating a suite of smart card standards.

SDK (software development kit)

A collection of software and software tools that is useful in building a particular kind of software application (e.g., a smart card software development kit or a graphics software development kit).

SET (secure electronic transactions)

A protocol developed by Visa and MasterCard for making credit card purchases on the Internet.

SIM (subscriber identity module)

The type of module used in GSM smart cards to allow personal access to the GSM network. The SIM contains the user's cellular telephone account information.

simulator

A computer program that runs on a personal computer, for example, that executes a program to eventually be executed on a smart card and provides tools to the smart card program developer to study and debug the smart card program. *See also* emulator.

SKA (secret key algorithm)

A cryptographic algorithm that uses a single key that is shared by the sender and the recipient of the encrypted message. The single key is used for both encryption and decryption and must be kept a secret shared between them.

smart card

A plastic card with a microprocessor chip that provides secure access to the memory of the card and performs other data processing and communication functions. Smart cards are used to store monetary value and personal identification information.

smart card editor

A program typically with a graphical user interface that enables you to see and change the contents of a smart card as well as send the smart card any command it supports.

Smart Card Forum

A smart card trade association. See *www.smartcard.com*.

soft mask

Executable code typically written in machine language that is written into a smart card's nonvolatile memory after the card is manufactured. Soft-mask code can correct errors in the smart card operating system stored in ROM or it can add additional capabilities to the smart card.

SPOM (self-programmable)

A one-chip microcomputer in which one integrated circuit contains all the electronic components of the microcomputer. Smart card chips are SPOMs.

stamp

A MAC additionally containing input data.

start bit

In an asynchronous communication protocol, the start bit signals the beginning of a new message and alerts the receiver to start collecting the bits of the message. The start bit typically serves only this heads-up function and is not part of the message itself.

SVC (stored value card)

A smart card that stores nonbearer values such as electronic cash. Some stored value cards can be reloaded with more value and some cannot.

swallow

To pull the smart card completely inside the reader so that the cardholder can't remove the card from the reader during a transaction.

SWIM (SIM WIM)

A smart card that contains both the SIM and WIM applications.

symmetric algorithms

A cryptographic algorithm or protocol in which the same key is held by both parties and is used for both encryption and decryption. DES is a symmetric algorithm.

symmetric key

A cryptographic key used in a symmetric cryptographic algorithm. It is called *symmetric* because the same key is used to decrypt a message as was used to encrypt the message. *See also* SKA (secret key algorithm).

synchronous protocol

A communication protocol that is premised on the existence of a common clock or synchronized clocks between the sender and the receiver of the data.

T=0

A communication protocol between a smart card and a smart card reader than transfers information one byte at a time; a byte-oriented smart card communication protocol.

T=1

A communication protocol between a smart card and a smart card reader that transfers information in blocks of multiple bytes; a block-oriented smart card communication protocol.

T3

The 3GPP technical committee that writes standards for the SIM in 3G networks.

tamper detection

Capabilities of a smart card such as low voltage or slow clock detection circuits that enable the card to detect an attempted unauthorized access to data it contains or to alter the calculations it performs.

tamper-evident

Physical aspects of a smart card that, when altered, will not return to their unaltered state and thus will show that the card has been tampered with.

tamper-resistant

Properties of a smart card—both in hardware and software—that make it difficult to perform unauthorized alternations of the data stored in the smart card or to make the smart card perform unauthorized computations.

tamper response

Actions such as zeroization taken by a smart card when tampering is detected.

TE (terminal equipment)

Another name for a smart card reader.

tear

To remove a smart card from the smart card reader in the middle of a transaction; may leave the data on the smart card in an inconsistent or incorrect state.

TESA-7

A cryptographic algorithm used in GSM telephony.

timing attack

An attack on a smart card's security system that is based on precise measurements of how long it takes the microprocessor to perform certain functions. For example, it takes longer to multiply by one than by zero.

TLV (tag length value)

A way of formatting arbitrary data for transmission between a smart card and a host application.

TPDU (transmission protocol data unit)

A block of data sent from the smart card to the host application.

transaction

A business or payment event for the exchange of value for goods or services.

transaction time

The amount of time between the start and finish of a transaction.

transparent file

A type of file organization. The EEPROM file contains a byte string. Data is accessed using the offset length relative to the first byte within the byte string.

transportation key or **transport key**

A key that prevents data being written into a smart card NVM when it is being transported from the chip manufacturer to the card manufacturer or from the card manufacturer to the card issuer.

UICC (*not* an acronym for Universal Integrated Circuit Card)

The smart card application platform that is being standardized by the ETSI Smart Card Platform (SCP) committee.

Unicode

A method for encoding characters from many alphabets in 2 bytes or 16 bits. For example, $03BE_{16}$ is the lowercase Greek letter epsilon Σ. *See also* ASCII (American Standard Code for Information Exchange).

USAT (UICC SIM Application Toolkit)

A set of command and response APDUs that enable an application resident on a smart card to communicate with the terminal and the network to which the terminal is attached.

USAT Interpreter

An interpreter that resides on a smart card for markup language pages written in languages such as XHTML and WML.

USB (Universal Serial Bus)

A standard, serial bus interface available as a standard I/O port on many PC and workstation computer systems.

USIM (UICC Subscriber Identity Module)

The application running on a UICC that implements subscriber identification in 3G networks.

V_{CC}

The contact or pad on a smart card module through which voltage is supplied to power the smart card processor; also the voltage itself, typically 5 volts.

V_{PP}

The contact or pad on a smart card module through which voltage is supplied to program or erase the nonvolatile memory of the smart card; also the voltage itself, typically 5 volts.

value checker

A battery-operated smart card reader for checking the current value held in a stored value card.

VisaCash card

A stored-value smart card produced by Visa that carries U.S. cash.

voltage attack

An attack on a smart card's security system that is based on making very precise measurements of how much voltage the smart card draws. For example, some smart card chips draw more voltage when they are multiplying by 1 than when they are multiplying by 0.

WfSC (Windows for Smart Cards)

Smart card operating system created by Microsoft.

WIM (WAP Identity Module)

A smart card used with a WAP mobile handset to provide security to WAP communication and transactions.

wired logic card

See intelligent memory card.

write/erase time

The amount of time it takes to write or erase a page of nonvolatile memory in a smart card. Typically on the order of 5 milliseconds for EEPROM memory.

zeroization

Setting the nonvolatile memory of a smart card to all null values (zero), wiping out all data stored on the smart card; typically done in response to tamper detection.

Index

A

Access control lists (ACLs), 106–7
ACK field, 82
Across Wireless, 132
Activation, smart cards, 334–35
Administrative commands, 124–26
    Envelope command, 125
    Get Data command, 125
    Get Response command, 124
    Manage Channel command, 124–25
    Put Data command, 125–26
AES algorithm, 109
Allen, Paul, 129–30
American National Standards Institute (ANSI)
    address, 83
    URL, 135
ANS IX3.118 (1984), 77
ANS IX3.15-1975 (R1996), 77
ANSI/ISO/IEC 7811-1, 59–61
ANSI/ISO/IEC 7811-2, 60
ANSI/ISO/IEC 7811-3, 60
ANSI/ISO/IEC 7811-4, 60–61
ANSI X9.15-1990(R1996), 76
Anti-counterfeiting, 6–7
APDUs, 79, 88–89, 111–12, 245
    command APDU, 111
    instruction APDU, 89
    response APDU, 89, 111, 113

SCADA card, 137–39
SIMs, 267–88
    TERMINAL PROFILE APDU, 269–77
    data field of, 270–77
Append Record command, 123
Application cooperation, 364
Application developer, 321
Application Identifiers (AIDs), 134–35
    Proprietary Application Identifier Extension
        (PIX), 135
    Registered Application Provider Identifier
        (RID), 134–35
Application-level protocols, 88–89
Application life-cycle states, 342–43
Application management
    locked cards, 349–50
    lost cards, 350
Application personalization, 351
Application programming interface (API), 238
Application protocol data units (APDUs), *See*
    ADPUs
Application state transitions, 343
Application system, convergence with card
        system and operating infrastructure,
        318
Applications, 91–126, *See also* Interindustry
        smart card commands (ISO 7816-4)
    access conditions, 109–11

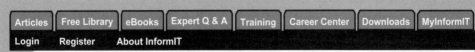

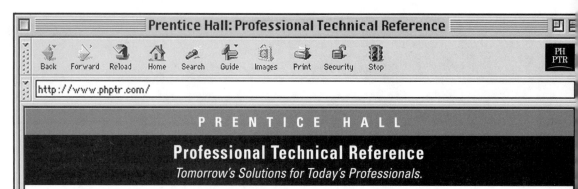